THE PROCESS OF COMMUNITY HEALTH EDUCATION AND PROMOTION

THE PROCESS OF COMMUNITY HEALTH EDUCATION AND PROMOTION

Eva Doyle
Baylor University

Susan Ward
Texas Woman's University

WAVELAND

PRESS, INC.

Long Grove, Illinois

For information about this book, contact:
Waveland Press, Inc.
4180 IL Route 83, Suite 101
Long Grove, IL 60047-9580
(847) 634-0081
info@waveland.com
www.waveland.com

To our families

Contents

2   Understanding Community Perspectives   26

3   Understanding Epidemiological Concepts   49

4   Understanding Health Through the Life Span   74

5   Understanding the Health of Ethnic Communities   95

PART II   *The Process of Health Programming*   121

6   Assessing Community Health Issues   123

7   Planning Health Programs   151

8 Implementing Health Programs   173

9 Program Evaluation   198

10 Coordinating Provision of Health Education Services   220

11   Acting as a Resource Person   239

12   Advocating for Health   258

PART III   *Communicating Health Education Needs*   283

13   Communicating Health and Health Education Needs   285

14 Quality of Life and Future Trends 308

Preface

Learning is a lifelong process, a constant necessity in a rapidly changing world. Learning can be fun and worthwhile when we reach for knowledge and skills that can take us somewhere new, exciting, and challenging. We wish that learning in universities was always exciting and challenging. But developing courses and textbooks to make it so is no easy task. It takes a willingness to constantly reexamine our health education profession in light of the world it serves and to adapt supporting courses and textbooks accordingly.

To understand our rationale for this textbook, we invite you to explore the health education profession, how it has evolved, where it is going, and how changing demands are calling for a different approach to professional preparation at the university level. We also ask you to consider the values and learning-style preferences of today's students and to think about how approaches to professional preparation must be adapted to those preferences if true learning and skill attainment are to occur.

PROFESSIONAL PREPARATION NEEDS

In the university setting, professional preparation programs for community health, health education, and health promotion have evolved from a content- to a skills-based orientation. This change began with the Role Delineation Project initiated to bring focus and consistency to the profession. When the project was complete, the National Commission for Health Education Credentialing established individual professional competencies known as the seven areas of responsibility of an entry-level health education specialist. These competencies serve as a framework for the individual credentialing of certified health education specialists (CHES) and the evaluation of university-level professional preparation programs by the SOPHE/AAHE Baccalaureate Program Approval Committee (SABPAC).

The move from a content- to a skills-oriented emphasis changed the focus of most professional preparation programs in community health. In the content-oriented programs, courses were largely topic-specific (for example, human sexuality, stress management) or population-specific (health promotion for the child, women's health), with the program's introductory courses merely providing a content overview of health issues related to these topics and groups. In skills-oriented programs, topic- and population-specific courses continue to play an important role. However, they are no longer the focal point of professional development. Instead, the program's core courses are based on the essential skills and strategies of our profession. This calls for courses and textbooks that introduce students to both health content and skills.

STUDENT NEEDS AND LEARNING STYLES

Not all students today fit the traditional mold of an 18-year-old recent high school graduate who is living in the dorm, has full financial support from mom and dad, and has nothing to do but study. Many students find themselves juggling work, studies, commuting time, and families. They are not interested in busy work or long lectures about information they can readily access via the Internet. They express impatience with textbooks full of quickly outdated information with no user-friendly application. They exemplify the "use-it-or-lose-it" learning philosophy in that they can better understand and retain facts that are embedded in experiential learning and that is readily connected to personal experience.

The degree to which course content and assignments are relevant, practical, and applicable to career development is a critical issue. Most health education students are willing to invest time and effort into courses and textbooks that help them accomplish their goals. Relevant, concise information presented in a hands-on application framework receives high marks from motivated students.

Students in the fields of health education and promotion desire to understand (1) what health educators do in various work settings, (2) how to gain the knowledge and skills needed to succeed in those settings, and (3) how to gain employment after graduation. If course information and projects are linked to these three motivators, student enthusiasm and learning are enhanced.

TEXTBOOK OVERVIEW

The Process of Community Health Education and Promotion can help students reach their goals through a critical-thinking, experiential learning approach that links the classroom to the real world. It provides an overview of the process of community health education with an emphasis on the seven areas of responsibility of an entry-level health education specialist. It introduces students to the (1) common health education philosophies and concepts, (2) settings in which health educators often work and ways to gain employment in them, and (3) knowledge and skills students will need to succeed as health educators.

Motivating Students to Read and Think

To engage the reader, we deliberately employ a relaxed and personal voice. The bulk of information provided is streamlined to introduce the topic without overloading the reader with excessive details. Where possible, topics are introduced in the context of why the student should take note of the information and how it can be useful. In the margins of some sections are invitations for the reader to pause and contemplate, create lists, recall personal experiences, or consider new ideas related to the subject. These suggestions are designed for the student's personal use and to promote critical analysis of the readings.

These margin prompts can also be used as a teaching tool by the course instructor. The instructor may prefer a low-structured format, allowing students to engage with the prompts on their own, only as needed, with no formal note-taking required. At moderate-structure levels, the instructor may choose to use the embedded margin activities as in-class discussion starters or as elective assignments for students desiring bonus points. In a high-structure approach, the instructor could require students to complete all margin activities as part of their course grade. The level of structure used is at the discretion of the instructor and should be considered in light of student ability and interest levels, class size, other course requirements, and time limitations. The review questions included at the end of each chapter provide another option for launching in-class discussions, written essay assignments, and test preparation. The same structure-level options are available for the chapter elements discussed next.

Project Links and Supporting Materials

Three types of textbook elements related to suggested activities and projects are provided in appropriate chapters. These elements are designed to capitalize on the student learning motivators described earlier: the desire to understand what health educators do and to prepare for health education employment. These three elements are titled "For Your Portfolio," "For Your Application," and "For Your Information."

For Your Portfolio   Some professional preparation programs require their students to develop a professional portfolio. This textbook encourages students to take the first step by developing what we refer to as a "skeletal" professional portfolio. Adhering to the introductory course format, the suggested portfolio guidelines (provided in Appendix C) provide for a three-ringed notebook that contains a one-page résumé and portfolio skeleton (title page, content page, and subheading dividers reflecting the seven areas of responsibility of an entry-level health education specialist). Descriptions of appropriate portfolio content (training, volunteer, and work evidence) are provided in the guidelines, and students are encouraged to add these as they progress through the degree program. Suggestions for how to build one's portfolio are presented in the "For Your Portfolio" sections at the end of each chapter. This element promotes a professional development perspective among students and encourages them to set long-range professional goals.

For Your Application   In addition to "For Your Portfolio," "For Your Application" elements relate textbook content and class discussions to the real world with opportunities to apply or further explore what has been read. In addition to serving as a reading-analysis aid for individual students, "For Your Application" can be used by the course instructor as in-class discussion launchers or individual assignments.

For Your Information   Each chapter contains at least one "For Your Information" (FYI) box that provides nutshell descriptions, how-to guidelines, and checklists useful for application of the health education process. The information in these boxes complements and expands on chapter content and serves as another prompt for application of course materials.

ACKNOWLEDGMENTS

The concept that "it takes a village" could be applied to this project. We thank the multitude of students whose input identified the need for and shaped the content of this book. We also thank a variety of colleagues whose encouragement and honest critique helped us reached our goal. They include Jill Black, Cleveland State University; Karen Camarata, Eastern Kentucky University; Dennis Daniels, Indiana University; Lyndall Ellingson, California State University at Chico; Dee Dee Glaskoff, East Carolina University; William Gross, Western Michigan University; Jeffrey Guidry, Texas A&M University; Mary Hawkins, North Carolina Central University, Durham; Bonni Hodges, State University of New York, Cortland; Gay James, Southwest Texas State University, San Marcos; Mark Kittleson, Southern Illinois University at Carbondale; Kiyoka Koizumi, Brooklyn College; and Shelia Simons, Eastern Illinois University.

PART I

Health
and Community
Perspectives

What Is Health?

YOU'VE MADE A DECISION TO MAJOR IN A HEALTH FIELD. It seems strange, but suddenly you realize that you've never even considered what health *means. Does the definition matter? Does how you think about health affect the way you behave and live?*

Chapter Objectives

1. Identify definitions of health that stem from varying perspectives.
2. Explain how immediate factors influence health.
3. Describe the ways in which health is influenced by social issues.
4. Compare global influences on health and social issues to immediate influences.
5. Explain the role of health education and the role of health educators in health.
6. Clarify personal beliefs about health and philosophy of health education.

DEFINITIONS OF HEALTH

- "Health is seeing the dentist and doctor regularly and particularly if you are sick." (Kyle, age 13)
- "It's not feeling sick, not having a cold." (Mary, age 7)
- "Health is how you feel. How your body works and how your systems work. The way you eat—not eating too much junk food. What activities you do, like swimming and running." (Katie, age 9)

Health Defined by Children, Parents, and Teachers

When you think of the word health, *what comes to mind?*

We interviewed 393 children, parents, and elementary school teachers to see how they defined **health.** Some, like Kyle and Mary, thought health was related to illness. Some, like Katie, thought health had something to do with the actions we take or the activities in which we participate. A number of the elementary school teachers we interviewed added other dimensions. They said that health was more than just physical well-being; their responses included "coordination of mind and body," "skills to perform effectively in life—socially, emotionally, and academically," "mind, body, and spirit," and "keeping safe, avoiding anything damaging, feeling good about self, and [having] socialization skills."

Community values and beliefs also influence our ideas about health. Other members of the same community as our 393 interviewees were also asked to define *health.* One individual said, "Health is a whole host of things from exercise to religion." Another said, "Health is all about diet, exercise, physical exams by the doctor, and relaxation." Does your definition match any of the ones we've cited?

Health Defined by Health Professionals

It shouldn't be much of a surprise that people have different definitions of health: Even health professionals can't agree on a single definition, and literally thousands can be found in the professional literature. Some definitions that have evolved over time are illustrated by the social-ecological model (Morris, 1975), the illness-wellness continuum (Travis, 1990), and the framework for health promotion (Epp, 1986). The definitions in the Report of the 1990 Joint Committee on Health Education Terminology are commonly used today, as are the components of wellness (Fahey, Insel, & Roth, 2001). These definitions reflect a shift in basic premises, away from a perspective focusing on the individual and disease and toward a perspective focusing on the whole person and community (a social perspective).

The social-ecological model (Figure 1.1) evolved from the ecological model, or epidemiological model, which illustrated the essential characteristics of infectious disease: the agent (cause), host (person), and environment. The ecological model, focused on the individual and disease, depicted absence of disease as a

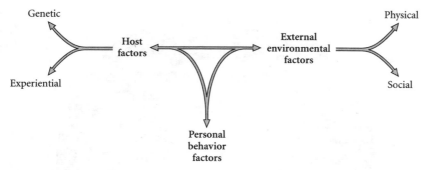

FIGURE 1.1　The social-ecological model.
From *Uses of Epidemiology* (3rd ed.), by J. N. Morris, 1975, Edinburgh: Churchill Livingstone.

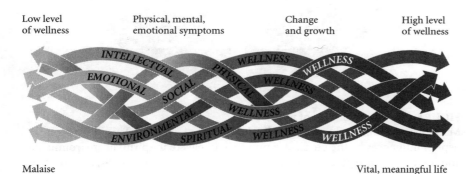

FIGURE 1.2　The illness-wellness continuum.
Wellness is composed of six interrelated dimensions, all of which must be developed in order to achieve overall wellness. From *Core Concepts in Health,* Insel and Roth (2000) Mountain View, CA: Mayfield.

balance between the host and the agent, with environment as the fulcrum. In other words, the environment influenced both the agent and host. If a person had an infectious disease, the agent side of the model would be heavier. Although still disease-oriented, the social-ecological model places the concepts from the original model into the context of today's disease patterns. This model indicates that the causes of disease are more than singular organisms or agents. The arrows point to the factors such as personal behaviors and environment that directly influence health. Host and environmental factors are multifaceted. Host factors can be genetic or produced through experience. Environmental factors include both physical and social aspects of a community.

The illness-wellness continuum (Figure 1.2) illustrates a range from premature death to high-level wellness. An individual fits somewhere in the range at any given time. In order to attain health, a person must go beyond absence of disease. This process requires individual knowledge about health, wellness-enhancing

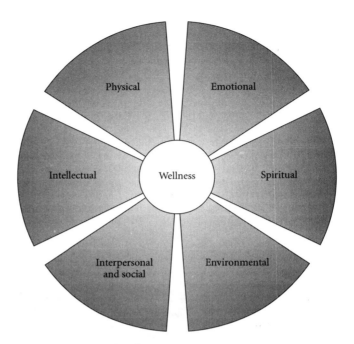

FIGURE 1.3   Components of wellness.
Many aspects of life influence an individual's level of wellness. This illustration depicts influences by the physical, emotional, intellectual, spiritual, environmental, and interpersonal aspects. From *Core Concepts in Health,* Insel and Roth (1994) Mountain View, CA: Mayfield.

actions, and healthy communities. A community could actually be placed in a similar continuum as well. Every community as a whole fits somewhere in a range of ill to well at any given time. The Joint Committee on Health Education Terminology (1991) provided three examples of definitions for the word *health* in its 1990 report:

> A state of complete physical, mental, and social well-being, and not merely the absence of disease and infirmity.

> A quality of life involving dynamic interaction and independence among the individual's physical well-being, his/her mental and emotional reactions, and the social complex in which he/she exists.

> An integrated method of functioning which is oriented toward maximizing the potential of which the individual is capable. It requires that the individual maintain a continuum of balance and purposeful direction with the environment where he/she is functioning. (pp. 105–106)

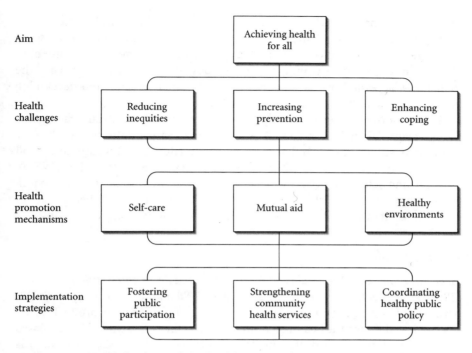

Aim		Achieving health for all	

FIGURE 1.4   Epp's framework for health promotion.

From "Achieving Health for All: A Framework for Health Promotion," by J. Epp, 1986, *Canadian Journal of Public Health* 77(6).

You can clearly see the shift from the focus on the individual and the absence of disease to the focus on the whole person and the community in the Joint Committee's definitions. Insel and Roth (1994) illustrate that many aspects of the "whole person"—intellectual, physical, emotional, spiritual, and environmental as well as social and interpersonal factors—influence health (Figure 1.3).

When defining health from a social perspective, we need to look beyond the health of individuals. We are not suggesting that the individual members of the community are less important than the whole, but only that when you are concerned with the health of the community you must view it from a larger perspective. Think of this perspective as analogous to viewing an individual as a whole (a person with beliefs, values, spirituality, and so forth) and not just a disease (that is, "a heart attack waiting to happen"). Epp's framework for health promotion Figure 1.4) describes accomplishing a goal—"achieving health for all"—through both individual participation and social change. As you can see, on the second tier of the model, Epp depicts the barriers to "achieving health for all" as social inequities, lack of prevention, and poor coping mechanisms. The third tier of the model indicates that individuals must increase their ability to care for themselves, receive more financial help for health problems, and live in healthier environments in order to decrease the barriers to health. The fourth tier describes some important strategies that communities can implement to foster the attainment of health. These include encouraging individuals to participate; improving the availability, accessibility, and quality of health-related services; and developing policies that focus on the improvement of health.

It is important to realize that health is not easy to define. Many factors influence people's beliefs about health as well as their actual health status. The very fact that health is difficult to define makes health education difficult, unless you understand the community with which you will be partnering (working). We use the following definition of health as a guide: a satisfactory interaction of physical, social, emotional, intellectual, and environmental aspects of well-being that occurs as a result of individual behavior choices and positive social conditions.

Healthy People 2000

Healthy People 2000: National Health Promotion and Disease Prevention Objectives (1991b) and *Healthy Communities 2000: Model Standards* (1991a) are U.S. Department of Health and Human Services reports that demonstrate products of actual work in defining the health of a community—the entire United States. Based on extensive input from professionals and reviews by the public, these reports and others that followed helped define health in this nation. These reports have a definite absence-of-disease perspective and are an important first step in working toward health for all. Health objectives for 2010, launched on January 25, 2000, are a guide for health professionals. According to Surgeon General David Satcher (2000), these objectives serve as "a roadmap showing opportunities for improvements in health that is grounded in science, built through public consensus, and designed to measure progress."

IMMEDIATE FACTORS THAT INFLUENCE HEALTH

It's no secret that our behavioral choices affect our health. Some bad choices that come to mind are smoking, drug abuse, drinking and driving, over- or undereating, and getting too little sleep. Even people who habitually engage in these behaviors are aware of the health risk. The important question for a health educator is, "If people know these behaviors endanger their health, why do they continue them?"

Knowledge, Attitude, Beliefs, Confidence, and Culture

Individual behavior is driven by a multitude of **influencing factors.** Immediate influences come from personal knowledge, attitudes, and beliefs and confidence in one's ability to perform a particular health behavior; life values that affect deci-

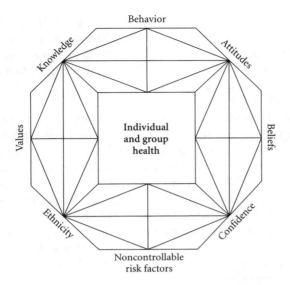

FIGURE 1.5   Community health web (right half).
Individual and group health could actually be considered a web, where many issues and aspects of life are interwoven and interconnected, all influencing each other and overall health.

sion making; and the degree to which one is influenced by significant people in one's life (culture and ethnicity). In Chapter 2 we discuss in more depth how culture influences health. **Noncontrollable risk factors,** such as age, gender, and genetic propensity to health risks, are also important components of health because they often shape the type and severity of health issues and concerns most critical to the welfare of the individual.

Figure 1.5 illustrates the right side of the community health web (shown in its entirety in Figure 1.6). Figure 1.5 depicts the relationships between individual and group factors (one of which is behavior) and health. To understand how health is influenced by the interrelationship of all these factors, think for a moment about adolescents who are considering smoking (behavior) for the first time. Even though they may know smoking is a health risk (knowledge), other factors may sway them to smoke. These could include the desire to be cool (a value), the conviction that smoking will help achieve popularity (a belief), and the stance that rules barring minors from smoking are old-fashioned and oppressive (an attitude). Although family members and teachers may attempt to dissuade these adolescents, they could belong to a social group (culture) whose own set of ideas and norms encourage members to light up.

As shown in Figure 1.5, the relationships between behavior and these other factors is reciprocal, meaning that behavior is influenced by and, in turn, influences each factor. For example, while the attitudes and beliefs mentioned above might motivate an adolescent to smoke, the actual smoking experience will also influence future attitudes and beliefs. The adolescent who experiences a negative physical reaction to those first puffs could develop a strong aversion to trying it again (a new attitude). On the other hand, an individual who enjoys attention from peers during the first experience could develop a new belief that only people who smoke are cool.

The reciprocal relationship just described also applies to the interaction of all nonbehavioral factors. For instance, increased knowledge about smoking and health risks can change smoking attitudes and beliefs. Conversely, increased concerns about the negative effects of smoking (an attitude) can increase knowledge by motivating an individual to learn more. The same is true about interactions between individuals and groups. Culture strongly shapes individual attitudes, and a single group leader's attitude change can change the perspectives of the whole group. This mutually influencing relationship between factors is referred to by Bandura (1977) as **reciprocal determinism.** It is an important concept to understand and capitalize on when attempting to implement health education and promotion programs.

Further complicating this web of influence is the fact that within each factor shown in Figure 1.5 there exists a subset of factor types and meanings. For example, under the label *beliefs* are a number of belief types. One example is **self-efficacy,** the degree to which one believes one can actually perform the behavior in question (Bandura, 1977). This type of belief is important, for example, if the targeted health behavior is the act of quitting smoking and the client's self-confidence in the ability to quit is low. Another belief type is behavioral **outcome expectation,** which refers to whether the smoker believes quitting will have desirable results. **Locus of control** is a third belief factor if the smoker believes another person or agent to be in control of the situation (for example, "I can't help myself"). You don't have to be an expert in psychology to understand that what happens in a person's head influences that person's behavior. If you want to help people develop consistently healthy behaviors, begin with health education strategies that influence attitudes, knowledge, and beliefs.

SOCIAL INFLUENCES AND HEALTH

Most people agree that human behavior plays a major role in the incidence of disease in today's world. In American society, our beliefs about health have developed, at least in part, from a disease perspective. We seem, however, to be moving toward a more holistic definition of health (Dever, 1990), at least in word if not in action. In this holistic definition, disease is only one aspect of community health, and other aspects—such as the psychosocial, spiritual, and environmental—must also be considered. This broader perspective calls for an understanding of societal characteristics that indicate a community's strengths and weaknesses. From strengths and weaknesses we can begin to help the community identify and focus on areas that need improvement.

Social Indicators

The characteristics to which we are referring are commonly called **social indicators,** or *social indices.* They include a number of characteristics like socioeconomic status, crime rates, employment rates, divorce rates, and even school attendance rates. Can you think of others? You might wonder what these have to do with health or to what use a health educator could put the information the indicators provide. What we learn from social indicators can be useful, whether the rates are high or low, good or bad. If, for example, the unemployment rate in a community is very low due to the presence of a large corporate headquarters, we would consider this a positive social indicator. Access to health care may be less of an issue in this community than in other communities because the corporate structure commonly provides health insurance to employees. Health insurance increases the likelihood that individuals can access health care, which may, in turn, decrease the incidence or severity of illness.

Another example of the relationship between social indicators and health is divorce rate and family stability. Divorce decreases the stability of a family: Among its consequences are a change in financial status and family-member roles, stressful personal interactions that evoke strong emotions and even provoke emotional outbursts, and the need to deal with negative perceptions of divorce by others. Family instability in turn has been documented to influence the incidence of crime and violence. The levels of crime and violence in a community are further social indicators. In a later chapter you will learn and practice strategies for mapping the assets of a community as well as identifying the negative social indicators.

Health as a Reflection of the Condition of Society

Social issues are important for health educators to understand because health status generally reflects the condition of our society (Cohen, 1989). As noted earlier, the relationship is actually circular, or reciprocal, in nature because a change in either a community's health or its societal conditions will bring about a change in the other. For instance, a decrease in childhood-illness rates could affect school attendance rates, which, in turn, could promote other positive health effects as students learn more and live more productive lives. The cyclical pattern can also become negative if, for instance, a slow economy forces massive layoffs and increased unemployment. The reduction in health insurance coverage that accompanies unemployment means fewer regular checkups and an increased severity of health problems. The unemployed have difficulty gaining new employment and then difficulties spiral. As society changes, individuals slowly adapt to those changes and once again health changes. According to Cohen (1989), "the task facing human societies is to design behavioral strategies that balance or minimize the risks" (p. 13). Health professionals have an opportunity not only to help individuals and communities improve health but also the society as a whole. Although the process sounds simple, Figure 1.6 illustrates the complex nature of the

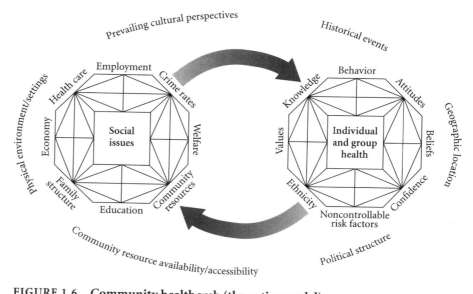

FIGURE 1.6   Community health web (the entire model).
The web effect continues with social issues. Many aspects of life influence social issues, and social issues, in turn, influence many aspects of life. Social issues also influence all of the factors that affect group and individual health, which, in turn, influence social issues.

relationship between social issues and health and the many factors that influence that relationship.

GLOBAL INFLUENCES ON SOCIAL ISSUES AND HEALTH

So far, we have described immediate influences on individual and group health. Yet, the community health web takes a more global perspective on the relationship between health and social issues within our complex society. Let's discuss the global issues in the outer circle of Figure 1. 6.

Community Resources

The resources available and accessible to a community affect its capacity to address social and health issues. In addition to monetary resources, to achieve positive change a community may need access to decision-making power and ability, health information and materials, facilities, equipment and technology, media channels, and enough people willing and able to do the work needed at various levels.

Political Structure

Prevailing political structures and philosophy at local and national levels often drive resource availability and accessibility. Because politicians must pay close attention to their voting constituencies, politics can be driven by prevailing cultural perspectives on a particular health or societal issue as well as by powerful lobbyists who represent industries with vested interests in those issues.

For years, the tobacco industry has vigorously lobbied U.S. lawmakers to protect its so-called political right to market its products and protect its economy-supporting business role. To counter this political force, organizations such as the American Cancer Society and the American Heart Association have used the media to accuse the tobacco industry of targeting children through sales marketing and even of ultimately killing people with tobacco products. As a result, society's prevailing anti-tobacco attitudes have led to smoke-free city and county movements; as this text is being written, the tobacco industry and lawmakers are debating the industry's legal accountability for smoking-related illness and death.

Geographic Location

The tobacco industry's defense has historically included the argument that non-tobacco factors potentially contribute to cancer and respiratory illnesses. These factors include other global influences that do contribute to some aspects of illness, such as living in pollution-prone geographic locations and experiencing other physical environmental conditions. Not only health but also one's attitudes toward health issues are determined in part by where one lives. In the United States, as we have seen, the tobacco lobby's arguments are countered by other groups and by health education programs. But in developing countries, where large tobacco companies also operate and to which U.S. firms export their products, there may be no adequate health education programs to help people stop smoking—or to keep them from starting. Even in the United States, where one lives can easily affect one's attitudes toward tobacco interests. Citizens of a tobacco-growing state are susceptible to arguments that their local economy and their own financial well-being depend on the continued prosperity of tobacco firms. It is easy—and only human—to allow fear of job loss and financial problems to overrule intellectual understanding of what tobacco does to health.

Historical Events

History teaches important lessons. Studies conducted over time show correlations (such as those between lung cancer and heart disease and tobacco use) that lead to new health recommendations. But catastrophic events in history also play a role. For example, where a toxic waste leak has occurred, communities are more likely to have environmental control policies and procedures. The illnesses that plagued the residents of Love Canal in western New York made Americans more aware of—and more willing to act on—problems of industrial waste. Safety is another health area where history serves as a teacher: After 90 children were killed in an elementary school fire in Chicago in 1958, not only did Chicago and the state of Illinois strengthen their fire codes, but also, according to the National Fire Protection Association, 68% of all U.S. communities examined their codes and practices (Chicago Public Library, 1997). Unfortunately, painful historical events seem to be the strongest teachers.

Prevailing Cultural Perspectives

The cultural perspectives that prevail in a community are not always easy to "see" or understand. It can be difficult to know specifically how culture influences health, but cultural perspectives are important. Cultural perspectives are integral to human life and to society, because each person influences the community in which he or she lives. Cultural perspectives influence activities as well as beliefs and attitudes and, therefore, health. Think for a minute about the eating patterns that are common in your extended family. If your family eats a lot of fruit and vegetables, you are likely to do the same, and you may even live in a community that makes similar food choices and shares other cultural perspectives. Smoking and drug use have become such a central part of some subcultures that education efforts must be carried out with special intensity and focus.

Physical Environment/Settings

Terrain, climate, and level of industrial activity all have an effect on health. Residents of tropical climates are susceptible to mosquito-borne illnesses. In the desert of the American Southwest, bubonic plague breaks out occasionally even today; and, in the same setting, a lethal strain of hantavirus made a recent appearance. Climate can influence exercise levels and activity in general. An industrial setting may produce more pollutants in water and air; where air pollution is severe, the effects of cigarette smoking on one's lungs are intensified.

But environment encompasses much more than obvious air and water issues. For example, the number of people residing and/or working in a location influences the number of buildings. The number of buildings in turn influences the number and types of plants and animals. Animals can carry and spread disease, so the presence of animals can increase the prevalance of disease in a location.

The degree to which environment influences health also depends on other issues, such as the prevailing economic and social structures in the community. If most individuals in the community are highly educated and well paid, the infrastructure (policies and procedures) of the community is more likely to involve planning for health and safety. Your role as a health educator may involve helping people understand the part that issues like environment play in health.

The complex web illustrated in Figure 1.6 can seem intimidating, especially if we assume that health educators must be experts in every detail of every influencing factor before beginning health promotion efforts. In reality, developing that level of community understanding should be viewed as a work in progress that takes time, patience, and careful planning. When first implemented, few health promotion programs truly address all factors affecting a health concern within a given community. However, the health educator's success depends on a willingness to revisit the community health web from time to time so that potential influences aren't overlooked or forgotten. This text will provide practical guidelines for how to assess those influences.

HEALTH EDUCATION AND HEALTH EDUCATORS

If few health promotion programs start out by addressing every factor that influences a particular community concern, with which factors should you begin? If you answer this question using a narrow definition of health, your answer might reflect only those factors that prevent disease. The problem is that prevention programs and lifestyle-change interventions that are said to improve health, in fact, often only decrease the incidence of disease. Decreasing disease improves health but only as a secondary benefit (Radley, 1995). It is important to understand that preventing disease is different from improving health because health is more than the absence of disease. Improving health involves helping individuals move beyond the absence of illness toward a positive, wellness orientation. It is about helping others develop an enjoyable, productive quality to their lives. To achieve that goal, you will need to understand individual and community perceptions of health and what shapes them.

Can anyone be a health educator? Some people consider knowledge of disease and its treatment all that is necessary for educating others about health. What do you think?

Even when approaching health from a broader perspective, we must understand that only the people whose health is in question can truly make a difference in their personal lives and the health of the community. Health professionals can easily find themselves tripped up by expert knowledge of a specific health problem, but such knowledge doesn't necessarily mean that specific problem needs to be addressed or that the health professional should force people to rectify the problem.

Health Education Defined

Health education involves much more than finding and addressing a problem. It is a process. The Joint Committee on Health Education Terminology (1991) defined the health education process as "the continuum of learning, which enables people, as individuals, and as members of social structures, to voluntarily make decisions, modify behaviors and change social conditions in ways that are health enhancing" (p. 105).

You may use or hear others use the term **health promotion.** The Joint Committee on Health Education Terminology (1991) defined health promotion and disease prevention as "the aggregate of all purposeful activities designed to improve personal and public health through a combination of strategies, including the competent implementation of behavioral change strategies, health education, health protection measures, risk factor detection, health enhancement and health maintenance."

We prefer to use the term *health education* because of the philosophical perspective on which it is based. Moreover, health education has recently been listed in the U.S. Bureau of Labor Statistics Dictionary of Occupational Titles. We believe that community programs (whether titled health education or health promotion) should focus on health rather than disease and should approach health from a social and reciprocal determinant context, which entails working with both groups and individuals.

Health Educators

What qualifications are necessary to become a health educator? Is it enough to know about diseases and their treatment? What other types of knowledge and skills are necessary if health is defined from a community and societal perspective?

The types of knowledge and skills a health educator needs have been debated for years. Discussion of the educational preparation necessary for professional health educators began in the early 1940s and continued through the 1970s. Many professional health organizations—such as the American Association for Health Education (AAHE), the American Public Health Association (APHA), the Society for Public Health Education (SOPHE), and the American School Health Association (ASHA)—participated in early discussions or even the writing of early professional standards. The 1985 National Task Force on the Preparation and Practice of Health Educators presented "A Framework for the Development of Competency-Based Curricula for Entry-Level Health Educators" (see Appendix A). The framework defined seven areas of responsibility that encompass the process of health education. The Competency Update Project, initiated in 1998, was created to review and update the areas of responsibility.

Seven Areas of Responsibility

In the following paragraphs we discuss the seven basic responsibilities of an entry-level health educator, but the framework also defines the competencies and subcompetencies needed for each one (see Appendix A). In addition, in the early 1990s, three graduate-level responsibilities were added.

Responsibility I: Assessing Individual and Community Needs for Health Education   Conducting needs assessments requires knowledge of the many factors, both intermediate and global, that can influence health, It also requires skills in information (data) collection. Information can be obtained from both primary and secondary sources. **Primary data** are those that you collect through methods such as surveys, interviews, and forums. **Secondary data** are those that have been collected previously; for example, you might get them from a voluntary health agency. Chapter 6 discusses assessment techniques and strategies.

Responsibility II: Planning Effective Health Education Programs   As a health educator, you must be able to communicate well in order to recruit agencies, resource people, and participants to assist in planning the health education program. The knowledge and skills you will need to plan a program include writing measurable objectives based on the assessment, matching program activities to those objectives, and developing appropriate sequencing and depth of content. Chapter 7 discusses the process of planning health education programs.

Responsibility III: Implementing Health Education Programs   Program implementation follows the planning process. As a health educator, you must understand and use a variety of instructional methods, including strategies for individuals and for groups, technology-based instruction, and experiential activities. An important aspect of implementation is ascertaining the knowledge and ability levels of participants. Program activities and objectives should be adjusted to match these levels. Chapter 8 discusses marketing, lesson plans, development of program materials, personnel guidelines, and other aspects of implementing health education programs.

Responsibility IV: Evaluating the Effectiveness of Health Education Programs Evaluation of program outcomes includes determining the standard of performance and establishing evaluation methods. As a health educator, you may have to select and/or develop surveys that will be used in the evaluation process. You must also be able to administer surveys, analyze data, and suggest appropriate actions based on the analysis. Chapter 9 describes types of evaluation techniques and how to design an evaluation plan.

Responsibility V: Coordinating the Provision of Health Education Services This responsibility involves determining the extent of and gaps in educational services. As a health educator, you must also be able to facilitate communication among program personnel and between personnel and outside agencies. You must promote collaborative efforts and help blend health education with other health programs. Training personnel is also an important part of coordinating health education services. Chapter 10 discusses cooperation, collaboration, conflict resolution, and the process of policy development.

Responsibility VI: Acting as a Resource Person in Health Education   All of the responsibilities discussed up to this point require that health educators serve as resource persons. As a resource person, you must be able to utilize computerized information-retrieval systems and interpret and respond to requests for health information. Further, you must be able to establish consultative relationships with individuals or groups requiring assistance with health-related problems. Chapter 11 describes types of resources, including online information, consultation, and networking. It also discusses how to navigate through the maze of various types of health care providers from Medicaid to HMOs.

Responsibility VII: Communicating Health and Health Education Needs, Concerns, and Resources   The final responsibility (but not the least important) requires that you understand health behavior theories and historical aspects of health education. This foundational knowledge will help you recognize potential problems, such as opposing viewpoints about health education. You must be prepared to use many types of techniques to resolve conflict, and you may serve as the liaison between individuals and other health care providers. Chapter 13 provides tips for effective oral and written communication, including how to deal with opposing views and how to understand the decision-making process.

As we've seen, definitions of health vary from person to person and from community to community. As you now know, differences in definitions result from many factors. Health educators play an important role in helping people understand their beliefs about health, in designing and implementing appropriate health education programs, and in evaluating outcomes. Many people without adequate preparation profess to conduct health education (for example, those who give out brochures on health-related topics without regard to reading level, teach a purchased unit without consideration of cultural appropriateness, or write a health education article without attention to the accuracy of content). Effective use of the health education process requires in-depth learning, critical thinking, decision-making skills, and practice.

The Competencies and Subcompetencies of Assessment

Responsibility I indicates that entry-level health educators should be skilled in assessing individual and community needs for health education. What does this responsibility actually mean? You will find as you read this section that assessment involves collecting information, analyzing the information collected, and making decisions based on the analyses. Chapter 6 presents an in-depth discussion of community assessment; but, for the purpose of understanding how competencies and subcompetencies are written and interpreted, we'll look at the competencies and subcompetencies of the first area of responsibility.

Think about an individual first. If you were asked to discover the health education needs of just one person, how would you go about doing so? Make a list of strategies. It is not an easy task, but the competencies and subcompetencies entailed in Responsibility I can assist you in a deeper understanding of it. When you have read our interpretation of the first area of responsibility, add to your list.

Competency A: Obtain Health-Related Data About Social and Cultural Environments, Growth and Development Factors, Needs, and Interests   This competency indicates that we should explore needs as well as interests. Perhaps needs and interests don't seem different to you. If not, think back to a time when someone told you to do something you "needed to do" but didn't want to do. Needs and interests can be vastly different. This competency reminds us to collect information (the first step in assessment) about both.

Competency A also gives us ideas about where to find information about the social and cultural environments and growth and development factors. The subcompetencies under Competency A give us specific guidelines for collection of useful information in determining health education needs. For example, Subcompetency 1, which states "select valid sources of information about health needs and interests," seems at first to be simple (of course, one would select only good sources). However, what is a good source? As parents we think we are good sources of information about the needs and interests of our children. Is this true? Are your parents or guardians always good sources of information about you? For some of you, yes; for others, emphatically no. The health educator must be able to identify and select valid sources.

Subcompetency 2 reads "utilize computerized sources of health-related information." What do you think this competency means? Does it mean you should go to the World Wide Web and look up health education? It would be nice if it were so easy. Use of the Internet is a skill that health educators must have, but we must know how to get the specific information we need. In addition, there are computerized, or electronic, sources of information other than the Internet. Universities and colleges provide access to immense databases (sometimes via the Internet but also on CD-ROMs). Some of these include Psychlit, Medline, and ERIC. We can easily access articles, books, abstracts, and reports written about any subject from almost anyplace in the world. Unfortunately, many of us use Internet search engines only and never access articles and books listed on the aforementioned databases. In truth, many of us don't even have access to the best information that can be found on the Web because we don't thoroughly understand the search process. FYI 1.1 contains a list of hints for using electronic media to collect information about health education needs.

Subcompetency 3 states "employ or develop appropriate data-gathering instruments." Again, this skill may seem easily attained at first; however, instrument selection is vital to the outcome of your assessment, and instrument development is a very difficult task. Let us define the word **instrument** first. We are not talking about a piece of medical equipment like a stethoscope. Common instruments used to gather health information include surveys, questionnaires, and interview questions. You might wonder, "What's the big deal? Just write down a few questions and let people answer them." Unfortunately, it is easy to ask a question that leads the participant to answer in a certain way. Let's examine an extreme case. What if you were interested in a person's perception of the value of exercise? You decide to use a **Likert scale format** that number-ranks responses. You ask the

FOR YOUR INFORMATION 1.1

Hints for Using Electronic Media

You are probably an expert in using technology for gathering information but don't forget that not all Web sites are appropriate. This list provides you with simple tips for using electronic media effectively.

1. Conduct some preliminary information gathering through verbal means. For example, ask people questions about their culture, social activities, recreational activities, health, health habits, and perceptions of needs in regard to health.
2. Use the preliminary data to determine in advance what specific written information you are seeking. For example, if the individual is a female athlete in her late teens, you would want to search for information about the health status of other female athletes in their teens. Be prepared with a list of key words.
3. Seek training about searching for information even if you think you know what you are doing. A few small tips can greatly enhance your searching capability. Your computer center and library can help you learn.
4. Access at least three different electronic sources of information (Web sites). If you can't get printouts, keep a record of URLs. You may need to document your research.
5. Use your library as well as your computer center.
6. When you find information that is beneficial, seek some of the references cited within it. Follow links at Web sites. Use the reference lists for articles and books.
7. Don't give up. Be persistent!

question "How important is exercise?" and give three rating choices: 1 = not important, 2 = somewhat important, and 3 = very important. Although it might seem the same, the question, "How unimportant is exercise?" would elicit different responses. The second question leads the participant to answer in a negative way.

It is also far too easy to ask a question that gives you information other than what you are looking for. For example, due to the dire consequences of contracting AIDS, many surveys have been developed to identify information about the behaviors that put people at risk. Having more than one sex partner is a known risk behavior. The survey items "I am in a monogamous relationship" and "I am sexually involved with only one person" may both elicit a yes response from individuals who indeed have more than one sex partner. Can you see why? The question does not address a time element; as a result, an individual having sex with just one person for only two weeks might consider it a monogamous relationship. Therefore, asking either of these questions would elicit incomplete or inaccurate information. The reading level and command of English of participants also influence their responses. The way survey items or questions are written, the content of the items, and the length of the questionnaire determine its reliability and validity. An instrument that is **reliable** measures the same thing every time, and a **valid** instrument measures what it is intended to measure. All instruments that are used to collect data must be analyzed for reliability and validity.

Subcompetency 4, "apply survey techniques to acquire health data," helps us to understand that instrument selection or development isn't the end of the process. We must know how to present the instruments and must understand the consequences of our selected presentation method. Some of the questions we must consider if we are using survey techniques include "Should the survey be mailed?" "Should data collectors meet with individuals and conduct direct interviews?" "Should a telephone survey be conducted?" and, if an individual doesn't respond to the first method of data collection, "Should a second method be tried?" As you can see, data collection through surveys is not easy but this shouldn't dissuade you from using them. It is, however, important for health educators to have skills in survey development and use.

Competency B: Distinguishing Behaviors That Foster and Hinder Well-Being
According to this competency, we should understand that health is heavily influenced by behaviors that can be modified or changed completely. Subcompetency 1, "investigate physical, social, emotional, and intellectual factors influencing health behaviors," helps us identify the information we will need to help us make the distinction. Subcompetency 2, "identify behaviors that tend to promote or compromise health," tells us to consider the relationship between behaviors and health status. We can give people the information they need about health promotion only if we can understand the relationship between behaviors and health.

Subcompetency 3, "recognize the role of learning and affective experiences in shaping patterns of health behavior," indicates that human behavior is complex. For example, consider how you feel when you hear the word *police*. Most of us have feelings, one way or the other, about this word. If we have received a speeding ticket, the word may evoke behaviors as well as feelings. Have you noticed how many people slow the speed of their car when they see a police car even if they are not speeding? This behavior has been learned either through direct experience or vicariously through another's experience. Past experiences, either direct or vicarious, play a powerful role in shaping behaviors. For example, people who observe others smoking are much more likely to smoke, especially if the person they observe is someone they care about. People who have a positive experience when they start an exercise program are more likely to continue exercising. This subcompetency helps us to understand that as health educators we may need to help people plan behavior changes that will result in positive experiences or help them identify positive role models.

Competency C: Analyzing Data and Decision Making   This competency—"infer needs for health education on the basis of obtained data"—indicates that data collection is meaningless unless the data are used appropriately. Subcompetency 1, "analyze needs-assessment data," suggests that we must "do something" with the data. Once again, it takes training to know what to do. Knowledge of statistics will assist you in decisions about whether information can be quantified (counted) and presented as **quantitative data.** Decisions about whether numbers from one person or group can be compared to the numbers from another person or group will have to be made.

In addition to quantitative data, **qualitative data** may also be needed to gain a broader understanding of a particular health issue. Qualitative data cannot be quantified because they rarely involve yes/no or numbered answers. Qualitative questions are usually open-ended, designed to detect consistent patterns or important themes about a health issue and what influences it.

Once data have been analyzed, a determination of "priority areas of need for health education" (Subcompetency 2) will be made. This determination relates to the third step in the assessment process, decision making. Certainly there would be no purpose in collecting data if decisions regarding that data were not made. We elaborate on useful decision-making strategies in Chapter 7.

As you can see, Responsibility I encompasses a great many skills. Now that you have had a chance to learn about the assessment area of responsibility, try to revise your list of ways to obtain information about the health needs of one individual. Keep in mind that everything that has been said about individuals is true at the community level also.

PROFESSIONAL DEVELOPMENT

You will need to study all of the seven areas of responsibility as you go through your undergraduate degree program. Each is equally important. You might think that once you have completed the entry-level educational experience (your undergraduate college degree) the learning process is finished. This is not the case. In any health field the magnitude of new information demands a need for continued learning. We hope you will see this need in a positive light. New information about health issues and new ways of approaching problems result from health research. We hope this fact creates a sense of excitement and wonder about the possibilities for the future.

Your first step toward continued learning might well be taking the certified health education specialist (CHES) exam. This exam was developed as a way of measuring mastery of the seven areas of responsibility. The National Council for Health Education Credentialing (NCHEC) developed the exam and maintains it. Examinees have 4 hours to answer multiple-choice questions from each of the seven areas. These questions are designed to measure your ability to think critically rather than your ability to memorize. Your college classes should prepare you for the exam; however, you may wish to purchase a practice book (Deeds, 1992). Once you have passed the exam, you will be a certified health education specialist.

As such, you will be required to complete 75 continuing health education credits (CHECs) in 5 years, or 15 per year. NCHEC accepts two types of credit (type I and type II). Type I credits are given to professional development programs that have been approved by NCHEC or other qualified approval agencies (those that have applied to NCHEC and have been formally given the responsibility to approve CHECs). Type II credits are given for professional development experiences that you select. At least 75% of your required continuing education credits must be type I. You should save materials that document attainment of both types of credit. When you attend a program that has type I credits you will receive a certificate. When you complete type II activities you will save items like registration materials and document the content of the sessions you attended.

Conferences are not the only way to attain continuing education credits. Some health education journals have special activities that can be completed and returned for type I credit. Many classes and meetings may also be appropriate for type I or II credits. The important thing is to continue your learning. Even if you are not certified as a health education specialist, you must continue to update your knowledge of health issues.

Professional development actually fits under the umbrella of ethical professional behavior. Most health issues are complex and ever-changing, and, therefore, you will have to make a special effort to keep abreast of new information and methods so that you are doing the best possible job for those you serve. We challenge you to remain updated and to think carefully about other issues of professional ethics.

Ethics and Professionalism in Health Education

Although ethics is complex and multifaceted, one aspect of acting ethically as an educator involves acting professionally. Professionalism includes many behaviors that have ethical implications—being honest, being courteous, fulfilling one's duties and role, providing support for others, and maintaining confidentiality—even being punctual. But such obvious elements of professionalism can be more complex than one might think. Although most of us would perceive punctuality as a positive aspect of professionalism, members of some cultures perceive time differently. It doesn't have the same importance or meaning. Therefore, we must understand that only in a time-oriented culture will punctuality be an aspect of professionalism.

Attitudes, beliefs, and behaviors interact as members of a profession define ethics. As with health, immediate and global factors influence definitions and actions in the field of ethics. However, health educators have agreed on some specific ethical standards. You may review them by reading the Code of Ethics of the American Association for Health Education (AAHE) and Society for Public Health Education (SOPHE) (see Appendix B). We suggest you study the code of ethics carefully but also that you maintain a deep respect for your program participants, colleagues, and community. Respect for others will serve as a guide to ethical behavior.

IN CONCLUSION

The role of a health educator is important and requires knowledge of content and attainment of many skills. As a health educator, we hope you will understand that *health* is not easy to define. Even so, you must be aware of your own definition of health and that of your program participants and other professionals. Many factors, both immediate and global, influence health. The health status of individuals and groups of people in turn affects social issues in the community. Health education provided by professional health educators has a vital role in helping individuals understand and change their beliefs, values, and behaviors. Health educators can help people affect the health of their communities. But to provide this help, they need knowledge and skills in the seven areas of responsibility and must undertake continuing professional development.

 ## REVIEW QUESTIONS

1. Define health.
2. Describe health education.
3. Analyze how health education and health are linked.
4. Describe immediate and global factors that influence health.
5. List some social indicators and discuss why they might influence health.
6. List the seven areas of responsibility.
7. Think ahead. Describe ways in which you might get updated health information.
8. Write a paragraph that indicates what professional ethics means to you.

 ## FOR YOUR APPLICATION

Cognitive Mapping

Now that you've begun to think about what health really means, let's brainstorm a moment about what influences it. Let's try a cognitive mapping exercise to identify contributing factors, the kinds of things that can affect a person's health.

In the middle of a piece of paper in your course notebook, write the word *health* and draw a small circle around it. Now ask yourself "What factors often affect a person's health?" Write anything and everything you can think of in the space surrounding your "health circle."

Think about the words you wrote. At least one of them probably has something to do with behavior. It's no secret that our behavioral choices affect our health. Some that immediately come to mind are smoking, drug abuse, drinking and driving, over- or undereating, and avoiding sleep at all costs. These are health-endangering behaviors that practically everyone knows about. The amazing thing is that even those who habitually engage in these behaviors are reportedly aware of the health risk. So, if people know these behaviors aren't a good idea, why do they continue them? The answer lies in a mature understanding of human behavior and how it is influenced.

 FOR YOUR PORTFOLIO

Creating the Framework

1. Purchase a 2-inch, three-ring binder.
2. Prepare the framework for your portfolio (see Appendix C).
   a. Make a title page for your portfolio.
   b. Begin a Table of Contents. (Be sure to complete it as you add documents.)
   c. Place 10 dividers in your notebook. (You will label them as you progress.)
   d. Label one divider "Philosophy of Education."
3. Prepare a draft of your portfolio document (your philosophy of education).
   a. Begin by defining health.
   b. Continue by describing health education.
   c. Analyze how health and health education are linked.
   d. Revise your draft as you learn more and grow as a health educator.

2

Understanding Community Perspectives

MARY STOPS AT A TRAFFIC LIGHT AND HER MIND WANders back over her day. She's been planning tomorrow's health fair for months. Yet she can't resist one last mental check. The newspaper ads are in place. Some volunteers have agreed to meet her early tomorrow to help with setup. Has she placed reminder calls to every booth representative? She thinks so. Door prizes! She'll call the volunteer in charge of those tonight, again, just to be sure. She has invited only the best to set up booths and has even persuaded the mayor to give a welcome speech. She is proud of that. But, will people in the community come? The question makes her nervous.

Chapter Objectives

1. Describe how communities are defined and function.
2. Apply the RISE approach to community identification.
3. Explain the connection between Maslow's hierarchy of needs and community bonds.
4. Describe how culture shapes a community and influences health.
5. Explain how politics and environmental factors influence community health.
6. Describe settings in which community health happens.

WHAT IS A COMMUNITY?

When you hear the word **community,** what comes to mind? Do you picture a small Midwestern town with neighbors calling to each other from front porches? If so, you can probably understand why the term seems to have lost its meaning in parts of urban America. In some communities, low-income apartment buildings stand next to factories and, miles away, high-income apartments are built near business districts. In the suburbs, residents may commute long hours to work or school, and life moves at a fast pace. In many cases, communities aren't what they used to be. If this is true, why does the health education profession spend so much time and energy on the concept of community health? This question is important because how you answer it and what you think about it will likely affect how you "do" health education in the future.

Understanding communities will be the key to your success as a health educator, regardless of where you work. Ignoring their structure and influence can bring death to your best-planned and critically needed health education program. In the scenario imagined at the beginning of this chapter, Mary is experiencing last-minute jitters about a health fair that is about to happen. She has apparently invested much time and energy in the event and yet is still afraid that people might not come. Despite extensive preparation and advertisement, low attendance is a possibility if the needs, interests, and character of a community are not fully understood. You can become a master of health education skills, capable of designing state-of-the art presentations, materials, and programs. However, your health education strategies will be effective only if you understand how communities are defined and function and capitalize on what is good about them.

Community Defined

A community is a group of individuals bound together by what they have in common. The common link may be structural, as in a shared neighborhood, workplace, or school. Or it may reflect common values, interests, or characteristics. Age, ethnicity, and sexual orientation can bond individuals into a community. Followers of a particular religion or spiritual belief may function as a community, especially if they belong to the same local organization, synagogue, or church. Even members of the same civic organization or club, such as a university sorority or amateur theater group, can function as a community with common goals, interests, and activities.

You have probably heard people speak of the "African American community" or the "gay community." These large groups and others are frequently mentioned in the news and in health education circles. But, as a health educator, will it be enough for you to identify communities so broadly? Do all members of the "elderly community," for example, share the same interests, concerns, and resources? Do they read the same newspapers and attend the same social functions?

Will the same type of health education message work for all? The answer to these questions is "no." And so a closer inspection of this concept called "community" is important. It can make a big difference in how you do your job and whether you do it well.

Identifying Your Community of Interest: Needs Versus Assets

As a health educator, the communities with which you will work are likely to be defined for you; you will be dealing with a specific health concern for a designated group. These assignments are often based on epidemiological data that have been interpreted to reveal a health problem in a particular community **subgroup** (a smaller group from within the larger community). For example, you might work in a local health department that provides HIV/AIDS education for low-income adults. Employed in a worksite wellness program, you could be asked to develop a back-injury prevention program for those who do heavy lifting or a fitness program for all workers. In a school setting, the focus might be on preventing unwanted teen pregnancies or adolescent alcohol abuse. In a voluntary health agency, your assignment could be to increase awareness of breast cancer or hypertension in a specific ethnic community. In each setting, your "community of interest" is identified by a particular health risk.

Attention to health risks is necessary in community health education in part because public health funding, corporate health initiatives, and school-based efforts often target groups at greatest risk of a particular health problem. Problems arise, however, when this needs-focused perspective becomes a community identity issue.

Few communities enjoy having real or implied weaknesses publicly announced. Lawrence Green (in Gilmore & Campbell), a well-known health education leader, explains "Many communities have grown weary...with yet another... initiative seeking to point out their needs, which usually translate as deficiencies embarrassingly catalogued and publicized, often without solution" (p. vii). Defining communities in terms of their problems (such as drug addiction, crime, and environmental hazards) can set a negative tone that decreases community enthusiasm for your health education efforts.

Does this consequence mean community health needs shouldn't be addressed? Of course they should. Such health concerns are often the reason health educators are employed. However, the health education profession has begun to identify communities in a more positive, capacity-focused manner that shifts the attention from community deficiencies to community assets (Gilmore & Campbell, 1996). Our goal in this chapter is to help you view the health needs of communities within the framework of their potential for creating solutions. That shift in focus will likely improve your chances of gaining community support and enthusiasm for health education.

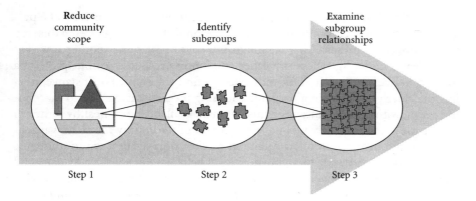

FIGURE 2.1   The RISE approach to community identification guides the health educator to *reduce* the community scope based on prioritized need, *identify subgroups* in that community whose perspectives may differ, and *examine* how these subgroups can work together.

The RISE Approach to Community Identification

We've created a three-step conceptual approach called "RISE" (Figure 2.1) to help you adopt a needs-to-assets perspective of the community with which you will work. In the RISE approach, the health educator **R**educes the community scope based on prioritized need, **I**dentifies **S**ubgroups within that community who may differ in their perspectives related to the health problem, and **E**xamines how these subgroups can potentially interact with one another and with organizations and agencies within the community to help create solutions.

To illustrate the RISE community-identification process, let's pretend you work for a local county health department and have been asked to promote heart-healthy dietary habits among low-income elderly county residents. Conceptually, you may have difficulty focusing on only low-income individuals within the broader elderly county population. But your resource availability and your organization's mission to serve the underserved will depend on your focus. For this reason, the first step of RISE is to *reduce* the scope of the whole community you plan to reach (your community of interest) by including only the audience of immediate need.

With your community of interest conceptually narrowed, you can then move to the second step of RISE, to *identify subgroups* in that community. Despite their common income situation, it is unlikely that all low-income elderly in the county share the same interests and concerns about heart disease and diet. Differing goals, values, lifestyles, and religious beliefs may call for variety in health education strategies. A community definition that includes varying subgroup characteristics will help you choose effective strategies tailored to those groups.

Step 3 of RISE allows you to *examine* the identified subgroups from the perspective of building community capacity. The connected puzzle pieces in this step (see Figure 2.1) represent what the subgroups have to offer one another as well as how organizations, agencies, and other community resources can help create a more cohesive community unit motivated to find solutions. For instance, low-income elderly who live in a particular housing project may be able to share information with other county residents about an available heart-healthy or health service program. Those living in a rural section of the county may have gardening skills and produce to offer. A church or civic organization within the same county could be searching for opportunities to help those in need. And faculty and students in a nearby university health or nutrition degree program could provide assistance in exchange for training experience. Careful examination could reveal these and other potential connections.

When you think of your community, use RISE to conceptualize it as a segment of the population made up of subgroups that are bound together by real and potential assets. But keep in mind that conceptualization is only the beginning. The real challenge will be to effectively tap into those assets for community health education. To accomplish this, you need to understand how communities are shaped by individual human needs (see the section, "People and Community"), cultural influences ("Culture and Community"), and the settings and resources through which community health education often occurs ("Places and Community").

PEOPLE AND COMMUNITY

List at least three groups of individuals with whom you regularly interact and the reasons why you interact with each.

People interact with one another for many reasons. Why do you interact with others? A list of people with whom you have daily contact would likely include significant others or family members, co-workers, and other students. You probably interact with some of those individuals "because you have to." But why do you "have to"? Perhaps you interact with the instructor and students in this course to meet your need for a college degree. You may interact with family members to satisfy needs for emotional and/or financial support.

Abraham Maslow (1954) would argue that you are motivated to act (and we would add "to interact with others") based on one of five levels of human need, often referred to as Maslow's hierarchy of needs (Figure 2.2). We believe this hierarchy explains why individuals bond into communities. Understanding it can help you become a more effective community health educator.

Maslow's Hierarchy of Needs

According to Maslow's hierarchy, one's physiological needs (food, water, oxygen) and the need for physical safety are the most basic and influential motivators of human behavior. You may have never experienced a long-lasting physiological or

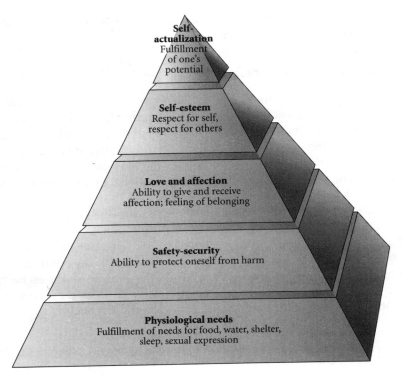

Self-actualization
Fulfillment of one's potential

Self-esteem
Respect for self, respect for others

Love and affection
Ability to give and receive affection; feeling of belonging

Safety-security
Ability to protect oneself from harm

Physiological needs
Fulfillment of needs for food, water, shelter, sleep, sexual expression

FIGURE 2.2 Maslow's hierarchy of needs reminds us that a community's basic physiological and safety needs must be met before efforts can focus on needs at higher levels such as self-actualization. Individuals sometimes bond into communities based on these need levels.

safety need that led to desperate action. Yet you can likely understand why a starving person would resort to stealing food or a teenager abused at home would prefer to live on the streets. When these physiological needs are at stake, nothing else seems to matter. That's why community health efforts to provide food and shelter for the homeless are so important. The homeless community's most basic needs must be met before other health education efforts can be put in motion.

On a higher level, needs are met by interaction with other people. The need for love and acceptance and for appreciation and respect can motivate people to join formally structured community churches, clubs, and organizations. Informal social networks are also formed because of this need, regardless of whether these groups support healthy or unhealthy lifestyles.

The highest level of need in Maslow's theory is for self-actualization. Self-actualization is characterized by emotional and spiritual health in which a person accepts self and others and possesses a keen sense of fulfillment and purpose in life. Individuals at this need level may be active in community organizations, work on college and graduate degrees, or choose a specific profession or interest area because these challenges provide opportunities for self-improvement and the chance to make a difference to society.

Why Community Subgroups Bond

Maslow's hierarchy explains why, within any given community, you will likely find smaller subgroups of individuals bound together by need. At lower hierarchy levels, individuals may join support groups to deal with addictions, abuse, disease, or other threats to their physical safety. And community volunteers working in these programs are likely to be people who have been personally touched by the problem, who understand the need for emotional support and acceptance, and who wish to make a difference for someone else.

The need for emotional acceptance and respect explains why individuals may more comfortably socialize in subgroups of people with common spiritual beliefs, interests, philosophies, and/or ethnic traditions. Because differences can be perceived as a threat to self-worth, subgroups who differ in any one of these areas may tend to avoid one another. How these collective subgroups address health issues is influenced by the cultures and environments in which they function and the settings in which community health education is delivered.

CULTURE AND COMMUNITY

We've already discussed how subgroups form out of a need for mutual acceptance. This sets the stage for an examination of how **culture** and **ethnic identity** shape and influence community subgroups. This section will define those concepts and describe their importance in community health education. It will also present ways for you to become a culturally sensitive and competent health educator.

Cultural Concepts and Definitions

Say the word *culture,* and a dozen different images and meanings come to mind. Some think of art and launch into discussions about music preferences and the theater. Others think culture is synonymous with **race** and use the two words interchangeably to refer to individuals whose customs, appearances, or languages differ from those of the mainstream in the United States. But what does culture really mean and why would it be discussed in a community health education text?

Race, Ethnicity, and Culture   Culture is a complex entity. To understand it requires an open mind and a great deal of patience. It is not synonymous with *race,* a word rapidly losing its usefulness because few genetic distinctions can be defined along racial lines; nor is it the same as **ethnicity,** a term used to indicate the degree to which an individual identifies and socializes with members of the same cultural group and consciously participates in its traditional cultural practices. Culture encompasses the knowledge, beliefs, practices, values, customs, and norms of a group of people that are passed from one generation to the next. It is learned from family and community members bonded by what is common among those factors and shaped by traditional religion, the environment, and historical events. Culture serves as a fibrous network that bonds individuals together within a close-knit community. Culture is a powerful shaper of human behavior and often dictates how people interact. For this reason, a consistently effective health educator is conscious of the three important principles listed below. You will find an opportunity to apply them at the end of the chapter (For Your Application 2.1).

- Every person is a member of a culture, regardless of the degree of membership awareness.
- Each person's culture influences his or her health-related beliefs and behaviors.
- Effective health education depends on the health professional's level of cultural sensitivity and cultural competence.

Cultural Sensitivity Defined   Aquiring **cultural sensitivity** means gaining awareness and insight. It begins with awareness of differences between one's personal cultural perspectives and those of one's clients and progresses to a respectful insight into the reasons behind those differences. For instance, direct eye contact has different meanings in different cultures. For many White, middle-class Americans, direct eye contact with others is maintained to convey confidence and respect. However, in some cultures, direct eye contact can be interpreted as a sign of aggression and disrespect, particularly when interacting with a person of authority. A culturally sensitive health professional is aware of potential differences regarding eye contact and is respectful of what that may mean to a client from another culture.

Cultural Competence Defined   For the health educator, **cultural competence** can be defined as the ability to respectfully interpret behaviors and promote health within the context of the client's culture. For example, an adolescent who consistently refuses to eat when others are eating may be considered at risk of developing an eating disorder. But what if the adolescent is Muslim, adheres to the Islamic faith, and is fasting because it is Ramadan, the Islamic month for prayer and spiritual cleansing (F. Youssefi, personal communication, April 4, 2000)? A culturally competent professional would avoid jumping to conclusions by exploring possible culture-specific interpretations and would seek ways to help the client simultaneously honor cultural beliefs and maintain health. Asking respectful questions may reveal the fact that Islamics fast only during daylight hours and that individuals with health problems are discouraged from fasting. A competent approach would be to carefully monitor the young person's health during those weeks and encourage eating nutrient-rich foods after sundown and before sunrise.

Developing Cultural Sensitivity and Competence in Community Identification

So how do we become culturally sensitive and competent community health educators when so many different cultural and ethnic perspectives exist? Can we truly become experts in all cultures? No, we can't know every detail about all cultures because their characteristics vary over time and across members. What we can and should do is develop an awareness of the influence of culture on our personal health beliefs and understand how those may shape our expectations in community health settings. We can then explore ways to avoid stereotyping individuals and become more culturally sensitive and competent among those whose cultures differ from our own.

Your Personal Culture   A good place to start is with a close look at your own culture. Yes, you are a product of at least one culture, whether or not you are aware of its influence. Do you remember how, in Chapter 1, we explored different perspectives about health? To identify the health-related cultural norms that influence you, let's explore your childhood memories.

Describe in one or two sentences how you think your family members would define health.

HEALTH DEFINITIONS   What health-related beliefs did you learn from your family and friends that have influenced your health behaviors? For example, was it a general assumption in your family that health is the absence of disease? That might be true if family members were concerned about your health only when you were sick. In contrast, you may have acquired a wellness-oriented perspective through the efforts of a family member who frequently stressed the value of proper diet and exercise for general well-being.

List memories you have of some specific disease-prevention practices in your family.

ILLNESS PREVENTION   What were your family's beliefs about the cause and prevention of illness? For instance, were you given vitamins on a regular basis and taken for medical checkups? Were you allowed to walk in the cold rain, or did someone in your family insist you would "catch your death of cold"? Some students recall having to take a laxative once a month or eat specific foods to keep one's health "well-regulated." Others were taught to be careful on the night of a full moon, wear amulets, light candles, and pray to ward off spirit-induced illness or injury.

ILLNESS TREATMENT   What happened when you became ill as a child? Did someone call the doctor right away, or were home remedies tried first? You may remember being given special foods or drinks such as soup, lemon tea, or a hot toddy to ward off a cold. Some older adults recall the use of hot compresses or special ointments for chest colds. For some, spiritual rituals, prayers, and candles were common treatments. One mother washed bed linens, bleached eating utensils, and sprayed disinfectant to protect the rest of the family when a child was ill.

Regardless of what specifically you learned in childhood, the fact remains that your ideas about health and how to maintain it were and still are driven by culture. Because of your education, you may have abandoned some family-influenced beliefs and practices, while continuing to hold others. You've also likely adopted new ideas and health behaviors you've learned from friends, school, or the media.

Describe your present health beliefs and practices and compare them to what you learned as a child.

Neither you nor your health clients will escape cultural influences on health-related ideas and practices. Remaining conscious of those influences and how they may differ between you and each client is the first step to cultural competence.

Cultural Competence Versus Stereotyping   With a healthy perspective on your own cultural influences and beliefs, you can begin the lifelong process of learning how to develop positive working relationships in ethnic-based community subgroups. The challenge when working with any client or group is to be sensitive to possible cultural influences and respectfully ask appropriate questions without prematurely assuming the clients adhere to all traditional cultural beliefs. We **stereotype** when we speak or act on those premature assumptions. Consider the case of a Hispanic American woman; you would be stereotyping her if you assumed her to be Catholic and not using birth control. The culturally competent professional is respectfully aware of traditional Catholic views on the subject, asks open-ended questions about the client's perspective, and acts in accordance with her responses. If traditional Catholicism does influence the client, appreciation for the culture can help the professional make appropriate suggestions. However, assuming that the client accepts traditional Catholic beliefs, without taking time to get to know her, can raise communication and trust barriers if the client is not Catholic or doesn't accept the Church's perspective on birth control. Becoming culturally competent and avoiding racial stereotyping are key to health promotion success.

Ethnic Community Identity   Self-identified ethnic communities or subgroups often have a strong sense of pride and community identity, as well as potential support organizations and networks that may not be evident at first glance. Though individual members of these communities will likely differ, the traditional norms and values of many ethnic communities in the United States are positive, health-enhancing assets. And, when emotional investment in the community is high, community volunteers can be a valuable resource to you in each of your seven areas of health education responsibility.

In the chapters that follow, we provide brief descriptions of norms for some U.S. ethnic groups, along with strategies for learning about ethnic subgroups in your local area. Then we explore ways to foster community involvement and ownership in health education efforts. In terms of our discussion here about how to define your community of interest, the critical point is to expect to find ethnic and cultural influences on the identity of your community and its subgroups.

PLACES AND COMMUNITY

So far, we have discussed how your community's identity can be shaped by the cultural norms and assets of its subgroups as well as by the needs of individual members. In this section, we present a third category of influence on your community's identity, referred to as the *places* in which your community functions and receives health education support. A community's "place" can refer to its location as defined by geography, political structure, and the institution or agency settings through which health education is delivered. These three place dimensions are important aspects of a community's identity.

A Community's Place in the Environment

Geographic and environmental locations can shape a community's identity and the health issues it faces. For example, Ocean City, Maryland, is a popular beach-front resort community that attracts thousands of summer tourists. The health issues in this geographic area include potential water and beach pollution, sun-exposure hazards, and the types of crime common to most high tourist-traffic areas. In contrast, a large inland city like Dallas, Texas, faces such health issues as air-quality control and traffic injuries in highly congested areas and maintenance of water supplies during drought periods. Thus, a community's geographic place can shape the health issue you are asked to address.

Geographic location can also influence the nature of community resources and support systems available for enhancing community health. Ocean City's climate and long beaches provide enjoyable, health-enhancing exercise and recreation opportunities, and the relaxed social atmosphere promotes stress-reducing rest. Partially because of its central-state location, Dallas serves as a hub for recreation and the arts, for social-support systems for a variety of community subgroups, and for quality health promotion and health care services.

Politics and Community Health

A community's identity is also shaped by its **political jurisdiction**—whether it is part of a village or city, a large state or a small one, an affluent county or one suffering from economic woes. The framework of government enables officials to regulate growth and expansion, as well as develop the tax revenues needed to maintain public services. Virtually every decision made by a community's political leadership affects the health of its citizens in some way. For example, a community's environmental health is addressed when city councils discuss water quality, wastewater treatment, landfills, or industry zoning laws. The funding and structure of police and fire departments influence injury and death rates that result from crime, fires, and traffic accidents. The availability and quality of city parks and recreational areas, libraries, and community theaters affect health because they offer opportunities for citizens to exercise mind and body and develop social skills.

Most communities are in a constant state of change due to variations in the economy, population growth, political climates, and funds available for community services. In all likelihood, these variations are even now affecting the community in which you will work as a health educator and the health of those you will serve. Some would argue that local communities could do more if they didn't have to depend so heavily on state and federal decision-making bodies and funding regulations (a decentralized government perspective). Others contend that a more centralized governing approach helps safeguard the health of those communities for which local resources are lacking. Regardless of your personal opinion, the political climate in which your community functions is a critical component of its identity and health.

Places Where Community Health Happens

Communities are targeted for health education by government and voluntary health agencies, philanthropic foundations, religious and service organizations, corporations, and educational institutions. These organizations can be a vital resource to your community as well as a personal employment opportunity. For both reasons, it is worth becoming familiar with some of these organizations and what they have to offer.

List three organizations where you think you would like to work. Contact them and ask questions.

In the discussion that follows, we describe some agencies and organizations. Appendix D lists a broader selection of health agencies, organizations, and resources you may want to learn more about. Local offices of these organizations provide opportunities for volunteer work and/or practicum and internship experiences that will enhance your professional portfolio.

Government Health Agencies   Many textbooks on community health describe the levels of **government agencies** from a top-down perspective because that is the direction in which funding flows. However, we believe that many community health educators moving into entry-level positions view and experience this hierarchy from the bottom up. For this reason, we begin where we think you will likely begin, at the local level.

LOCAL HEALTH DEPARTMENTS   Depending on the size of the community, a **local health department** (LHD) can fall under city or county government jurisdictions. Cities with populations larger than 50,000 usually have their own health departments, which can, in some cases, also serve surrounding sparsely populated areas. A county health department may be the only available LHD in more rural regions, and in some regions a single LHD may serve more than one county.

Regardless of the nature of your employment as a health educator, your community's LHD can shape the health of your clients and the resources available to you both. Through the local health agency, your clients may have access to immunization clinics, HIV/AIDS counseling and testing, and health education programs. It is also from the LHD that you can obtain statistics about community births, deaths, and the incidence and prevalence of certain diseases. This important needs-assessment information can help you design more effective programs. Public buildings, transportation systems, and restaurants are also inspected through the environmental health and food service divisions of your community's LHD (American Public Health Association [APHA], 1975).

Although LHDs are funded largely through local property taxes and, in some cases, fee-for-service income, most receive some state and federal support. These monies provide leverage for more centralized health departments (state and federal) to mandate services that must be provided by LHDs (such as vital statistics and disease reporting and restaurant and public building inspections). These specific services are regulated by state-level standards. If you are familiar with your state's standards and goals, you will be better equipped to tap into state-level resources.

STATE HEALTH DEPARTMENTS   A step up in the hierarchy are **state health departments** (SHDs), a critical link between the clients you serve in your community and needed **federal funds** for health education programs. The federal government provides funding to SHDs through block grants designated for specific health problems. The grants are proportioned out to LHDs in accordance with prioritized needs. For this reason, a collaborative relationship between your organization and your community's LHD can be mutually beneficial. For example, you could be employed by a school system or community clinic whose goals are to decrease unwanted pregnancy among low-income teens. The LHD in your area may be eligible to receive from the state a portion of the block funds designated to address that health issue. With these funds available, the LHD staff could benefit from your organization's access to the community and, simultaneously, help you obtain your program goals.

SHDs also support LHD efforts (and, indirectly, your efforts) by providing expensive laboratory testing services, equipment, and experts that LHDs may not be able to afford. They also serve as an information and reporting link to the federal government by providing national agencies with local statistics. This allows the agencies to match national health statistics to local records. Specific health issues are frequently addressed through specific divisions: environmental, maternal and child, mental, occupational and industrial, dental, and veterinary public health. The SHD structure often includes separate divisions for communicable and chronic diseases, vital and health statistics, public health nursing, and health education or promotion. As you might expect, the health education and promotion division can serve as a direct resource for both needs assessment and health education programming efforts.

NATIONAL HEALTH AGENCIES   A number of **national health agencies** (see Appendix D) address various health issues and concerns in the United States; these agencies can also affect your local community health education efforts. For example, if you are concerned about health-related working conditions in a particular company, the Occupational Safety and Health Administration (OSHA, under the Department of Labor) may provide assistance. The Environmental Protection Agency (EPA) is a resource for hazardous-waste questions if you are working with a population whose water or air quality seem threatened.

When working with low-income pregnant women and/or single women with children, Women, Infants, and Children (WIC, Department of Agriculture) and Aid to Families with Dependent Children (AFDC, Social Security Administration) are good programs to know about. The WIC program provides pre- and postnatal nutrition education and supplemental food assistance for pregnant, postnatal, and breastfeeding women and their children up to 5 years of age. The AFDC program provides financial supplements to single mothers who experience difficulty making ends meet.

Of all the federal health agencies at your disposal, the Department of Health and Human Services (DHHS, Figure 2.3) may be the most inclusive federal resource: It houses programs from which you can glean the most current health-related information about specific health problems in population subgroups and geographic regions, and it offers assistance in state-of-the-art health education program development and implementation. The DHHS Web site (see Appendix D) also provides links through the "U.S. State and Local Gateway: Health" to health-related information pertinent to your state, county, and city. DHHS subdivisions include the National Institutes of Health and the Centers for Disease Control and Prevention.

You probably noted in Chapter 1 that one of the seven areas of responsibility of a certified health education specialist is the ability to serve as a resource person for health-related information. To be an effective resource for health information doesn't entail carrying a great many facts in one's head but, rather, knowing where to go to obtain the most accurate and current information available. The National Institutes of Health (NIH) provide that information through ongoing research efforts in the Bethesda, Maryland, laboratories and, to a larger degree, through highly competitive research grants awarded to health scientists at universities and research laboratories. The health-influencing factors described in Chapter 1, along with recognized prevention techniques and medical treatments, were identified and confirmed through NIH research efforts. Use the NIH Web site listed in Appendix D for more information about the NIH and to access current health information.

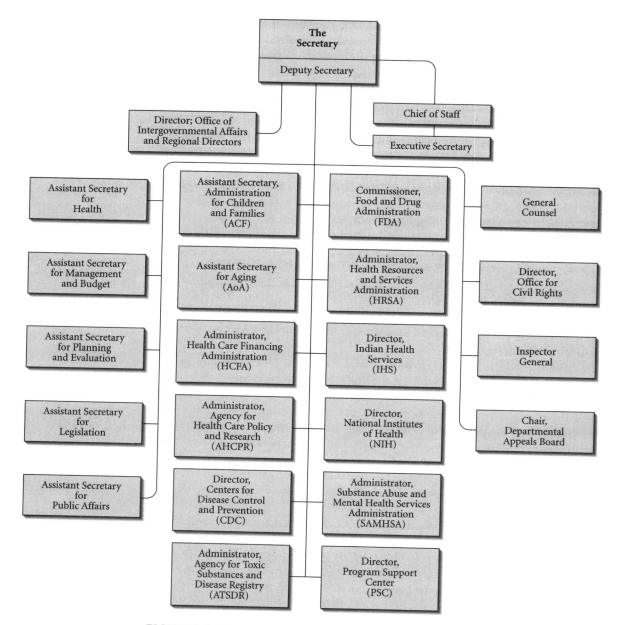

FIGURE 2.3   Department of Health and Human Services organizational chart.
From U.S. Department of Health and Human Services Web site: http://www.hhs.gov/about/
orgchart.html.

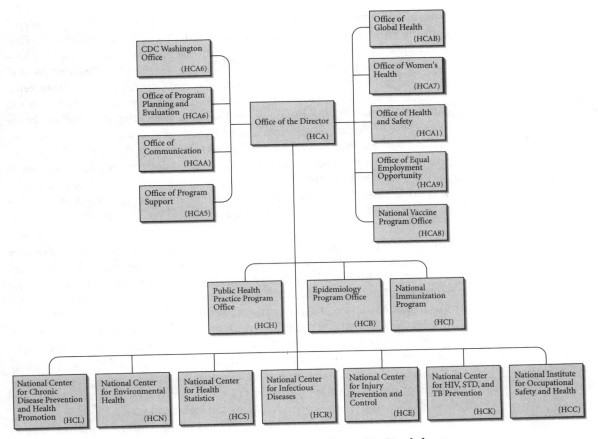

FIGURE 2.4   Centers for Disease Control and Prevention organizational chart.

From Centers for Disease Control and Prevention Web site: http://www.cdc.gov/maso/.

For health statistics regarding the incidence and prevalence of communicable and chronic diseases in the United States, contact the Centers for Disease Control and Prevention (CDC, Figure 2.4). Located in Atlanta, Georgia, the CDC maintains surveillance data, conducts epidemiological investigations, and uses its diagnostic laboratories to track and develop control programs for diseases and other health problems. It also serves as an information link to comparable government health agencies in the international community through the World Health Organization.

Health education and illness prevention are among CDC's primary objectives, and the organization is a valuable resource for health information and support of health education efforts. The CDC Wonder Web site listed in Appendix D is a good resource for identifying primary health problems of age- and ethnicity-specific groups.

WORLD HEALTH ORGANIZATION   The World Health Organization (WHO) comprises and is funded by member nations of the World Health Assembly. WHO is headquartered in Geneva, Switzerland, with six regional offices located in strategic areas. One regional office, the Pan American Health Organization (PAHO), is located in Washington, D.C., and serves North, Central, and South America.

WHO and PAHO may seem far removed from the community in which you will work. However, the programs and services they offer may still affect the health of your clients. WHO's goal is to help communities around the world identify and address local health needs. The organization works toward this goal by providing technical support and funds, training, and expert advice for health workers. WHO efforts greatly contributed to the eradication of smallpox, once a worldwide killer disease, and current efforts include a services support program called "Health for All" (World Health Organization [WHO], 1999a).

Voluntary Health Agencies   From a health education perspective, **voluntary health agencies** (VHAs) are an important part of your community's identity because they predominantly draw on community volunteers for leadership, people power, and funding. As a result, they can provide a natural connection between your health education program and community members.

Most VHAs focus on a specific health problem such as heart disease, cancer, or diabetes. A common goal is fund-raising (through, for instance, telethons, special dinners, and walk-a-thons) for research on the cause, treatment, or cure of the disease. A popular example of an effective voluntary health program is the March of Dimes support for polio research over several decades. Today, the deadly disease has been nearly eradicated through vaccines.

Two additionally important VHA goals are community and professional education about the health problem and service to those who suffer from it. The health education skills you develop can be particularly useful in these areas, especially in relation to communication and acting as a resource.

Most VHAs have local, state, and national offices; each level is analogous to similar levels in government health departments and agencies. The paid staff members of local community VHA chapters particularly depend on the efforts and generosity of community volunteers to make things happen.

A multitude of voluntary health agencies exist, and there isn't room here to describe them all. We've provided a brief description of the American Heart Association (FYI 2.1). You can use this as a model for obtaining information about other VHAs (see Appendix D).

Philanthropic Foundations   A philanthropic foundation is a private, nonprofit organization that funds special projects ranging from humanitarian and educational causes to health improvement efforts in special populations. The Foundation Center of New York (1999) lists more than 47,000 U.S. philanthropic foundations established by families, corporations, special interest groups, and

FOR YOUR INFORMATION 2.1

American Heart Association

The American Heart Association is a well-known voluntary health agency. A list of other agencies can be found in Appendix D.

Type of Organization
Voluntary health agency

Contact Information
7272 Greenville Avenue
Dallas, TX 75231-4596
214-373-6300
http://www.americanheart.org

Funding Sources
Donations and fund-raisers

Primary Mission

"The American Heart Association (AHA), representing 4.6 million volunteers, is dedicated to the reduction of disability and death from cardiovascular diseases and stroke."

Communities of Interest
General public
Health professionals who treat
    heart patients

Common Activities and Services
Fund-raising for research
Teacher training
Information and referrals
Political lobbying and advocacy

Health Education Focus
Cardiovascular health
Proper nutrition and exercise
Detrimental effects of smoking
Detection and treatment of
    hypertension

Health Education Channels
Literature and audiovisual materials
Conferences and presentations
Public service messages
Professional publications
School and worksite programs

From the American Heart Association Web site: http://www.americanheart.org

communities (see Appendix D). For example, the Rockefeller Foundation supports projects to ease world hunger and control disease as well as programs in family planning and reproductive health. The Robert Wood Johnson Foundation (FYI 2.2) actively supports health-related endeavors and could be a resource for your efforts, depending on your employment status and the characteristics of your community of interest. A list of philanthropic foundations is included in Appendix D.

The Robert Wood Johnson Foundation

The Robert Wood Johnson Foundation supports efforts to improve America's health. A list of other foundations can be found in Appendix D.

Type of Organization
Special-interest foundation

Contact Information
Post Office Box 2316
Princeton, NJ 08543-2316
609-452-8701
http://www.rwjf.org

Funding Sources
General Robert Wood Johnson Estate

Primary Mission

The Foundation concentrates its grant-making in three goal areas: to assure that all Americans have access to basic health care at reasonable cost; to improve the way services are organized and provided to people with chronic health conditions; and to reduce the personal, social and economic harm caused by substance abuse—tobacco, alcohol, and illicit drugs.

Communities of Interest
Populations at risk of
  inadequate health care
  (low-income communities,
  elderly, children,
  ethnic communities,
  mothers/infants)

Common Activities and Services
Child psychiatric illness treatment
Day care for Alzheimer's patients
AIDS patient/family assistance
General practitioner training
Rural and inner-city health care
Funding for training/fellowship programs
Funding for research/technical assistance

Health Education Focus
AIDS/HIV infection
Drug abuse prevention
Youth tobacco education
How to cope with cancer

Health Education Channels
Government agencies
Native American tribes
Universities and schools
Community organizations

From the Robert Wood Johnson Foundation Web site: http://www.rwjf.org.

Religious and Service Organizations   Churches, synagogues, and mosques can be effective places for health education programs to happen. Religious leaders are often respected and trusted by community members. Members of religious groups may serve as volunteers in your program if they view what you do as potentially helpful to others. Church and synagogue facilities are often ideal for a variety of programs, providing classroom and recreational areas and equipment. They are also frequently located in areas that are easily accessible and familiar to the surrounding community.

The type of health education and health care services offered through places of worship range from health clinics, counseling services and referrals, and immunization programs to aerobic-exercise, weight-management, and stress-management classes. Pregnancy crisis centers, homeless shelters, soup kitchens, and clothing distribution centers are among the many free or low-cost services provided by religious organizations. In some cases, these organizations employ a nurse or health minister to coordinate these activities. Others cooperate with local health agencies and other health organizations to serve the needy in their communities. Regardless of your place of employment, the local religious organizations in your community of interest can be valued supporters of your health education efforts.

Service organizations such as the Rotary, Kiwanis, Lions, and Masons can be another good resource for community leadership, volunteers, and other types of collaboration for health education. University fraternities, sororities, and service clubs often require, or at least encourage, their members to complete community service hours. Interaction with these groups can sometimes give you access to facilities and resources in the community that would otherwise be unavailable to you. When you view these types of organizations as part of the fabric and identity of your community of interest, the possibilities become endless.

Educational Institutions   School health education is an important component of our profession because it can potentially reach a large percentage of the entire community. Although the extent to which health is part of the school curriculum differs from state to state, most states do include health in the curriculum at some learning level. Whether or not you plan to teach health in schools, that health education "place" will likely be an important avenue for community access.

Think for a moment about the types of health information you learned in elementary school. Did any of your teachers address health topics in your classes? If so, what do you remember studying? Classroom students are a captive health education audience and a direct information line to their families. But school health is no longer viewed by our profession as something that happens only in the classroom. Many of the community health concepts and strategies you will study in this text are just as viable on school campuses as in the community at large. The school classroom is only one component of a much broader school-centered community.

Figure 2.5 illustrates the Eight-Component Model of School Health Programs developed by the CDC (Centers for Disease Control and Prevention, 1999). This model represents interactive approaches to school health in which classroom health and physical education teachers are encouraged and trained to collaborate with school personnel (administrators, nurses, nutritionists, counselors, and other staff), parents, community volunteers (medical and allied

List educational levels at which you studied health (such as elementary and middle school) and name topics you liked most and least, plus some you wish you'd been able to study.

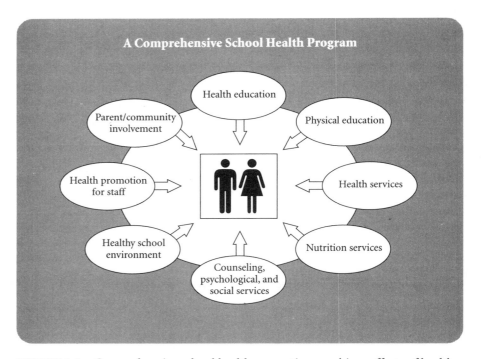

FIGURE 2.5   Comprehensive school health promotion combines efforts of health and physical education teachers, other school personnel, parents, community volunteers, community organizations, and universities to promote healthy lifestyles and a healthy environment. From CDC Web site: http://www.cdc.gov/nccdphp/dash/model-1.gif.

health professionals, community health educators), community organizations, and universities to promote healthy lifestyles and environments. School health fairs, parenting classes, medical referrals, immunization programs, teacher/staff fitness programs, and special-topic awareness campaigns are among the many health-related programs offered on school campuses. For more information about school health and the comprehensive school health model, visit the CDC Web site for the National Center for Chronic Disease Prevention and Health Promotion (see Appendix D). Their Adolescent and School Health section is an excellent information resource.

Corporate Settings   Worksite health promotion and employee wellness programs are another important "place" in which you may find yourself offering health education. Business leaders who support these programs often do so to reduce employee absenteeism, increase productivity and job satisfaction, and lower insurance and health care costs.

Worksite program size and content vary greatly. Some companies house their own worksite wellness programs, while others contract out for part or all of their health education efforts. Common health education classes include stress management, fitness, smoking cessation, nutrition, weight management, parenting, and drug abuse prevention; programs in cancer and cardiovascular disease awareness and prevention are also common. Health fairs, screenings, and **health-risk appraisals** (measures of health risk based on behaviors and genetic history) are regular components of most programs. Some emphasize after-work and weekend recreation programs that involve employees and their families in friendly sports competitions such as basketball, volleyball, handball, and golf. Company picnics, marathons, ropes courses for professional development, and other one-time events may also fall under your umbrella of responsibility in this setting. In larger programs, the management of fitness facilities, recreation areas, equipment, and personnel may be part of your job.

Many of the community health perspectives and skills presented in this textbook are useful in worksite health settings. The employees of the company or, in some cases, a particular employee subgroup can become your community of interest. And, as in any community, the needs, characteristics, and resources of that employee subgroup will shape the nature of what you do. For example, you may find that a back-strengthening or injury-prevention program is essential for assembly-line workers, while those in the company who work at a desk all day are interested in exercise opportunities and stress-management training. The Association for Worksite Health Promotion listed in Appendix D provides more information about worksite health education and promotion.

IN CONCLUSION

We began this chapter with the idea that how you define and operationalize the term *community* will be your key to success in health education. We hope you now understand that any community in which you will work will be complex in its structure, needs, and potential. The RISE model should help you develop a fuller appreciation of that community's collective subgroups and the networks and resources available to them. As you seek to learn more about those subgroups, note reasons why individuals bond together and how culture and politics influence individual perceptions and interests. Consider the community in light of its positive resources and potential for developing its own solutions. Work to help make the organizations and settings in which health education happen a place where individuals are treated with respect and community potential is celebrated.

REVIEW QUESTIONS

1. Define *community* and name some commonalities that may bond community members together.
2. Describe the RISE approach to community identification and explain how it can be used to identify community needs and assets.

3. Explain the connection between Maslow's hierarchy of needs and community bonds.
4. Describe how culture shapes a community and influences health.
5. Explain how political and environmental factors can influence community health.
6. Name at least four work settings in which community health education happens and describe some typical responsibilities of a health educator working in each setting.

 FOR YOUR APPLICATION

Three Principles of Health and Culture

- *Every person is a member of a culture, regardless of the degree of membership awareness.* Describe the culture(s) or group(s) to which you belong.
- *Each person's culture influences his or her health-related beliefs and behaviors.* Describe some health-related beliefs or behaviors of the group(s) you identified for the first principle.
- *Effective health education depends on the health professional's level of cultural sensitivity and cultural competence.* Describe a moment in your life when you interacted with an individual whose cultural beliefs or practices differed from yours. Describe your thoughts about and reactions to those differences.

 FOR YOUR PORTFOLIO

Creating a Personal Résumé

Contact the student career services or career development support office on your campus and ask for help in developing a one-page résumé to include in your portfolio. Consider your work and volunteer experience in light of the discussion in this chapter about community subgroups and places in which health educators often work. Contact representatives of at least two potential employers and ask for their advice about the knowledge and skills you need to work in those environments. Visit Web sites and/or local offices of several health organizations and note key skills and concepts highlighted in their job descriptions and other documents. Examine the skills described in the seven areas of responsibility (Appendix A). On your résumé, adapt the descriptions of your skills and experiences in accordance with what you learn from these sources. Then, make plans to volunteer, work part-time, or do both for organizations that will prepare you for the job market and enhance your résumé.

3

Understanding Epidemiological Concepts

YOU HAVE JUST STARTED A NEW JOB AT THE LOCAL PUB-lic health department. The director notifies you that a local physician has reported a case of measles (a disease that is preventable through vaccination). He says that he and other health officials are concerned about the potential for an epidemic. You are not absolutely sure what he means or how they will know an epidemic has started. In fact, even though measles is a disease almost everyone has heard about, you can't remember many specifics. You wonder what role you will play if there is an epidemic.

Chapter Objectives

1. Describe the epidemiological approach to understanding patterns of disease among humans.
2. List the purposes of epidemiology.
3. Compare current and historical life expectancies in the United States.
4. Identify measures of mortality.
5. Classify causes of disease.
6. Describe the factors that influence morbidity.
7. List sources of morbidity information.
8. Discuss measures of morbidity.
9. Describe concepts related to infectious disease, such as agent, host, environment, mode of transmission, and spectrum of disease.
10. Identify concepts related to noninfectious disease, such as acute illness, chronic illness, and the web of causation.
11. Define primary, secondary, and tertiary prevention.

THE EPIDEMIOLOGICAL APPROACH
IN THE COMMUNITY

The word *epidemiology* originally comes from Greek. If you have studied medical terminology, you know that the suffix *ology* means "study of" and the prefix *epi* means "among or upon." The root word *deme* means "commune or group of people." Therefore, the literal definition would be "the study of groups of people." We think a good working definition of **epidemiology** is the study of disease, the determinants of health, and/or behaviors that prevent or cause disease or injury among groups of people. This definition implies that epidemiology serves many purposes. Some of these purposes are to

Study past or current trends in health status or level of disease

Identify causes of death

Establish **etiology** (cause) of disease

Define risk factors and determinants of disease

Determine need for health services

Identify feasible disease-prevention and health promotion strategies

Suggest need for future research in health and disease

Predict future disease outbreaks

How would you describe the job of an epidemiologist?

An **epidemiologist** is a specialist in **epidemics,** or outbreaks of disease. In a sense, epidemiologists are detectives. They seek answers. In general, epidemiologists consider the population as a whole, or the community, in their investigations. They ask questions of individuals so that they can understand the disease or prevention strategy in the group.

If you were an epidemiologist, responsible for gathering information about diseases, and there was an outbreak of a disease in your community, how would you start your investigation? Some obvious questions might be "How many people are sick now?" and "How quickly is it spreading?" With our hypothetical case of measles, you would first find out as much as possible about measles. Even if you knew a lot about the disease already, you would find out if new information had been discovered. Next, you would talk with the girl who had measles, her physician, and family. Other people with similar symptoms would be interviewed to determine if more cases of measles were present in the community. The long-term purpose of your investigation would be to protect the community from an epidemic.

Even if you weren't yet sure of the name of the disease or its cause, you would probably start with questions like "How many cases?" and "How fast is it spreading?" to determine incidence and prevalence. You may have heard the words before, but they are sometimes used incorrectly even in professional literature. **Incidence** is the number of new cases of a specific disease among a specific group of people in a specific period of time. For example, in 1996 there were 68,885 new cases of AIDS in the United States (CDC, 1997b). **Prevalence** is all of the cases (not just the new ones) of a specific disease among a specific group of people in a specific period of time.

As the investigating epidemiologist, you should determine prevalence and incidence in order to make decisions about whether an outbreak, or epidemic, of a disease is present. That's important because an epidemic is an increase in the normal prevalence of a disease. You might plot an epidemic curve to assist in the decision-making process. The epidemic curve would illustrate the first infection (**index case**) and the number of new cases at selected intervals in time until there are no further new cases. In our measles example, the case reported to the health department would be the index case. Any others that were found during interviews would be plotted. Historical prevalence rates for measles in the community would be compared to the current rate. If the current rates are higher, an outbreak is occurring. If people die as result of a disease outbreak, you might also determine disease-specific death rates early in the investigation.

Mortality

Of course, you would want to move as quickly as possible in collecting epidemiological information to minimize risk of mortality. **Mortality** means death. Epidemiologists compute crude mortality, or death, rates in order to get an overall picture of the level of death in a community. Mortality rates are computed by dividing the number of deaths in a specific place by the number of people in the population at a given period of time. FYI 3.1 lists formulas commonly used in epidemiology. A **crude mortality rate** cannot be used to estimate the degree of risk an individual has of dying in a community because many factors have powerful influences on death rates. The most powerful is age. If the community you are investigating has a large number of older individuals, it will have a higher mortality rate than a community with many young individuals—not because it is a riskier place to live, but because older people are more likely to die.

What if you suspect that a disease outbreak is specific to a particular age group? To test your assumption, you can compute rates. Sometimes epidemiologists will compute **age-specific mortality** rates in order to study the frequency of death among people of a selected age group. This mortality rate is computed by dividing the number of deaths among people in a specific age group (for example, 13- to 18-year-olds) by the number of people in the age category at a specific period of time. You can also compute the mortality rate for other age groups to compare across groups. Performing calculations to remove age influences on crude mortality rates makes it more feasible to compare risk of death between communities because you have removed the effect of the factor that influences rates the most.

Morbidity

Morbidity means illness. We've already stated that incidence and prevalence are morbidity rates commonly used by epidemiologists and other health professionals to determine the level of illness in a community. The morbidity rates of different

FOR YOUR INFORMATION 3.1

Formulas for Selected Rates and Ratios Used in Epidemiology

Rates and ratios play important roles in epidemiology. They are not difficult to use when you know the formulas. Some of the most common are listed here.

Morbidity

Incidence =

$$\frac{\text{Number of new cases of a disease}}{\text{Total number of people at risk}} \text{ over a period of time} \times 100,000$$

Attack Rate =

$$\frac{\text{Number of people sick}}{\text{Number of people both sick and well}} \text{ during a period of time} \times 100$$

Prevalence =

$$\frac{\text{Total number of people with a disease}}{\text{Average number of people}} \text{ during a period of time} \times 100,000$$

Mortality

Crude mortality =

$$\frac{\text{Number of deaths in a selected year}}{\text{Number of people in the population}} \times 100,000$$

Infant mortality* =

$$\frac{\text{Number of infant deaths during a year}}{\text{Number of live births during a year}} \times 1,000$$

Disease-specific mortality =

$$\frac{\text{Number of deaths due to a specific disease}}{\text{Number in population}} \times 100,000$$

Age-specific mortality =

$$\frac{\text{Number of deaths in a specific age group}}{\text{Number of people in the same age group}} \times 100,000$$

*Infant deaths are defined as deaths among babies from 0 to 365 days old.

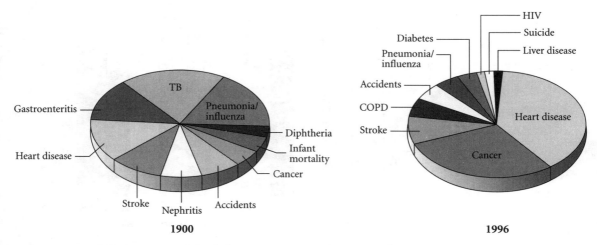

FIGURE 3.1   Shifts in causes of death from 1900 to 1996 (COPD is chronic obstructive pulmonary disease).
As you can see from these two charts, the types of diseases that cause death have shifted over time. Even though we are currently seeing some infectious diseases, such as tuberculosis, becoming more prevalent today, the major causes of death are related to lifestyle choices. From *Epidemiology for Public Health Practice* (2nd ed.), by R. H. Friis and T. A. Sellers, 1999, Gaithersburg, MD: Aspen.

types of diseases that affect communities vary over time, according to the place, and with the characteristics of the people. If you review Figure 3.1 you will note shifts in the types of disease that occurred in the twentieth century (illustrated though causes of death). As you can see, early in the century, completely different types of disease were the leading causes of death. Two major categories of morbidity are the two types of disease, infectious and noninfectious. Infectious diseases, such as tuberculosis (TB), pneumonia, and gastroenteritis, were much more common causes of death in the early 1900s than were noninfectious diseases (Friis & Sellers, 1999). Today, noninfectious diseases, like heart disease, cancer, and stroke, are the most common causes of death (Friis & Sellers, 1999), although we may be seeing another shift as infectious diseases like TB and AIDS become highly prevalent. Morbidity and mortality influence both life expectancy and quality of life, which are two issues that make the understanding of epidemiology imperative for health educators.

Life Expectancy   Fluctuations in morbidity and mortality rates in a community will, of course, affect the life expectancy of its residents. **Life expectancy** refers to the average number of years groups of people are expected to live. Life expectancy rates have changed over time. Advances in available treatments, prevention methods, and healthier lifestyles have contributed to the change. In the 1900s the life expectancy in the United States was 49.24 years, whereas in 1990 the life expectancy in the United States was 76.1 years. Figure 3.2 graphs life expectancies

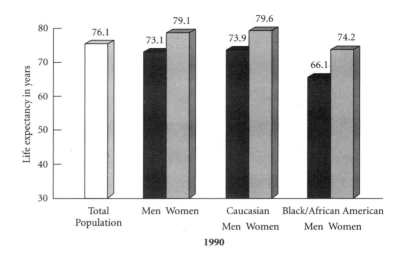

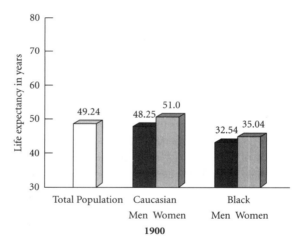

FIGURE 3.2   Life expectancy charts reported by USDHHS, 1900 and 1990.
Life expectancy has increased dramatically over time for all people in the United
States; however, disparities still exist between people of different ethnicities. These
charts illustrate both the increase in life expectancy and some of the disparities.

Information from United States Department of Health and Human Services, Public Health Service
(1996). Hyattsville, MD: CDC National Center for Health Statistics.

for genders and Blacks and Caucasians in the United States. The reasons behind
these differences in genders and ethnic groups are not easy to understand; however, it is imperative to both seek the causes of the differences and actively address them.

According to Cohen (1989), differences in life expectancy are directly related
to poverty. Low socioeconomic status influences insurance coverage, which in
turn influences access to medical care. Even if medical care is accessible, people

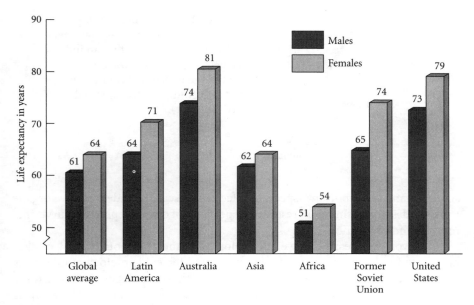

FIGURE 3.3   Life expectancies for selected regions.
Life expectancies have not increased for all regions of the world. As you can see from this chart, some countries/regions fall well below the United States and other developed countries. Data from Centers for Disease Control Web site: http://www.cdc.gov/nchs/fastats/fastats.htm.

in poverty may not be able to afford nutritious food or even enough food. Their housing may be inadequate and safety may be a major issue. Education may not be attainable; and this problem alone influences all of the aforementioned. Poverty and its influence on health will be discussed in more detail in later chapters.

Figure 3.3 illustrates the life expectancies of selected regions of the world. Note the differences in life expectancies and try to identify some of the reasons they exist. Life expectancy rates sometimes differ as a result of the level of development of a country or region. Some regions just don't have the technology to address medical problems that is available to developed countries. Other regions have environmental problems or cultural practices that influence life expectancies. For example, the nuclear power plant accident in Chernobyl, Ukraine, in 1986 has resulted in increased thyroid cancer among the people of that area. These increases will continue to be seen. Health educators have an opportunity to broaden the scope of their work in communities by seeking answers to root causes of death and disease.

INFECTIOUS DISEASE

Infectious diseases spread from individual to individual or from insects, animals, or other carriers to humans. They are generally caused by an easily identified

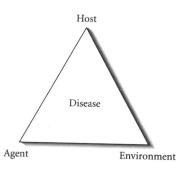

Host

Disease

Agent   Environment

FIGURE 3.4   **The epidemiological triangle.**   There are three major factors that influence whether an individual gets an infectious disease. They are the agent, external environment, and host (individual, or internal environment).

single organism. Important aspects of infectious disease include causative organisms, modes of transmission, reservoirs, spectrum of disease, epidemic curve, immunity, and prevention.

Have you ever heard of the epidemiological triangle? Although many models have been used to illustrate the basic concepts of the epidemiology of infectious disease, the triangle is still relevant and easy to understand (Figure 3.4). The three apexes of the triangle represent the agent, host, and environment. The **agent** is the cause of the disease or causative microorganism. In infectious diseases it is almost always biological. Another term used for agent in infectious diseases is **pathogen** (disease-causing microorganism). The **host** is the recipient of the disease. Anything internally in the host that influences the disease process should be considered part of the host. The **environment** consists of the external surroundings that influence the host.

Agent

The most common agents in infectious disease are viruses, bacteria, fungi, and worms. Viruses are the smallest agents and most difficult to treat. **Antibiotics,** which are substances that arrest the growth of or destroy pathogens, do not kill viruses. They do kill bacteria, which are also microscopic and come in shapes that range from rectangular to spiral. Although some bacteria are becoming antibiotic-resistant, most are still controllable with standard treatments. Fungi, yeast, and molds cause many common conditions, such as vaginal yeast infections and athlete's foot. Worms, such as tapeworms (which can be many feet long), cause a variety of illnesses. See Figure 3.5 for common biological agents and examples of the diseases that they cause.

The effects of agents on a host depend on many characteristics, such as their **virulence, infectivity, pathogenicity, resistance,** and the number of microorganisms that enter the host. For example, rabies, a very severe illness, almost always causes death in humans. The virus that causes it is therefore *virulent.* An agent that can easily enter a body and multiply is *infective.* A highly infective agent causes measles. Measles is also a disease of high *pathogenicity;* once in the body, the measles agent almost always causes full-blown disease, not just a light case. HIV has low *resistance,* which means that outside of the body it is easy to kill.

Pathogen	Examples
Viruses	Common cold
	Influenza
	Poliomyelitis
	Hepatitis B
	Herpes
	HIV/AIDS
	Chicken pox
	Mononucleosis
	(Epstein-Barr)

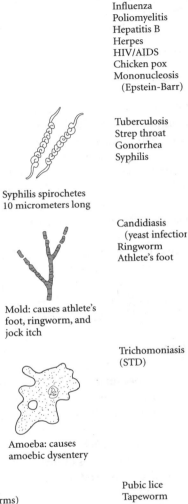

Poliovirus
0.03 micrometer
in diameter

Bacteria

Tuberculosis
Strep throat
Gonorrhea
Syphilis

Tuberculosis bacilli
3 micrometers long

Syphilis spirochetes
10 micrometers long

Fungi

Candidiasis
 (yeast infection
Ringworm
Athlete's foot

Yeast: causes vaginal
infections; 5–30
micrometers long

Mold: causes athlete's
foot, ringworm, and
jock itch

Protozoa

Trichomoniasis
(STD)

Trichomonas: causes
genital tract infections;
50–100 micrometers long

Amoeba: causes
amoebic dysentery

Metazoa
(helminths or parasitic worms)

Pubic lice
Tapeworm

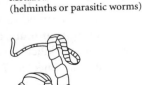

Tapeworm
up to several meters long

FIGURE 3.5 Common biological agents.

Infectious diseases are caused by a number of organisms. Some of the most common are shown in this illustration along with the types of diseases they cause. From *Environmental Health* (2nd ed.), by M. T. Morgan, 1997, Englewood, CO: Morton.

It will be helpful for you to know the common biological agents because as a health educator you may be asked to teach people about the causes of their infectious diseases. Understanding terms like *virulence, infectivity, pathogenicity,* and *resistance* will also help you help others communicate with their health care providers.

Host

The host is the individual who has the disease; *host* can be thought of as a person's internal environment. Try to think about the internal things that influence you. Did you come up with things like what you eat, how much you sleep, the presence of other diseases or disorders, genetics, and the ability to develop immunity? If so, you were absolutely right. Anything that influences the body internally has the potential to influence the outcome of a disease. Even factors like stress, exercise, and body temperature influence disease processes in the body. These things don't cause the disease but rather determine to some extent how an individual will react to or fight a disease.

The host's first line of defense is skin. What an amazing organ! It serves as a barrier to many agents. Tears and saliva do the same. The body's inflammatory response serves as the second line of defense. In an inflammatory response, the body sends fluids containing white blood cells and other substances to fight off the agent. The body's third line of defense is **immunity.**

Immunity   *Immunity* means that an individual is resistant or not susceptible to a specific disease. Immunity occurs when antibodies are produced in the body. **Antibodies** kill microorganisms or prevent them from multiplying and infecting the host. A person isn't immune to all diseases just because he/she is immune to one. In other words, immunity is disease-specific, and not all diseases stimulate antibody production. There are several ways in which immunity occurs. Individuals can produce it in their own body or receive the ingredients of immunity from outside the body. These two types of immunity are called **active** (body produces) and **passive** (body does not produce) immunity. Both active and passive immunity occur either naturally or artificially. In **natural immunity,** individuals produce antibodies after having had a disease or received antibodies from their mother in utero. In **artificial immunity,** individuals become immune to a disease by producing antibodies after having had the weakened or killed agent responsible for the disease injected or by having actual antibodies injected. FYI 3.2 lists the types of immunity.

Herd immunity occurs when a significant number of people in a population are immune to a disease. If many people in a community have a disease, it is much more likely that the disease-free people will get it; if few people have the disease, its spread to people who aren't immune will be less likely. Think of a specific disease while looking at Figures 3.6 and 3.7. The first figure illustrates the typical progression of an epidemic when few people are immune. If a large number of people

FOR YOUR INFORMATION 3.2

Examples of Immunity

Immunity can be acquired in two ways as shown here. Immunity is one of the human body's major lines of defense against disease.

Active Immunity
Artificially acquired active immunity (Vaccination)

Passive Immunity
Artificially acquired passive immunity
(Antibodies injected)

Naturally acquired active immunity
(Having had a disease)

Naturally acquired passive immunity
(Antibodies passing from mother to baby)

become immune—by vaccine, for example—a protective barrier is created for those who are susceptible. People who don't have the disease, due to immunity or no contact, won't spread it. Almost the entire population, or "herd," is protected.

As a health educator, you may help people gain the knowledge necessary to make good decisions about health. The range of information people might need concerning the internal environment of the host may vary from healthy food choices to reducing stress to the side effects of vaccines as well as their benefits. As we have mentioned before, it is important for you to be able to access information; in this case, you would need to research host issues. Return to Appendix D to review Internet resources.

Environment

The external environment influences both the outcomes of disease and the very presence of the disease. The external environment has physical aspects (such as terrain, precipitation, and temperature) as well as social aspects (such as cultural characteristics). The numbers of people, plants, and animals influence the external environment. Insects or animals spread some diseases. If an insect carrier (vector) of a specific disease doesn't live in an environment, the disease is less likely to be present in the environment. If a disease is spread via tiny droplets in the air, a place crowded with people is going to have disease spread at a higher rate than will a location with very few people. Certain organisms live and spread best in places that are very hot and humid. The cultural environment influences everything from food choices to types of housing and stress-coping strategies.

How an epidemic spreads in a population

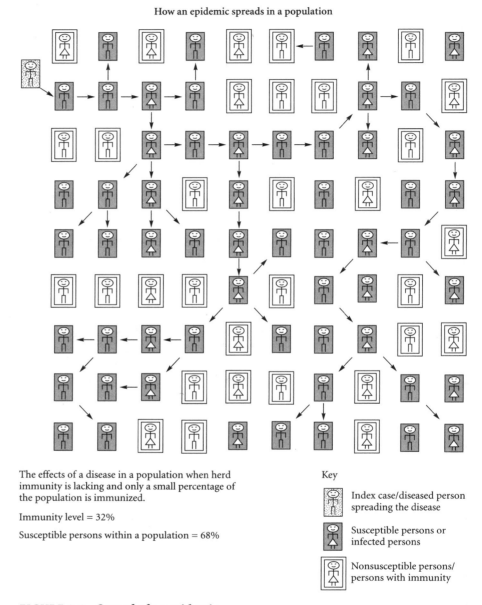

The effects of a disease in a population when herd immunity is lacking and only a small percentage of the population is immunized.

Immunity level = 32%

Susceptible persons within a population = 68%

Key

Index case/diseased person spreading the disease

Susceptible persons or infected persons

Nonsusceptible persons/ persons with immunity

FIGURE 3.6   Spread of an epidemic.
Diagram of a population, showing a low immunization level that falls short of protecting individuals within the group. From *An Introduction to Epidemiology* (2nd ed.), by T. C. Timmreck, 1998, Sudbury, MA: Jones and Bartlett.

The protection given a population through immunizations

The effects of a disease in a population when herd immunity is complete with a large percentage of the population being immunized.

Immunity level = 85%

Susceptible persons within a population = 15%

Key:

 Infected person

 Susceptible persons

 Nonsusceptible persons/ persons with immunity

FIGURE 3.7   Herd immunity.

Diagram of a population showing a high level of immunizations within the group so that it affords a good level of protection to most of the individuals within the group.

From *An Introduction to Epidemiology* (2nd ed), by T. C. Timmreck, 1998, Sudbury, MA: Jones and Bartlett.

Although all cultural characteristics do not influence the external environment, all influence an individual's likelihood of contracting certain diseases. Again, as a health educator, you will need to be prepared to answer questions about the environment and how it affects disease. If, for example, you live in a place where deer ticks (which carry Lyme disease) are common, your job may be to teach people that tick bites can be prevented by wearing long sleeves and tucking in loose clothing.

The agent, host, and environment interact with one another in the big picture of infectious disease. One example of the interaction occurs in the modes of transmission of diseases. Characteristics of hosts, agents, and environments affect how the agent is transmitted from one person to another.

Mode of Transmission

The **mode of transmission** is the way in which agents travel from one host to another. Some agents travel through the air, whereas others have to be picked up from a hard surface. As noted earlier, insects and animals also carry some agents from one host to another. Modes of transmission are direct or indirect. A *direct* mode of transmission means that an agent is passed directly from one person to another (person to person). *Indirect* modes involve a third element—an animal, insect, hard surface, or food. All modes of transmission fall within these two broad categories. Airborne transmission occurs when the agent is carried on small droplets of moisture or dust. Small droplets, forcefully expelled from someone's mouth or nose via a cough or a sneeze, can travel great distances if they aren't blocked. Vectorborne transmission occurs when an animal or insect serves as the agent's transportation. **Vectors** are living but nonhuman (Timmreck, 1998). **Fomites** are inanimate objects, such as cups, tables, doorknobs, and toys, that also can serve as a means of transportation for some agents. Sometimes an agent remains in a **reservoir** and multiplies until it is transmitted to a host. Anything living or nonliving might serve as a reservoir—including the human body. Some humans or animals carry an agent and transmit it to others but do not get sick themselves. These *carriers* make prevention a challenge because their carrier status often goes undetected until many people around them get the disease (Typhoid Mary is the most famous example).

Modes of transmission involve the way agents get from person to person but do not determine how an agent enters the body (*portal of entry*) or exits the body (*portal of exit*). Portals of entry and exit and modes of transmission play important roles in the prevention as well as transmission of diseases.

Once an agent enters a body, if the conditions are right, the disease will progress through a fairly consistent set of stages. These phases are illustrated in Figure 3.8. The *incubation period* is the time from the agent's entry in the body (*point of infection*) to the occurrence of signs or symptoms of disease. During the *prodromal period,* signs (measurable changes in the body such as increases in body

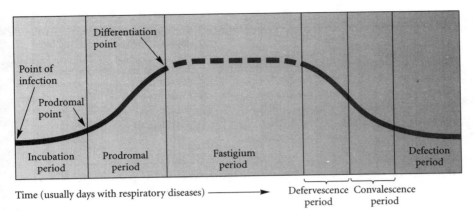

FIGURE 3.8   Progression of an infectious disease.
In this case, the disease affects the respiratory tract. From *An Introduction to Epidemiology* (2nd ed.), by T. C. Timmreck, 1998, Sudbury, MA: Jones and Bartlett.

temperature) and symptoms (subjective changes in the body such as pain) begin to occur. The disease is in its peak during the *fastigium period*. Signs and symptoms decline during the *defervescence period,* and the individual recovers during *convalescence.*

Noteworthy Infectious Diseases

Some infectious diseases are short term, or **acute,** and others are long term, or **chronic.** Although there are many acute and chronic diseases that we might discuss, we have selected three that have been in the news in the recent past. Other significant infectious diseases, and their modes of transmission, are listed in Table 3.1.

Escherichia coli   Some forms of the bacterium *Escherichia coli* (*E. coli*) are virulent pathogens. *E. coli* is generally foodborne (carried by food). You may have heard about recent outbreaks from contaminated and undercooked hamburger in fast-food restaurants. Individuals who contract the illness caused by the O157:H7 strain frequently have bloody diarrhea for short periods of time. Unfortunately, some individuals—especially very young children—die as a result. This illness is severe and acute in nature but can be prevented by adequate heating of the food reservoirs.

Hepatitis A   Several types of hepatitis virus are infectious; however, hepatitis A is the most easily transmitted. It is commonly transmitted to humans via uncooked foods, such as oysters, or foods that have been contaminated by a food worker with the disease. An individual with hepatitis A might experience extreme

TABLE 3.1   Selected Infectious Diseases

Spread by Water or Food	Spread from Person to Person	Spread Through Sexual Contact	Spread by Bugs or Animals
Salmonellosis	Hepatitis A	Gonorrhea	Lyme disease
Botulism	Respiratory illnesses	Syphilis	Bubonic plague
Cholera	Streptococcal disease	Chlamydia	Rabies
Giardiasis	Tuberculosis	Candidiasis	Malaria
Legionellosis	Hansen's disease (leprosy)	AIDS	Rocky Mountain spotted fever

Information from *Public Health and Preventive Medicine* (13th ed.), by J. M. Last and R. B. Wallace, 1992, New York: Appleton & Lange.

fatigue, tenderness over the liver, and jaundice (yellow coloring of the skin). Restaurant workers must practice proper hygiene in order to prevent the spread of hepatitis A through food.

Group A Streptococci   Some strains of this bacterial agent cause tissue to deteriorate. Recent serious illnesses may have been caused by a new strain or one that has not been prevalent in the past (Friis & Sellers, 1999). Transmission occurs through inhalation or wound infection. In many cases, it has been resistant to common treatments; it is the pathogen that killed Jim Henson and others. It can also cause gangrene.

NONINFECTIOUS DISEASES

The definition of noninfectious disease seems simple enough: diseases that are not transmitted from one person to another. Noninfectious diseases are brought about by chemical, metallic, electrical, psychosocial, genetic, or other agents. The agent is not generally a pathogen, although it can be. In fact, noninfectious diseases are commonly caused by a combination of agents. A visual schematic of how agents work together to cause disease is found in Figure 3.9. The schematic, called a *web of causation*, demonstrates the relationship between agents. Finding the agents that cause a noninfectious disease or discovering how several agents work together to cause the disease is not simple. Robert Koch developed a list of postulates for determining infectious disease causation. They were adjusted to be helpful with chronic diseases.

1. The suspected characteristics of a chronic disease must be found more frequently in persons with the disease in question than in persons without the disease.

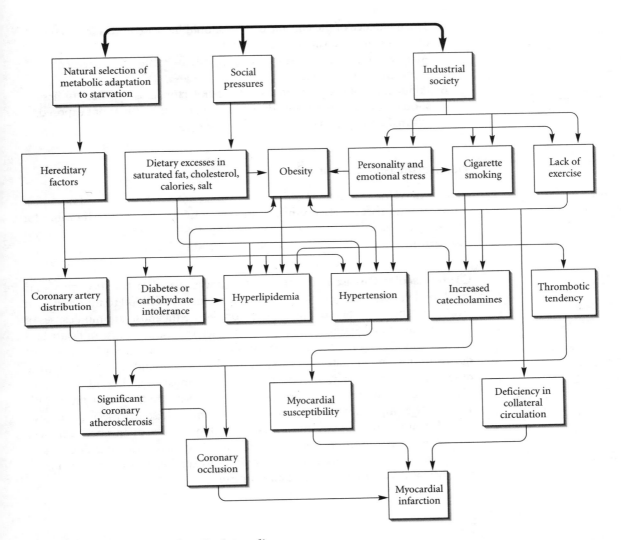

FIGURE 3.9   Web of causation for heart disease.
The cause of a myocardial infarction, or heart attack, is not simple to track. As you can see from this illustration many things from hereditary factors to lack of exercise influence the onset of heart disease. When no single cause can be determined, a web of causation must be created. From *Primer of Epidemiology* (4th ed., p. 4), by G. D. Friedman, 1994, New York: McGraw-Hill.

2. Individuals possessing the chronic disease characteristic must develop the disease more frequently than do persons not possessing the characteristic.

3. Exposure to a risk factor must occur before the chronic disease.

4. The incidence of the chronic disease should increase in relation to the duration and intensity of the risk factor.
5. All facets of a chronic disease illness should be related to the level of exposure to the risk factor.
6. Populations of people exposed to the risk factors in controlled studies should develop the chronic disease more often than those not exposed. (Evans, 1978, p. 254)

Noteworthy Noninfectious Diseases

In the United States and most other developed countries the burden of noninfectious chronic diseases is very heavy. In fact, four diseases are responsible for 71.6% of all deaths in the United States (CDC, 1998a). They are coronary heart disease, cancer, stroke, and chronic obstructive lung disease.

Cardiovascular Disease and Cancer   Cardiovascular diseases affect the heart and blood vessels. Ischemic heart disease (a deficiency of blood to the heart) and stroke (a deficiency of blood, often in the brain) are the most common causes of death in the United States. All cancers are the second leading cause of death, and cancers and cardiovascular diseases together account for almost two thirds of deaths in the United States. The loss of life alone commands attention, but the other aspect of chronic noninfectious disease that must be addressed is the cost. The medical costs for these diseases is around $400 billion annually (CDC, 1998a). The important issue is the extent to which these diseases can be prevented. Many noninfectious diseases are related in one way or another to choices people make. For example, the major risk factors of cardiovascular disease and some cancers include tobacco use, insufficient exercise, and poor nutrition— mainly matters of personal choice and control.

PREVENTION

What types of activities would you list as examples of prevention?

Helping people get the information they need to make healthy choices is one important aspect of prevention. You may even think that your involvement in prevention occurs only before an individual becomes ill. But two of the three categories of prevention take place after the onset of disease.

Primary Prevention

Primary prevention involves efforts that occur before individuals become sick. Programs that help people stop smoking before they develop heart disease or cancer reflect primary prevention efforts. Another example of primary prevention is vaccination of children against infectious diseases. Vaccination triggers the production of antibodies, which in turn prevents future cases of the disease. These types of primary prevention have to do with the host. It is also possible to change the environment to bring about primary prevention. For example, mosquito control and water fluoridation programs are primary prevention efforts.

Secondary Prevention

Once a disease occurs in an individual, efforts to prevent its progression are called **secondary prevention.** Screening tools like mammography (breast X-rays that screen for cancer) are secondary in nature. They may identify a cancerous lesion at an early stage when it can be treated successfully—thereby preventing progression. Many women believe that if they have yearly mammograms they will not get breast cancer. In fact, mammograms do not prevent breast cancer.

Tertiary Prevention

Tertiary prevention is concerned with the quality of life with disease. Regardless of the effect of a disease on an individual, tertiary prevention is practiced when efforts are made to improve the quality of life as much as possible. This may not seem like prevention at all but the idea is to prevent situations from becoming worse—in other words, to help people with serious diseases live the best life possible. Try to think of some actions that you could take to improve the quality of life for someone who has suffered a major heart attack.

SOURCES OF DATA

Prevention efforts may begin with the collection of health-related data or the completion of epidemiological research. Plans for health education programs of all types should be based on assessment of relevant information. Health-related data are collected systematically in the United States. Some of the existing sources of data are discussed in the following paragraphs.

Census

Censuses originated in combination with the process of taxation in ancient Egypt and Rome. In the United States, the census occurs every 10 years in order to determine seats in the U.S. House of Representatives. Federal funding of some health and social services programs also depends on number and distribution of people as measured by the U.S. Census (Timmreck, 1998). Caution is needed when using census data in epidemiological research, however. The ethnic and racial categories listed on the census, for example, have been matters of controversy. There is such diversity in this country that some experts wonder if it is possible to categorize ethnicity and race at all. Other data collected in censuses include gender, age, marital status, type of housing, ancestry, language spoken in the home, year the residence was built, place of birth, education level, employment status, plumbing and kitchen facilities, telephone and vehicle availability, and types of heating and cooling. Combining census data with data about disease can assist health educators gain a clearer picture of a community's health status.

Vital Statistics

In the United States vital life events are recorded and then counted. For example, each newborn receives a birth certificate, and death certificates are written for each person who dies. The numbers of marriages and divorces also become vital statistics in the United States. Certain diseases that occur in this country are considered reportable: Physicians or other health care providers who diagnose these illnesses are required to record and report the diseases to their health departments.

With censuses and other kinds of record keeping, there are inaccuracies. Sometimes diseases aren't diagnosed properly or the cause of death is inaccurately listed. As time progresses, diagnostic criteria change, making comparisons of vital statistics between years less meaningful. Nevertheless, vital statistics provide a great deal of information that helps program planners.

In the United States the National Center for Health Statistics has computerized systems for collecting vital statistics nationally. The Center also conducts many surveys that provide exceptional information about the nation's health. Included are the National Survey of Family Growth (demographic and social factors associated with maternal and child health); the National Health Interview Survey (demographic and morbidity information); the National Health and Nutrition Examination Survey, or NHANES (prevalence of selected diseases, disorders, and risk factors); and the National Hospital Discharge Study (hospital discharges).

The Centers for Disease Control and Prevention also conduct very large data-collection projects. CDC makes the data from these projects available to researchers across the nation. The CDC operates the National Notifiable Diseases Surveillance System and conducts the U.S. Immunization and Youth Risk Behavior surveys. If you are conducting an assessment or research project, consider using some of the extensive data currently available.

RESEARCH IN EPIDEMIOLOGY

Epidemiologists use four major types of studies to discover patterns in risk factors, disease, and healthy behaviors: cross-sectional, cohort, case-control, and experimental studies.

Cross-Sectional Studies

Cross-sectional studies involve a "snapshot" of a group of people. It is a one-time data-collection effort (by survey or some other means) that often uses a self-report format. **Self-report** simply means that no clinical or official measurement is made; rather, people report information about themselves. This type of study is also called a *prevalence study* if the researcher is studying the presence of a disease. Why would a cross-sectional study determine prevalence? Check out the definition of prevalence given earlier in the chapter if you have difficulty answering this question. The title of the study (cross-sectional) describes the sample; a cross section of a population is selected for study. Many types of information can be gathered during the data-collection process, including anything from health behaviors to attitudes and beliefs. Relationships can be inferred as a result of this type of data collection. For example, you might find that when many people report a concern about pollution, many people also recycle trash. This kind of association does not mean that the concern about pollution causes the degree of recycling; it just means there is a relationship of some sort. Although cross-sectional studies can provide you with a lot of information about relationships, you must be careful not to make unwarranted assumptions about cause and effect.

Cohort Studies

Cohort studies are sometimes called *incidence studies*. As you know, the frequency of new cases of a disease is used to compute an incidence rate. In this type of study, a cohort of healthy people is followed through time to see if they develop a specific disease of interest. Other information is also collected, such as health behaviors, beliefs, and exposures. As a result, the incidence rate for the disease of interest can be computed. Cohort studies allow comparisons of incidence rates between people who report a specific behavior (such as exercise) and those who report they do not engage in the specific behavior (exercise in this case).

A **cohort** is any group whose members have something in common. The commonality might be age, place of location, gender, occupation, or virtually any other characteristic. Cohort studies cost more than other types of studies because they are carried out over a long period of time. These studies are also referred to as *longitudinal* because of the length of time they take or *prospective* because they are future-oriented. One of the best-known cohort studies is the Framingham study in which more than 5,000 people in one community were assessed and followed over many years. The study provided some outstanding information about risk factors for heart disease.

Case-Control Studies

In case-control studies, a specific disease is generally the focus of the research. In the most common use of case-control, a group of people with the disease is selected to be *cases* in the study. A second group, without the disease but otherwise very similar to the first in regard to characteristics like age, gender, ethnicity, and socioeconomic status, is selected to be *controls*. Researchers ask people in both groups to recall behaviors or health determinants from the past, or they use retrospective (past) medical records to study how the two groups differ. The objective is to discover how and/or why the disease occurs.

Experimental Studies

The experiment is the only type of study in which researchers can really isolate the cause of a disease or the effectiveness of treatments. In this type of study, participants (called *subjects* in the case of an experiment) are **randomly selected** from the population of interest. A computerized process, much like throwing every person's name into a hat and drawing out the number needed, is used to randomly choose those who will be in the study. This selection process gives each person the same chance at being in the study as anyone else. In other words, one type of person won't be over- or underrepresented in the study. Subjects are also randomly assigned to either the intervention or control group. Subjects in the intervention group will receive a treatment, exposure, or other intervention. The control group will not receive the treatment or intervention but will be treated the same in every other way. Differences in the groups will be analyzed in order to determine the efficacy of the intervention.

HISTORICAL PERSPECTIVES

Although the science of epidemiology as we know it developed in the 1800s, the search for the cause of disease goes back to ancient times. Through observation, study, and experience, early physicians and scientists gained knowledge about the spread of disease. Quarantine and sanitary practices were instituted in some areas long before people understood that infectious diseases are caused by microbial agents. A few of the significant events in the history of epidemiology are charted on Figure 3.10. In recent years, epidemiologists have been challenged by Ebola fever and hantavirus, as well as human immunodeficiency virus. We encourage you to learn more about this topic; seek out some of the books that have been written about the epidemiological "adventure."

IN CONCLUSION

Epidemiological studies provide much valuable information to health educators. Morbidity (incidence and prevalence) and mortality rates alone can assist health educators in helping individuals and communities obtain information about prevalent infectious or noninfectious diseases and plan appropriate education and prevention programs.

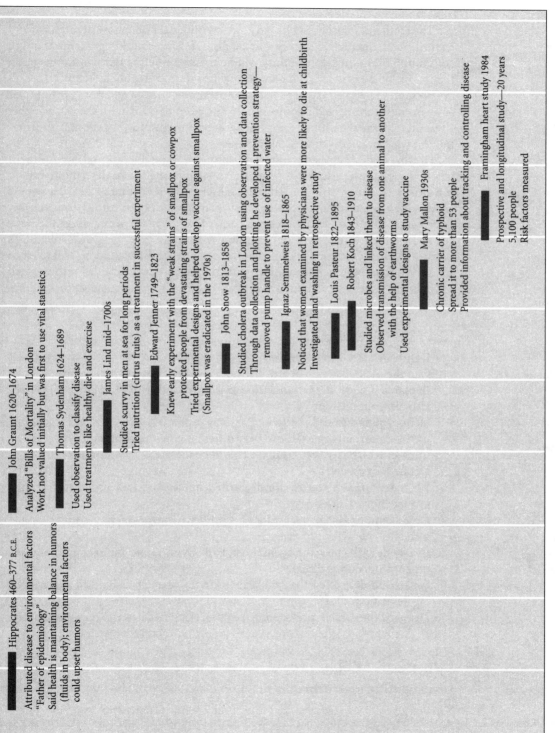

FIGURE 3.10   Timeline: A few significant events in the history of epidemiology.
Historical events have had a powerful influence on our lives and health. It is impossible to note them all in one brief illustration;
however, some important events are found in this figure.

The epidemiological triangle is a guide to understanding how agent, host, and environment interact in the spread of disease. Understanding agents that are commonly found in a community will help determine the types of information that might be presented in an educational program. If highly infectious diseases are present, ill people may need to learn the importance of remaining at home or away from the uninfected population. On the other hand, if a disease that is highly resistant to normal treatments is present, people may need very specific information on what preventive measures to take.

Health educators play an important role in keeping the external environment healthy. You may be asked to help plan a recycling program or determine ways to solve overcrowding. Your largest role, however, may well be in helping people change their internal environments. You may have an opportunity to plan programs about food choices, exercise, or other lifestyle matters that affect the host.

You may be involved in determining what epidemiological information is needed to plan effective health programs. As a health educator you will need to know how to use the vast amount of epidemiological data available for the benefit of your community. Epidemiology is likely to be an important aspect of your job.

 ## REVIEW QUESTIONS

1. Define *incidence* and *prevalence.*
2. Can the incidence rate of any disease be higher than the prevalence rate for the same disease, at the same time and place, and with the same people? Explain your answer.
3. Define *morbidity* and *mortality.*
4. Can the mortality rates of two very different cities be compared to determine in which city there is more risk of death? Explain your answer.
5. Define *life expectancy.*
6. What are possible reasons for disparities in life expectancies between ethnic groups in the United States?
7. Give examples of agents, host issues, and environmental issues that influence the spread of disease.
8. Briefly describe how the agent, host, and environment interact with one another in infectious diseases.
9. Give examples (other than those listed in the text) of each of the three types of prevention.
10. Describe the three types of epidemiological studies described in the chapter.

 ## FOR YOUR APPLICATION

Investigating an Outbreak

You are a health educator at the local public health department in a community of approximately 50,000 people. The university in your community enrolls about

15,000 students at any given time. During the summer, the university sponsors cheerleading, art, science, and other camps. One summer the local emergency room reports seven cases of severe vomiting and diarrhea within a 30-hour period. All of the victims are between 10 and 14 years old. Each had been attending a camp at the local university.

You are on the team of individuals who will investigate these illnesses. List five questions you might ask to gather the information that you will need to find the source of the illness. Indicate to whom you would address the questions and why they are important.

FOR YOUR PORTFOLIO

Documenting Professional Development

1. Label a notebook divider "Professional Development."
2. Contact a local or regional health department or another medical institution.
3. Ask to speak with an epidemiologist.
4. Make an appointment to visit the epidemiologist at his/her worksite.
5. During your visit find out what types of activities are accomplished in an average day.
6. Get information about the process that was followed in a local disease outbreak.
7. Summarize your findings and place your summary in the Professional Development section of your portfolio.

4

Understanding Health Through the Life Span

YOU'VE DECIDED TO WORK ON GAINING SOME COMMU-nity experience and build your résumé as you work through your degree program. Bravo! You decide to begin with some volunteer work at a local community center where most programs are designed for adults over the age of 65. The director asks you to develop a one-day workshop that focuses on preventing drug abuse. You enthusiastically agree. You particularly enjoyed learning about the prevention of adolescent drug abuse in the drug education course you completed. Addressing drug abuse among older adults couldn't be that different . . . could it?

Chapter Objectives

1. Explain the importance of viewing the health status of Americans in age-specific groups.
2. Discuss strengths and weaknesses of health-status data sources in the United States.
3. Describe the underlying role of socioeconomic status and its effect on health status in the United States.
4. Describe demographic characteristics of age-specific groups in the United States.
5. Describe health issues among each of the age-specific groups.
6. Explain the factors that influence the health of each age-specific group.
7. Identify information and support resources that can be used to understand and address health issues specific to each group.

WHY LOOK AT AGE-SPECIFIC GROUPS?

The first two chapters of this book were designed to help you develop a foundation of understanding about health and communities, and Chapter 3 introduced you to the epidemiological processes used to identify the health status of a population. This chapter provides an overview of what we know about the health issues of greatest concern in the United States as they relate to specific age groups. As you read this chapter, keep in mind our discussion in Chapter 2 about how most health education efforts begin with identified health needs.

America's Health Status and Leading Causes of Death

The Pan American Health Organization periodically publishes a document (*Healthy Conditions in the Americas;* PAHO, 1998) that describes the health status of every country in the Americas. According to this report, citizens of the United States have improved their health status and are living longer. Fertility rates have increased, while infant mortality rates and the age-adjusted death rates of the U.S. population have dropped.

Why do you think U.S. citizens are living longer? If your reasons include advances in medical technology and improved living conditions, you are partially correct. Considering the amount of money spent on medical technology, one could readily assume that high-technology medicine is a major contributing factor in better health. However, increased life expectancy at birth can be attributed primarily to low-technology public health efforts in prenatal care, improved diet, sanitation, and childhood immunization projects (Miller & Price, 1997). These efforts were undertaken largely because of national initiatives to identify factors that influence U.S. health status and the assets available for health improvement within our country. These influences and assets were then targeted for health education and illness-prevention programs through public health organizations and other community channels. In health education terminology, this process is called needs assessment and capacity building, and it is followed by program planning and implementation. In Part II of this book, you will have the opportunity to learn about and practice these processes. They have resulted in an increased public awareness about and reduction in disease risk factors (PAHO, 1998).

List reasons why you think U.S. citizens are living longer.

Improved life expectancy in the United States is not representative of the whole picture of our nation's health status. Our country continues to face health problems, although specific health issues change over time (see Figure 3.1). Today the five leading causes of death in America are heart disease, cancer, stroke, chronic obstructive pulmonary disease (COPD), and unintentional injuries (National Center for Health Statistics [NCHS], 1999a). The Centers for Disease Control and Prevention (1998a) report that two-thirds of those mortalities and a great portion of morbidity result from heart disease, cancer, and stroke. Heart disease (34%) and cancer (25%) account for more than half.

The existence of these statistics would seem to make our health education job simple, wouldn't it? We know that the majority of Americans are at risk of developing one or more chronic diseases within their life span. Thus, our prevention efforts should focus primarily on these concerns, and health education should begin at early ages. If only it were that simple.

Go back in your memory to the days of your adolescence. Recall Maslow's hierarchy of needs from Chapter 2 and apply it to who you were then: Think about your life priorities at that point in time. What motivated you? What were you concerned about most? Was it the possibility of developing heart disease? Did the previous question make you laugh? Most adolescents grapple with issues that affect their health, but the three leading causes of death in the United States are seldom at the top of their list of concerns.

Some pressing health concerns for age- and ethnicity-specific subgroups may not show up in statistics for the total population. That is why it is important for you to learn about the specific health concerns of different age and ethnic groups (see Chapter 5 for information specific to ethnic groups). When we look at America's health status within the context of specific groups, we begin to see a clearer picture of life's complexity and the amazing challenges faced by our profession. We also begin to find needed direction for our health promotion efforts.

Strengths and Weaknesses of Data Sources

Have you ever wondered about how we know the leading causes of death in our country? Or have you simply taken for granted that competent people are compiling the information somewhere in a federal building? National health statistics are an important foundation for your future employment because many decisions to fund disease-prevention and health promotion programs are based on those numbers. Without data sources, the decision makers would be more susceptible to sensationalized news accounts that tend to focus on such issues as violence and AIDS to the exclusion of "less newsworthy" health concerns (Benbow, Wang, & Whitman, 1998). The political agendas of specific groups and the sometimes inaccurate perceptions held by decision makers would not be balanced with statistical evidence to clarify the broader picture of a community's health. We need statistically sound health data sources to help us identify existing health needs, prioritize our health promotion efforts, and track the process of how our health promotion programs affect America's health.

As a health educator, one of your areas of responsibility (see Chapter 1), is acting as a resource person. It is likely that you will, from time to time, need to access national health statistics databases to retrieve needed information as part of needs-assessment and program-planning efforts. That information can also be very useful in educating your local community about real health risks. For these reasons, it is important that you not only know where and how to access the information but also are aware of the strengths and weaknesses of your sources.

In Chapter 3, you read that epidemiologists study incidence and prevalence rates of disease to monitor the health status of a given population. They are often concerned about the accurate reporting of births, deaths, and disease diagnoses so that fluctuations in health status can be adequately tracked. By law, physicians, clinics, and hospitals must report information about some diseases to their local health departments. The local health departments summarize local data and report to their state health departments who, in turn, report to the Centers for Disease Control and Prevention (CDC). Through its National Center for Health Statistics, the CDC maintains and disseminates this information in the *Monthly Vital Statistics Report* (see Appendix D for access information).

This system sounds admirably efficient and, for the most part, it is. However, the accuracy of the data at the national level strongly depends on the efficiency of local reporting. In some cases, the medical-records personnel in hospitals and clinics are overwhelmed by high patient loads and busy schedules. Personnel turnover and lack of training affect reporting frequency and accuracy. Low-risk diseases may not be reported as frequently as those considered more serious, and the exact cause of communicable diseases in particular can be lost in reporting. The complexity of contributing factors can distort cause-of-death determination. Attempts to categorize morbidity and mortality data according to patient age, ethnicity, or both can also be a challenge. These complexities slow the data-collection process to the extent that access to final reports for use at the local level can be delayed up to three years.

These weaknesses do not negate the usefulness of national health statistics. They do, however, serve to caution us about depending too heavily on exact numbers. National health statistics databases are reliable sources for exploring health trends and serve as a good starting point for decisions about how to prioritize health promotion efforts. When coupled with a careful assessment of the health-status trends in your local community, the information can be extremely valuable.

This chapter discusses the leading causes of death in the United States among infants (those less than 1 year old), children (1–14 years), adolescents and young adults (15–24 years), adults (25–64 years), and older adults (65 years and older). Here we survey the general health concerns of each age-specific group and invite you to contact the age-specific information sources highlighted in Appendix D for more details.

The Underlying Role of Socioeconomics

As you study health issues faced by Americans across age groups and ethnic communities (Chapter 5), it is vitally important that you not lose sight of what is likely the single most influential factor on health status. That is the **socioeconomic status** (SES) of individuals across those groups (Salpolsky, 1998; Sebastian, 1999). The term *socioeconomic status* refers to both social class and income; people of low socioeconomic status face cultural deprivation as well as poverty. In 1995 Americans who lived in poverty were three times as likely as those living above the poverty level to report fair or poor health status (USDHHS, 1997a). They were also two and a half times more likely to experience a chronic health condition that limited their activity. Children living in poverty were less likely to have enough food to eat, to be immunized, and to have health insurance. Individuals who never finished high school were more likely than those who did finish to have poor prenatal care and low-birth-weight babies. In fact, the 1995 age-adjusted death rates among adults aged 25 – 64 years were more than twice as high for those with no high school degree than for those who had at least completed high school (USDHHS, 1997a).

Name factors that place low-income individuals at greater health risks than middle- and upper-class Americans.

Why? Why would individuals at lower socioeconomic levels be at greater risk of these health problems than most middle- and upper-class Americans? You can probably think of several contributing factors. Poor nutrition is one. It thwarts the immune system and increases disease risk. So it makes sense, doesn't it? People with lower incomes have less access to adequate food supplies. They also tend to perform at lower levels academically and become school dropouts, thus reducing exposure to classroom programs on proper nutrition and other health issues.

Individuals at lower socioeconomic levels also have less money for early medical care. When money is available to buy over-the-counter medications, small health problems can sometimes be arrested before they worsen. Aspirin or ibuprofen can reduce inflammation so that injuries heal more quickly, and cough medicines can help keep lungs clear so that more serious illness doesn't develop. Money also helps pay for regular medical checkups and office visits during the early stages of an illness. When health insurance is not available to cover medical expenses, people are more likely to ignore or delay getting help, and disabilities and life-threatening situations are more likely to develop.

What about lack of knowledge about, and low regard for, developing healthy lifestyles? Individuals who drop out before completing high school may be exposed to fewer opportunities to learn about health and wellness in general. They may also be more susceptible to other health risks, such as cigarette smoking, physical inactivity, drinking and driving, and failure to use seat belts. Low-income adults (particularly single mothers) are more likely to work two jobs, have less time for themselves, and often function at high stress levels as they juggle work and family obligations. In the face of daily struggles for enough money and enough food, spending time on stress-managing leisure activities, for example, may seem like an unaffordable luxury.

Do only low-income individuals have health problems? No. America's middle- and upper-class citizens also struggle with some of the same health issues (such as heart disease and diabetes). But the factors contributing to the cause, diagnosis, and treatment of those health problems can differ across SES categories. Health, like life, is complex. Income and education levels can make a difference in the health status of the clients you serve. They can also shape your search for solutions.

As you read the remainder of this chapter about health through the life span, note the health concerns and specific health education areas you think you should master to work effectively with each group. Use Appendix D and your local phone book listings to identify national and local organizations or information sources that can help you begin developing expertise in those areas. We also urge you to complete other university health education courses that provide more in-depth information about specific health topics (such as stress management, nutrition, and weight management) and particular subgroups (such as women, children, adolescents, and older adults).

INFANT AND MATERNAL HEALTH

Demographic Characteristics

According to the National Center for Health Statistics (1999b), 3,880,894 babies were born in the United States in 1997 for a birthrate of 14.5 per 1,000 live births and a fertility rate of 65.0 per 1,000 women aged 15 – 44 years. A growing number of babies are raised by their single-parent mothers, 31.6% of whom lived in poverty in 1997.

Mortality and Morbidity Statistics

A nation's **infant mortality** rate is considered a strong indicator of its health status. In the past 40 years, the United States has made great strides in this area, moving from an infant mortality rate of about 29 per 1,000 live births in 1950 to a rate of 7.6 in 1990 (NCHS, 1996). Those rates further decreased between 1990 and 1995 for White infants (7.6 to 6.3 deaths per 1,000 live births, a 17.1% decrease) and for African American infants (18.0 to 14.8, a 17.2% decrease) (PAHO, 1998). Yet concerns still exist because of the tremendous gaps between rates for White and nonwhite infants, with particularly high infant death rates occurring in economically disadvantaged families. Despite its wealth, the United States ranks a low 24th in the world in terms of infant mortality rate compared to other industrialized nations (USDHHS, 1998a). As depicted in Figure 4.1, the five leading causes of U.S. infant death in 1997 were (1) congenital anomalies, (2) disorders relating to short gestation and unspecified low birth weight, (3) sudden infant death syndrome, (4) respiratory distress syndrome, and (5) maternal complications of pregnancy (NCHS, 1999a).

The March of Dimes Foundation for Birth Defects (1999b; see Appendix D) developed a Web site titled "On an Average Day in the United States." In it, the organization's perinatal data center estimated (from 1995 national statistics) that 10,662 babies are born in the United States "on an average day." Of those, more than 1,300 are born to teenage mothers and just under 800 are born at low birth weights.

"On an average day," 78 babies under the age of 1 year die (March of Dimes, 1999b). Based on these approximations, more than 200 babies will die over the next 3 days. Would it surprise you to know that most of those deaths could be

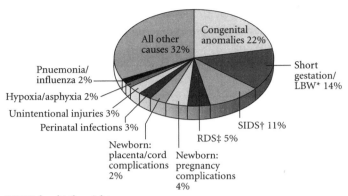

* LBW: low birth weight
† SIDS: sudden infant death syndrome
‡ RDS: respiratory distress syndrome

FIGURE 4.1   Most of these leading causes of death in the United States, 1997, for infants (1 year of age and younger) could be avoided with appropriate pre- and postnatal care. Raw data from *Health, United States, 1999*, National Center for Health Statistics, 1999. Retrieved January 11, 2000 from the World Wide Web: http://www.cdc.gov/nchswww/products/pubs/pubd/hus/99mortal.htm.

avoided with appropriate pre- and postnatal care? What you learn about infant and maternal health and how you apply it in the real world could make a difference in these numbers.

Factors That Influence Health

Almost two-thirds of U.S. infant deaths are attributable to **low birth weight** (LBW). LBW, which is defined as less than 5.5 pounds, is highly associated with inadequate prenatal care; low socioeconomic status; race; the mother's age and marital status; environmental exposure to viruses, chemicals, and radiation; and a number of unhealthy behaviors—including smoking, inadequate diet, and alcohol and other drug abuse (PAHO, 1998; Swartz, 1990). These factors and the high rate of maternal mortality among low-income mothers are reasons why prenatal care and health education are important aspects of community health.

Information and Support Resources

A list of information and resources related to infant and maternal health can be found in Appendix D. As for all age-specific groups, the National Center for Health Statistics and the Center for Disease Prevention and Health Promotion provide health-related data, descriptions of key health issues, and guides to organizations and programs that support health solutions. The U.S. Department of Agriculture (USDA, 1993) sponsors a Special Supplemental Food Program for

Women, Infants, and Children (WIC) that provides access to food and health services for low-income individuals at nutritional risk. The Maternal and Child Health Bureau sponsors such efforts as the National Healthy Mothers, Healthy Babies Coalition (HMHB, 1999). The March of Dimes Foundation mentioned earlier is another good place to start when seeking health information related to infant and maternal health.

Just as you should when working with any group or community, begin with these national information sources to become well-versed in national trends and resources available to you in your local health education efforts. However, make sure to also communicate with local health organizations and community leaders to learn about factors and issues unique to the local population you serve.

CHILD HEALTH

Demographic Characteristics

Based on U.S. Census Bureau (USCB, 1999a) data, an estimated 58 million children under the age of 15 lived in the United States in 1999. The government often reports health status for these children within two age-specific subcategories, 1–4 and 5–14 years. Reasons for these age distinctions include differences in leading causes of death and their contributing factors, as well as lifestyle-altering changes commonly experienced when a child reaches the common public school eligibility age of 5 years.

Mortality and Morbidity Statistics

Unintentional injuries account for 42% of all deaths in U.S. children, with close to half of those a result of motor vehicle crashes. Drownings, burns, suffocation, and firearms cause the rest. Statistics for 1997 are depicted in Figures 4.2 and 4.3. In differing rank orders, congenital anomalies (problems present at birth), cancer, and homicide rank second to unintentional injuries as leading causes of death among children (NCHS, 1999a).

As you can see, homicide is the fourth leading cause of death among those 1–4 years old and the third leading cause among those 5–14 years old (NCHS, 1999a). Gun-control efforts have fueled heated debates about the rights of gun owners and the need to protect America's children. This attention may have helped lead to the reduction of gun-related deaths observed in 1995. Yet, according to the Children's Defense Fund (1998), an average of 16 children and youth are still killed by guns every day in the United States.

Suicide ranks sixth among causes of death for 5- to 14-year-olds (NCHS, 1999a). This fact is unnerving in the face of how much life has yet to be experienced at that age. The health professional who assumes that children are largely resilient to life's ups and downs should take careful note. As we discussed in

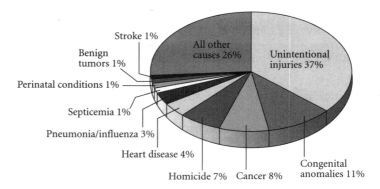

FIGURE 4.2 The leading cause of death in the United States, 1997, for younger children (1–4 years of age) is unintentional injuries, which account for 36.5% of deaths in this age group. Raw data from *Health, United States, 1999,* National Center for Health Statistics, 1999. Retrieved January 11, 2000 from the World Wide Web: http://www.cdc.gov/nchsww/products/pubs/pubd/hus/99mortal.htm.

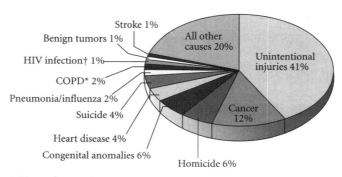

* COPD: chronic obstructive pulmonary diseases
† HIV: human immunodeficiency virus

FIGURE 4.3 Unintentional injuries (41.8%) top the list of leading causes of death in the United States, 1997, among older children (5–14 years of age). Raw data from *Health, United States, 1999,* National Center for Health Statistics, 1999. Retrieved January 11, 2000 from the World Wide Web: http://www.cdc.gov/nchsww/products/pubs/pubd/hus/99mortal.htm.

Chapter 1, emotional wellness is a critical component of overall health and should never be taken lightly, even among the young.

Heart disease is often considered a condition that emerges in one's later years. However, it also ranks among the leading causes of death among children (fifth for both age groups). Pneumonia and influenza also rank high among causes of death in children (sixth for those 1–4 years old; seventh for those 5–14 years old).

Heart disease and pneumonia/influenza represent opposite ends of the chronic-versus-infectious disease spectrum and illustrate the broad scope of issues you may face when working in child-health settings (NCHS, 1999a).

Factors That Influence Health

Although the majority of U.S. children are immunized, communicable disease outbreaks still occur, particularly in rural and inner-city areas where vaccination programs have not adequately reached many children (PAHO, 1998). In fact, the United States has been accused of failing to protect its children from communicable childhood diseases as effectively as do other industrialized nations (McKenzie, Pinger, & Kotecki, 1998). However, with the exception of a 1989–1990 measles outbreak, PAHO (1998) reports that there have been no vaccine-preventable disease outbreaks in recent years. Accelerated immunization and education efforts are largely targeting underserved populations living in large urban areas (USDHHS, 1998a).

Child abuse and neglect affected 1 million U.S. children in 1995 (USDHHS, 1997a). Physical abuse accounted for 25% of cases investigated by child protective services that year. Other leading forms of maltreatment were sexual (13%) and emotional (5%) abuse and medical neglect (3%). The mental and emotional scars abused children carry affect their ability to function in school and society. Some run away from home to escape oppressive home environments, while others may resort to a more permanent escape through suicide. Adults who were abused as children are more likely to abuse others and commit violent crimes, and the cycle continues.

Cliché though it may be, children really are our future. If you work with children in health education settings, you may discover a need to address health education programs to issues of injury prevention, immunizations and communicable disease, oral health, and child abuse and neglect prevention. Understanding the world of a child and the way adults influence it will be of benefit to you and the children you serve.

Information and Support Resources

We have already mentioned the National Center for Health Statistics and the Center for Disease Prevention and Health Promotion as excellent age-specific information resources. Other organizations focus primarily on the health of children and adolescents. The American Academy of Child and Adolescent Psychiatry provides information about the developmental aspects of children. Some state-based organizations, such as the Texas Youth Commission Office of Prevention, serve as resources for extensive information related to the health of children and adolescents worldwide. Appendix D contains an extensive list.

ADOLESCENT AND YOUNG ADULT HEALTH

Demographic Characteristics

U.S. Census Bureau (1999a) estimates reported 37.7 million adolescents and young adults (those 15–24 years of age) living in the United States in 1999. This number represented 13.8% of the total population. Approximately 19.7 million (7%) ranged in age from 15 to 19 years, an age span commonly referred to as adolescence.

Mortality and Morbidity Statistics

As can be noted in Figure 4.4, the five leading causes of death among teenagers and young adults were unintentional injuries, homicide, suicide, cancer, and heart disease (NCHS, 1999a). Alcohol-related motor vehicle accidents cause most deaths among White males, while homicide is the leading killer among African American males in this age group. According to the 1997 National Youth Risk Behavior Surveillance System report (CDC, 1998b), 52% of high school respondents had consumed alcohol, 39% had ridden with a drinking driver, and 35% had smoked cigarettes within the past month. Of the 38% who had had sexual intercourse during the preceding three months, only 17% were using birth control pills and 54% had used a condom. Regular exercise and proper diet were practiced by only a few, yet 41% were attempting to lose weight. According to CDC (1999c), nearly one quarter of all new HIV infections and infections with other sexually transmitted diseases, as well as 1 million pregnancies, occur among our nation's teenagers (FYI 4.1).

Factors That Influence Health

List five people whose opinions you valued during your adolescence. List the age and type of relationship you shared (for example, best friend, teacher) with each.

The health educator who works with adolescents and young adults must understand the nature of *peer pressure* and the sense of immortality that strongly contribute to health behaviors in this age group. Think back for a moment to your own experience as an adolescent and the people whose opinions counted most for you then. Some may have been adults, but those who wielded the strongest influence on your day-to-day behavior were likely closer to your age. Although most of us hate to admit it, peer pressure is a powerful influence on us all. It causes some of us to change clothes more than once in preparation for an important event and others to gasp or giggle if we dress or behave in a way that is outside of the accepted norm. Peer pressure isn't necessarily bad. It can actually influence us to adopt healthy behaviors such as joining aerobics classes and participating in community service projects. It can, however, wreak havoc in our lives when "what everyone is doing" presents a health risk.

Many adolescents find themselves in a developmental stage of life: Their self-identity is forming, exploration of new ideas is common, and sensitivity to

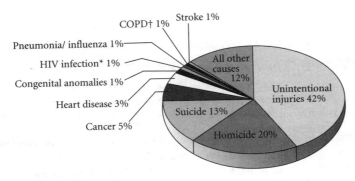

COPD† 1% Stroke 1%
Pneumonia/ influenza 1%
HIV infection* 1%
Congenital anomalies 1%
Heart disease 3%
Cancer 5%

All other causes 12%
Unintentional injuries 42%
Suicide 13%
Homicide 20%

* HIV: human immunodeficiency virus
† COPD: chronic obstructive pulmonary diseases

FIGURE 4.4   Unintentional injuries (42.4%), homicide (19.5%) and suicide (13.2%) are the leading causes of death among adolescents and young adults (15–24 years of age) in the United States, 1997. Raw data from *Health, United States, 1999,* National Center for Health Statistics, 1999. Retrieved January 11, 2000 from the World Wide Web: http://www.cdc.gov/nchsww/products/pubs/pubd/hus/99mortal.htm.

criticism and rejection is high. This stage renders many adolescents particularly vulnerable to peer pressure at a time when they also tend to live more in the present and are less concerned with long-term consequences. When these vulnerabilities are challenged by risk-promoting peer pressure, the results can be life-threatening.

Alcohol use is a frequently accepted **behavioral norm** among adolescents and young adults (Komro, Perry, Veblen-Mortenson, Williams, & Roel, 1999) and has long been significantly related to the three leading causes of death in that age group (Office of Disease Prevention and Health Promotion [ODPHP], 1988). Alcohol use usually begins during adolescence (Komro et al., 1999), and approximately one third of teenagers are alcohol abusers (National Institute on Alcohol Abuse and Alcoholism [NIAAA], 1998). Peer leadership programs designed to reduce underage drinking have been proven effective (Komro et al., 1999). In particular, some programs have successfully changed normative perceptions about the number of peers who drink, have enhanced understanding of benefits of not using alcohol, and have improved parent-child communication about alcohol-use consequences (Perry et al., 1996).

Homicide is another cause of adolescent deaths that is often alcohol-related (Powell, 1999). The homicide rate among young U.S. males is alarmingly high, approximately 20 times higher than in other industrialized nations. Among Black youth, homicide rates are four times higher for females and eight times higher for males than for their White counterparts. An epidemic of students opening fire on school campuses has added a new dimension to the discussion of adolescents and homicide (Hill & Drolet, 1999). Public reaction has resulted in widespread

FOR YOUR INFORMATION 4.1

Adolescents: The Risks They Take...

Adolescents in the United States are prone to a variety of behaviors that place them at risk for health problems.

- **Exercise** Nearly half of American youths aged 12–21 years do not engage in vigorous physical activity on a regular basis.
- **Diet** Almost three fourths of those aged 12–21 years do not eat the recommended number of servings of fruits and vegetables.
- **Smoking** Every day, nearly 3,000 young people take up daily smoking. Thirty-six percent of high school students currently smoke and 70% have tried smoking at least once.
- **Sex** Forty-eight percent of 9th–12th graders have had sexual intercourse; 57% of those who are sexually active used a condom at last intercourse. Every year, about 3 million adolescents become infected with a sexually transmitted disease.
- **Pregnancy** The United States has the highest teenage pregnancy rate of all developed countries. About 1 million teenagers become pregnant each year; 95% of those pregnancies are unintended, and almost one third end in abortions.
- **Crashes** In 1998, 5,606 teenagers died of injuries caused by motor vehicle crashes. Nearly 20% of high school students report they rarely or never wear safety belts when riding in a vehicle with someone else. They are also more likely than older drivers to speed, run red lights, make illegal turns, ride with an intoxicated driver, and drive after using alcohol or drugs.
- **Violence** Thirty-seven percent of high school students were in a physical fight in the past year. Eighteen percent carried a weapon in the last month. Twenty percent have seriously considered suicide.

From *Health Topics: Adolescents and Teens,* by the Centers for Disease Control and Prevention, April 7, 2000. Retrieved April 22, 2000 from the World Wide Web: http://www.cdc.gov/health/adolescent.htm

concern for school safety, and the issue has been designated a national public health and education priority (Weiler, Dorman, & Pealer, 1999).

Factors believed to contribute to *violence* among adolescents include increased exposure to violence involving weapons and escalating incidences of substance abuse, gang membership, victimization, hopelessness, and low academic performance (Powell, 1999). Poverty, a factor highly associated with violent behavior, has been said to rob young people of important deterrents such as positive role models, educational opportunities, and important social support systems. Attention to these factors and, particularly, to the fostering of adult social support and religious commitment, are recommended to promote nonviolent behavior among those at greatest risk (Powell, 1999).

Alcohol consumption also has negative effects on *sexual activity* (Dinger & Parsons, 1999). It increases the likelihood that young people will engage in sexual intercourse and decreases the chances that precautions will be taken to prevent unintended pregnancies and sexually transmitted diseases (STDs; CDC, 1999c). Unintended pregnancies can lead to abortions and/or a host of other long-range problems for both mother and child. And among those STDs on the rise is AIDS, the fifth leading cause of death in this age group (CDC, 1999c). Sexuality education for adolescents is a controversial issue in some political settings. But the consequences are grave when we fail to address this issue among sexually active teens.

As you work with adolescents, you may find a need to educate them about *safe sex* or *sexual abstinence,* preventing alcohol and other drug abuse, and preventing violence. The challenge of working with adolescents is sometimes tough, and the stakes can be very high. Yet fostering family and school connectedness and instilling in adolescents an optimistic sense of purpose about their future have been proven to positively affect risk-taking behavior (Fors, Crepaz, & Hayes, 1999). The more equipped you are with adolescent-specific knowledge and skills, the more likely will be your chances of making a difference.

Information and Support Resources

The Centers for Disease Control and Prevention provide a wealth of information related to adolescent health (see Appendix D for access information). This organization sponsors various adolescent-related projects and programs, including the Youth Risk Behavior Surveillance project (CDC, 1998b). In this project, a comprehensive survey of high school students across the nation collected information about health behaviors and identified risky behaviors.

Another good resource for understanding the health issues of adolescents is a Web site developed by the U.S. Department of Health and Human Services called the "Youth Info Directory." It provides useful adolescent-related information, including a profile of America's youth, recent reports and publications, speeches on youth topics, resources for parents, and links to related Web sites.

The American Medical Association maintains a Web site titled "Adolescent Health On-Line" that provides information about the latest research, special health topics, guidelines for preventive services, and links to related sites. These and other organizations, and their URLs, are listed in Appendix D.

ADULT HEALTH IN THE MIDDLE YEARS

Demographic Characteristics

The leading causes of death for two adult groups are depicted in Figures 4.5 (ages 25–44) and 4.6 (ages 45–64). The term *adult* can be misleading because it is commonly used to describe a wide range of age and experience. We use the term *middle adult* here to refer to those who range from 25 to 64 years of age, a group that commonly faces a different set of life challenges than do people in, for example, the adolescent and elderly categories. We recognize the vast array of experiences and perspectives this category represents. However, this age group includes most of the body of working Americans whose age and wages earn them the status of important health service consumers who are apt to vote on health-affecting decisions and policies.

In 1999, an estimated 141.7 million middle adults (25–64 years of age) lived in the United States, representing approximately 52% of all Americans (USCB, 1999a). Of the total U.S. population, approximately 14% were 25–34, 16% were 35–44, 13% were 45–54, and 8.6% were 55–64 years of age.

Mortality and Morbidity Statistics

Cancer and heart disease dominate the leading causes of death among adults 25 to 64 years old, accounting for approximately 60% of all deaths (PAHO, 1998). The good news is that death rates due to heart, or cardiovascular, disease have dropped dramatically since 1950, a change attributed to the large numbers of people who have stopped smoking and adopted heart-healthy exercise and dietary habits. The bad news is that cancer death rates have remained fairly constant over that same period of time, with lung cancer topping the list for both genders, followed by breast cancer for women and colorectal cancer for men. Although a large number of adults have quit smoking, 85% of all lung cancer deaths are still attributed to that behavior. In fact, smoking is often named as the number one killer because it contributes to more U.S. deaths than does any other health-related behavior (CDC, 1998a).

Factors That Influence Health

List at least five lifestyle behaviors that you think contribute to the prevalence of chronic diseases.

What contributes to the high rates of heart disease and cancer in the United States? Before answering that question, we must first acknowledge that decreased incidences of communicable diseases are part of the reason these chronic diseases have risen to the top of the list. That's the good news. The bad news is that, in addition to noncontrollable genetic and environmental factors, certain lifestyle behaviors contribute greatly to the continued prevalence of these chronic diseases.

The three **controllable risk factors** that contribute enormously to heart disease and cancer are tobacco use, unhealthy dietary patterns, and physical inactivity (CDC, 1998a). As a health educator, it will be to your employment advantage to become well-versed in how exercise, diet, and smoking relate to illness and health. These aspects include the specific physiological connections between these behaviors and disease; the factors that influence choices related to these behaviors; and the methods commonly recommended for effective exercise, diet, and smoking cessation.

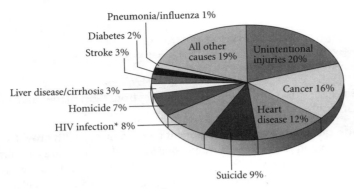

FIGURE 4.5   Unintentional injuries (20.1%), cancer (16.1%), and heart disease (12.2%) are leading causes of death among younger middle adults (25 – 44 years of age) in the United States, 1997. Raw data from *Health, United States, 1999,* National Center for Health Statistics, 1999. Retrieved January 11, 2000 from the World Wide Web: http://www.cdc.gov/ nchswww/products/pubs/pubd/hus/99mortal.htm.

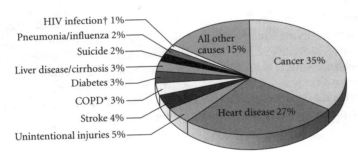

FIGURE 4.6   Cancer (35.0%) and heart disease (26.9%) account for a large proportion of the leading causes of death among older middle adults (45 – 64 years of age) in the United States, 1997. Raw data from *Health, United States, 1999,* National Center for Health Statistics, 1999. Retrieved January 11, 2000 from the World Wide Web: http://www.cdc.gov/ nchswww/products/pubs/pubd/hus/99mortal.htm.

Most adults know that regular exercise, proper diet, and abstinence from tobacco use are good for them. So, why don't adults do what we might consider to be "the right thing" when it comes to these three behaviors? To understand this, other influencing factors must be considered.

Middle adults (25 – 64 years of age) form a diverse group with a variety of needs and interests. Some common health-influencing factors for this age group

FOR YOUR INFORMATION 4.2

Facts About Women's Health . . .

Women's health risks and problems often differ from those of men and, in some cases, are more prevalent.

- **Health care** Compared with treatment given to men, health providers tend to give women less thorough evaluations for similar complaints, minimize their symptoms, provide fewer interventions for the same diagnoses, prescribe some types of medications more often, and provide less explanation in response to questions.
- **HIV/AIDS** HIV/AIDS is the third leading cause of death among women aged 25 to 44 and the leading cause of death among African American women in this age group.
- **Autoimmune diseases** About 75% of autoimmune diseases, such as lupus and rheumatoid arthritis, occur among women. They represent the fourth largest cause of disability among women in the United States.
- **Eating disorders** At least 90% of all cases of eating disorders occur in women.
- **Alcohol** Though women are less likely than men to use or abuse alcohol, death rates among female alcoholics are 50–100% higher than those of men.
- **Violence** More than 2.5 million women are victims of violence each year. Women are 6 times more likely than men to be abused by someone they know and 10 times more likely to be victims of sexual assault.
- **Depression** Approximately 7% of American women will suffer from a major depression during their lifetime compared to 2.6% of men.

include financial pressures at all levels of the socioeconomic scale, relationship and responsibility stressors at home and work, and low motivation to attend to personal health in light of these other pressures. The health educator who understands these needs will be better equipped to work in adult-based health education settings. FYI 4.2 considers health factors for women.

Information and Support Resources

In addition to the national information sources mentioned in previous sections, the Pan American Health Organization's "Health Conditions of the Americas" provides a periodically updated health-status report for age-specific groups. This and other sources are listed in Appendix D where you can also find groups that deal with specific threats to adult health (such as American Cancer Society, American Heart Association).

- **STDs** Women suffer more frequent and severe long-term consequences of STDs than men do because they are more susceptible to infection and less likely to experience symptoms.
- **Pregnancies** Eighty-two percent of pregnancies among women 15 to 19 and 61% of pregnancies among women 20 to 24 are unintended.
- **Arthritis** Nearly 23 million of the 38 million Americans with arthritis are women. It is the most common and disabling chronic condition reported by women.
- **Heart disease** Women (44%) are more likely than men (27%) to die within a year following a heart attack, and women who recover from a heart attack are more likely than men to have a stroke or have another heart attack.
- **Stroke** Stroke is the third leading cause of death for American women and kills more than twice as many women each year as breast cancer. Yet, in 1997, only 8% of American women recognized heart disease and stroke as leading causes of women's deaths.
- **Cancer and smoking** Over the past 10 years, the mortality rate from lung cancer has declined in men but has continued to rise in women. Currently, 23% of women smoke, a primary contributing factor.
- **Chronic disabilities** Women are more likely than men to be affected by such chronic disabling conditions as diabetes, osteoporosis, osteoarthritis, obesity, urinary incontinence, and Alzheimer's disease.

From *General Women's Health Information,* by National Women's Health Information Center, Office on Women's Health, U.S. Department of Health and Human Services (2000, April 21). Retrieved from the World Wide Web April 23, 2000: http://www.4women.gov/media/general.htm

OLDER ADULT HEALTH

Demographic Characteristics

The proportion of U.S. citizens over 65 years of age was an estimated 35 million in 2000 (13% of the population). That proportion is expected to climb as high as 23% by 2040 (PAHO, 1998). Contributing factors will likely include a consistently low death rate and an influx of baby boomers into that age bracket.

Mortality and Morbidity Statistics

The five leading causes of death in this age group (Figure 4.7) are heart disease, cancer, stroke, chronic obstructive pulmonary disease, and pneumonia and influenza (NCHS, 1999a). Deaths due to heart disease and stroke are on the decline

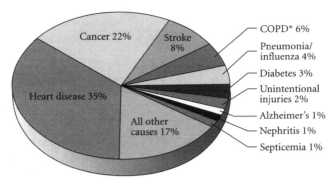

*COPD: chronic obstructive pulmonary diseases

FIGURE 4.7   Heart disease (35.1%) is followed by cancer (22.2%) as the primary causes of death among older adults (65 years of age or older) in the United States, 1997. Raw data from *Health, United States, 1999,* National Center for Health Statistics, 1999. Retrieved January 11, 2000 from the World Wide Web: http://www.cdc.gov/nchswww/products/pubs/pubd/hus/99mortal.htm.

in this age group, while lung cancer deaths are increasing. However, heart disease remains at this point the number one killer of America's seniors.

Factors That Influence Health

The face of health among older Americans is changing. A person who had reached the age of 60 years by 1995 could expect to live to the age of 81.1 years, while a 65-year-old individual could expect to live to the age of 82.4 (PAHO, 1998). In 1997, the life expectancy for all Americans was at an all-time high of 76.5 years (NCHS, 1999a).

People are living longer. But increased longevity and reduced risk of life-threatening diseases are only part of the picture. Arthritis, osteoporosis, incontinence, and visual and hearing impairments remain health problems. For this reason, an enhanced quality of life can be of particular importance to this age group. We will address quality-of-life issues more fully in subsequent chapters. But for now we invite you to note the significance of quality of life in older-adult health education programs. Maintenance of positive self-esteem and independence can be an important goal for seniors who are interested in enjoying more of life. It can also greatly affect health status among members of this age group.

Information and Support Resources

The sources named in previous sections as a good place to access age-specific health information will be helpful to you. Information about specific health issues as they relate to older adults can also be obtained from some of the problem-specific organizations we named in the "middle adult" section. Some agencies and organizations, however, focus primarily on the well-being of older adults. Those include the Administration on Aging (of the U.S. Department of Heath and Human Services), the National Institute on Aging (one of the National Institutes of Health), and the American Association of Retired Persons (AARP). Access information for these and others can be found in Appendix D.

IN CONCLUSION

This chapter provides a brief overview of the health issues of age-specific groups in the United States. We hope you will use the information and resources presented to enhance your understanding of health through the life span. The "For Your Application" activity at the end of this chapter can help you explore what you know. Of course, simply reading this chapter and visiting some selected Web sites will not render you fully equipped to effectively work with any of these age groups. Although a sound knowledge base is a good place to start, true learning and skills development come through experience.

Experience is something you can provide for yourself. The "For Your Portfolio" suggestion is designed to help you develop experience opportunities. It might prove helpful for you to follow that portfolio suggestion with a different age-specific group each semester. Through such experiences, you can gain insight into the values and issues faced by, for example, an adolescent who just joined a gang, a college student who drinks to fit in, a young single mother with no health insurance, or a widowed grandmother who is afraid to exercise. Experience working with a broad range of age-specific groups can help you in two ways. Each volunteer experience can be added to your résumé as evidence of your ability to work with various age groups. And encounters with individuals from all walks of life can broaden your professional perspective.

REVIEW QUESTIONS

1. Explain the importance of viewing the health status of Americans in age-specific groups.
2. Discuss strengths and weaknesses of health-status data sources in the United States.
3. Describe the underlying role of socioeconomic status and its effect on health status in the United States.
4. Describe some general demographic characteristics of each of these age-specific groups in the United States: infants, children, adolescents/young adults, middle adults, older adults.
5. Name some leading causes of death and prominent health issues for each of the groups listed in question 4.

6. Explain the factors that influence the health of each age-specific group.
7. Identify information and support resources that can be used to understand and address health issues specific to each group.

FOR YOUR APPLICATION

Tracking Health Issues Through the Life Span

Select a health problem (such as alcohol abuse) that can be "tracked" through the life span. Create a three-column table and label those columns "Age-Specific Group," "Potential Risks/Problems," and "Potential Solutions." Add a row to the table for each of the age-specific groups addressed in this chapter (for example, infants, children, adolescents). Place those labels in the "Age-Specific Group" column of each row. At the top of the paper, give your table an appropriate title (such as "Alcohol Abuse Through the Life Span"). Then, in the "Potential Risks/Problems" column, list what a person in each age group might face if exposed to the health problem. For example, if exposed to alcohol abuse, an infant might be born with fetal alcohol syndrome; a child might be abused/neglected by alcoholic parents; an adolescent might be in an alcohol-related traffic accident; a middle adult could develop chronic liver disease; and an older adult could suffer from other illnesses known to be intensified by alcohol misuse (such as diabetes and heart disease). For the "Potential Solutions" column, list capacities and resources available to individuals in each age group that could reduce potential alcohol-related problems or reduce exposure to alcohol misuse. Note differences across the life span. Check your answers with what you can find through library and Internet searches.

FOR YOUR PORTFOLIO

Gaining Life Span Experience

Volunteer in a variety of local school, church, and recreational programs to gain experience with individuals from across the life span. Child-care facilities, day camps, and youth clubs can provide access to infants, children, and adolescents. Shelters for the homeless or abused or other special programs can give you insight into various adult subpopulations. Senior citizen centers can be ideal for interaction with older adults. In the beginning, you may be asked to perform seemingly trivial tasks. However, demonstrating consistent dependability and maturity can build trust and confidence in your ability to do more. Document your experiences in your portfolio with letters, flyers, snapshots, and the like.

5

Understanding the Health of Ethnic Communities

"WHY WON'T SHE LOOK AT ME WHEN I'M TALKING TO her? Doesn't she understand that I'm trying to help?" You're frustrated. You've worked so hard putting together this health education program, and now nothing seems to be working. Participants drop out but won't tell you why. Others keep coming but don't practice at home what the program teaches. You're on the verge of giving up.

Chapter Objectives

1. Explain how use of ethnic labels as health-status categories can be misleading.
2. Describe limitations of data sources as they relate to minority health status.
3. Explain how the PEN-3 model can be used to distinguish between positive, existential, and negative cultural influences on health.
4. Describe the demographic characteristics of four broad ethnicity-specific populations in the United States—and the names they choose for themselves.
5. Describe the primary health issues of ethnicity-specific populations in the United States.
6. Explain the socioeconomics, cultural beliefs and practices, and community dynamics that influence health within each ethnic community.
7. Identify information and support resources that can be used to understand and address health issues specific to each group.

WHAT'S IN A LABEL?

The face of America is rapidly changing. The proportion of **minority groups** in the U.S. population rose from 16.9% in 1980 to 19.7% in 1990 and 28% in 1997 (U.S. Census Bureau [USCB], 1999b). By 2050, nearly half of the total U.S. population is expected to identify with a minority group. The future of our nation depends on its ability to embrace this change and capitalize on the strengths of its diversity.

Yet, with that diversity come the challenges of communicating across cultural barriers and developing health education programs that are effective in different cultural settings. The frustration expressed in the opening scenario could be a result of culture-based miscommunication or lack of understanding. A careful study of common communication styles and ways of thinking within a particular community can help educators avoid these problems. However, one danger of studying information about selected **ethnic communities** is that individuals and subgroups within those communities can be vastly different from one another. Without a clear understanding of data limitations, we all can be guilty of mislabeling and stereotyping. It may help you to revisit the cultural sensitivity discussion in Chapter 2 before reading this chapter about the health needs of selected ethnic communities so that you can avoid the misinterpretation and misuse of the information presented here.

The Nature of Data Sources

In Chapter 4 we discussed the strengths and weaknesses of data sources, including the need to categorize reported health statistics by age so that health issues important to one age group are not masked by whole-population data groupings. This is also important for America's ethnic communities because the health-status picture—problems and possible solutions—within each community can differ from that of the U.S. population as a whole. The problem with creating these data categories lies in what those categories truly mean and the potential for mislabeling individuals and misinterpreting grouped data.

To illustrate this problem, consider for a moment what it means to be "Hispanic." The U.S. Census Bureau created this data category to distinguish between U.S. citizens who are and aren't of Hispanic descent. The same category is used in reports of morbidity and mortality cases to the CDC. But what if your father's family is of German descent and your mother is Mexican American? Would you consider yourself Hispanic? If you were delivered unconscious to an emergency room, what might the professional who completed the paperwork guess about your ethnicity? Would she guess by your physical appearance or the name on your driver's license? What if you viewed yourself as Hispanic but, when asked, told them you were White out of fear of discrimination? Statistical mislabeling can occur for many reasons and affects the accuracy of what we think we know about health trends in a particular ethnic community.

Existing ethnic-specific health data can also be misinterpreted. In earlier chapters we identified a variety of factors that influence individual health status, including income, education, environment, lifestyle choices, age, gender, and service access. We know these variables account for most health variations among Hispanic individuals. We also know that different cultural characteristics can be found within Hispanic subgroups and that only a portion of Hispanic Americans closely follow traditional cultural beliefs and practices. Thus, it would be inappropriate to think of Hispanic Americans as a **homogeneous,** or mostly similar, cultural group for which a single health promotion intervention will work.

Another factor to be considered as you explore the relationship between culture and health is your personal view about what constitutes a cultural norm. Some prefer to use the term *norm* to refer to something that is unique to (owned exclusively by) a group. By that definition, very few cultural characteristics could be called *norms* because most can also be found among more traditional members of other ethnic communities. In contrast, we present this chapter from the perspective that a cultural norm is a common rule or standard of behavior within that group regardless of whether or not it can be found in other populations. Thus, a particular belief or behavior can be a norm in one ethnic group and can still be found in other ethnic groups.

So, if the data collection process is so abysmal, what is the value of studying health trends prevalent in a particular ethnic community? Some benefits have already been addressed in Chapter 4, such as the ability to identify and address health issues unique to a group. Ethnic-specific data also allow us to view health issues within the context of a particular community's unique environment, history, and culture (see Chapter 1) to more fully understand contributing factors. Two additional benefits can be addressed within the context of the culture of poverty and the PEN-3 model's (Airhihenbuwa, 1990) concept of capitalizing on community strengths.

List some potential benefits of studying ethnic-specific health data.

The Culture of Poverty

Chronic diseases remain a leading cause of death for all adult groups, regardless of minority or nonminority status. But minority communities experience disproportionate levels of complications, disabilities, and early deaths associated with disease. Why do health-status gaps exist between minorities and Whites? **Poverty,** the state of having insufficient resources, is the primary reason (U.S. Department of Health and Human Services [USDHHS], 1997a). A greater proportion of minority adults receive inadequate incomes, drop out of school, and have inadequate health insurance coverage than do Whites. This reduces the frequency of medical checkups and early treatment that could prevent complications for minority individuals (USDHHS, 1998a). It also decreases opportunities to gain health knowledge and skills needed to develop healthy lifestyles.

Poverty not only affects one's health but also shapes one's life priorities and interactions with others. In Chapter 2, we discussed Maslow's hierarchy of needs and saw that individuals with unmet physical needs have a different set of priorities and motivators than do those whose physical needs are being met. Ruby Payne (1998), a recognized expert in children's education, points out that physical and financial resources are not the only unmet needs in an impoverished environment. Impoverished individuals may also lack emotional, mental, and spiritual resources; family and friend support systems; role models who demonstrate how to overcome difficulty; and knowledge about the hidden or unspoken rules or norms that are necessary for navigating middle-class school and health care systems. As you study the health status and general cultural norms of various U.S. ethnic communities, it will be useful for you to understand the underlying culture of poverty that affects the health habits and status of individuals across all groups.

Name three skills a person living in poverty would need to survive.

According to Payne (1998), you can survive in poverty if you know how to do such things as live without a checking account or a car, keep your clothes from being stolen at a laundromat, physically fight and defend yourself, or obtain and use food stamps. Perhaps, as a student, you are thinking "Wait a minute! I know all about some of that stuff. Going to school has made me very, very poor!" It is possible, however, that you are in a "situational poverty" rather than a "generational poverty" situation (Payne, 1998, p. 64). That is, you may be experiencing temporary financial setbacks while trying to work through a degree program, but may still adhere to middle-class norms and priorities. A person living in generational poverty (one whose parents and grandparents were also poor) might not be as equipped to navigate the middle-class world of Little League baseball, piano lessons, college enrollment, credit card payments, checking accounts, and medical insurance claims.

Though class lines are not always distinct, individuals from differing class systems may require different levels of understanding, communication styles, and health education approaches, depending on the values and rules to which they adhere. For instance a person in poverty may view his or her current health status as part of personal destiny or fate, something one can do little to change. This attitude poses a greater challenge to health educators proposing behavioral change than does the perspective held by some middle-class individuals that choices make a difference. Conversely, the sense of humor often found among impoverished individuals can be a positive stress-management tool that is sometimes lacking among middle-class high achievers. These class differences cannot be automatically labeled "good" or "bad." They are simply different. Awareness of those distinctions, when properly infused into your approach, can work to your advantage as a health educator.

The picture of American minority health is not entirely dismal. Not all minority citizens fit the low-income, poor-health profile we just described. Many minority individuals belong to middle- and upper-class groups who are well educated and well aware of health promotion concepts. Some low-income minority communities have also demonstrated an impressive capacity for developing their own resources and solutions to health issues. The key is to be aware of health-enhancement barriers that exist for some minorities and to view each community member as an individual.

The PEN-3 Concept

Another important part of the minority health picture is how you view your professional role in relation to it. It would be a sad mistake for you to see yourself as the "knight in shining armor" who arrives at a community's doorstep with all the health answers and resources in hand. That isn't how effective community health education usually works. Most individuals and communities prefer to "fight their own battles" and shape their own futures. Ideally, your role in those situations will be to serve as a catalyst and support person rather than a bearer of all the right answers. This difference in perspective may seem slight, but making that shift can greatly influence the results of your effort.

PEN-3 (Figure 5.1) is a conceptual model designed by Collins Airhihenbuwa (1990), a leader in multicultural health education, as a guide for culturally appropriate health education. Each of the three model dimensions contains components health educators should consider when working with a particular ethnic community. In each dimension, the first letter of these components compose the acronym PEN. In the dimension labeled Health Education, we are encouraged to consider whether our health education program is designed to reach only an individual **p**erson or the broader scope of that person's **e**xtended family or **n**eighborhood (school, community). In most instances, efforts that encompass the entire community result in more effective and long-lasting results.

In the dimension labeled Educational Diagnosis of Health Behavior, we are encouraged to assess community **p**erceptions (such as attitudes, knowledge, beliefs), **e**nablers (that is, available and accessible resources), and **n**urturers (such as family, peers, religious leaders, health professionals) that influence health behaviors and health status within the community. This dimension was derived from a well-known health needs-assessment model called PRECEDE/PROCEED that you will read about later. Its primary precept is that few people live in a vacuum with no need for human or resource support. Most are dependent to some extent on the influence of others and the accessibility of health services. Thus, to bring about health-related improvements, our health education programs should address attitudes, beliefs, and behaviors not only of the individuals we serve but also of the people who influence them. And, of course, enhancing health service availability and accessibility is another important component of health promotion efforts.

The third PEN-3 dimension, Cultural Appropriateness of Health Behavior, calls on us to carefully examine cultural characteristics in light of how they truly affect the health status of the community. Airhihenbuwa (1990) pointed out that culture-based knowledge, attitudes, beliefs, and practices of a group can exert **p**ositive, **e**xistential, or **n**egative influences on the community's health. (*Existential* means "affirming existence"; existential effects are neutral or harmless, though

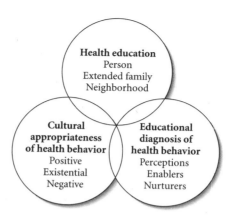

FIGURE 5.1   PEN-3 model.
The PEN-3 model encourages us to consider the health-related influences of an individual person's extended family or neighborhood (health education); community perceptions, enablers, and nurturers (educational diagnosis); and positive, existential (exotic but harmless), and negative cultural norms (cultural appropriateness). From "A Conceptual Model for Cultural Appropriate Health Education Programs in Developing Countries," by C. O. Airhihenbuwa, 1990, *International Quarterly of Community Health Education, II,* pp. 53–62.

they might seem exotic to someone from another culture.) Unfortunately, negative influences are sometimes the only characteristics of a culture that receive attention in health promotion. Although minimizing negative influences is an important aspect of promoting wellness, problems arise when all cultural influences are assumed to be negative and when positive cultural aspects are ignored.

Many cultures foster health-enhancing beliefs and practices that, when used as motivators in your health promotion program, can make your job easier. For example, traditional Chinese respect for older family members (Matocha, 1998) can foster support for health promotion programs designed for the elderly. The traditional African American belief that personal choices and behaviors affect one's destiny (Spector, 1996) can be useful when health-related behavior change is needed. The positive cultural influences of a traditional community can and should be integrated into your health education program to enhance program acceptance and participation.

Airhihenbuwa (1990) maintains that some health beliefs and practices may be existential; they may seem exotic or strange to the Western medical perspective but, in truth, are harmless. One example is the practice of "coining" in some traditional Asian communities where illness is believed to be caused by evil spirits who gain control of one's body (L. Rasbridge, personal communication, December 15, 1999). A traditional healer scrapes the skin with a coin to release illness-bearing spirits. The resulting red marks are usually harmless but can alarm an untrained school or health official, particularly when they appear on a child. Recognizing this practice as an existential influence could prevent you from reacting inappropriately and help you avoid jeopardizing community trust.

As you study each of the following sections regarding the health of selected ethnic communities, we encourage you to do so from a balanced perspective. Keep in mind that

- Existing databases are limited but can offer insight into overall health-status trends
- Ethnic labels rarely reflect the diversity of individuals to whom they are applied
- Traditional cultural health beliefs and practices are usually engaged in by only a few within an ethnic community
- A complete picture of a community's health often encompasses positive, existential, and negative influences

FYI 5.1 and 5.2 are intended to help you begin your search for understanding the community you will serve.

HISPANIC AMERICANS

Demographic and Socioeconomic Characteristics

In 1999, just over 31 million individuals of Hispanic origin were living in the United States (U.S. Census Bureau, 1999b). That number represented 11.4% of the total U.S. population (see FYI 5.1) as compared to 8.9% in 1993 (del Pinal, 1998). The rate is expected to climb to 13% by 2010 (USDHHS, 1997b) and 21% by 2050 (Norbeck, 1995), making this the fastest growing and soon-to-be largest U.S. minority group.

The estimated Hispanic median age of 26.4 (U.S. Census Bureau, 1999b) is younger than the median age of non-Hispanic groups (see FYI 5.1). Although educational attainment is improving, school dropout rates remain much higher in this group, with only 43.6% of Mexican Americans completing a high school education, compared to 80.5% of non-Hispanics (Purnell, 1998). As in all U.S. groups, the poverty rate for Hispanics has declined, moving from 29.4% in 1996 to 27.1% in 1997 (U.S. Census Bureau, 1997a). Yet, it still lags behind the overall U.S. rate of 13.3% (U.S. Census Bureau, 1997a).

A large portion of Hispanic American citizens are Mexican Americans (64%), followed by Central and South Americans (13%) and Puerto Rican Americans (11%) (USDHHS, 1997b). Distinctive subgroup labels are complex due to individual choice of descriptive terms. Many people prefer to identify with their specific cultural heritage, using such terms as Mexican American, Latin American, Spanish American, Chicano (Americans of Mexican descent), Latino, or Ladino (Purnell, 1998; Spector, 1996). Some can trace their heritage back to marriages among Mexican, Indian, and European ancestors.

An Overview of Selection Information for U.S. Whites, African Americans, Asian Americans, Hispanics, and Native American Indians.

	Whites / European Americans (non-Hispanic)	Blacks / African Americans (non-Hispanic)
U.S. population %	72.0	12.1
Median age	38.0 yrs	30.2 yrs
Median income *	$38,972	$25,050
% Living in poverty, 1997	11	26.5

Subgroup labels / countries of origin		*Preferred labels:* African American, Black, Black American, colored, Negro
		Nations of origin: Many West African countries, West Indian islands, Dominican Republic, Haiti, Jamaica

| Leading causes of death (all ages) | 1. Heart disease
2. Cancer
3. Stroke
4. COPD ‡
5. Pneumonia/ influenza
6. Unintentional injuries
7. Diabetes
8. Suicide
9. HIV infection
10. Alzheimer's disease | 1. Heart disease
2. Cancer
3. Stroke
4. HIV infection
5. Unintentional injuries
6. Homicide & legal intervention
7. Diabetes
8. Pneumonia/ influenza
9. COPD‡
10. Perinatal-related conditions |

* Median household income, 1997   † 1990 data   ‡ COPD: chronic obstructive pulmonary disease

From U.S. Census Bureau (1997a,b; 1996b,c); Centers for Disease Control and Prevention (1997a); Schust (1997); Spector (1996); and Campinha-Bacote (1998).

Hispanic Americans	Asian and Pacific Islander Americans (non-Hispanic)	Native American Indians, Eskimos, Aleuts (non-Hispanic)
11.4	3.7	0.7
26.4 yrs	31.9 yrs	28.2
$26,628	$45,249	$19,900 †
27.1	14	31 †

Hispanic Americans	Asian and Pacific Islander Americans	Native American Indians, Eskimos, Aleuts
Colombian	Asian Indian	Cherokee
Cuban	Cambodian	Chippewa
Guatemalan	Chinese	Choctaw
Honduran	Filipino	Navajo
Mexican/Chicano	Guamanian	Sioux
Nicaraguan	Hawaiian	Over 545 others
Puerto Rican	Japanese	
Salvadoran	Korean	
Others	Laotian	
	Samoan	
	Vietnamese	
	Others	

Hispanic Americans

1. Heart disease
2. Cancer
3. Unintentional injuries
4. HIV infection
5. Stroke
6. Diabetes
7. Homicide & legal intervention
8. Pneumonia/influenza
9. Chronic liver disease/cirrhosis
10. COPD‡

Asian and Pacific Islander Americans

1. Heart disease
2. Cancer
3. Stroke
4. Unintentional injuries
5. Pneumonia/influenza
6. COPD‡
7. Diabetes
8. Suicide
9. HIV infection
10. Alzheimer's disease

Native American Indians, Eskimos, Aleuts

1. Heart disease
2. Cancer
3. Unintentional injuries
4. Diabetes
5. Alcoholism
6. Stroke
7. Pneumonia/influenza
8. COPD‡
9. Suicide
10. Homicide & legal intervention

FOR YOUR INFORMATION 5.2

Checklist for Assessing the Health Needs of Ethnic Communities

The following checklist is a helpful guide for the first steps of information gathering and staff training.

Check off the items on this list as you complete the important steps to your own satisfaction.

1. Have you gathered information on and increased your understanding of the following?
   - The demographics of the target community
   - The major historical issues of the community
   - The community's economic and political concerns
   - The major cultural beliefs, values, and practices of the target community
   - The health problem as it can be addressed within the cultural context(s) of this community
   - Other questions you have chosen to explore

2. Have you also consulted the following sources?
   Library resources such as
   - Census data, government documents, reports, and statistics
   - Public health literature

Mortality, Morbidity, and Influencing Factors

The overall age difference between the Hispanic and non-Hispanic White populations partially explains why chronic disease deaths rank higher among Whites, whereas deaths due to unintentional injuries, homicide or legal intervention, and HIV infection are higher among Hispanics (USDHHS, 1997b). As with other minorities, Hispanics are less likely than non-Hispanic Whites to receive medical screenings and treatment, and they often have limited access to health facilities and physicians (USDHHS, 1998a).

Obesity, diabetes, and cardiovascular disease are strongly related, and Hispanics suffer from disproportionate rates in all three areas when compared to non-Hispanic Whites (USDHHS, 1998a). The prevalence of diabetes among Hispanics is almost twice that of non-Hispanic Whites, and age-adjusted Hispanic blood pressure rates are also high. Yet, only 38% of Hispanic Americans report having their cholesterol checked within the past 2 years, and 52% of Hispanic women (compared to 34% of non-Hispanic White women) are overweight.

- Behavioral and social science literature
- Local newspapers

Experts such as

- Academicians with knowledge of or experience working with specific ethnic or cultural groups
- Health professionals working in similar communities or with similar problems
- Other professionals working in diverse communities or in the target community
- Individuals from the target community

3. Have you prepared your staff to work in the community through the following activities?
   - Summarized research findings in a report for your staff
   - Discussed this information and included staff's input
   - Explored staff's cultural attitudes and beliefs and how these might influence their behavior in the community
   - Assessed your and your staff's past experience in working with diverse communities to determine who has the necessary skills
   - Planned for training and/or ongoing support for staff to help them resolve personal and professional issues as they arise in the community

From *Health Promotion in Diverse Cultural Communities* (p. 11), by V. M Gonzalez, J. T. Gonzalez, V. Freeman, and B. Howard-Pitney, 1994, Palo Alto, CA: Stanford Center for Research in Disease Prevention.

The 1996 infant mortality rate for Hispanics was 7.6 per 1,000 live births, a contrast to the non-Hispanic White rate of 6.0 (USDHHS, 1998a). This is consistent with what we know about the need for prenatal care and the fact that Hispanic pregnant women are less likely to receive it than are non-Hispanic Whites (70% versus 84% in 1995). Although teen birthrates for all groups are declining (Simpson, 1998), continued efforts are needed to ensure that Hispanic pregnant women receive appropriate prenatal education and care.

Health-Related Cultural Norms

Familism   Traditional Hispanic Americans place great value on a family unit that extends beyond biological parents and children to include aunts and uncles, cousins, grandparents, godparents, and close friends (Purnell, 1998). These close relational ties contribute to a strong sense of community. Elderly family members usually move in with their children when they can no longer care for themselves.

Sick relatives and friends are likely to receive hospital visits from many caring people. Health programs that promote nurturing family approaches can work well in these traditional settings.

Machismo   The word *macho* may conjure up an image of a tough guy who believes himself superior to women. Its original meaning, however, was more positive; it referred to a man with "strength, valor, and self-confidence" (Purnell, 1998, p. 401). In patriarchal Hispanic tradition, male family members are the primary decision makers and women monitor daily home and health care (Burk, Wieser, & Keegan, 1995; Purnell, 1998).

Communication Styles   Spanish is often the language of choice among traditional Hispanic families. Communication styles are rooted in views about *respeto, simpatía, personalismo,* and *confianza* (Purnell, 1998; Spector, 1996). *Respeto* (respect and courtesy to others) is often demonstrated by using titles (Señor or Señora) rather than first names and by avoiding direct eye contact, a sign of aggression. To uphold *simpatía* (avoiding conflict) and *respeto* for authority, traditional clients may not openly voice disagreement or dissatisfaction with your health promotion program. They may appear to agree in person and then simply not return. It helps to listen to what people *don't* say.

An overbooked health educator can suffer from a shortage of a critical commodity: time. In an ideal world, there would be enough hours in the day to embrace a more leisurely, caring approach when working with our clients. We sometimes forget that "rushing" client visits can result in having more time on our hands than we'd like when those clients quit coming back. To counter this, *personalismo* (personalizing interaction) can be established with traditional Hispanic clients by first asking about the well-being and recent activities of the family. This approach often puts clients at ease and helps them feel as though you truly care about them. If you can recall interacting with a person who always took time to ask about your life, you can likely understand the significance of doing so with your clients.

Adapting your health education style to the traditional Hispanic views of *respeto, simpatía,* and *personalismo* will enhance the degree to which community members trust and accept you and your program. But don't expect to win their *confianza* (trust) overnight. You probably regard newcomers in your life with a bit of preliminary caution. Expect the same from your new clients. Be as consistent as possible in your efforts, openly admit when you make mistakes, and keep working at it. Patience pays.

Traditional Health Beliefs and Practices

Hot and Cold Theory   Some traditional Hispanics believe illness is caused by improper balances of "hot" and "cold" foods (based on healing properties, not temperature) (Purnell, 1998; Spector, 1996). Hot illnesses (such as infections, fever, diarrhea, and sore throat) are treated with "cold" foods like fresh fruits and vegetables, milk, fish, and chicken. Cold diseases (such as arthritis, pneumonia, menstrual cramps, and cancer) are treated with hot foods like eggs, beef, pork, cheeses, liquor, and spicy dishes (Purnell, 1998).

Mal de Ojo Some people associate *mal de ojo* or "evil eye" with what they've seen in movies about witches casting spells with wicked looks. But, in Hispanic traditions, *mal de ojo* is an illness (such as fever, vomiting, irritability) that can be passed on to another person through well-meaning but excessive admiration and direct eye contact; an example is an adult making a great fuss over a cute baby. The spell can be broken, however, if the admirer touches the child as she looks. You may notice a child wearing a seed bracelet or a bag of seeds pinned to her clothing to prevent *mal de ojo* (Purnell, 1998).

Susto The condition called *susto* (fright or soul loss) is believed to result from a traumatic event that causes the soul to leave the body, sometimes while one is dreaming. Spector (1996) reported three common symptoms: restless sleep; listlessness, anorexia, or lack of interest in personal appearance and hygiene; and malaise, depression, and introversion. Treatment often involves a *curandero* (a traditional healer; see "Gatekeepers" section) and herbs to coax the soul back into the body (Purnell, 1998; Spector, 1996).

Empacho The blocked intestines that characterize *empacho* are believed by traditionalists to occur when one fails to eat a proper balance of hot and cold foods (Purnell, 1998) or when one lies about the amount of food consumed (Spector, 1996). The block is thought to be caused by a lump of food that sticks to the gastrointestinal tract. Treatment includes massaging the back or stomach area.

Caida de la Mollera A serious condition that occurs among infants is *caida de la mollera,* or "fallen fontanel." The anterior fontanel can become depressed beneath the contour of the skull when an infant is dehydrated from diarrhea or vomiting (Spector, 1996) or handled too roughly (Purnell, 1998). Superstition embraces the belief that it happens when a health professional touches the baby's head (Spector, 1996). You can likely imagine the difficulty this belief invokes in areas where diarrhea is rampant, infant mortality rates are high, and medical professionals are distrusted. Culturally sensitive public health education could go a long way to make a difference in this situation.

Gatekeepers and Community Dynamics

A **gatekeeper** is a formal or informal community leader who influences the political and social climate of a community (McKenzie, Pinger, & Kotecki, 1999).

One community gatekeeper you may encounter within traditional Hispanic communities is the local Catholic priest, particularly if many community members still practice this dominant Hispanic religion (Purnell, 1998) and if the local church plays an active role in community functions. Another gatekeeper could be a local *curandero* or *curandera,* a holistic faith healer believed to have the gift of healing and whose healing services may be combined with care from a licensed medical physician (Spector, 1996). Because individuals with academic degrees or titled positions command great respect (Purnell, 1998), they may also serve as important community gatekeepers in some instances.

Information and Support Resources

Several government and organizational sources provide information about ethnic communities and minority health (for example, the Office of Minority Health, Ethnomed, CDC's Office of the Associate Director for Minority Health, USDHHS's Directory of Minority Data Resources); see Appendix D, "Ethnic/Minority Information Resources and Organizations." The National Alliance for Hispanic Health provides a host of publications and other information sources, including a Web page called the "Hispanic Health Link" (see Appendix D).

AFRICAN/BLACK AMERICANS

Demographic and Socioeconomic Characteristics

According to the U.S. Census Bureau (1999a), an estimated 33 million non-Hispanic Black Americans were living in the United States in 1999. At that time, this was the largest ethnic group in the United States, representing 12.1% of the total population (see FYI 5.1), with a median age of 30.2 years (compared to 38.0 for Whites) (U.S. Census Bureau, 1999a).

Like all minority groups, African/Black Americans occupy all socioeconomic levels (U.S. Census Bureau, 1997a). As with Hispanics, the poverty rate among African Americans is decreasing (from 28% in 1996 to 26.5% in 1997) but remains starkly high in comparison to the overall U.S. rate of 13.3% (U.S. Census Bureau, 1997a, 1997b). In 1998 the percentage of African American families headed by single mothers was 46.7% (compared to 12.9% for Whites), with more African American single mothers (39.8%) living in poverty than were White single mothers (23.4%) (U.S. Census Bureau, 1998). Despite these odds, 87% of African Americans had earned a high school degree or more in 1998 (compared to 93.3% for Whites) and 15.3% had earned a bachelor's degree (compared to 31.9% for Whites) (U.S. Census Bureau, 1998).

You may wonder about the appropriate term to use when referring to members of this ethnic population. Most ancestors came from the western coast of Africa, from which millions were captured and brought to the United States as slaves (Campinha-Bacote, 1998). Yet not all Black Americans are of African descent. Preferred identification labels vary, particularly across generations. The terms *Negro* and *colored,* sometimes preferred by older Black Americans have been replaced by self-identification as *Black, Black American,* or *African American* (Campinha-Bacote, 1998). When in doubt, the best course of action is to ask for and use the term preferred by each individual.

Mortality, Morbidity, and Influencing Factors

Death rates among African/Black Americans are 58.8% higher than those of White Americans (PAHO, 1998). As can be noted in FYI 5.1, the top three leading causes of death for African Americans mirror those of Whites, but the number of these deaths in proportion to population size is much higher among African Americans (McKenzie, Pinger, & Kotecki, 1999). As with other minority groups, low income and lack of insurance cause African Americans to wait longer to seek help for these medical problems, which become more severe before treatment is obtained (USDHHS, 1998a). A recent upward trend in cigarette smoking among Black teenagers (USDHHS, 1998b) may contribute to more chronic disease problems in the future.

HIV infection/AIDS is the leading cause of death for all Americans (of all ethnicities) between the ages of 25 and 44 years, and 62% of all those who have developed AIDS have died from it (USDHHS, 1998a). Though racial and ethnic communities constitute only 25% of the U.S. population, 54% of all AIDS cases occur within these groups. AIDS death rates are declining in the United States, but the rates of decrease have been much smaller for Blacks (a 13% decrease from 1995 to 1996) than for non-Hispanic Whites (23%). And, although the AIDS death rate for Blacks decreased by 40% between 1996 and 1997, over 40% of new AIDS cases still emerge among Blacks (USDHHS, 1998b). With HIV/AIDS the fourth leading cause of death for the total African American population (USDHHS, 1997a), education about and prevention of the disease is a primary health issue in this community.

Violent deaths claim more African American males than White males, with accidental deaths and homicides ranking as the fifth and sixth leading causes of death in 1995 among African Americans (USDHHS, 1997a). In that same year, the age-adjusted homicide rate was six times higher for Blacks than for Whites and was the leading cause of death for African American males aged 15–24 (PAHO, 1998). The recent call for public health initiatives in violence prevention (McKenzie et al., 1999) could place you at the forefront of this effort in your future employment.

The birthrate among Black teenagers decreased by 23% between 1991 and 1997. However, "while less than 20% of all births are to Black women, they account for over 40% of all maternal deaths" (USDHHS, 1998b, p. 1). For that reason, the need for increased prenatal education and care among African American women continues.

Despite these disheartening health-status gaps, improvements in the health of African Americans have occurred. Black women are now as likely as White women to have a mammogram (Simpson, 1998). Blacks were 96% more likely in 1980 and only 30% more likely in 1995 to die of chronic liver disease and cirrhosis than Whites (Simpson, 1998). These improvements, coupled with positive changes in education, income, and the general health of African Americans, are encouraging evidence that health promotion and prevention can make a difference.

Health-Related Cultural Norms

Family Dynamics   Traditional African American culture is matriarchal, meaning that the head of the household is often the mother (Campinha-Bacote, 1998). This deviation from the patriarchal nature of most other groups has been traced to the slavery era, when fathers were often sold to other plantations and mothers were left to raise families. Elders in the African American community are treated with respect, and the role of grandmother is central to family identity and function.

Nguzo Sabo   The traditional Afrocentric worldview embraces the seven principles of *Nguzo Sabo* (Campinha-Bacote, 1998) as a guide to appropriate living. The principles include "*Umjo* (unity), *Kujichagula* (self-determination), *Ujima* (collective work and responsibility), *Nia* (purpose), *Imani* (faith), *Ujamaa* (cooperative economics), and *Kuumba* (creativity)" (p. 57). These seven principles contribute to a traditional culture that values hard work, self-discipline, and a cooperative community spirit.

Communication Styles   English is the dominant language spoken among African Americans and is sometimes manifested in a dialect called "Black English" (Campinha-Bacote, 1998), or **Ebonics.** Grammar and sentence structure used in this dialect sometimes differ from what is considered to be standard English. For example, the verb *be* is sometimes used in a nonstandard way, as in "He be going there." Nouns are sometimes followed by a repetitive pronoun, as in "My mother, she lives in New York" (Landrum-Brown, 2000). You may be or know an African American who uses Ebonics to interact with grandparents or older family friends, but uses a more formal English articulation and sentence structure in school and business settings. This is an admirable example of how individuals can move in and out of differing cultural environments and enjoy the benefits of membership in both.

Traditional African American communication is dynamic and expressive, with feelings openly expressed among trusted friends and family. A louder voice volume doesn't necessarily correlate with anger or aggression. In fact, wit and humor are greatly valued among African Americans. Thus, loud verbal put-downs passed between African Americans are more likely reflective of an acceptable friendly joking relationship than serious conflict (Campinha-Bacote, 1998).

Traditional African Americans are reportedly more comfortable with closer personal space than are Whites. However, touch is personal and reserved for close family members and eye contact with an authority figure can be viewed as aggressive behavior (Campinha-Bacote, 1998). As with Hispanic Americans, we suggest that you call older African American clients by their title (such as Dr., Mr., Mrs.) unless invited to do otherwise.

Traditional Health Beliefs and Practices

Spirituality   Christian teachings have played a strong historical role in the African American community (Campinha-Bacote, 1998; Spector, 1996). The Black church is an integral part of community function regardless of the degree of religious commitment among individual community members (Campinha-Bacote, 1998). In some traditional circles, illness is believed to be caused by evil spirits or sinful deeds. Healing comes from God through the power of prayer and "the laying on of hands" (Spector, 1996, p. 66). Belief in Satan-induced illness may lead some to a fatalistic view about sickness prevention (Campinha-Bacote, 1998), but belief in a spiritual source of strength and healing can also have positive health-enhancing results. We invite you to develop a healthy respect for the spiritual beliefs of traditional African Americans and infuse positive spiritual components into your health education programs.

Voodoo   A very small portion of the African American community reportedly practices voodoo, which derives its name from a West Indies god, Vodu (Spector, 1996). Over time, traditional voodoo rites and ceremonies merged with Catholic beliefs so that today's ceremonies are a mixture of tribal dance, sacrifice and blood drinking, and the attribution of special powers to Catholic saints and relics. Health-related voodoo treatments include the use of good and bad gris-gris (spirit-powered oils and powders) and lighting candles of various colors for positive or negative hexes and spells (Spector, 1996).

Rooting   In the practice of rooting, derived from voodoo, a folk healer or root doctor may prescribe a variety of treatments. Many of these home remedies involve herbs or household products, such as a herbal tea made from goldenrod root used to treat pain and fever or a potato poultice used to fight infection and inflammation (Spector, 1996). The degree to which rooting remedies work varies. The PEN-3 components—positive, existential, and negative influences—can help you discern appropriate approaches.

Geophagy and Pica   Some Africans who were brought to the United States as slaves believed that eating iron-rich clay (*geophagy*) was good for a pregnant woman and her baby (Spector, 1996). This practice was later replaced with *pica*, eating Arco starch. Because these practices can lead to anemia and other health problems (Campinha-Bacote, 1998), culturally sensitive health education is needed among those who follow them.

Gatekeepers and Community Dynamics

As in most communities, social status is important in traditional African American communities. Those with titled achievements, such as doctors and lawyers, may serve as recognized community gatekeepers. In communities with traditional spiritual roots, clergy members play a critical role in community function (Campinha-Bacote, 1998).

Spirituality among traditional African Americans can be a positive health motivator. Support from local African American religious leaders can be critical to community acceptance of your program. Folk healers, such as herbalists and spiritualists, may also play an important health role for some traditional individuals.

Information and Support Resources

As with Hispanics, a number of government and volunteer agencies provide information and resources for health issues specific to African Americans. In its Initiatives to Eliminate Racial and Ethnic Disparities, the U.S. Department of Health and Human Services describes four Internet Web sites that may be "of special interest to African Americans." One of those is the Family and Community Violence Prevention Program that involves historically Black colleges and universities in youth violence prevention efforts. The Minority Health Professional Foundation involves many of those same universities in supporting optimum health among poor and minority individuals. The Black Health Net Web site provides health-related information for African Americans. And the American Diabetes Association has developed a special African American Program that is specific to diabetes in this population. (See Appendix D.)

ASIAN AMERICANS AND PACIFIC ISLANDERS

Demographic and Socioeconomic Characteristics

In 1999, approximately 10 million non-Hispanic Asian Americans and Pacific Islanders (AAPIs), 3.7% of the total population, were living in the United States (U.S. Census Bureau, 1999a) and had a median age of 31.9 years (see FYI 5.1). Like other ethnic populations, this group is growing rapidly and is expected to constitute 7.9% of the population by 2050 (McKenzie et al., 1999).

The AAPI community consists of a widely diverse group of more than 30 different primary languages and subcultures (Spector, 1996). In 1996, an estimated 60.7% were foreign-born (USDHHS, 1997c). Countries of origin for Asian

Americans include China, Japan, Korea, Cambodia, Vietnam, and Laos. Pacific Islanders are predominantly of Hawaiian, Samoan, or Guamanian descent (McKenzie et al., 1999).

The 1997 poverty rate (see FYI 5.1) among AAPIs was much closer to that of White Americans than to that of African and Hispanic Americans (U.S. Census Bureau, 1997a, 1997b). The AAPI median household income (see FYI 5.1) was higher than for all other groups, including Whites (U.S. Census Bureau, 1997b). High school completion rates have varied widely across AAPI subgroups, ranging from 31% among Hmongs to 88% among Japanese Americans in 1995 (Bennett & Martin, 1998). In 1994, two fifths of AAPIs 25 years old and over had completed at least a bachelor's degree, a number one and one-half times higher than the rate for non-Hispanic Whites (Bennett & Martin, 1998).

Mortality, Morbidity, and Influencing Factors

Overall, the health of AAPIs has compared favorably to that of other ethnic groups (USDHHS, 1997a). In 1995, this group had the lowest rates of any (including Whites) for infant mortality, suicides, homicides, and deaths caused by lung cancer, cardiovascular disease, and motor vehicle crashes. It also experienced the lowest reported incidences of teen births (2.2 in comparison to 5.3 for the total population) and AIDS (5.8 in comparison to 25.7 for the total population). Yet there is some indication that these comparative statistics may be misleading.

According to a Healthy People 2000 Progress Review (USDHHS, 1997a), cancer is the leading cause of death among Chinese and Vietnamese Americans. Stomach cancer incidence is five times higher among Korean Americans than among the total U.S. population. Cerebrovascular disease deaths are increasing among AAPIs, and three times as many Asian American women smoke as is indicated in self-report studies. AAPI suicide rates equal or exceed the total state rates in California and Hawaii (where large numbers of AAPIs live), and Asian American women have the highest suicide rate among all women age 65 and older nationwide. Of particular import is the incidence of tuberculosis, which is five times higher among AAPIs than among other groups (USDHHS, 1997c).

On a positive note, the AAPI community has enjoyed recent increases in the use of clinical preventive services. More individuals in this group than ever before now have a regular source of primary care. However, approximately 36% of AAPIs under the age of 65 still have no health insurance (compared to 16% in the total U.S. population) (USDHHS, 1997c). Though much has been gained in the health status of Asian Americans, more is needed.

Health-Related Cultural Norms

Family and Honor   You have probably noticed a pattern by now in the importance of family in most traditional ethnic cultures. In Asian traditions, individual success is most valuable in light of the honor it brings to the family (Spector, 1996). Obedience and respect, particularly in relation to age and status ranks, are very important. Relatives are expected to use their connections to support each other (*guan xi* in Chinese) and adult children are obligated to care for their aging parents (Matocha, 1998). Traditional family leaders and decision makers are usually the oldest male in the family. Traditional women are considered family nurturers and caregivers (Matocha, 1998).

Religious Beliefs   As in most cultures, religion provides a rich context for health beliefs and practices among traditional AAPIs (Spector, 1996). The four traditional religions of Buddhism, Confucianism, Taoism, and shamanism share a central theme of harmony and balance (Spector, 1996). Buddhism teaches respect for life, moderation in behavior, self-discipline, and selflessness. Confucianism emphasizes harmonious relationships, a behavioral code, respect for superiors, and the pursuit of learning. Harmony with nature and between humans is a primary principle of Taoism (see next paragraph), and shamanism supports the belief that everything in nature possesses a spirit.

Yin and Yang   The yin-yang philosophy originated in ancient China, where it was commonly believed that all life is regulated by two forces that constantly work in opposition to each other (Spector, 1996). *Yang* is the positive and dynamic energy force (light, hot or warm, full) and *yin,* the negative and static energy force (dark, cold, empty). Traditional belief says that if one is to function in harmony with self and the world, an appropriate balance of this yin-yang life force must be maintained (Matocha, 1998).

Communication Styles   The diversity of languages represented within the AAPI population is as vast as the number of existing countries of origin and subcultures. Among Filipinos, the fastest growing Asian group in North America, more than 100 languages are spoken (Miranda, McBride, & Spangler, 1998). Because modesty is considered a virtue, some people in the AAPI group may closely guard against public embarrassment over health-related issues that imply personal failure (marital difficulties and mental disorders, for example) (Jack, Harrison, & Airhihenbuwa, 1994). To maintain "face," a traditional client may pretend to understand and agree with your instructions or suggestions. When working with traditional Asian American clients, you may need to maintain a respectful distance (arrange chair choices at varying distances), minimize direct eye contact (try sitting side by side) and touch (explain why and how when touch is necessary), and ask for ample communication feedback (use short, simple sentences and list directions) (Matocha, 1998).

Traditional Health Beliefs and Practices

Qi   Some traditional Asian Americans believe the human body contains an invisible system of channels or meridians through which energy (*Qi*) flows (Matocha, 1998). Traditional healers are trained to know the precise points along these meridians at which an acupuncture needle, physical pressure or massage, or moxibustion (heat application) can be applied to induce healing.

T'ai Chi   T'ai chi is an ancient practice in which individuals attempt to achieve a healthy balance in energy flow (called *chi*) through a variety of movements or exercises. Some seek chi through the martial arts. Others prefer less definitive movement patterns that are dictated by one's inner sense of the yin-yang balance. T'ai chi could be labeled a positive cultural influence as defined within the PEN-3 model because it has been found to reduce stress levels and benefit the circulatory system (Matocha, 1998).

Coining and Cupping   You may recall the PEN-3 example we provided earlier of an existential Asian American health belief called *coining*. Traditional healers may provide spiritual cleansing through coining (lightly scraping the skin with a coin) or *cupping* (creating suction through heat on the skin with a "cup") to rid the body of illness-causing spirits (Matocha, 1998). Demonstrated respect for these existential practices can foster community acceptance of your health education programs.

Traditional Remedies   Traditionally, herbal roots, plants, and other products are ground and boiled in water for the patient to ingest or use as a poultice (Spector, 1996). Examples include eating snake flesh for clear vision; applying rhinoceros horn to boils; and taking ginseng tablets or tea for anemia, digestive problems, impotence, and depression. Because it can be dangerous to combine these treatments with physician-prescribed medicines, you should be aware of home remedies used by your clients.

Gatekeepers and Community Dynamics

Health care practitioners are usually respected authority figures in the AAPI community. However, traditional healers may not respect Western health practitioners because Western treatments are viewed as invasive and painful (Matocha, 1998). Depending on the local religious practices, a shaman (faith healer) or Buddhist priest may be an important community gatekeeper for your community health education efforts.

Information and Support Resources

The Asian and Pacific Islander American Health Forum promotes AAPI health by advocating on a national basis for health-enhancing policies, programs, and research. The Association of Asian Pacific Community Health Organizations is supported by the Office of Minority Health and is a good resource for information about the current health status and issues of Asian Americans. See Appendix D for URLs.

NATIVE AMERICAN INDIANS, ESKIMOS, AND ALEUTS

Demographic and Socioeconomic Characteristics

Some Native American Indians prefer to be called Native Americans, while others prefer American Indians. Some trace their heritage to ancient Eskimo or Aleut communities rather than to those commonly referred to as the American Indian tribes. This label issue may seem trivial. However, because this community has experienced a history of mislabeling and mistreatment, your sensitivity to local label preferences will be important. For convenience, in this section we will refer to them as American Indians.

Just over 2 million American Indians resided in the United States in 1999 (0.7% of the total population). More than 550 federally recognized tribes reside on reservations in 34 states (predominantly Oklahoma, California, Arizona, and New Mexico) (Indian Health Service [IHS], 1999; USDHHS, 1995). The largest American Indian nation is the Cherokee (approximately 370,000 members), followed by the Navajo, Sioux, Chippewa, and Choctaw nations (U.S. Census Bureau, 1999d).

A smaller proportion of American Indians enroll in colleges and universities than do any other U.S. minority group (Still & Hodgins, 1998). Although education rates are improving, the estimated percentage of American Indians who complete high school degrees remains at approximately 55% (compared to 93.3% for Whites) (Paisano, 1998).

Mortality, Morbidity, and Influencing Factors

Despite declining rates of coronary heart disease (CHD) among other ethnic groups, CHD incidences among American Indians are increasing, and it is now their leading cause of death (see FYI 5.1) (Howard et al., 1999). High rates of diabetes (70 per 1,000 versus 30 per 1,000 in the total population) may be contributing to this increase (Howard et al., 1999; USDHHS, 1995). Once diagnosed, American Indians are more likely than their White counterparts to suffer the serious complications associated with these illnesses and are more likely to die from them (Howard et al., 1999; USDHHS, 1995). Low income, lack of insurance, and delayed health care explain why.

Although fewer American Indians than Whites reportedly consume alcohol, alcoholism-related deaths are four to eight times higher than the national average (McKenzie et al., 1999). Rates of alcohol-related homicides, suicides, and deaths in motor vehicle crashes are nearly twice those for Whites (USDHHS, 1997a). The cirrhosis death rate is triple the rate for Whites (USDHHS, 1995).

Infant mortality and lack of prenatal care are major health problems among American Indian women. In 1995, the infant mortality rate (11.3 per 1,000 live births) was second only to that of African Americans (15.1) and much higher than that of Whites (6.3) (USDHHS, 1997a). The percentage of total live births to American Indian teenagers that year was 8.7% (compared to 4.3% for Whites). Over 33% of mothers who delivered babies did not receive prenatal care during the first trimester; the figure for Whites is 16.8%.

Health-Related Cultural Norms

Clans and Families   It is time to say it again. The family unit is important to this traditional culture, and elderly members are highly respected (Still & Hodgins, 1998). Competition is often discouraged and, in some tribes (such as the Navajo), families with more wealth are expected to provide for those with less (Still & Hodgins, 1998). Family leadership roles differ across American Indian subgroups, but many tribes are matriarchal, meaning that mothers and grandmothers are the center of society and are common health-related decision makers (Still & Hodgins, 1998).

Mother Earth   Health-related beliefs vary across cultures, and individuals. However, common tradition embraces the concept of *Mother Earth* (Spector, 1996), the idea that the earth is a living organism with which one must seek harmony to be well and happy. Caring for one's body and the land on which one lives create a harmonious environment in which a person can fulfill one's spiritual destiny. Disharmony results in illness.

Communication Styles   Language and dialect differences across more than 550 tribes sometimes serve as communication barriers between tribes (Still & Hodgins, 1998). Like some Asian-oriented languages, some American Indian languages rely heavily on differing voice inflections to convey different meanings. Talking loudly or using the wrong voice inflection when trying to pronounce an Indian word can be insulting. For that reason, using an interpreter in professional settings is often a good idea (Still & Hodgins, 1998).

When working with a traditional American Indian, don't be alarmed if you are met with a deadpan expression or if direct eye contact is avoided. Some individuals may seem aloof until they know you better, and those who interpret eye contact as a sign of aggression may avoid it. Although touch is usually reserved for intimate friends, a handshake is often the appropriate greeting.

Traditional medical healers are expected to know the cause of illness without asking the patient. In a clinical setting, physicians may be considered incompetent if they have to ask many questions. With traditional clients, it may help to begin with observational statements (such as "You appear to have a chest cold") rather than questions.

Traditional Health Beliefs and Practices

Divination   Traditional American Indian healing is rooted in beliefs about the mind-body-spirit connection and the place of plants, animals, and humans in the spirit world (Spector, 1996). Medicine men and women are often believed to possess a spiritual gift that allows them to first diagnose the cause of an illness without asking the patient (called *divination*). Hopi medicine men and women often use *meditation* to determine the cause of an illness. They sometimes use a crystal ball or chew on trance-inducing jimsonweed to identify the evil that caused the disease. A Navajo medicine man or woman may be gifted with the *motion of the hand* in which sand or pollen is ceremonially sprinkled around the patient while the diviner chants and waves a hand to determine the cause of illness. Sand art is sometimes created in these ceremonies or incorporated into *stargazing* (determining the cause by noting the colors of light shafts) or *listening* (interpreting various sounds) (Spector, 1996).

The Singer   The diviner often meets with the family to discuss the discovered diagnosis, discuss treatment, and recommend a healer or *singer* if the diviner does not have the healing gift or training. A singer may be called on to treat the condition through "the laying on of hands" or by drawing disease-causing elements out of the body while singing.

Purification   *Purification* (cleansing the body and spirit) is brought about by total water immersion and the use of sweat lodges and herbal remedies in special rituals. Remedies differ across groups. For example, the Micmac Indians of Canada use milkweed plant to cure warts and juniper berries to treat rheumatism. The Oneida Indians treat colds with witch hazel and ear infections with skunk oil. The Hopi Indians use sunflowers to treat spider bites and the ground stem of the yucca plant as a laxative.

Gatekeepers and Community Dynamics

In traditional settings, the spiritual leaders we've described can serve as valuable gatekeepers among traditional American Indians. But care must be taken to avoid stereotyping individuals and offending community leaders. Local leaders in American Indian organizations and those in political office on reservations may hold the keys to community access and acceptance of your program.

Information and Support Resources

The Indian Health Service is an agency within the U.S. Department of Health and Human Services responsible for health services to all American Indians and Alaska Natives. The IHS helps Indian tribes develop and coordinate health services and programs and advocates in the health field for comprehensive health services to American Indians. The IHS is a good place to start when looking for information about American Indian health (see Appendix D).

IN CONCLUSION

Wouldn't it be wonderful to be able to read a chapter like this one and instantly become fully prepared to address the health issues of all ethnic communities? It doesn't work that way, does it? This chapter has provided you with only a small sampling of information, which may or may not appear to be immediately useful to you, depending on the settings in which you intend to work. But keep in mind that every individual is a product of culture and that culture will always influence how you "do" health education, regardless of the setting and regardless of the visibility of its influence. Like most textbooks, this one can only provide "food for thought." True learning will begin when you start to apply what you've read. The activity described in "For Your Application" encourages you to explore what you know, discover what you don't, and begin expanding your cultural horizons. The "For Your Portfolio" can help you take those first steps toward cultural competence. The journey takes a lifetime, but it's worth the time.

REVIEW QUESTIONS

1. Explain how broad ethnic labels, when used as health-status categories, can be misleading.
2. Describe the limitations of existing data sources as they relate to minority health status.
3. Explain how the PEN-3 model can be used to distinguish between positive, existential, and negative cultural influences on health.
4. Briefly describe the demographic characteristics of Hispanic American, African American, Asian American, and American Indian populations and list some of the terms they use to identify themselves.
5. Describe the primary health issues of each of the populations listed in question 5.
6. Explain the socioeconomics, cultural beliefs and practices, and community dynamics that influence health within each ethnic community.
7. Identify information and support resources that can be used to understand and address health issues specific to each group.

FOR YOUR APPLICATION

Mapping America's Communities

Select an ethnic community and a health problem it faces. Write both in small letters in the middle of a blank sheet of paper. In the area surrounding those words, place other words or symbols that represent factors you think contribute to the selected health problem among more traditional members of the ethnic community. Connect the words or symbols with lines and arrows to show the direction of influence between them. Then, expand the "map" by adding words, symbols, or both that represent positive community and cultural influences that could serve as potential solutions to the health problem. Connect these to other words and symbols with dotted lines and arrows to show the direction of potential influence. Be prepared to explain to others what the lines and arrows mean (how factors you've identified can influence each other). When finished, you'll have created a cognitive map that represents how you view the complex picture of health (both problems and potential solutions) within this community. Validate your map by checking information sources provided in Appendix D and researching more about the health and cultural diversity of your selected community.

 ## FOR YOUR PORTFOLIO

Gaining Cross-Cultural Experience

Volunteer at your local health department or other health organizations or agencies that commonly serve individuals from a wide array of cultural backgrounds and ethnicities. Ask the agency's volunteer supervisor to write a brief summary and evaluation of your responsibilities, demonstrated skills, and performance quality, paying specific attention to your cross-cultural communication skills.

Attend workshops and seminars that specialize in language mastery, cultural sensitivity, or both. Document your attendance and describe the nature of the training in your portfolio.

PART II

The Process of
Health Programming

6

Assessing Community Health Issues

CONGRATULATIONS! YOU GOT THE JOB! YOU REPORT TO work at the local health department and meet with the director for an hour to discuss health education goals and priorities. You're excited about your assignment to various projects but are a little nervous about getting started. You sit down at your new desk and wonder, "Where do I begin?"

Chapter Objectives

1. Define needs-assessment concepts.
2. Discuss the difference between actual and perceived needs and explain why it is useful to assess both.
3. Describe the usefulness and processes of APEX/PH and PATCH in community needs assessment.
4. Discuss how models and theories can be useful in the needs-assessment process.
5. Use the PRECEDE/PROCEED model to identify factors that influence community health problems.
6. Describe the primary components of the health belief model, transtheoretical model, and theory of planned behavior.
7. Describe a four-step process for assessing the health issues within a community.
8. Practice assessing health issues in a hypothetical situation.

NEEDS-ASSESSMENT CONCEPTS AND DEFINITIONS

Now that you have a general picture of America's health problems, it is time to consider the process through which those problems were identified and the methods you should use to develop a broader RISE-oriented view of America's subgroups. In Chapter 1, we introduced the seven areas of responsibility of a health education specialist and described the specific subcompetencies of one of those seven, needs assessment. Our goal here is to expand your understanding of the purpose and character of needs assessment, how it is evolving in our profession, and how it relates to other assessment and community organization terms and principles.

We know our health education programs are on target when we base them on accurate **needs assessment** data and a careful interpretation of their meaning. The goal of needs assessment is to identify gaps between what exists and what ought to exist so that you can design a program to reduce those gaps (Windsor, Baranowski, Clark, & Cutter, 1994).

Actual and Perceived Needs

Gilmore and Campbell (1996) define needs assessment as "a planned process that identifies the reported needs of an individual or a group" (p. 5). They explain that two important groups of people are expected to provide input in needs identification. Those are the health professionals and community members who, hopefully, will both be involved in planning and implementing the proposed health education program. The needs identified by these groups may be **actual needs** (often based on documented incidence and prevalence rates) or **perceived needs** (sometimes based on real or perceived risks). These two types of needs can sometimes differ, but they are both important pieces of assessment information.

Why Both Are Important

Why would perceived needs be as important as actual needs? The answer can be readily understood if you picture, for example, a community in which a high rate of HIV infection has been documented, although most community members deny that the problem exists. Health professionals would likely suggest you implement an HIV/AIDS education program to address this actual need, but community members might be less than cooperative. The community might be more concerned about a recent single and well-publicized incident of domestic violence and prefer a violence prevention program rather than an HIV/AIDS education program. The more information you have about actual and perceived needs in the community you serve, the more equipped you will be to educate the community as needed and work with others to prioritize program goals.

A slightly different scenario could exist if the community actually wished to address both health concerns but was still more concerned about violence (perceived needs) than HIV/AIDS (actual needs). Finding the "common ground" (Green & Kreuter, 1999, p. 58) where data-based evidence and community concerns match is an ideal place to begin community health promotion efforts, but it doesn't always exist. When it doesn't, it helps to respectfully acknowledge perceived needs, build community awareness about real needs, and work from a partnership format to maintain a collaborative spirit.

COMMUNITY PARTICIPATION AND CAPACITY BUILDING

We explained in Chapter 2 that our profession is moving toward a community empowerment approach that involves community members in the health education process. **Community empowerment** is "a social-action process that promotes participation of people, organizations, and communities towards the goals of increased individual and community control, political efficacy, improved quality of community life, and social justice" (Wallerstein, 1992, p. 198). In other words, community empowerment is about helping people help themselves in a way that encourages them to take ownership of their health problems and use their abilities and resources to develop solutions.

Capacity-focused, or assets-based, assessment is one strategy that helps foster community empowerment and place the focus on potential solutions rather than community needs and deficiencies. Specifically, capacity-focused assessment identifies capacities, skills, assets, or contributions that can be provided by community individuals, associations, and institutions (Gilmore & Campbell, 1996). The information collected in capacity assessment (or assets mapping) can be used later to form community coalitions and advisory panels for program planning and implementation (see Chapter 7). Two frequently used models for capacity assessment and community involvement in program planning are described next.

Assessment Protocol for Excellence in Public Health (APEX/PH)

APEX/PH (National Association of County Health Officials [NACHO], 1991) was developed in the late 1980s through the cooperation of a number of health organizations and agencies, including the American Public Health Association (APHA) and the Centers for Disease Control and Prevention (CDC). This three-part assessment plan provides a broad framework in which you can appropriately balance information collected through both needs and capacity assessments. Part 1 of the APEX/PH is the "organizational capacity assessment" in which your agency or department is evaluated by an internal self-assessment team made up of the agency director and staff members. The goal is to identify strengths and weaknesses of the agency as they relate to its ability to deliver health programs and services to your community of interest.

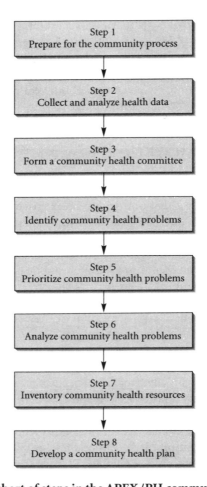

FIGURE 6.1   Flowchart of steps in the APEX/PH community process.
The steps in the APEX/PH community process flow from preliminary health data collection (steps 1–2), through community-driven needs identification and prioritization (steps 3–6), to an inventory of resources and plan development (steps 7–8).
From *APEX/PH Assessment Protocol for Excellence in Public Health* (p. 78), by National Association of County Health Officials, 1991, Washington, DC: Author.

Part 2 of APEX/PH is the "community process" that mobilizes the community to identify and prioritize its own health needs and assets and develop a plan for intervention. Figure 6.1 outlines the eight-step process for community involvement in needs and capacity assessments. Note how the steps progress from preliminary health-data collection (usually incidence and prevalence of disease or health problems) through community-driven needs identification and prioritization to an inventory of resources and plan development.

Part 3 of APEX/PH is called "completing the cycle." In it, local health-influencing policies and the results of parts 1 and 2 are periodically reviewed and

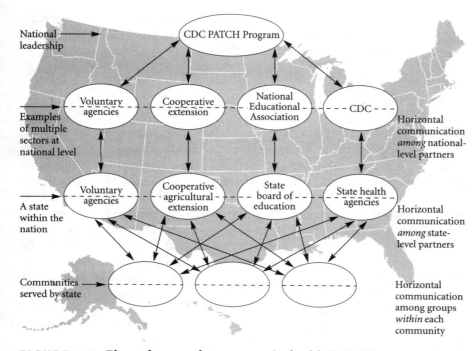

FIGURE 6.2   Planned approach to community health (PATCH).
PATCH guides communities to plan, implement, and evaluate health education
programs. From *Community Health Education and Promotion* (p. 197), edited by C. S. Schust, 1997,
Gaithersberg, MD: Aspen.

evaluated to ensure that efforts now in progress are still on track. It is recommended that part 3 be implemented at least every 4 years.

Planned Approach to Community Health (PATCH)

PATCH (Figure 6.2) is a community-health-planning model developed by CDC
in 1983 (Green & Kreuter, 1999). The row of ovals at the bottom of Figure 6.2
represents local community groups. The other two rows represent state and national agencies and associations who can contribute to local community health
interventions. The arrows in the model represent partnership links between
groups that form a supportive network.

The purpose of PATCH is to involve local communities in needs assessment
and health intervention that is supported by collaborating agencies at the state
and national levels. The PATCH process begins by forming an advisory group that
is representative of the whole community, with at least 20% consisting of lay leaders or gatekeepers (formally or informally recognized community leaders). This
group works with a steering committee comprising 6–12 key members of the
community group and the local coordinator, which will likely be you. This team

works together to collect and organize needs-assessment data and prioritize health issues. The results are then used to develop an intervention or program plan and program evaluation protocol.

KNOWING WHAT TO LOOK FOR

So far, we have discussed how needs- and capacity-assessment data are collected and how that information is used to develop a health education program plan. What we haven't addressed is what to look for in those assessments. To emphasize the importance of knowing what to look for, we'll tell you a story about an international public health group that once decided to build a hospital in a very remote region of a developing country. The group decided to build the hospital because of the high rate of maternal and infant deaths in childbirth in that region, a problem attributed to the scarcity of trained physicians and appropriate medical facilities. So the group diligently raised the money needed, built an amazingly modern facility in view of the surrounding conditions, and flew in well-trained professionals to do the work. But after some time, childbirth death rates remained high and few local people had even visited the new facility. Someone decided to ask "Why?" and learned from the people who lived there that they trusted the local midwives and preferred to remain in their familiar home surroundings to give birth rather than move to a new and unfamiliar building to be cared for by strangers. The public health group realized it had failed to accurately assess the situation. It decided to try again, this time armed with needed information about the local community, its interests and perceived needs. With time, the health group was able to reach the local people by inviting their midwives to train in the facility and work in the birthing room along with the "imported" professionals. Had someone fully understood the need to assess the whole picture before the plan was implemented, things might have progressed quite differently.

If it's easy to miss some important aspects of the needs and capacities of a community, how can we approach the assessment process with any assurance of knowing what to look for? That process may seem simple, but it rarely is because each community has its own unique characteristics and a variety of influences that have shaped it (see Chapter 2). However, some helpful guidelines and models used in the health education profession can increase our chances of identifying a full assessment picture. Their appropriate application calls for a patient, mature understanding of how they work.

The Elephant Story

Having to memorize theories and models for a college course can be a nuisance. You may suspect that some professors include them in required materials just to keep you busy or to satisfy some egotistical "ivory tower" personality quirk. We don't deny that in some cases you could be correct. However, theories and models can be useful in the real world when they serve as a framework for accuracy and efficiency. Used appropriately, they can help you to know what you are doing and do it well. To illustrate the value of using a model in needs assessment and program planning, we invite you to consider a fictitious story we lovingly refer to as "The Elephant Story."

Our story is derived from a well-known poem called "The Blind Men and the Elephant" written by John Godfrey Saxe in the 1800s (Bornstein, 1996). The poem was fashioned after a part of the Udana, canonical Hindu scripture (Ireland, 1999). Both are about blind men who believed they understood all there was to know about an elephant but, in reality, understood only certain parts. Our "elephant" story helps make our point about needing to see the whole assessment picture. We hope you'll find it useful.

The Story   Once upon a time, there were a number of different research groups who were all attempting to assess a certain "health phenomenon" called "the elephant." Part of the problem inherent in seeing the full picture of this "elephant phenomenon" was that these research groups were not cooperating with each other. Members of each group feared that sharing information with others would threaten their access to limited resources. The result was that each group had only a partial picture of the whole elephant issue. This, of course, distorted the truth about the elephant phenomenon and crippled any effective attempts to address the issue as a whole.

One day, a student who had recently joined one of the research teams voiced the unspeakable. She suggested that all of the teams be invited to a conference to share what they'd learned about the elephant phenomenon. She even launched an awareness campaign to help each team realize the advantages of being able to see the whole elephant picture. She then booked the conference in the Bahamas to add to the appeal. Miraculously, it worked! The teams came.

On the first day of the conference, all of the big names in "elephant phenomenon research" entered the conference hall, and the excitement (not to mention the competitive tension) was high. The first research team representative walked to the podium and the crowd expectantly hushed. He started speaking: "Ladies and gentlemen, I am honored to be the first to speak on this momentous occasion about the phenomenon we all know to be the elephant. As you know, our research team has been tirelessly working for a number of years to carefully assess the elephant and we have clearly identified some interesting physical characteristics and movement patterns. We now know that the elephant is shaped much like a tree trunk, is flat on the bottom, and often appears in clusters of four" (Figure 6.3). With a self-satisfied look on his face, the researcher returned to his seat.

A representative of another research group then came to the podium with a slight frown on her face. She leaned into the microphone and stated "Ladies and gentlemen, I respectfully submit that the previous speaker may think he's been researching the elephant. However, I can only surmise that he must be mistaken." The first speaker gasped from his seat, and his face turned red. But she continued,

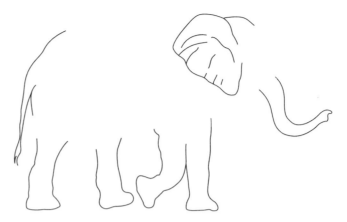

FIGURE 6.3   The elephant story.
The "elephant story" illustrates how a model can be used to create a more complete picture of a community health issue from previously isolated pieces of information.

"My team has been researching the elephant phenomenon for over a decade and we've found our data to accurately reflect its characteristics." She paused for effect. "The elephant is not at all shaped like a tree trunk, nor does it move in clusters of four." The first speaker angrily grasped the arms of his chair. "To the contrary, elephants almost always move in pairs. (We believe they mate for life.) They are shaped much like a huge, flat fan and, under certain conditions, may move in wavelike motions." She shot a pointed look at the first speaker and returned to her seat.

The tension mounted as a representative of yet a third research group approached the microphone. He solemnly eyed his audience and, with a thoughtful expression, said "Distinguished colleagues, I am perplexed by what we have heard today. There is nothing in my 20-year experience of elephant phenomenon research to validate the previous two speakers' descriptions. In our assessments, we have never encountered elephants in close proximity to each other. Each elephant is shaped like a garden hose and often behaves like one with an occasional spray of water coming out the end." He sat down amidst the hubbub of agitated whispers and angry looks between research teams.

Just as total crowd chaos was about to break forth, a tall, white-haired, distinguished-looking gentleman suddenly stood from the back of the room and shouted above the noise "Enough!" Heads turned toward his voice and, in an instant, you could have heard a pin drop. This man was recognized by all as a longtime researcher and scholar in the field. Though he, too, had selfishly guarded his findings over the years, he remained a recognized authority in elephant research, predominantly because he'd been researching the longest. All eyes were on him as he purposefully made his way to the front. He turned his intense gaze onto the hushed audience and said "I've heard quite *enough!* I am *appalled* at your lack of understanding and true knowledge about a phenomenon that affects the lives of so many people. This elephant phenomenon is no joking matter!" Fixing his fiery gaze on each of the three speakers, he virtually shouted "You have embarrassed our profession with your misguided attempts to describe the elephant! The elephant is like . . . it's like a small . . ."

The crowd leaned toward him, sensing that what he was about to say would change forever how they saw the elephant. But the intensity of the moment became too much and, before he could finish his sentence, the gentleman fell to the floor in a dead faint. The crowd rushed to his aid, almost smothering him in the process. Some were shouting instructions to unbutton his collar, get him some water, call 911. Others shouted for the crowd to back up and give him some breathing space. In a moment, the gentleman came to himself and instantly grabbed the collar of the researcher who kneeled beside him. Pulling him close, the gentleman urgently whispered in a hoarse, strained voice "The elephant is like a very large, stiff worm with no eyes." Those close enough to hear him looked at each other in surprise. "A worm?" someone asked incredulously. "Yes," he hissed. "A worm that grows out of the rump of a hill." He paused to catch his breath and then moaned, "But, to this day, I can't for the life of me determine the source of that awful smell."

The Meaning   Okay. So it's a silly story. It's difficult to imagine any thinking human having difficulty seeing the full picture of an elephant. After all, we all know what an elephant looks like, right? But what if we were talking about a real community health issue that was a little more difficult to define and assess? What if it were something that affects the well-being of a large array of community members, such as violence in schools? Imagine that some teenagers walk into a high school and open fire on students with automatic weapons. The aftermath is devastating, and the whole country gets in on the act of trying to assess what happened and why.

The discussions could sound a lot like the comments of those researchers who saw only parts of the elephant. Some might blame the school system for loose security and call for metal detectors at all doors or specialized training for school personnel. Others might point to violent media sources and demand that they be banned. The parents would certainly be scrutinized, and cries could arise for more counseling programs for troubled families or for stricter laws holding parents accountable. Most assuredly, a large array of resources and potential solutions would be suggested, some of which might actually work within the context of the whole picture. However, without a broad understanding of all potential influences and solutions, some "parts of that elephant" might be overlooked.

That's how theories and models help. They provide a framework through which we can accurately assess large, complex health issues and their potential solutions. They remind us to look for common relationships between factors and help us ask the right questions. A number of theories and models are used in the health education field. We've addressed only a portion of them in this textbook.

Most are useful in a number of ways, including needs assessment; program planning, implementation, and evaluation; and program marketing. For that reason, we encourage you to avoid thinking of each model only within the context of the chapter in which it is presented. The specific models and theories you use will depend on your unique work situation and preferences.

The PRECEDE/PROCEED Model

One of the most widely-used health assessment and planning models is that developed by Green and Kreuter (1999) called **PRECEDE/PROCEED.** As you can see in Figure 6.4, this model is big and can seem a bit overwhelming at first, until you realize that its purpose is not to belabor the process with needless attention to detail. Instead, it is designed to help us develop a full picture of our community of interest—its health needs and the factors that influence them. It isn't the only existing needs-assessment and program-planning model, but it is a good place to begin your exploration of needs because it offers a broad community-assessment perspective and provides a framework in which community members can participate in the process.

The model originally focused on the assessed health problems of communities and the ability of a central agency or organization to develop programs as solutions. It has been adapted, however, to promote community involvement in the needs-assessment and program-planning process and incorporate a more positive approach through assets mapping, capacity building, and resource and policy development (Green & Kreuter, 1999). How it works is the opposite of the "elephant research" illustration in Figure 6.3. With a lot of teamwork and careful attention to a variety of contributing components, you can help a community develop a full picture of the quality of life and health status of its members and develop a plan of action to enhance them.

In needs assessment, the PRECEDE portion (phases 1–5, Figure 6.4) is implemented phase by phase, from right to left in the model. Phase 1, on the far right, entails the social assessment of the community's quality of life. This is the ideal place to start because the ultimate goal of health education is to foster life satisfaction and total well-being among community members. Starting here enables you to involve the community in subjectively defining the social issues of greatest import and determining how they can be addressed for the common good (Green & Kreuter, 1999).

In the *social assessment,* community members are encouraged to identify social indicators that reflect the community's levels of satisfaction with their quality of life. These indicators vary depending on the community members' unique perspectives. Figure 6.5 provides examples of social indicators that may be used during Phase 1 of the assessment. Assets mapping is also conducted during this phase to identify available resources and the individuals and organizations who control them (Green & Kreuter, 1999)

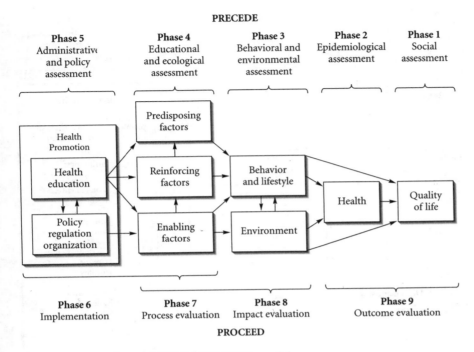

PRECEDE

Phase 5	Phase 4	Phase 3	Phase 2	Phase 1
Administrative and policy assessment	Educational and ecological assessment	Behavioral and environmental assessment	Epidemiological assessment	Social assessment

Phase 6	Phase 7	Phase 8	Phase 9
Implementation	Process evaluation	Impact evaluation	Outcome evaluation

PROCEED

FIGURE 6.4 The PRECEDE/PROCEED model.
This model can be used to identify factors that contribute to health and quality of life within a community. The arrows depict lines of causation and how health promotion efforts can produce positive impacts and outcomes. From *Health Promotion Planning: An Educational and Ecological Approach* (3rd ed., p. 35), by L. W. Green and M. W. Kreuter, 1999, Mountain View, CA: Mayfield.

In the *epidemiological assessment,* (phase 2), data are collected to determine the incidence and prevalence of community health problems that affect the community's quality of life (see Figure 6.5 for indicators). These can include communicable diseases (such as measles and hepatitis), chronic diseases (such as cancer and heart disease), health-related risk factors (such as malnutrition, anemia, and hypertension), and other recognized health problems (such as domestic violence and adolescent pregnancy). In this phase, the APEX/PH and PATCH methods of community and health professional involvement can be used to prioritize these issues in terms of their degree of importance to and changeability within the community.

We stated earlier that beginning with phase 1 (social assessment) of the model is the ideal. We should point out here, however, that phase 2 (epidemiological assessment) may be where you actually begin. Why? Because most health education jobs have a predefined focus. For example, if you were hired by the American Heart Association, you would know during job interviews that the "health

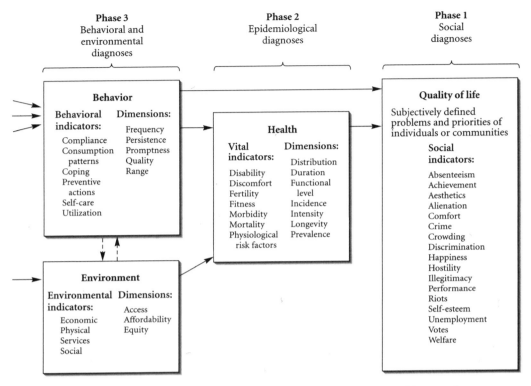

FIGURE 6.5   **Relationships, indicators, and dimensions of factors that might be identified in Phases 1, 2, and 3 of the PRECEDE diagnostic process or evaluated in the extension of PROCEED.**

From *Health Promotion Planning: An Educational and Ecological Approach* (3rd ed., p. 39), by L. W. Green and M. W. Kreuter, 1999, Mountain View, CA: Mayfield.

problem" focus (phase 2) is heart disease. Under those circumstances, it would pay for you to first devote attention to how the community of interest perceives heart disease and its effects on their quality of life. Thus, in this instance, you would move from phase 2 to phase 1 and then back to phase 3 (Green & Kreuter, 1999).

Specific behaviors and environmental factors that contribute to the targeted health problem(s) are identified and prioritized in phase 3 (see *behavioral and environmental diagnoses* in Figure 6.5). Targeted behaviors can be positive, negative, or both, depending on the health issue in question. For example, if heart disease is targeted in the epidemiological assessment, the targeted behaviors may be to increase exercise, decrease high-fat dietary intake, and eliminate smoking in the community. Environmental factors may be those beyond the individual's control, such as the lack of low-fat selections in fast-food restaurants. If so, you may need to include long-range environmental change efforts in your action plan.

Phase 4, the *educational and ecological assessment,* is composed of predisposing, reinforcing, and enabling factors. Distinguishing among these three categories can be a challenge when you are first learning the model, but recognizing their different but related influences will be critical for your health education program. **Predisposing factors** (attitudes, values, beliefs, knowledge) in community members involve those thought processes that motivate the targeted behaviors. For example, predisposing factors that sometimes influence adolescents to smoke include the belief that smoking is cool, the desire (value) to be accepted by peers, and an attitude of rebellion against authority figures who say they shouldn't. On a more positive note, adolescents may exercise regularly if they know about and value its benefits and are motivated by a desire to stay "fit and trim."

Reinforcing factors are rewards or encouraging feedback (positive or negative) that community members receive from other people. In our example, smoking adolescents may receive encouragement from smoking peers but can be positively influenced by nonsmoking role models (such as popular athletes) willing to help in your health education program. Individuals who are providing negative reinforcement may also be educated or trained through your program to shift to a more positive influence, as in the case of physical education teachers being trained to tailor their classes to the abilities and interests of their students so that adolescents develop positive attitudes about exercise.

Enabling factors include resources and skills needed for behavior change to occur or barriers that may prevent it from happening—or both. Regular exercise will be easier to maintain if exercise resources, such as a safe and convenient place to jog or engage in recreational sports, are available and accessible. Because improper exercise can cause needless muscle soreness and injury, adolescents also need training in appropriate exercise skills. Enabling factors that contribute to negative health behaviors may also need to be targeted as in the case of cigarette accessibility for minors.

The first step of the *administrative and policy assessment* (phase 5) is to assess the resources needed to develop and implement the health education program. The second is to compare those needs to available resources in the community. Time, personnel, and budget are three primary resource considerations that can be matched at this point with identified community assets and capacities. The third step is to assess barriers to implementation such as staff commitment and attitudes or community concerns. In the policy assessment, local politics and organizational systems that may influence program implementation are also considered. This is a good place to begin emphasizing your community of interest's resources and develop community coalitions to develop solutions.

Now that you've looked at this portion of the PRECEDE/PROCEED model, we encourage you to use it. Figure 6.6 presents a sample "PRECEDE assessment" of adolescent smoking. The words or phrases in each PRECEDE box represent factors we might identify and target if we were conducting a needs assessment among adolescents in a local school system. We invite you to use this visual as

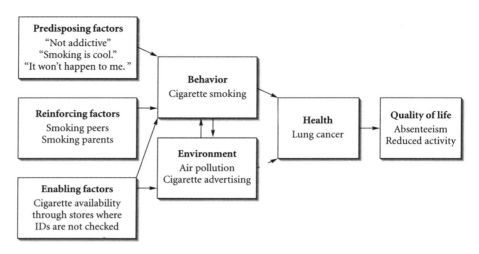

FIGURE 6.6   A sample PRECEDE assessment of adolescent smoking.
This sample shows selected factors known to influence smoking behavior and its
long-range effects.

Draw a small "quality of life" box on the far right side of a sheet of paper. Record in it social indicators you think would emerge from a needs assessment about high school drug abuse.

Draw a "health" box to the immediate left of the quality-of-life box and list in it some possible "drug health indicators."

Add behavioral, environmental, predisposing, reinforcing, and enabling boxes to your drug abuse model and insert relevant examples in each.

a guideline and create your own PRECEDE assessment of a similar adolescent health issue, such as drug abuse.

Let's pretend there have been a number of incidents related to drug abuse in a local high school; various students have been involved in alcohol-related traffic accidents, drug overdoses, and the like. School authorities and parents are alarmed about drugs pervading the school system, and the issue is a primary discussion topic among students. You've been asked to develop a school-based drug education program and you wish to apply the PRECEDE/PROCEED model to assess influencing factors. What quality-of-life factors would you expect to emerge in the social assessment? In other words, what social indicators might be detected as evidence that drugs are a problem in the school? Any number of indices could emerge, including drug-influenced domestic problems, school absenteeism and dropouts, and even arrests.

How would you know whether drug abuse is actually prevalent in the school and should be a health education priority? You would look for incidence and prevalence rates of specific drug-related health problems. Examples of indicators you could name include the frequency of alcohol-related traffic accidents, drug overdoses, and diagnosed drug addictions recorded over the past year. These statistics could be compared to other possible health problems such as injuries or sexually transmitted diseases to validate drug problems as an important priority.

With drug problems confirmed as an important target, what behavioral and environmental factors might you find to be contributing to the drug problems? In an educational and ecological assessment, what predisposing, reinforcing, and enabling factors might emerge? Individual surveys and group assessments could reveal important answers, such as the need to address social drinking and drug experimentation (behaviors) commonly practiced at parties and sporting events (a social environment factor). Common adolescent attitudes, values, misconceptions, and beliefs about drug and alcohol use (predisposing factors) could be found similar to those associated with cigarette smoking, and just as damaging. Your needs assessment might reveal that a well-designed health education campaign could counter the usual negative peer pressure if it involved recognized role models and school heroes (reinforcing factors). The assessment could also help you understand drug accessibility issues and identify the skills needed to refuse drugs in a social setting (enabling factors).

The PRECEDE assessment results we just described could serve as a visual framework for a needs-specific drug abuse prevention program. Specific aspects of program development, including goals and objectives writing and implementation, will be addressed in Chapter 7. Then, in Chapter 8, we will visit the model once more to discuss program evaluation plans and strategies. These two components constitute the PROCEED portion of the PRECEDE/PROCEED model.

As good as the PRECEDE/PROCEED model is for broad-based community assessment and program planning, it does not address every aspect of what health educators should know about human nature and the factors that often influence the way people think. For example, the model includes "attitudes" among the predisposing factors that often influence health behavior, but it doesn't provide detailed descriptions of the types of attitudes or perceptions that influence health most often. The theories and models described in the following sections can help you further explore these psychological influences. Understanding them can help you be more specific in your chosen health education strategies.

Health Belief Model

Did you ever watch a film or video in school that was designed to scare you away from drinking and driving? If so, you may still remember some of the more graphic scenes of automobiles ripped in half and human blood everywhere. Did the scare tactics work? If so, for how long did the message influence your behavior?

What if you had been the person hired to make that video? Would you have done anything differently? You might have, if you understood the average adolescent mind-set. Adolescents who take risks rarely believe that behavioral consequences affect them. They may fully accept statistical evidence that shows a high correlation between fatal accidents and drinking while driving. But they may not fully believe themselves to be at risk, even though they drink and drive. Their attitude may be "I know it can happen to the other guy. But that doesn't mean it's going to happen to me." In some cases, showing a dozen graphic videos about the severity of the consequences may do little to change that perception.

List circumstances under which using scare tactics (such as graphic videos) might and might not motivate people to change behavior.

That's why using existing theories and models in needs-assessment efforts is important. They can guide us to ask critical questions about specific types of attitudes and beliefs so we can later design health education strategies that are

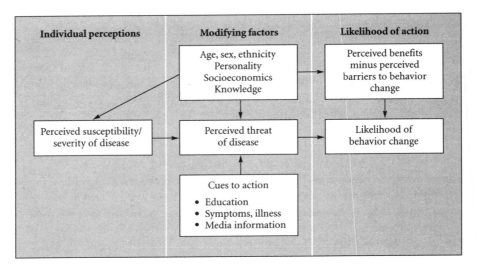

FIGURE 6.7   Health belief model.
According to the health belief model, adequate levels of perceived severity and
perceived susceptibility must both be present for perceived threat to be a behavior-
motivating factor. From "The Health Belief Model," by V. J. Strecher and I. M. Rosenstock, in
Health Behavior and Health Education: Theory, Research, and Practice (p. 48), edited by K. Glanz, F. M.
Lewis, and B. K. Rimer, 1997, San Francisco: Jossey-Bass.

specifically adapted to them. The **health belief model** (Hochbaum, 1958) is a clas-
sic health education model that could apply in our drinking-and-driving example.
As you can see in Figure 6.7, the model illustrates how the "size of the threat"
(perceived threat of disease) will influence a person's behavior as it relates to that
threat (likelihood of behavior change). In other words, those adolescents we
talked about are more likely to refrain from drinking when they drive if they truly
feel threatened or at risk of experiencing the potentially awful consequences. So
how would you convince them they are at risk? How would you raise their levels
of "perceived threat?" The graphic video might not work if it addressed only one
of the two types of individual perceptions that often influence perceived threat.

The type of video we described would likely focus on raising the watcher's *perceived severity of disease* (or severity of injury/death in our example). The video
could show actual footage of alcohol-related accidents, simulations of just how
the driver's alcohol-impaired performance could result in bad driving choices,
statistical charts and graphs depicting high correlations between drunken driving
and deaths in our country. All of this information could convince the watcher
that, indeed, a person who drives while intoxicated is at higher risk of accidents.
However, as we said earlier, the video might bring about higher levels of perceived severity without truly convincing the watcher of personal risk or *perceived
susceptibility* to death and injury. In other words, an adolescent can truly believe
bad stuff can happen when a person drinks and drives (high perceived severity)
but still think "It just won't happen to *me!*" (low perceived susceptibility).

According to the health belief model, adequate levels of perceived severity and perceived susceptibility must be present for perceived threat to be a behavior-motivating factor. And even with both those elements in place, other *modifying factors* sometimes come into play (Strecher & Rosenstock, 1997). Of course, we already know that differences in age, personality, and so forth can influence perceptions about threat as well as about the perceived benefits and barriers (pros and cons) to engaging in healthy behavior (see Figure 6.7). But even with all those health-enhancing components in place, individuals sometimes still need a little nudge to help them get started on changing behavior for the better. In the health belief model, that little nudge is referred to as a *cue to action,* usually a single event that serves as a jump start to behavior change. In our example, a cue to action among adolescents might be personal involvement or the loss of a close friend or admired celebrity in an alcohol-related accident. Any event that brings the threat closer to home can serve as a cue to action.

Now that you've studied the health belief model, how would you heighten perceived threat in the adolescent situation we've been describing? We'll look at that more closely in Chapter 7 where we'll talk about how to plan and implement programs that work. For now, it's enough to understand that our needs-assessment process must incorporate efforts to find out the exact types of health-influencing attitudes and perceptions prevalent in a particular community. The use of theories and models like the health belief model can keep us from overlooking some important influences.

Theory of Planned Behavior

Have you ever done something you knew was risky? If so, think for a moment about why you did it. Though you may have had a number of reasons, none may have been related to your perceptions about the severity of the consequences or your susceptibility to them. That's why the health belief model doesn't work in every situation. There are times when people know all about severity and susceptibility and still forge ahead. So, if you are looking for the right questions to ask in a needs assessment, we suggest that you also consider some of the influencing factors in Figure 6.8, which represents the **theory of planned behavior** (Ajzen, 1991).

Like the PRECEDE/PROCEED and health belief models, the theory of planned behavior includes an attitude component that reminds us to think about community members' behavior-related perceptions, beliefs, and expected outcomes. The theory also prompts us to think about another common influencing factor among adolescents that we've not yet discussed. It's called **subjective norm** (see Figure 6.8). A person's subjective norm is made up of (1) his or her perceptions about whether others approve or disapprove of the behavior (normative beliefs) plus (2) the degree to which he or she values their opinion (motivation to comply) (Montano, Kasprzyk, & Taplin, 1997). If this sounds a lot like perceived peer pressure, you're beginning to get the picture. As those adolescents begin to

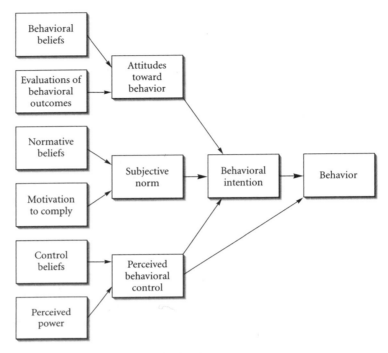

FIGURE 6.8   Theory of planned behavior.
In the theory of planned behavior, subjective norm is measured as a person's perceptions about and motivation to comply with the opinions of others. From "The Theory of Reasoned Action and the Theory of Planned Behavior," by D. E. Montano, D. Kasprzyk, and S. H. Taplin, in *Health Behavior and Health Education: Theory, Research, and Practice* (p. 92), edited by K. Glanz, F. M. Lewis, and B. K. Rimer, 1997, San Francisco: Jossey-Bass.

think about the dangers of drinking and driving, they are also likely to weigh those risks against what they perceive their friends to think. For some, the desire to be accepted by others has a powerful influence on behavior. As you conduct needs assessments, don't forget to ask questions about subjective norm influences.

Transtheoretical Model or Stages of Change

If all of the people in your community of interest acted like clones, if they all had the same perceptions and moved at the same pace in their decision-making processes, we could stop here with our "model discussion." After all, we've already covered a broad base of community influences on health (PRECEDE/ PROCEED) so that you can understand how individuals are influenced by factors that go beyond themselves. We also gave you an example of how your assessment should encompass different types of behavior-related attitudes and beliefs (health belief model) and the powerful influence of peers (theory of planned behavior). What we haven't covered, however, is how the behavior-change process can

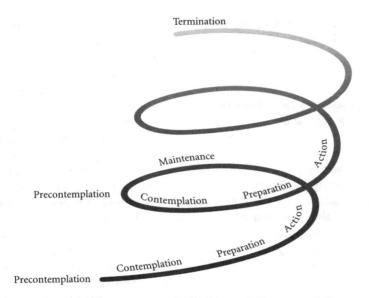

FIGURE 6.9   Transtheoretical model (or stages of change model).
The transtheoretical model (stages of change) illustrates how a person can progress through a series of stages, from not even considering a behavior change to actually infusing the behavior change into one's lifestyle. Loops and repeated stages depict potential relapse and repeated change cycles. "Termination" originally referred to the desired outcome of no longer engaging in unhealthy behaviors such as drug abuse. However, the model is also used in the adoption of health-enhancing behaviors.
From "The Transtheoretical Model of Change and HIV Prevention: A Review," by J. O. Prochaska, C. A. Redding, L. L. Harlow, J. S. Rossi, and W. F. Velicer, *Health Education Quarterly 21*(4), pp. 471–486.

evolve over time. We think that's important because we don't want you to become impatient or discouraged if you don't witness immediate results with your health education efforts. The process of educating a community about health and observing positive changes is sometimes like planting a seed and watching it slowly grow into a full flowering plant. You have to be patient and willing to "feed and water" the behavior-change process along the way. You also have to understand what that process needs at each stage of growth. That's one of the benefits of referring to the **transtheoretical model,** or **stages of change model** (Figure 6.9) when assessing your community's needs. It will help you determine where community members are in the decision-making process so you can adapt your health education strategies to fit those stages.

In our discussion about behavior-related attitudes and beliefs, we've assumed that our group of adolescents have already formulated some opinions about drinking and driving that you need to address in your drug abuse prevention program. However, some of those adolescents, even the ones who drink and drive, may have never really thought about it at all. They may have been too busy with the ups and downs of adolescent life, hormone changes, and school events to contemplate the risks of drinking and driving. According to the transtheoretical model (Prochaska, Redding, & Evers, 1997), those who "just haven't thought" would be in the *precontemplation* stage. If, in your assessment efforts, you learned that a large majority of the population was in this stage, you would likely need to launch an awareness campaign to motivate people to start thinking about the benefits of staying sober while driving.

But, what if most of the adolescents *had* already thought about it a great deal due to some recent alcohol-related deaths in their school? In that case, spending all your limited time and money on an awareness campaign might be a waste. The majority would be in the *contemplation* stage (Prochaska et al., 1997), meaning they had been thinking about the need to change their drinking and driving habits but were, perhaps, hesitating because of what they'd have to give up (popularity and outings, for example). Your health education efforts in this instance would need to focus more strongly on minimizing those perceived barriers.

As you've likely guessed by now, each stage of change has its own characteristics and information needs. Individuals in the *preparation* stage have already decided to make a change and are planning to do something about it in the very near future. They are the ones who need more information about *how* to avoid drunk driving situations in the face of peer pressure (Prochaska et al., 1997). However, it would be a waste to start with this "how to" information if individuals are in the precontemplation stage and haven't even decided yet that they need to know how.

Those in the *action* and *maintenance* stages have already been practicing the desired behavior at different levels of success (Prochaska et al., 1997). They need different health education strategies to promote consistency in practicing the newly acquired behavior change and prevent relapse. Strong support groups can help individuals who have reached these last stages to continue making good choices.

ASSESSMENT STRATEGIES: FOUR STEPS TO NEEDS ASSESSMENT

We hope that by now, you've formulated some ideas about the nature and purpose of needs and capacity assessment, along with a general understanding of some models and theories used to mobilize communities. We've encouraged you to involve community members in data collection and needs prioritization and given you some ideas about the type of information to gather, but we haven't yet given you specific strategies for how to accomplish these tasks. McKenzie and Smeltzer (1997) present a four-step process for conducting needs assessment we think will help you.

Step 1: Determining the Present State of Health of the Target Population

This first step involves collecting information about the existing health status of your community. As outlined in APEX/PH and PATCH, the information you collect should reflect needs from a variety of perspectives, including those of the community and the health professionals who hope to make a difference there. Though some situations may call for using either primary or secondary data, we encourage you to always consider using both to some degree.

Primary and Secondary Data   Secondary data collected from national sources are a good place to start because they can help you determine how the nature and extent of needs identified in your community compare to those of other communities who face similar issues. You can learn from those sources about effective and ineffective approaches attempted in other places and may gain some insight you might otherwise have missed. You can then consider the specific characteristics and needs of your community and adapt what you learned from those secondary sources.

An even more important secondary source can be other organizations and groups who have worked or are presently working in your community of interest. Although leaders of some organizations within that community may view you as competition and respond in a territorial fashion, others will likely welcome what you are able to bring to the community and be willing to share what they know. Tapping into these local secondary sources before you begin any primary data-collection efforts can save you time and resources by helping you avoid needless collection duplication. It can also be a very useful way to learn from the experience of other professionals about the culture, history, and characteristics of your community; who the real leaders and gatekeepers are; and how to best establish trust and mutual respect between you and community members. These secondary source connections can also develop into future collaborative relations that can strengthen and broaden your efforts.

Primary data collection is also a critical component of this step because it helps accomplish two things. The most obvious is that it can provide accurate, community-specific data about problems, influences, and potential solutions to health issues. If conducted appropriately, the process can also help you establish important relationships with community members. Involving them in the early stages of your work helps develop community ownership. From this process of community involvement, you can gain an inside perspective on community culture and characteristics and the degree to which members will likely respond to your efforts. Their input will help you adapt to perceived needs and establish a working camaraderie. It will also help you determine the best methods of primary data collection and the types of questions that need to be asked. The primary data collection methods you can choose from are usually categorized as individual or group assessments.

Individual Assessments: Surveys, Delphi, Interviewing   FYI 6.1 provides an overview of the three types of individual survey methods (mailings, telephone, and face-to-face) and two commonly used group assessment processes. The information provided there is outlined and described in great detail by Gilmore and

FOR YOUR INFORMATION 6.1

Overview of Some Individual Survey and Group Assessment Strategies

This overview of individual survey and group assessment strategies highlights the advantages and disadvantages of using each in the needs-assessment process.

Individual Surveys	Advantages	Disadvantages
Mail surveys	Low cost, wide distribution possible, valid information (allows time for thinking before answering)	Lengthy process, low response rate, limited questions, no control over answers (no clarification possible), mailing list required
Telephone surveys	Shorter process than mailing, better response rate, more/different questions possible, better control over answers (can ask for clarification)	More costly than mailing, less valid information (may receive socially desirable answers)

Campbell (1996), experts in needs assessment. They define a **survey** as "a structured process for gathering information directly from individuals by asking questions" (p. 29). They suggest using a mailed survey if the type of information you need could be considered private and more personal contacts would seem threatening to survey participants. Mail-outs are also less expensive and require fewer personnel. However, telephone and face-to-face surveys usually result in higher response rates than do mail-outs; and face-to-face surveys in particular can be more effective among those with low literacy or minimal English. Telephone surveys can be conducted more quickly, but face-to-face interviews are best for open-ended questions. It is important to carefully consider all of these factors—type of information, audience, money, time, and personnel—when choosing the survey method that works best for you.

Another individual assessment method that bears mentioning is the **Delphi technique;** it is used when objective information is not available from other sources and generates "a consensus through a series of questionnaires" (Gilmore & Campbell, 1996, p. 45). It is often used to identify goals and establish priorities,

Face-to-face surveys	Best opportunity for questioning, most control over answers (can read nonverbal expressions), effective for low-literacy individuals	Most costly (time & travel expense), least valid information (socially desirable answers), is becoming difficult to gain access to participants (privacy & security issues)
Group Participation	**Advantages**	**Disadvantages**
Nominal group	Direct involvement, planned interactivity, allows for diverse opinions, full participation of all group members, creative atmosphere, recognition of common ground fostered	Time commitment, competing issues may slow process, participant bias can emerge, segmented planning involvement
Focus group	Low cost, convenient, creative atmosphere, ease of clarification, high flexibility potential	Qualitative information only, limited representativeness, dependence on moderator skill, preliminary insights only, some group members dominate

brainstorm possible alternatives, or gather information about group values and perspectives. The process usually involves three to five rounds of mailed questionnaires in which participants are first asked to respond to a few broad questions; and, from those responses, more specific questionnaires are developed to further clarify and specify the information. Although this approach can be useful in clarifying important issues, it is more likely that you will be involved in various local survey methods when you first enter the profession.

Group Assessments: Nominal, Focus, Forums   Advantages and disadvantages of the nominal and focus group processes are also outlined in FYI 6.1. As can be deduced from the description there, the **nominal group** process is more structured than the **focus group** process. In the nominal group process, five to seven individuals who are knowledgeable about community issues meet to address a particular issue. In the beginning, each member is asked to write down, without discussion, personal responses to a single question (such as, "What do you think are the most pressing health concerns in our community?").

Each written response is shared with the group in round-robin fashion, until every response is recorded. The group then discusses and clarifies items on the list and ranks them according to what is considered most important. The process continues until a prioritized list is agreed on, through a vote if needed. This high-structure approach is designed to foster equal input for every member.

The **focus group** process is a much more relaxed approach where 6 to 12 fairly homogenous group members answer questions asked by a trained moderator. The moderator's role is to help the group stay focused, stimulate interaction, and encourage clarification and expansion of ideas without biasing the results. These sessions are usually taped so that ideas expressed in this free format will not be lost or forgotten. This format is designed to encourage spontaneity in the building of ideas through the process of free expression. It is particularly useful in collecting qualitative information for a preliminary assessment of community opinions and goals. It does, however, call for a well-trained, experienced moderator who will remain impartial and focused on the assigned group task.

Not included in FYI 6.1 is another group assessment process called the **community forum.** Of all the individual and group strategies mentioned here, the forum is the least structured and can involve the greatest number of participants. Community forums, or public meetings, are often used to distribute information but can also be helpful in gaining initial feedback from any community member who wishes to voice an opinion about a particular health issue. Although it is not considered the most rigorous approach to community assessments, it does allow all community subgroups or segments to voice their views and can be a positive communication channel when carefully planned and implemented. The key is to maintain a positive, objective tone during the meeting and avoid possible degeneration into a gripe session.

Because each data-collection method has its strong points, we suggest you consider using multiple strategies, depending on your available time and resources. The nominal or focus group processes can be a good way to get started because they can provide insight into community values and concerns in a relatively short amount of time. We recommend, however, that information gleaned from group processes be used to develop surveys or questionnaires for implementation among larger representative groups within the community. An appropriately balanced collection of group and individual assessment data can help you develop a truer picture of your whole community.

Step 2: Analyzing the Data Collected

Collecting needed data can be hard work and takes time and patience. However, once data are collected, knowing how to interpret them can also be a challenge. **Data analysis** can be either formal (as in using computerized statistical analysis) or informal ("eyeballing" the data in search of obvious differences between what is and what should be). If your community's perceived needs match obvious gaps in health education or services, the less formal eyeball approach will suffice. For example, community members may be concerned about alcohol-related traffic accidents, and on surveys some community subgroups may report a high propensity to driving under the influence. Local police and hospital emergency room records may confirm that alcohol-related accidents are a frequent problem, with often tragic results. And a review of community settings in which the needed education could occur may reveal inadequate efforts. If so, more rigorous data analysis isn't necessary because the prioritized need is obvious.

But what if the real need isn't so obvious? What if data about the community's perceived needs, local secondary data, and available service or education needs don't match? Or, what if several needs from each of these sources are evident and the results are mixed?

There are no foolproof solutions to this common dilemma but there are some steps you can take to help clarify the issue. The first is that you may need to collect more data. If local records indicate a high incidence or prevalence of a health risk, you may need to go back to your community for more primary data about their perspectives and experiences with that specific issue. If a particular health issue is evident in the primary data but not showing up in secondary data, you may need to consult local health professionals and community members to determine why the issue is evident in local records. These decisions about "what is" should be driven by input from all stakeholders with the desired end result being a list of identified problems, their nature, and their extent.

Step 3: Prioritizing the Identified Needs

Now comes the hard part, deciding which needs to address first. This important step determines the direction your health education program will take. It is difficult because there may be several important needs on the list and people may disagree about which should receive immediate attention. Yet limited resources and time will rarely allow you to address them all at once. You have to start somewhere.

McKenzie and Smeltzer (1997) suggest you consider each listed need in light of four questions:

1. What is the most pressing need?
2. Are resources adequate to deal with the problem?
3. Can the problem best be solved by a health promotion intervention, or could it be handled better through administration, politics, or changes in the economy?
4. Can the problem be solved in a reasonable amount of time? (pp. 52–53)

As unfeeling as it may sound, questions 2 through 4 are important due to time and resource constraints you will likely experience through your employment or because of deadlines and expectations from funding sources who have agreed to support your efforts. Green and Kreuter (1999) would likely categorize these four questions under the heading of how "changeable" the health situation is.

FOR YOUR INFORMATION 6.2

Prioritizing Health Needs

A community's health needs should be prioritized according to their importance and changeability as deemed by community members and the health professionals who serve them.

	More important	Less important
More changeable	Needs that are highly *changeable* and *important*	Needs that are highly *changeable* but are less important
Less changeable	Needs that are highly *important* but are less changeable	Needs that are neither changeable nor important

They suggest you assign each of the identified needs to one of four areas (FYI 6.2) that weigh levels of pressing need (importance) with the potential for change (changeability) as a result of health education efforts. The decision should also be made in light of the degree to which other community agencies and organizations are providing similar programs. This can help you avoid duplication of existing services and minimize potential territorial issues with leaders of other organizations.

Step 4: Validating Prioritized Needs

Validating needs may seem unnecessary because it calls for a return to some of the previous steps, such as conducting focus groups to determine the community's reaction to the prioritized need or gaining second opinions from other health professionals. If careful groundwork has already been established, this fourth step may be less important. However, because so many people have likely provided input to the process, some may have lost sight of the final decision along the way. If the needs are not properly validated, you could possibly proceed with costly programs that are less effective than expected. For that reason, we suggest you consider this fourth step an important reminder to constantly validate your prioritized needs as you go. You can confirm your decisions through careful, consistent communication with community members and collaborating health professionals as you move from the assessment to the program-planning stages.

Even if you arrive in a new employment situation where much of the data collection and prioritizing groundwork has been completed, we encourage you to at least spend time establishing personal relationships with primary and secondary source contacts to foster your awareness of the situation. The time invested will help you apply the RISE approach to more quickly identify the connecting links (as well as possible barriers).

IN CONCLUSION

In this chapter, we have presented needs- and capacity-assessment concepts and models that should serve you well in the future. Not only will they help guide your efforts as a future health educator, but the PRECEDE/PROCEED model will also be of particular use to you throughout the remainder of this course. Gold, Green, and Kreuter (1998) have developed a computer-based needs-assessment program called Enabling Methods of Planning and Organizing Within Everyone's Reach (EMPOWER) that can guide you step-by-step through the PRECEDE/PROCEED model components. We suggest you seek more information about EMPOWER access opportunities once you master basic needs-assessment concepts. In Chapter 7, you will have the opportunity to learn how to use the model to move from needs assessment to program development.

REVIEW QUESTIONS

1. Define needs-assessment concepts.
2. Discuss the difference between actual and perceived needs and explain the value of assessing both.
3. Describe the usefulness and processes of APEX/PH and PATCH in community-needs assessment.
4. Describe how models and theories can be useful in the needs-assessment process.
5. Draw the PRECEDE portion of the PRECEDE/PROCEED model and explain how its components can influence a community's health.
6. Describe the primary components of the health belief model, theory of planned behavior, and transtheoretical model.
7. Describe the four-step process for assessing the health issues within a community as described by McKenzie and Smeltzer (1997).

FOR YOUR APPLICATION

Developing a PRECEDE Assessment

Choose a specific health problem in an age- or ethnicity-specific community and use the PRECEDE/PROCEED model to identify factors contributing to the health problem and subsequent quality-of-life issues.

1. Draw the same PRECEDE boxes you see in Figure 6.4 on a sheet of notebook paper. Write the PRECEDE labels (quality of life, health, behavior, and so forth) at the top of each box.
2. Write your chosen health problem inside the "health" box. (If it's a behavior, such as smoking, enter it in the "behavior" box instead.)
3. Move to the right and enter some quality-of-life issues you think arise in your chosen community as a result of this health problem. (If you began with a health behavior, complete both the health and quality-of-life boxes.)
4. Now move back toward the left. Fill in each box with factors you think contribute to the problem. Try to be specific to your chosen community.
5. Use resources provided in Appendix D to verify your entries. Make a list of potential community resources, capacities, and solutions.

FOR YOUR PORTFOLIO

Creating Assessment Opportunities

Contact a local health department or health agency that provides health education programs. Ask about health issues and programs the agency is planning to address in the future. Volunteer to conduct a literature search to (1) clearly define the health issue, (2) identify factors that could potentially influence the targeted health problem, and (3) locate existing needs-assessment survey instruments that could be used by the agency. Use the PRECEDE model as a guide, and create a brief report of your findings. Give one copy to the agency and place one in your portfolio. Create a division in your portfolio labeled "Needs Assessment (Responsibility I)." Ask an agency representative to write a brief evaluation of your efforts to include in that portfolio division.

7

Planning Health

Programs

YOU GO TO A WORKSHOP AND LEARN ABOUT A NEW PRO-
gram for teen mothers. You decide to try it with a group of
teen mothers in the community. Not only are the outcomes of
the program different from what you expected, but in addi-
tion your participants didn't even enjoy the program. This
result can be very frustrating, but it is fairly common. Did
you assess the needs of your audience first? Was your pro-
gram plan based on the assessment? Were the methods you
used—as well as the content—appropriate for the audience?
Program planning involves much more than just finding a
preprepared program.

Chapter Objectives

1. Write process objectives for a hypothetical health education program.
2. Identify theory-based methods.
3. Identify methods that include experiential and critical thinking activities.
4. Identify technology-based methods.
5. Select methods for a hypothetical health education program.
6. Describe the components of a budget for a health education program.
7. Identify barriers to a health education program before implementation.

WRITING GOALS AND OBJECTIVES

After reading Chapter 6 you have a good idea of how important assessment is to the success of your program. Health care professionals often make the mistake of collecting data but not properly using it. Much information may be gathered, but little is actually put to use in program planning. Let's discover how to change that.

Program planning involves writing goals and objectives, selecting methods to present your program, creating a budget, and developing a timeline. Figure 7.1 illustrates the post-assessment steps in program planning.

The goals and objectives of your health education program evolve from the assessment process. Otherwise, what would be the use of identifying your community's needs or capacities? Developing goals that address the community's needs and use the capacities you've discovered requires something of a visionary perspective. But the information collected in the assessment can be a helpful guide. **Program goals** are future-oriented and broad but not extensively so. One overall goal of your program for teen mothers might be to decrease pregnancy rates over a given period of time. If you write your goals using PRECEDE, as we suggest in this section, they will also address quality of life and health.

Objectives serve as guidelines for the accomplishment of your goals. The three broad categories of objectives (outcome, impact, and process) each play a role in accomplishing the goal of the program. We will look at each category more carefully in this chapter.

Imagine for a moment that you used the PRECEDE/PROCEED model (Green & Kreuter, 1999) to assess your population. When you conducted the social assessment, you found that a large number of people in the community lacked formal education beyond the eighth grade and many had a low socioeconomic status. During the epidemiological assessment you discovered that a high teen pregnancy rate existed in the community. In the behavioral and environmental assessments you found that teen mothers often chose to raise their babies using practices not conducive to healthy development and that, although available, housing was frequently located in unsafe neighborhoods. Figure 7.2 illustrates the information you collected in phases 1–3 of your PRECEDE assessment. Goals are developed for each assessment phase.

Keep in mind that the first phase of PRECEDE involves a social assessment (quality of life). One way to make changes in quality of life would be to focus on issues of health that influence problematic social factors. In fact, you would focus primarily on the behaviors that influence the health issues (those things you found in your behavioral assessment). Therefore, your goals from the social and epidemiological assessments should be very broad and much more visionary in nature. The later goals dealing with your primary program focuses would be more specific. An example of a goal for the first phase of assessment might be to improve socioeconomic status (SES) levels in the community. From the second phase of assessment, an example of a goal might be to decrease teen pregnancy; and in phase three it might be to increase educational levels among teen mothers

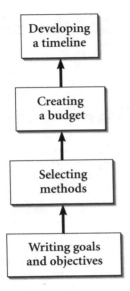

FIGURE 7.1   **Guidelines for program planning after community assessment is complete.**   Program planning makes the most sense when you follow a process. This figure illustrates a simple set of guidelines for program development.

in the community. Some health education professionals feel that you should also include a time frame and an expected amount of change in the goals, but we suggest you keep them broad for now. Figure 7.3 illustrates assessment information and the associated goals.

Categories of Objectives

The educational and ecological assessments of phase 4 begin to provide you with detail to place into your objectives. Objectives are very specific and should contain common elements including what, how much, whom, where, when, and who. We'll examine the three categories.

Outcome Objectives   A health outcome generally deals with determinants of health, such as blood pressure, or health behaviors, such as smoking, rather than health in a broader sense. Health determinants and behaviors can be measured. The key to writing an objective that will truly be a map for your goals is that it can be measured. Only then will you be able to track your progress. **Outcome objectives** are long-term but realistic. They are based on expected achievements of your program, but they are not supposed to happen immediately. They will be measured months or even years after the program has begun.

Impact Objectives   The purpose of **impact objectives** is to assist in ensuring that positive health outcomes will occur. In a sense they are intermediate objectives. They deal with aspects of health that are changed more quickly than health outcomes. Some examples of these include health knowledge levels,

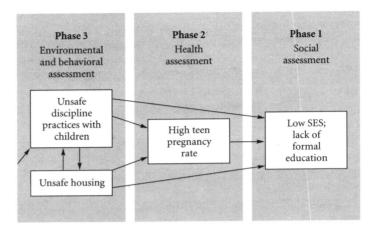

FIGURE 7.2   PRECEDE phases 1–3.
The social assessment documents social issues that are of concern in a community. The health assessment uses epidemiological data to determine health issues that influence the documented social concerns. The environmental and behavioral assessments identify the actual behaviors and environmental situations that influence the health issue.

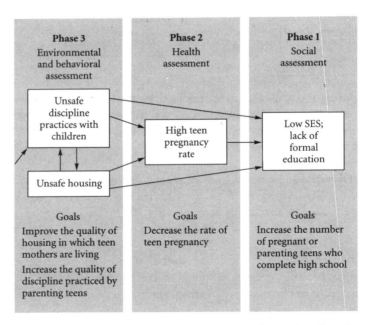

FIGURE 7.3   Examples of assessment information and associated goals.
Once assessment data has been collected, goals that correspond to each level of assessment must be written. These broad statements provide the overall direction for the program.

weight, and number of cigarettes smoked in a day. Sometimes health determinants and behaviors are both outcomes (long-term results) or impacts (short-term results) of health programs. **Impact objectives** should be measurable, realistic, and short-term.

Process Objectives   The term *process* refers to a series of behaviors that produce an end. In a **process objective** the target is the function of the program, which includes things like the number of participants, accessibility of the program to the population, and satisfaction of participants. Process objectives should also be measurable, realistic, and short-term.

Writing Objectives

Objectives vary in their focus. An objective might focus on health status, knowledge, or behavior. For now, let's discuss how to develop a behavioral objective. The purpose of a behavioral objective is to help your program participants adopt health-enhancing behaviors. Use the following six steps to help you write objectives:

1. Identify your audience (who).
2. Clarify the specific behavior (what).
3. Determine the degree of change expected in the behavior (how much).
4. Describe the individual responsible for conducting the program (another who).
5. Identify the time when the program will occur (when).
6. Identify the place where changes will take place or where the program will occur (where).

Identifying Audience   The audience is made up of the members of the target population, sometimes called program partners. These are the people for whom the program is designed, those who will benefit from changing their behaviors. It is important to identify the program audience first because, as you know, the program must be matched to the audience's specific needs. It must also be culturally appropriate and match educational levels of the population. The information you use in writing objectives and developing the program should have been collected through the needs assessment, but as the program is developed you might want further information. Don't be afraid to collect more information as you need it. When you write behavioral objectives, describe your audience as specifically as possible. FYI 7.1 contains examples of ways to describe the audience in your objectives.

Clarifying the Behavior   Most health care providers and educators realize that unless an objective is measurable, it won't be useful in helping attain a goal. Think about what makes something measurable. What if the objective said that a program would help people "understand . . ."? Would you be able to measure understanding? Is there an instrument like a stethoscope or a written questionnaire that measures understanding? No, there really isn't because we don't know whether people understand something until they actively demonstrate their understanding. For that reason, the word *understand,* which isn't directly observable, should be replaced with an observable action verb such as *list, explain,* or *describe.* If the participant lists, explains, or describes the information correctly, you will know he or she understands it. As a program planner, you will clarify the *what* so that it can be measured. Behaviors, specific determinants of health, and risk factors are the easiest to measure. Behaviors might not be just physical in nature. They might also include increases in knowledge (generally measured by a written tool), change in beliefs (also often measured by a written tool), and thought processes like decision making and analysis of information (measured through observation or written solutions to problems). FYI 7.2 contains a list of some measurable and observable behaviors.

Determining the Degree of Change   Determining how much change is expected is probably the most difficult decision you will make in program planning. The effectiveness of the program is eventually determined by this component of the objective. Problems occur when the amount of change possible is overestimated or underestimated. Overestimating the change that program participants can make quite simply makes the program look bad. As you know, change is never easy. Have you ever tried to quit eating fast food, chocolate, or something else that you enjoy and eat frequently? Would you call it easy? It is easy, however, for a program planner to be overconfident in the effectiveness of the program and overestimate the level of change it will effect in the participants.

On the other hand, underestimating results can have a devastating effect on the program participants. Fear of failure can cause some program planners to lower their expectations of the participants too far. It would be truly negative to see program participants blocked from progress because the planner didn't have confidence in their potential.

You might be wondering how you determine the degree of change participants might or should make. To do so, you can review professional literature, consider your own observations of the participants, and analyze programs that have been successful in the past in the same location. Degree of change is frequently written as percentage of change. For example, teen pregnancy rates will decrease by 10% from 1999. If you use a percentage, be sure to list the reference on which that percentage should be based. FYI 7.1 contains examples of phrases that might be used in describing degree of change.

Describing the Person or Group Responsible   In this step you identify the individual responsible for conducting the program. On some occasions, "who" will

Components of Objectives

Each objective should contain the components listed in this table including audience, behavior, degree of change expected, person or group responsible, time, and place. There are many potential words or phrases to use for each component. The key is to make certain that objectives describe your program adequately.

Audience (generally a noun and descriptor)

Pregnant teens
Animals in shelters
College freshmen
People with heart disease

Behavior (measurable verb)

Exercise
Illustrate
Select
List

Degree of change

By 10%
From 60% to 65%
Three times
Five servings

Person or Group Responsible

Health educator
Veterinarians
Teachers
Physicians

Time

By the end of the program
By the end of fiscal year 2005
During the year
One year after program completion

Place

In the city
At personal residence
At fitness center

FOR YOUR INFORMATION 7.2

Measurable and Observable Behaviors

Describing behaviors in measurable terms becomes difficult at times. This chart provides some examples but, of course, there are endless possibilities.

Cognitive (with increasing levels of cognitive ability)

Count	Express	Apply	Analyze	Assess
Define	Locate	Examine	Calculate	Judge
List	Review	Practice	Debate	Evaluate
Identify	Compute	Illustrate	Compare	Revise

Affective

Accept	Seek	Display
Observe	Complete	Discriminate

Psychomotor

Taste	Position	Copy	Create	Walk
Place	Repeat	Build	Produce	Climb

not be an individual but an agency, committee, or group of people. The determination will be situation-specific. FYI 7.1 contains examples.

Identifying the Time   A description of when the program will occur is developed in this step. "When" may be a specific date or period of time. A common description of a time is a fiscal year. FYI 7.1 contains examples.

Identifying the Place   Identification of place can actually have two meanings. The first, where changes will take place, might be used if a change will be apparent throughout an entire community. The second, where the program will occur, might be used if the objectives are more individual in nature. FYI 7.1 contains examples of both.

If you were using the assessment information discussed in the chapter so far, what objectives would you write?

Study Figure 7.4 for an example of information that might have been gathered in phase 4 of the PRECEDE assessment discussed earlier. Note that you will want to write specific objectives for predisposing, reinforcing, and enabling factors.

Once objectives have been written, the program planner must determine how information will be presented or how opportunities for making behavior changes will be offered. These are the program methods.

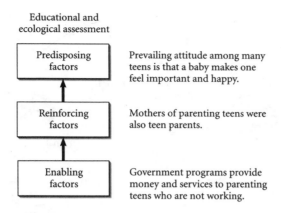

FIGURE 7.4   PRECEDE phase 4.
The educational and ecological assessment provides specific information on attitudes, beliefs, and environmental situations that influence behavior. These factors would be important to address in your program.

SELECTING METHODS

The way in which information is presented to program participants will make a great difference in their level of understanding and future use of what they learn. Many resources that describe instructional methods are available, but we would like you to be aware of several broad categories of methods.

Theoretical-Based Methods

As we explained in Chapter 6, theories about behavior help explain why people act the way they do. Many have been researched extensively and have been shown to be effective predictors of behavior. Theory-based educational methods may well prove to be the most effective in helping people change health-related behaviors. Several were described in relationship to assessment, and two will be described here. Keep in mind that most theories can be used in several ways. It will be up to you to determine which theories you will use and how you will use them. A review of professional literature can assist you by providing information about how theories have been used effectively in the past.

Multiple Intelligences   One theory that has been very useful in many educational settings is **multiple intelligences (MI)** (Armstrong, 1994). This theory suggests that many types of intelligence influence learning. Each individual will learn in different ways, depending on the dominant type of intelligence. Figure 7.5 depicts the MI pizza, which illustrates the different types of intelligences. They include being word-smart, logic-smart, picture-smart, body-smart, music-smart, people-smart, and self-smart.

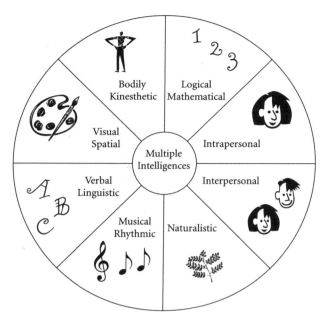

FIGURE 7.5   MI pizza: the different types of intelligence.
Each person expresses intelligence in a unique way. An individual's form of intelligence influences the way he or she will learn. It is important to use methods that make sense to individuals with varying types of intelligence.

Word-smart people learn through the use of words. They read well and understand what they read. These individuals will enjoy receiving brochures or other written material about health issues and will gather useful information from them. Logic-smart individuals use and appreciate analytical thinking in their daily lives. Understanding how health information applies to real life will help logic-smart people learn the information you want to convey.

Picture-smart individuals have a feel for shapes, colors, and pictures. They enjoy using their hands to create visually pleasing products. Information given to picture-smart people is most effective if it is combined with visual effects. Movement is very important to those who are body-smart. They learn best if activity is part of the learning process. Music-smart individuals love sounds and learn best through auditory means. Incorporating pleasing sound as you present health information will improve the likelihood that your message will get across.

People-smart individuals are social; they communicate and relate well with others. Providing opportunities for them to socialize while learning will help them. Self-smart individuals are strongly in tune with themselves. They understand their own feelings and express them well to others. Providing opportunities for self-smart individuals to stretch their knowledge of self while learning new information will make your program more successful.

We encourage you to get to know your participants well enough to know the ways in which they learn best. If this is not possible, plan programs that involve multiple intelligences. Use pleasing sounds or music as part of the program; provide activities with movement; give information in writing as well as verbally; make sure that written material is visually pleasing and uses colors, shapes, and pictures; allow opportunities for socialization in the program; and ask participants to apply the new information to real life.

Social Cognitive Theory   The second useful theory is **social cognitive theory** (Bandura, 1977), which provides information about why people behave the way they do as well as how people change behavior. Figure 7.6 illustrates our conceptualization of social cognitive theory (SCT); it has not been verified through empirical research, but it might help clarify the theory's components.

An underlying assumption of the theory is the dynamic relationship between a behavior, an individual, and the environment. They continuously interact with one another; as one changes, so do the others.

According to SCT, the environment and situation, outcome expectations and behavioral capabilities, and self-efficacy perceptions and expectancies will influence an individual's behavior. *Environment,* as we stated in Chapter 3, includes anything external to the individual, including social, cultural, and physical aspects. The *situation* is an individual's perception of the environment. As you know from personal experience, perceptions aren't always 100% accurate. Accurate or not, the situation influences both the environment and behaviors.

Outcome expectations are an individual's beliefs about potential outcomes of a behavior. When individuals state that they believe they will lose weight as a result of exercise, they are expressing outcome expectations. *Behavioral capabilities* are the skills and knowledge necessary to make behavior change. According to SCT, outcome expectations and behavioral capabilities influence behavior directly. For example, a person who believes that exercise will result in weight loss or maintenance and has knowledge about nutritious, low-calorie food will likely behave differently from individuals without these beliefs and skills. However, the individuals who place importance on weight loss and believe they can exercise and eat right are more likely to follow through. The value an individual places on an outcome is called *expectancy*. *Self-efficacy* is the belief that one can perform a specific behavior.

Bandura (1977) believes that values (expectancies), beliefs (self-efficacy), and skills (capabilities) can be influenced through **observational** or **vicarious learning.** Observational or vicarious learning occurs when individuals watch someone else perform the behavior successfully. The next step would be actual practice with small parts of the final behavior until each is performed successfully.

Once a behavior is performed, consequences of the behavior will influence expectancies, self-efficacy, and capabilities. These, in turn, influence future behavior and the environment. This interactive influence is called reciprocal determinism. Social support from individuals in the environment can influence the individual and behavior in a powerful way.

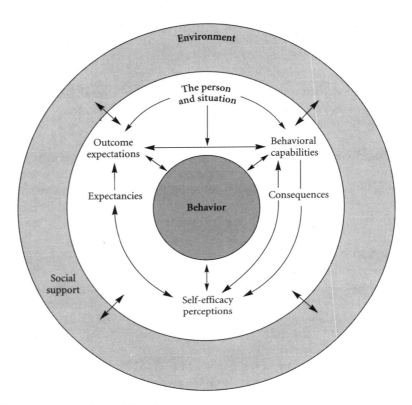

FIGURE 7.6   Social cognitive theory.
Social cognitive theory helps to explain why people choose behaviors. Among other things, it suggests that a person's belief about an outcome of a behavior and confidence in his or her ability to perform it will influence the frequency of the behavior. It also suggests that the environment influences a person and the behavior, which in turn influence the environment.

Experiential Methods

Think about the environment in which you live. Would you say it is fast-paced, visual, and interactive? Many of us deal with many images and activities and much change on a daily basis. As a result, the participants in our health education programs are likely to expect fast-paced programs, filled with images and activities. You will want to select methods that are creative and engaging. One of the oldest of all forms of teaching—providing experience—is often the most interesting and offers the most long-term learning benefits (Marlowe & Page, 1998; Reed, 1996).

Experiential Model   The basic experiential education model presented in Figure 7.7 has five stages: asking participants to set personal goals, engaging partici-

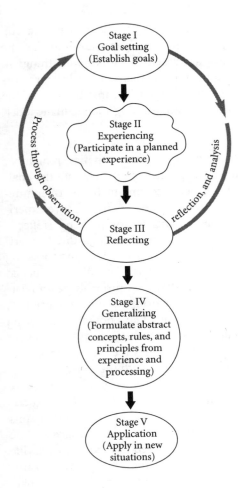

FIGURE 7.7 **Experiential model.** Experiential learning requires more than just an experience. As this model depicts, goals must be set, the experience should be planned, and participants should be allowed an opportunity to reflect, generalize, and then apply what they have learned to the "real" world.

pants in planned experiences, facilitating the processing of the experience (helping people find personal meaning), assisting participants to develop concepts or guidelines from the processing, and guiding application of the concepts and guidelines to other situations. This model is based on three assumptions:

- Learning is most effective when the learner is personally involved in the learning experience.
- Knowledge has to be personally discovered if it is to have meaning or make a difference in behavior.
- Commitment to learning is highest when the learner sets personal learning goals and actively pursues them within a given framework.

A quick and easy experiential activity to help people understand stressors and stress reduction uses a bowl, sponge, and water. A volunteer is asked to hold a large sponge above a large bowl. A second volunteer is asked to hold a cup of water above the bowl and sponge. The other participants are told that the sponge represents the human body. They are asked to think about things in their lives that cause stress (stressors) and then to call them out. A little water is poured onto the sponge each time a stressor is called out. The instructor stops the activity when the sponge is totally waterlogged and dripping and facilitates a discussion about the activity.

Processing the Experience   As you conduct experiential activities, remember that your role is one of *facilitator*. You will help participants navigate the challenges presented to them through planned experiences and then help them integrate the learning that results from performing the activity into future experiences (Henry & Ward, 1999). Assisting participants to comprehend (reflect), internalize, and transfer (generalize) the lessons learned through these experiences is called *processing* (Lankard, 1995; Schon, 1987; Snow, 1992). In processing the sponge activity, the instructor would ask something like "What happened here?" The participants would describe what they saw and probably begin relating it to real life. They might comment on how the dripping sponge represents someone who is not coping well with stress. They might also note that squeezing the sponge would represent using coping and stress reduction strategies effectively. Rather than giving a lecture, the instructor guides the discussion so that students understand stressors through their experience with the activity.

Thus, the keys to getting meaningful learning out of experiential activities are to design them to create the same decision-making skills used in real-life experiences and then to process the issues that arise from the activity. Participants should encounter challenges similar to those they are expected to face and be given the opportunity to use the same skills they will need to solve these real-life problems (skills such as critical thinking, problem solving, collaboration, teamwork, and the like) (Steinaker & Bell, 1979). Processing the activities helps participants alter future behaviors. Failing to process the experience could negate the benefits of the activity.

BASIC GROUND RULES FOR PROCESSING   It is important to establish some basic ground rules for processing to help establish a sense of security and trust for disclosing personal thoughts and feelings within a group setting. The ground rules will be different for different groups. What might be appropriate and acceptable for a group of adolescents might not work as well for a group of college students or businesspeople. Some groups will need more structure and more clearly stated rules. Other groups may thrive on a more open and flexible environment. Whatever the specifics of the ground rules, the overriding rule of processing is that all persons are treated with respect and caring.

SAMPLE PROCESSING GUIDELINES   The following list of guidelines for conducting the processing part of an activity is not expected to cover all eventualities—sometimes flexibility and common sense are the right guides for a specific moment.

- Have the group sit or stand in a circle—everyone can make eye contact.
- Keep group members within the circle. Participants communicate best when they are facing one another.
- Introduce the group process:
  - to speak honestly and openly with others.
  - to create a safe environment to explore feelings and what has been learned from the experience.
  - to listen and receive constructive feedback from others.
- Emphasize that comments are confidential among the group members, unless an individual gives specific permission to share his or her comments outside the group.
- No physical violence or verbal abuse (put-downs, name-calling) in the group.
- One person speaks at a time without interrupting others.
- Everyone is a valid group member. If the group is unhappy with one person (or a person with the group), it becomes a group responsibility to resolve the issue.
- Everyone is ultimately responsible for his or her own behavior.
- A person's emotions belong to him or her and may be considered true for him or her. (Henry & Ward, 1999, p. 3)

Examples of issues that could arise during some activities and a few questions that could be asked during the processing, both reflecting and generalizing, can be found in FYI 7.3. These are only some of the issues that could emerge from an experiential activity. By allowing participants sufficient time to respond in the reflection stage, the issues that *they* feel are important should emerge, and these are the issues that should receive the most focus in the processing stage.

The processing done during the generalizing stage should elicit from participants concrete ways to transfer the learning from their experience in the activity to their experience in real life.

Computer-Based Methods

Computer-based methods of education use computers and sometimes computer networks for communicating information. Information is communicated through various types of media like text, audio, video, or images. Although you have used computers extensively, it is important that you are able to define simple terms for some of your less experienced participants in health education programs. *Text* is essentially just letters and numbers without pictures or shapes. *Graphics* are shapes like circles and squares with shading and lines. *Images* are pictures, including photographs or paintings. *Audio* includes sounds likes voices,

FOR YOUR INFORMATION 7.3

Potential Processing Issues and Questions from Processing

Allowing participants time to process their experience provides them with the opportunity to derive meaning from it. The following provide some sample questions that would maximize successful processing.

Reflection

General Opening Questions (getting the issues "out in the middle of the circle")

1. So, what just happened?
2. Tell me what you just experienced as you prepared for, moved through, this activity.
3. What were some of your thoughts and feelings during this activity?

Recognizing / Understanding / Expressing Feelings

1. Can you name a feeling you had at any point in completing the activity? Where in your body did you feel it most? Did it influence your behavior?
2. What beliefs were responsible for generating that feeling?
3. Did any of the feelings you had remind you of feelings you have experienced during stressful situations?
4. What did you do with these feelings? Were they expressed? If so, how? If not, why not?

Cooperating

1. Can you think of specific examples of when the group or specific classmates cooperated in completing the activity? Explain.
2. What does cooperation look like? Give behaviors you saw today.

music, and other effects; and *video* consists of moving pictures. People using computer networks will be able to communicate with each other instantaneously (as on a telephone) or over time (as in e-mail).

As you are already aware, many systems can be used in computer-based learning. Some of these include e-mail, the Web, bulletin boards, conferencing (with or without video), and MOO. You probably already have some understanding of e-mail and the Web. *Electronic bulletin boards* are something like wall-mounted bulletin boards. Individuals post discussion items, and others sit at their computers, read what has been written, and respond in turn. It is not generally "real time" or live. Newsgroups are similar to bulletin boards. Conferencing has be-

3. Were there any actions or efforts that seemed to block the group from achieving its goal? Explain.
4. What were some of the observed results of cooperating and helping others?

Appreciating Self

1. What kind of self-talk did you do during the initiative?
2. Do you sometimes put yourself down when you make a mistake? What effect might that have on your actions? On the function of the group?
3. What could you say to yourself to counteract the put-down message?

Generalizing

Transfer of Learning (essential if you want to make a difference)

1. What did you learn in this activity that you think will be helpful to you in getting through this or another class successfully?
2. Can you think of an example in school where you have faced a similar challenge as an individual? In a group situation?
3. What abilities or skills did you or your group exhibit that will help you in future courses or semesters?
4. How will you use what you learned to make school, work, and life better?

Closure Questions

1. What did you learn about yourself? What did you learn about others?
2. Was there a specific person who did something you think worthy of recognition?
3. Is there anything else you would like to say to a specific person or to the group?
4. What was the highlight of the day for you?

Henry, J. & Ward, S. (1999). Unpublished paper

come very sophisticated, allowing real-time discussion and even video, depending on the nature of the software that is being used. *Software* is the program that runs the systems. It can be purchased and loaded into your computer, although many of us purchase computers with the software already loaded and ready to use. *MOO* stands for MUD-object-oriented; and MUD is multi-user dungeon (or domain). Participants can hold real-time discussions in text. MOO has the added dimension of textual descriptions of places in which the participant should imagine himself or herself. You might use MOO to help health education program participants imagine themselves in situations where continuing a healthy behavior change is difficult. For example, a person who is trying to quit smoking might be asked to read a description of being with friends who are smoking and encouraging him or her to "smoke just one." Using MOO the participant can respond to the situation as he or she would in real life and others can provide immediate feedback. The individual trying to quit gets practice and comments on his or her strategies while sitting at home.

The two broad categories of computer-based learning methods include online courses and computer-based communication. An *online course* involves a carefully designed format with thoughtfully selected content through which a student will work. Participants might find links to sites on the Web within an online course. *Computer-based communication* involves the systems discussed earlier. There is not generally a predesigned content, although a set of questions or thoughts from the instructor might guide the discussion in one way or another. Many instructors use a combination of the two types of computer-based methods. Advances in technology and software are bringing the two together in much more user-friendly ways. It won't be long before computer-based technologies will be as easy to use as turning on the television.

Even if the technology advances to the point where it is easy to plan, computer-based methods are not for every participant. Many of the methods assume that participants are good readers and, for interactive types of systems, good writers. Although you may use computers on a daily basis as a student, there are many individuals in your communities who don't have access to computers and therefore do not know how to use them. This is not to say that they would not want to learn or couldn't learn, but learning the technology might have to be part of the program for some participants. Unfortunately, even many health care professionals do not have access to computer technology at their worksites.

Selecting methods is a challenging and exciting part of program planning. It should be conducted with a great deal of thought. Unfortunately, some aspects of program planning aren't as exciting. They are, however, just as important. These include planning the budget and developing a timeline for implementation.

OTHER ASPECTS OF PROGRAM PLANNING

Budgets

When you are planning a health education program, you need to consider many aspects of budget. We will discuss a few briefly now. **Budgets** are predictions of the revenues and expenses expected for the program. **Budgeting** is the process of developing the budget. That process includes gathering information and reviewing similar programs to identify potential program costs. According to Walter (1997), there are six basic steps in budgeting:

1. Select the cost categories for your budget.
2. Decide if you will divide your program budget into sections by time slices or phases.

3. Estimate costs for all the cost categories in your budget.
4. Document anticipated monetary or in-kind contributions to the project.
5. Add an allowance for contingencies.
6. Calculate the total amount of funding needed.

Selecting Cost Categories   Common categories in health education budgets include personnel, consultants, equipment/furniture, communications, travel, facilities, supplies, and indirect costs. Both wages and benefits (such as health and life insurance) must be considered in the personnel costs. If the program requires the services of a consultant, those costs will be identified in the consultant category. There is generally little opportunity to include new furniture and expensive new equipment in your budget due to lack of funds, but if this type of purchase will be made for the program it is contained in a separate category. Telephone, fax, post, and any other types of communication costs are identified in the communications category. The travel category identifies travel expenses incurred by both the program staff and at times the program participants. The travel category might include travel directly related to the program implementation as well as getting to and from conferences where you would present information about the program. The facilities category includes costs like rent. All of the consumable products that are used in the program are put in the supplies category. This might include paper, writing, printing, and other supplies that cannot be reused. All of these categories are direct costs to the program. Sometimes the program is housed within an agency that requires that indirect costs be included in the budget. These are funds for things like lighting, heating, and cooling that the program will use even though exact costs cannot be determined.

Determining Budgeting Phases   If a program-planning project is large, it may be easier to break it into phases. For example, you might want to have three divisions: planning, implementing, and evaluating. If phases are used, the budget will reflect the three phases so that it is very clear where expenditures will be made.

Estimating Costs   For the personnel category, you must determine how many people will be needed to conduct the program, what type of personnel these individuals will be (that is, health educators, secretaries, and so forth) how much time it will take each person to do his or her job, and the wages required. Benefits are generally included if the personnel will be spending more than 50% of their time on the project. Benefits often include medical and life insurance packages, plus retirement. Agencies often estimate 15–20% of the wages for each person's benefits (Green & Kreuter, 1999). Ways to estimate communication and travel costs include reviewing similar programs and mapping out the expected communication and travel needs. Agencies that are funded with government monies can often use telecommunication and travel rates that are negotiated at the state level. You will need to check with your agency to see if any special rates apply.

Think about your personal budget. Would preparing a budget for a health education program be similar in any ways?

TABLE 7.1   Sample Budget for an Immunization Education Program.

Initial budget estimates based on analysis of resource requirements before assessment of resources available

Budget Items	Hours	Rate	Totals
Personnel			
Administrator	480	$29	$ 13,920
Health educator	960	23	22,080
Nurses	800	20	16,000
Secretary	480	14	6,720
Subtotal			$ 58,720
Personnel benefits (fringe) @20%			$ 11,744
Total personnel costs			**$ 70,464**
Supplies			
Printing brochure			$ 2,000
Postage (20,000 × .32)			6,400
Office supplies			300
Vaccination supplies (800 × $3)			2,400
Total supplies			**$ 11,100**
Services			
Telephone			$ 500
Photocopying			400
Consultants			
Data processing	25	$12	$ 300
Medical consultant	62	75	4,650
Graphic artist	16	25	400
Total services			**$ 6,250**
Travel			
Local (400 mi. @ .31)			$ 124
State conference ($650 air; $150 per diem)			800
Total travel			**$ 924**
Total direct costs			**$ 88,738**
Indirect costs (20% of direct costs)			**$ 17,748**
Total budget estimate			**$106,486**

From *Health Promotion Planning: An Educational and Ecological Approach* (3rd ed., p. 195), by L. Green and M. Kreuter, 1999, Mountain View, CA: Mayfield.

Consumable products can be tricky. Again, we suggest mapping out needs. Think about the actual number of handouts, brochures, and other consumable items that will be used. Identify how much these items cost in your geographical location and multiply. Budgeting can be both fun and a challenge if you approach it with a positive attitude. Program budgets may vary significantly, but most con-

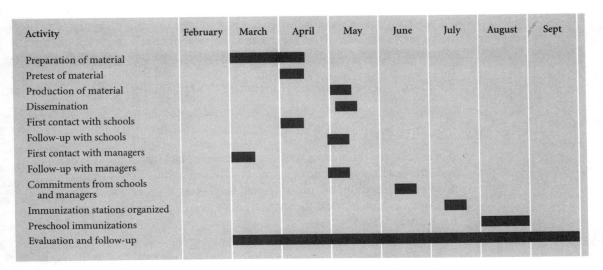

Activity	February	March	April	May	June	July	August	Sept
Preparation of material								
Pretest of material								
Production of material								
Dissemination								
First contact with schools								
Follow-up with schools								
First contact with managers								
Follow-up with managers								
Commitments from schools and managers								
Immunization stations organized								
Preschool immunizations								
Evaluation and follow-up								

FIGURE 7.8   Gantt chart for an immunization program.
Although projecting an accurate timeline can be a challenge, it is a vital part of program planning. It influences all aspects of the program from start to finish. From *Health Promotion Planning: An Educational and Ecological Approach* (3rd ed., p. 192), by L. Green and M. Kreuter, 1999, Mountain View, CA: Mayfield.

tain the subheadings found in Table 7.1, which shows an actual budget for a health education program. These subheadings include personnel, supplies, services, travel, and indirect costs.

Creating Timelines

The appropriate timing of each aspect of your health program will help guarantee your success and help keep you within your budget. We suggest that you use some type of charting system to illustrate when each part of the program will take place. One of the most effective charting methods for timelines is called a Gantt chart (Figure 7.8). In this type of chart you can visualize when an activity will start, how long it will last, and what activities are overlapping.

IN CONCLUSION

We hope that you now have a fairly clear picture of how to use a PRECEDE assessment in program planning. Writing goals and objectives are skills of such importance that you should master them before continuing to read. Your goals and objectives will assist you in selecting methods, creating your budgets, and developing timelines.

Selecting methods is challenging and exciting. You might choose computer-based teaching methods or other hands-on experiential activities. A theoretical foundation may be the most beneficial way to begin your program method selection. Each part of program planning requires time and thought. You won't regret the effort, however. Excellent planning will lead to a smooth implementation.

REVIEW QUESTIONS

1. Describe the differences between goals and objectives.
2. Define each of the three types of objectives described in this chapter.
3. Discuss the components that should be present in every objective.
4. Compare and contrast the three types of learning methods described in this chapter.
5. Give a sample application of each of the three types of objectives.
6. List and describe the categories that are commonly used in a health program budget.
7. Provide an example of a Gantt chart that you have created.

FOR YOUR APPLICATION

Planning a Program for Teen Mothers

- Use the information and goals established in phases 1–4 of the PRECEDE assessment presented in the chapter.
- Write one impact and one process objective for your program.
- Select a method for fulfilling your impact objective.

FOR YOUR PORTFOLIO

Documenting Goal and Objective Writing

1. Make a divider titled "Program Planning."
2. Ask your instructor to review the goal and objective you wrote in the For Your Application activity.
3. Make revisions.
4. Put the completed goal and objective in the Program Planning section of your portfolio.

8

Implementing
Health Programs

YOU ARE EXCITED ABOUT GETTING STARTED WITH THE new program you developed for pregnant teens. You have taken all of the right steps. You conducted a needs assessment and carefully planned your program, based on the perceived and documented needs of the population. You are ready to go! But wait, there are still a few missing links. You find that you need money to conduct the program and you need to make sure that information about the program reaches the people it is meant to serve. You also have materials to develop and schedules to create. Don't let the excitement die, because the success of the programs you implement will be tied to the time you take to address these issues.

Chapter Objectives

1. Discuss methods such as grant writing, seeking sponsors, and conducting special-event fund-raisers for health education programs.
2. Describe methods of social marketing.
3. List ways of assessing marketing effectiveness.
4. Discuss hiring and training for individuals who will deliver the health education programs.
5. Describe appropriate program record keeping.
6. Practice developing action plans.
7. Describe techniques for establishing the readability of program materials.
8. Describe ways to assist individuals with vision or hearing impairments use materials on the World Wide Web.

All of us think of money as a resource, but what other things might also be considered resources?

Program implementation (putting your program into action) requires giving attention to everything we've already discussed as well as some matters that will seemingly pop up out of the blue. Implementation issues range from important, difficult issues like money to important but small issues like an overhead projector that doesn't work correctly. Of course, money is one of the largest concerns because all programs require funding to some degree.

FUNDING THE PROGRAM

Resources, including personnel, equipment, materials, the site, and so forth, make or break the program. Although, in reality, these issues must be addressed early in your planning, they make such an impact on the implementation of the program that we want to discuss them in this chapter. Unfortunately, almost all resources depend on whatever money is available. So let's talk about funding your programs. Although there are many ways to seek funds, the primary methods include grants, contracts, sponsorships and other types of donations, and special-event fund-raisers. Many of you will be working with all of these methods for funding health education programs. Be sure to check with your agency, however, to make certain that the agency policy allows the type of fund-raising activity you are considering.

Grant Writing

For some reason, the idea of writing a grant proposal makes many people fearful. Perhaps it seems like too large a job, or perhaps the idea that the proposal could be turned down is what scares people. We suggest that you think about your program ideas with pride and set about to describe them in the best possible light so that others will learn about their benefits and be willing to provide funds. We are not going to tell you that grant writing is easy and that anyone can do it. According to Bing Burton, the Director of the Denton County Health Department in Texas, all health educators should consciously develop their writing skills (personal communication, November 9, 1999). He says that his department funds approximately 40% of its programs through grants and that grant writing requires excellent writing skills.

The good news is that grant writing is really another application of program planning. If you master the program-planning skills a health educator needs, you will have the knowledge necessary to write a grant. Let's talk about the components of a grant so that you can see for yourself how much they are like planning components. All grants require slightly different components, to be placed in slightly different order, but they are alike enough that you will always be able to see the similarities. Many grant applications, or **requests for proposals (RFPs),** include extensive directions and explicit descriptions of the content expected. Follow the directions; don't vary from what is requested. The directions were written for a reason. Sometimes funding agencies offer grant-writing workshops for a specific request for proposals. We strongly encourage you to attend these workshops whenever possible. They can only increase your chances of getting the money you need. Most grant applications will call for a cover page, purpose statement, list of objectives, review of literature or presentation of the problem, description of the population, description of methods or procedures, evaluation plan, budget and timeline, references, vitas, and appendixes (MacKenzie & Brown, 1986). See FYI 8.1 for tips on successful grant writing.

Cover Page   Most grant agencies have a cover page that they wish you to use or follow. This page generally asks for the name and address of the responsible individual, sometimes called the **principal investigator.** It will also require the name and address of the person responsible for fiscal (money) management of the grant, the amount of the grant request; the time period for the project; and a brief description of the agency. Be sure to complete the cover page as requested. If you have questions about this page or any other request for information, you should not hesitate to call the funding agency. Part of the job of its employees is to answer questions and assist in the application process.

Purpose   You will be asked to write an introductory statement or a purpose statement, or both. In an introduction, you briefly describe the problem that your project will address and discuss the importance of addressing it. The statement of purpose must be a clear and concise description of why you will conduct the program.

Objectives   You learned about writing program objectives in Chapter 7. Grant objectives are no different except that they address only the aspects of the program that would be funded by the grant for which you are applying. If you are still unsure about writing objectives, you might want to review Chapter 7.

Review of Related Literature or Presentation of the Problem   A thorough discussion of the problem that your program will address is of vital importance. In this section of the grant proposal, you demonstrate that there is a health problem. Can you see how data from your needs assessment fits here? Once you have accurately demonstrated that a problem exists, you must also convince the granting agency that programs like yours are successful in addressing the problem. You will do this by writing a review of literature related to programs like yours that have been successful. This section especially demands excellent writing skills.

Target Population   In this section of the grant proposal, you describe the group of people for whom the program will be given. You might include demographic information such as age ranges, educational levels, and gender. You give information about the size of the population and even the location and type of environment in which they live.

FOR YOUR INFORMATION 8.1

Tips for Successful Grant Writing

Although grant writing as a process has much in common with program development, the major difference is that the funds for your program depend on the attainment of grant monies. The tips listed here have been shown to help make a grant successful.

A successful grant proposal

Is based on an innovative idea
Is likely to advance the practice of health education
Fills a critical gap in our knowledge
Is driven by previous research
Works toward a long-term goal
Includes a thoughtful up-to-date literature review
Is well written
Provides evidence of feasibility
Demonstrates an appropriate choice of methods
Is well focused

Methods/Procedures   In this part of the grant proposal, you provide a complete description of what the program entails. In a way, it is like a recipe, describing specifically what, how much, and how. You should offer enough detail that another individual could read it and actually do what you are planning to do.

Evaluation   It's important to be able to know whether your program is effective (McDermott & Sarvela, 1999). After all, why continue a program that doesn't accomplish its objectives? When you write a grant proposal, the funding agency will want to see your evaluation plan. In this section of the proposal, you describe your evaluation plans (see Chapter 9, where we discuss evaluation in detail).

Budget/Timeline   Remember the discussions of budget and timelines in Chapter 7? Developing a budget and timeline for your grant requires a similar process. Review Chapter 7 if you have questions.

References   List all the sources you used in preparing the grant proposal in this section. It should look like the reference list in a research paper. We encourage you to use many types of references. It is very easy to just go to the Internet, but you will need to access journal articles and books too. Be sure you evaluate the information you get for accuracy and credibility.

Vitas/Résumés   In this section of the proposal, you give the funding agency information about yourself and the others involved in the project. Keep in mind that reviewers are looking for someone who has expertise in the area of the program. If you are not a specialist in the area the program will cover, ask someone with expertise to serve on the project with you.

Appendixes   The appendixes in a grant will include any documents that you want the granting agency reviewers to see but that do not fit in the other categories. For example, you might include copies of surveys that you will use to collect information from participants. You might also include letters of support for the program written by leaders in the community.

Grant Sources

Believe it or not, a great number of grants are available for health programs. The federal government, state agencies (such as state health departments), voluntary agencies (such as the American Heart Association or the American Cancer Society), foundations (such as the Kellogg Foundation), and even professional organizations (such as the American Alliance for Health, Physical Education, Recreation, and Dance) offer money for health programs. The World Wide Web is the best place for finding information about grants. We suggest that you go to the Web pages for the agency, state, or foundation you think might support your program. Revisit Appendix D for URLs of some of these agencies. Try it; you'll see that finding grant sources is not as difficult as it seems.

Seeking Donations or Sponsors

If no grants are available for a particular program at a particular time, you might seek a **corporate sponsorship** or donations from individuals who believe health is important. With a corporate sponsorship, a business pays for a program or segment of a program. As you can probably imagine, there is no single method for seeking donations. Sometimes you write a letter and, at other times, you make personal contact via a face-to-face meeting or telephone call. However, there are some important things to remember, regardless of your method. For example, check with your agency about policies regarding donations. In some circumstances you won't be able to accept donations at all. In other circumstances, you will be allowed to seek donations but will be required to follow a well-defined set of guidelines.

If you receive approval to seek donations, make certain that other divisions in your agency are not requesting money from the same company or individual at the same time. It is simply not fair to overwhelm a corporation or individual who has been generous in the past with numerous new requests for money. If you request funds from a corporation, ask about the procedure you will be expected to follow. Most donate money frequently but have specific procedural requirements (such as submission of something like a grant proposal).

Regardless of whether you will be writing letters or proposals or making phone calls, put thoughtful preparation into the project. Proofread your letters, have others read them for clarity and flow, and revise them several times. In the case of telephone contacts, develop a script and practice before you make the call. And, of course, if you receive a donation or sponsorship, give appropriate thanks. In addition to written thank-you notes, you might consider thanking donors on program handouts.

Special-Event Fund-Raisers

Almost any activity can be a fund-raiser. Some of the most common today include fun runs, golf tournaments, and silent auctions. Individuals pay to participate or purchase something. Fund-raisers can be highly successful, but they can also cause many headaches if the planners are not experienced. For example, one of our local service clubs planned a chili supper fund-raiser. The planners understood promotion but were not skilled at the total marketing picture. They advertised very effectively. In fact, approximately 500 people attended. However, the organizers did not assess the effectiveness of their promotion or the likelihood that so many people would attend. They cooked for only 100. Can you imagine the chaos? Although this mistake was somewhat humorous, some planning errors can be dangerous to participants. What if you planned a 6-mile fun run but did not offer runners water or first aid? You could easily put participants in danger. Our suggestion is that you involve an experienced special-events planner on your fund-raising committee.

SOCIAL MARKETING

Social marketing is "the design, implementation and control of programs aimed at increasing the acceptability of a social idea or practice in one or more groups of target adoptors" (Novartis Foundation for Sustainable Development, 1999). Social marketing uses the strategies of commercial marketing.

Understanding Social Marketing

In social marketing, decisions must be made about the product, price, place, and promotion, often called the four P's of marketing. Other P's to consider include partnership, policy, and politics. Philip Kotler and Gerald Zaltman (1971) developed the idea of social marketing when they realized that traditional marketing principles could apply to attitudes and behaviors that influence social issues. Prior to the creation of social marketing, large social campaigns often succeeded only in increasing people's awareness of a specific health issue. On the other hand, large advertising campaigns for new products continued to effectively increase use of specific products. Today, social marketing uses the methods of commercial marketing, with differences in content and objectives. Like commercial marketing, social marketing addresses product, price, place, and promotion, but it is also wise to address partnerships, policy, and politics (Weinrich Communications, 1999).

Product   Your *product* has actually been determined before you implement your program. In social marketing, the product can range from an actual product (a physical object) to a health-related service or even an idea. Keeping this in mind, you can see that the product is actually developed during program planning. Some potential products that you might be interested in marketing for a smoking cessation program are a device or invention to help an individual stop smoking (like a patch), the idea that smoking is not healthful even for teens, or an actual smoking cessation program (service).

Price   By *price* we mean more than just money. Although monetary cost is one aspect of price, other intangible things like time, effort, and risk of embarrassment must also be considered. In general, people will weigh the benefits of the product against the costs. Their use of the product will depend on a perception that benefits outweigh the costs.

Place   The means of distribution for the product defines *place*. In the traditional form of marketing you might decide that your product would be distributed from a warehouse via trucks to retail stores. In social marketing you would make decisions about the "channel of communication." The channel of communication might be a newspaper, a television show or commercial, a counseling session with a physician, or face-to-face interviews at the consumers' homes.

Promotion   It can be easy to confuse promotion and place in social marketing. *Promotion* deals with keeping consumers interested and motivated to use the product. It might also involve news and telephone media. But whereas *place* would refer to the channel or mode of communication you choose to use (such as a newspaper ad), the promotion aspect refers to how your message is worded to motivate or persuade the reader. The purpose differs from place; you might think of promotion as advertising and place as the medium you choose for your advertisement.

Partnership   Health-related social problems are complex. In most cases, the complexity requires collaboration among health agencies. *Partnerships* between agencies facilitate effective decisions about price and place.

Policy   According to Weinrich Communications (1999), "Social marketing programs can do well in motivating individual behavior change, but that is difficult to sustain unless the environment they are in supports that change for the long run. Often, *policy* (a planned course of action to guide decisions) change is needed, and media advocacy programs can be an effective complement to a social marketing program" (p. 3).

Politics   Your social marketing plan will require making decisions about the political environment. Suppose the product involved is controversial—for example, discussing birth control methods in public high schools. Unless an assessment of the politics surrounding the product is made, difficulties can snowball. *Politics* can destroy even the most beneficial program. There are times when it is best to wait until the political environment is more conducive to successful completion of the program.

Developing a Marketing Plan

Creating a market plan requires focusing on the people who will be using a product rather than on the product itself. Research and evaluation are the key to an effective plan (Weinrich Communications, 1999). Keeping in mind that the product has already been determined, marketing objectives must be set, assessments of the target audience must be made, pricing and placing that correspond with the population needs must be developed, and promotion or advertising must occur. Once a product has been identified during planning, we think of the acronym MAPP (Figure 8.1) as a guide to developing a marketing plan. This process of developing a marketing plan should remind you of the PRECEDE portion of the PRECEDE/PROCEED model. As you know, assessments come first, followed by planning, implementing, and evaluating. In fact, if you have used PRECEDE, writing a marketing plan will be much easier.

Writing Marketing Objectives   Marketing objectives relate directly to the program objectives. As we stated earlier, the product is determined during program planning; therefore, those very program objectives are part of the marketing objectives. Other marketing objectives specifically address promotion. Let's look at an example of a promotion objective. "During the year 2000, center staff will improve potential participants' perception of the program by creating updated and distinctive brochures with the assistance of a professional graphic designer." As you can see, the objective contains all of the components of program planning objectives. The difference is in the focus on promotion rather than actual programming.

Thinking back to Chapter 6, what are some methods for assessing the needs of your population?

Assessing the Target Audience   This aspect of the marketing plan includes knowing the demographic makeup of the audience, such as the economic status, education levels, and age structure. It also includes psychosocial information such as attitudes and beliefs. Cultural and religious beliefs and behaviors are im-

Marketing objectives

Assessment of population

Price

Promotion

FIGURE 8.1   MAPP.
The MAPP acronym is a simple way to remember the steps to marketing a program.
At least some form of marketing will be necessary for any program to be a success.
Having at least a rudimentary understanding of marketing will improve your
chances of implementing a successful program.

portant to understand when you are creating a social marketing plan. Fortunately,
you can achieve an understanding of your target audience for marketing purposes
at the same time you conduct the initial needs assessment for program planning.

Both qualitative and quantitative methods of audience assessment can be
used. A combination of methods might be best. Surveys, a frequently used quantitative method, can be mailed, conducted via the telephone, or conducted in
face-to-face settings. Focus groups and interviews, commonly used qualitative
methods, also involve primary data collection. Can you name some secondary
sources of data that might be helpful in your needs assessment and marketing research? You might have considered reviewing the literature or accessing previously collected morbidity and mortality data.

Place—Determining Distribution Channels   Communications media are the
most commonly used channel for distribution in social marketing. Media include
television, radio, newsprint, magazines, and cinema. Other types of distribution
channels are personal face-to-face communication, telephone contact, posters,
the mail, direct sales, and distribution of brochures and other written documents.
The selection of the appropriate channel depends on both the target audience and
the product. For example, you won't want to choose the business section of a local paper to provide program information that you want teens to read. Again, you
must get to know your audience before you will be able to determine the appropriate channel. An important theoretical basis from which to identify an appropriate channel is the theory of the diffusion of innovation.

The **theory of the diffusion of innovation** describes the ways that an innovation spreads through a population of people. An *innovation* can be anything from

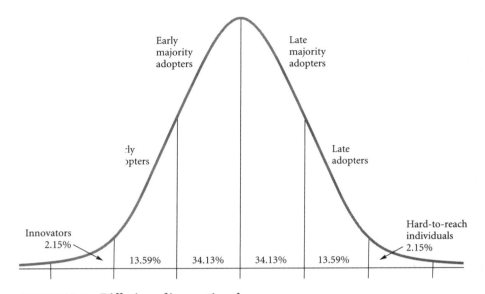

FIGURE 8.2   Diffusion of innovation theory.
This theory describes acceptance of change as following a bell-curve pattern. It also suggests that innovators will accept a new product or program much more quickly than individuals who are late adopters or hard to reach.

a product (like new athletic shoes) to an idea (like the belief that smoking kills). In marketing terms, this is considered the product. Understanding the theory can help you determine what channels to use to advertise your innovation (health program). As you can see from Figure 8.2, the theory can be depicted as a bell-shaped curve. Theorists believe that consumers can be categorized into five groups by the rate at which they adopt an innovation. As you read through this information, think about where you fit into the curve. You may find that it is not easy to determine your exact speed of adoption. Each of us adopts innovations according to the type of innovation and the current environment. In other words, the speed of adoption is not necessarily a stable characteristic; however, most of us fall into patterns of adoption.

Innovators adopt change easily. In general, they are highly educated and can be reached through mass media channels. If they determine that an innovation might benefit them, they will change quickly. Let us pretend that we are promoting a new, effective stress-reduction strategy across the United States. For innovators, we could put an article in a national publication like *USA Today* or *Newsweek*. Innovators would be more likely than others to read the article and choose to try the new plan as a result. *Early adopters* are often public leaders and highly respected in communities. Others often follow their adoption patterns. Like innovators, they can be reached via mass media, although state or regional channels may be more effective. Again, a newspaper might be the place for dissemination of our stress-reduction plan; but, instead of an article, we might want to place an advertisement that suggests how effective the plan has been with individuals who have tried it. *Early majority adopters* accept innovations once they determine that others they respect have done so. Demonstrating the adoption patterns of innovators and early adopters is often the most effective way to reach most of these people. Local newspapers and other types of media can be effective means of spreading the innovation. For the promotion of our stress-reduction plan, we might use the same strategy that we used for early adopters except that we would place our advertisement in a regional or local newspaper. *Late majority adopters* are somewhat skeptical of change. They will adopt an innovation most readily if they are required to do so (public law) or they believe that the change will benefit them dramatically. In order to reach late majority adopters, we might work directly with leaders in corporate worksites. Our goal would be to encourage corporations to require use of our stress-reduction plan. *Late adopters* and *hard-to-reach individuals* (called laggards by early theorists) accept change only with difficulty. They tend to have lower levels of education and often live in poverty. One-on-one, face-to-face means of communicating the innovations seem to be the most effective with this group of individuals. For our stress-reduction plan, we might have individuals from the late adopter population who use the plan make personal contact with others.

The relative advantage, complexity, compatibility, testability, reversibility, and observability of an innovation also influence the rate of adoption (Glanz, Lewis, & Rimer, 1997). FYI 8.2 defines some of these terms and others associated with the theory of the diffusion of innovation.

Pricing   Although seemingly simple and easy to define, pricing is complex. On the one hand, price determines the accessibility of the service or product; and, on the other hand, price can imply credibility or quality (Alward & Camunas, 1991). People often believe that a product is not worth much unless it is associated with a high price. In order to determine the price, you must consider your objectives. See FYI 8.3 for using pricing objectives for tangible products.

Assessing Marketing Effectiveness

In Chapter 9, you will read more extensively about program evaluation. We hope it is evident to you now, however, that you must always check to see if your plans are working. One of the biggest wastes of time and money comes from continuing with activities that don't work. You will learn about a number of evaluation methods in Chapter 9; but for now, we would like to offer a few questions that you might ask about your marketing plan to assess its effectiveness:

- Does the product meet the needs of the population? Or, in other words, Are the participants making the planned changes? Do the participants perceive the program to be useful? Are people healthier as a result of the program?

FOR YOUR INFORMATION 8.2

Diffusion of Innovative Terms

According to the theory of diffusion of innovations, innovations have seven characteristics. Each will be important for you to understand when projecting how a new program or product will be accepted by the target participants.

Compatibility   When innovations are consistent with the economic, sociocultural, and philosophical value system of the adopter, adoption is more likely to take place.

Flexibility   Innovations that can be unbundled and used as separate components will be applicable in a wider variety of user settings.

Reversibility   If for any reason, the adopting individual or organization wants to revert to its previous practices, it is desirable that an innovation be capable of termination. Innovations that are not are less likely to be adopted.

Relative advantage   If an innovation appears to be beneficial when compared to current and previous methods, adoption is more likely.

Complexity   Complex innovations are more difficult to communicate and to understand and are therefore less likely to be adopted.

Cost-efficiency   For an innovation to be considered desirable, its perceived benefits, both tangible and intangible, must outweigh its perceived costs.

Risk   The degree of uncertainty introduced by an innovation helps determine its potential for adoption. Innovations that involve higher risk are less likely to be adopted.

From "Implementing Comprehensive School Health Education: Educational Innovations and Social Change," by L. J. Kolbe and D. C. Iverson, 1981, *Health Education Quarterly 8,* 57–80.

- Can the population access the product? Or, Are people attending the program? Do participants perceive the price of the program to be appropriate? Do participants perceive the benefits of the program to outweigh the barriers to attending?
- Are the distribution channels effective? Or, Do participants report hearing about the program through your selected channels of advertising? How did participants hear about the program?
- Do policies and politics serve as barriers or boosters to the product? Or, How do agency politics affect the program? How do local politics affect the program?

FOR YOUR INFORMATION 8.3

Using Pricing Objectives for Tangible Products

The price of your product or program will be determined by the type of outcome desired. The following provides suggestions for determining price.

Goal of Marketing	Pricing Activity	Consequence of Activity
High number of population to accept health product or service	Offer product or service at a low cost	Potential perception of a product or service of low worth
Equal distribution of health product or service	Offer product or service at a flexible price structure	Individuals with high income pay more, potential perception of inequality
Expense and income are balanced	Offer product or service at a price that defrays the cost	Cost may be too high at first
Maximizing profit	Offer service or product at a price that improves the demand	Cost may be too low at first
Minimizing excessive demand of an unhealthful service or product	Offer service or product at a very high price	Negative perception of pricing

From *A short course in social marketing,* by Novartis Foundation for Sustainable Development, 1999. Retrieved September 22, 1999, from the World Wide Web: http:www.foundation.novartis. com /social_marketing.htm.

OTHER ASPECTS OF IMPLEMENTATION

Implementing your program requires that you attend to every aspect of the program, not just money and marketing. Going with the flow (that is, letting whatever happens, happen) is not appropriate. Some of the other aspects of program implementation that you will want to address include selecting and training staff or volunteers, developing curricula, identifying equipment and facilities, determining program logistics, preparing materials, and program follow-up.

Selecting Staff

Randy Pennington, the owner of a leadership consulting firm in Dallas, states that an effective way of viewing staff is to consider them as essential volunteers (personal communication, November 8, 1999). Adopting this attitude requires you to spend adequate time training your employees and demonstrating to them that they are valued. This approach is necessary if you want to keep good employees.

Staff should understand the organizational culture and practices, have experience working with the target audience, demonstrate professionalism, and have content expertise and skills (Carnevale, Gainer, & Meltzer, 1990). How would you go about finding people who fit these criteria?

Begin the process of selecting employees by asking for a portfolio and continue by interviewing those who demonstrate the knowledge and skills that you require. Most professional preparation programs encourage students to develop portfolios. As the potential employer, you can see the health educator's work for yourself. For example, if the individual will be asked to write pieces for a newsletter, you will want to read sample articles or other written documents that demonstrate effective written communication skills.

Begin the interviewing process by modeling professionalism. Professionalism is not easy to define, but it includes actions like being on time, preparing in advance, selecting appropriate attire, communicating effectively, and acting with integrity. The first time you meet the prospective employee will be your first training session. If you demonstrate a lack of preparation or ineffective communication, you are essentially giving permission for the individual to act in a like manner if hired. Remember that new employees want to do a good job and they will follow your lead.

We suggest that you ask potential employees to demonstrate their skills. If you will expect your new employees to make presentations to small groups, ask applicants to do so as part of their interview. If they will be conducting program evaluations, give them an actual scenario to discuss. We also encourage you to wait for the right person rather than resorting to panic placement (selecting anyone just to get someone in the position). It may be a relief to just hire someone; but in the end you will spend a lot more time, effort, and money if you have to begin again because the individual did not match the position.

If you are seeking volunteers rather than paid employees, you should still ask for information about their educational backgrounds and skills. You will want to place volunteers in an area that matches their skills and desired type of work. Unlike job applicants, they are not usually turned away. But in a hiring situation, you will look for an individual who has the skills required for a specific job. Unqualified individuals are not hired.

Unfortunately, there are times when prospective employees or volunteers do not hold the same beliefs that serve as the philosophical foundation of the agency. For example, an individual who does not approve of abortion may not support a policy that requires women to be given information about abortions. You will have the responsibility of making certain that the individuals you hire or invite to volunteer support the agency's philosophy.

Training New Employees

We asked people who had recently started new jobs to comment on their training needs. Seven themes appeared in their comments. Every person noted that clear and honest descriptions of expectations were vital. Some also stated that they needed to know the extent to which they could develop their own goals. The people in our small study indicated in various ways that they needed to understand the agency mission as well as the purpose of the specific job they would be performing. Some mentioned that explanations of their benefits and important agency policies were necessary. They also valued identification of available resources and identification of resources that were not available through the agency but helpful if the employee could access them. Last, but not least, all of the individuals mentioned that they needed training for new skills as well as feedback on the acquisition of those skills.

Interestingly, the people we talked with regarded the training process as a reflection of the philosophical basis from which their employer worked. They seemed to feel that an agency that offered appropriate training was likely to value its employees. Agencies that value employees provide opportunities to help them succeed rather than just indicate performance problem areas.

Facilities

The physical environment can make a major difference in people's ability to learn. Have you ever attended a lecture in a room that was very hot or very cold? How did the temperature affect your ability to listen? Room temperature, amount of light, colors, room setup, room size, and type of furniture create the environment. The effectiveness of your program will be partially determined by the environment. Consider your options carefully.

What aspects of a room influence your ability to learn?

Choosing the Site   Many types of locations might be selected for your health education programs. If you do not have space available in your agency, other choices might include hotels, conference centers, universities, ships, resorts, other public buildings, and corporate settings (Nadler & Nadler, 1987). Your choices will depend on your budget, program objectives, size of audience, and location of potential sites. Table 8.1 provides a comparison of different types of sites.

Room Size and Setup   Don't forget to plan how the tables and chairs will be placed. It may sound like busywork, but think again about your own learning experiences. Have you ever been asked to have a discussion with a small group of people in a classroom where you can't move the chairs? That room setup

TABLE 8.1   Comparison of Site Types

The type of site you select for your program will make a difference in attendance and participant satisfaction. However, the type of site also influences the cost of your program, so you
will want to compare and contrast the advantages and disadvantages of different types of sites
before you make a selection.

Site	Description	Advantage	Disadvantage
Hotels	Buildings that pro-vide sleeping rooms, meeting rooms, and restaurants	Staff available to help coordinate Needs are met in one location	Possibly expensive
Convention centers	Special facilities that provide meeting rooms and resources	Able to host large groups of people Resources readily accessible	Hotels and restau-rants may not be within walking distance May be expensive
Universities	Institutions with a primary purpose of educating	Rooms of various sizes available May be less costly	Distance between rooms may cause difficulties Meeting equipment may not be as read-ily available
Resorts	Sites designed for recreation	Provide other activi-ties for participants	Participants may not attend meetings May be expensive

probably caused a barrier to both the discussion and the learning. Room setup
should be determined only after you have decided on the method of instruction
for each program. Remember the discussion of methods in Chapter 7? If your
program requires face-to-face interaction, you will want to make decisions about
whether individual rooms are needed for each face-to-face meeting, if a table will
separate you and your participants, and how many people will be able to attend.
In the case of presentations to a group of individuals, there are numerous ways to
set up the room. Figure 8.3 illustrates some of the most common.

The Content

In all educational environments there are two types of curriculum: planned and
unplanned. According to Doll (1992), a **curriculum** is "the formal and informal content and process by which learners gain knowledge and understanding,

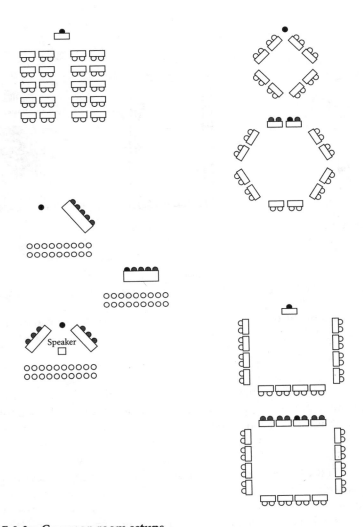

FIGURE 8.3   Common room setups.
Rooms can be arranged in a number of different ways. Careful consideration of the type of meeting, activities, and/or presentations that will be conducted should be made before the room setup is selected. From *The Comprehensive Guide to Successful Conferences and Meetings,* by L. Nadler and Z. Nadler, 1987, San Francisco: Jossey-Bass (a John Wiley Company).

develop skills, and alter attitudes, appreciations, and values" (p. 6). A curriculum pertains to all programs, not just those in an educational institution. As a health educator, it will be important to purposefully and thoughtfully develop the curriculum you will use in the health education program. You have already done a significant amount of planning, but now you must put in the detail.

Some like it hot—

BOOM!

Shot through with the
fireworks of spur-of-the-
moment innovation

Some like it cold—

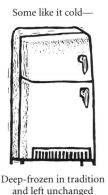

Deep-frozen in tradition
and left unchanged

Some like it rebuilt,
no matter how old—

Continually inspected,
revised, and changed

FIGURE 8.4   Curriculum development.
Curriculum generally fits into one of three categories as shown in this illustration:
hot, cold, or rebuilt. Each has a time and place but the type of curriculum should be
part of a well-thought-out plan. From *Curriculum Improvement: Decision Making and Process*
(9th ed., p. 17), by R. Doll, 1996, Boston, MA: Allyn and Bacon.

Developing Curricula   There are three paths you might choose for curriculum
development (Figure 8.4). You might choose to select a new idea (innovation),
continue with what has been used in the agency for a long time, or revise the old
curriculum. The important thing is that you make these decisions in advance of
your educational program based on some logical reasoning. Consider the learning tips in FYI 8.4 to help you make decisions about curriculum development.

Your written curriculum might take several forms. For example, you might
create a chart that includes the name of the program, a list of objectives that will
be accomplished via the program, methods matched with each objective, and a
content outline. Some curricula include actual materials, action plans (lesson
plans), and a list of necessary resources.

The Action Plan   An **action plan,** called a lesson plan in an educational setting,
is an important component of any program. The action plan is a small piece of
the total curriculum or program. Most programs have several parts. For example,
they might include a series of classes, or they might include discussion groups as
well as face-to-face meetings. An action or lesson plan would be developed for
each small piece of the program. They are not long documents but just enough to
guide each part of the program. We strongly encourage you to develop them even
if others in your agency don't use them. As usual, many sample forms exist for
action/lesson plans. See Figure 8.5 for an example.

Program Logistics

Record Keeping   Record keeping is both painful and joyful. Accurate records help you document that your program is working and that you are managing the funds adequately. This is only the case, however, if your records are consistent, accurate, and accessible. We encourage the use of the computer as a tool for record keeping. A number of software programs provide effective tracking and organization of program data. The types of records you must keep are related to process, impact, and outcome (see Chapter 7) and will relate directly to your objectives. In regard to process, you will certainly keep attendance records, but you may want to collect information about the participants' perceptions of the program, content, and learning environments. Statistical programs for computers, such as the Statistical Packages for the Social Sciences PC, allow you to enter and store data easily. They will produce descriptive statistics (frequencies, averages, and percentages) at a click of a button. These same programs will help you store and analyze your impact and outcome information. These are the data that will document the effectiveness of your program, so they become, in a sense, the lifeblood of the program.

Schedules   Another aspect of the program is the timing or scheduling of the activities. As always, there are a number of ways that you can illustrate and distribute your schedules. One of the most common methods involves the use of a monthly calendar as a flyer. The program activities are simply placed on the

Activity:

Instructor:

Date:

Description of participants:

Objectives:

Schedule	Description of activity	Content to be covered	Resources

FIGURE 8.5   Sample action plan.
As with every other aspect of program planning and implementation, individual lessons or contacts with participants should be well planned. Most professionals find it easiest to use a consistent planning tool like the action plan shown in this illustration.

correct day of the month. Participants can then post their monthly schedules in an easily accessible location. Another method is a program-like document that lists the days and times of upcoming events. Participants receive a brochure or small booklet that provides a quick look at upcoming events. The key is to carefully plan your schedule and get the word out to participants. Keep in mind that if a schedule isn't working, it should be changed.

CREATING MATERIALS

Language Disorders and Literacy Levels

"The ability to read and write is strongly influenced by the ability to understand and use language. Individuals who are good listeners and speakers tend to be strong readers and writers" (American Speech-Language-Hearing Association, 1999). **Language disorder** refers to any impairment in form, semantics, or pragmatics (American Speech-Language-Hearing Association, 1999). At one time or another you will have people with all of these problems in your programs. An individual who has difficulties with *form* might misunderstand the information provided by word endings. Individuals who have difficulties with *semantics* may have difficulty understanding *idiom* (a phrase or expression that cannot be understood from the ordinary meanings of the words in it). For example, when we were writing a later section of this chapter, we referred to the "nuts and bolts" of the program. What is meant by "nuts and bolts" in such usage is not explained by the definition of the two words as pieces of hardware. Other examples of idiom include "butterflies in the stomach," "kick the bucket," and so on. *Pragmatics* means using the same phrases or words for different purposes; for example, the word *cool* might indicate temperature or it might indicate a value judgment. You will need to prepare materials that are useful to individuals with language disorders.

You will also have individuals with varying **literacy levels** in your programs. If you are working with college students, you know that the **readability** level of your materials can be high; but for the general population, you will want to keep the reading level around the eighth grade and around the sixth grade for audiences of lower literacy (McDermott & Sarvela, 1999). Readability refers to reading ease as well as other aspects of reading. There are many methods for determining readability, but one common procedure is the SMOG Index (McLaughlin, 1969). It gives a grade level for written materials. Fortunately, many word-processing programs have readability indexes built into them.

There are several actions you can take in developing materials that will help individuals with language disorders as well as low literacy levels. See FYI 8.5 for a list of tips for developing materials. As you can see from the list, including words with fewer syllables, writing shorter sentences, and using pictures will increase comprehension.

Creating Web Pages

Web pages are an excellent resource for your program. A Web page is like an informational brochure or flyer that is posted for all to see. The good news about developing Web pages is that, like other aspects of implementation, computer software makes it easy. "The Web exists to communicate information" (Parker, 1999, p. 2). In other words, although color and fonts are important, work first on the content of your pages. To get started with Web page development, answer the

FOR YOUR INFORMATION 8.5

Tips for Developing Materials

The materials you select or develop will be one of the influencing factors on learning. This list provides ways in which to make appropriate materials.

- Keep the readability level below the eighth grade unless you know the specific level of your audience.
- Use pictures to supplement text. Make certain that the pictures are relevant to your audience.
- Unless the members of your audience have medical backgrounds, assume that they are not familiar with medical terms.
- Ask a member of the target population to check the language and adjust it. It should be meaningful to the people who will read it.
- Ask a second member of the target audience to read the adjusted material and describe the content. Make certain that the adjusted material still means what you intend it to.
- Provide examples that are relevant to your audience.
- Field-test your material by asking several members of the target audience to preview the materials and provide feedback.

question "What is the purpose of the Web site?" Then derive your content from the information your participants will need and want.

Once your content has been selected, consider the design. The best Web pages are simple, which means they are easier to make and easier to read. According to Roger Parker (1999), there are nine guidelines for Web page design:

1. Design should be purposeful.
2. Design should simplify complicated information.
3. Design should provide visual contrast.
4. Design should make your program competitive.
5. Design should show how the program pieces fit together.
6. Design should help the participant know what is important.
7. Design should involve a few effective font and color changes.
8. Design should save the participant time.
9. Design should involve editing.

Individuals with special needs can have difficulty with a poorly designed Web page. Tips for creating an effective Web page for them (and for everyone else) are provided in FYI 8.6.

FOR YOUR INFORMATION 8.6

Creating Web Pages for Individuals with Special Needs

Some individuals have special needs that will require changes made to the materials they use in a program, including Web-based programs or pages. Following are some ideas for meeting the needs of individuals with visual or hearing impairments or learning disabilities.

Visual Impairments

Eliminate screen cluttering.
Avoid placing more than one hyperlink on each line.
Eliminate tiled background that obscures texts.
Design high-contrast texts and background.
Provide a text-only option.
For pictures, provide a text description.

Hearing Impairments

Explain sound clips using text.
Provide text descriptions for all video clips that include sound.

Learning Disabilities

Have lots of descriptive pictures.
Have step-by-step explanations for all instructions and commands.

From Designing access to the WWW pages, by Alliance for Technology Access, 1999. Retrieved May 5, 2000, from the World Wide Web: http://www.ataccess.org/design.html.

That old saying "practice makes perfect" is certainly true with Web pages. You should begin learning to develop them now.

KEEPING THE PROGRAM ALIVE

"A positive self concept gives people a firm foundation from which to reach their maximum potential in the workplace and other areas of life" (Carnevale et al., 1990, p. 215). *Self-concept* is made up of self-awareness, self-image, and self-esteem. *Self-awareness* is a knowledge of one's skills and abilities, and awareness of one's impact on others, emotional capacity, and needs. *Self-image* is a view of oneself. *Self-esteem* is an expression of happiness or dissatisfaction with one's self-image.

These aspects of the self have a dramatic influence on your program's longevity. If your participants feel a decrease in self-concept (either consciously or unconsciously) as they attend the program, they won't come back. It happens all too often. The attitude of an instructor, the difficulty of the activities or materials, and the degree to which participants have to demonstrate new skills in embarrassing situations can all influence self-concept. Thoughtful planning is the best way to prevent a program from dying because participants are uncomfortable.

IN CONCLUSION

Program implementation seems easy at first, but it must be approached with an understanding of its importance. Ongoing funding for the program is necessary to keep the program going. Grant writing is a common method for seeking funds, but you might also want to consider conducting a special-event fund-raiser or seeking donations. Once the program has been planned and has appropriate funding, your next goal will be effective marketing. Marketing encompasses much more than advertising. You'll revisit your needs assessment to define the market, address issues of place and price, and develop promotion strategies. You will also want to consider partnering with other agencies, and you'll need to review current policies and politics.

The nuts and bolts of the program will also be fine-tuned in program implementation. Appropriate program materials and schedules should be developed with the target population in mind. Records, although not always fun, will document your ability to manage the program and produce positive impacts and outcomes. Treat program implementation seriously. Don't let your energy lapse just when the participant becomes involved.

REVIEW QUESTIONS

1. List common components of a grant proposal.
2. Discuss briefly why each is important.
3. List the components of marketing.
4. Detail the differences between the components of marketing.
5. Describe the strategies you might use to select a new employee and discuss why.
6. List tips for developing materials.
7. Analyze why each is useful.
8. Describe and identify ways in which you can keep the program alive.

FOR YOUR APPLICATION

Locating Potential Grant Sources

- *Try your local government or public health agency.* Many communities can be accessed by using the URL: http://www.name of city.gov.

- *Try your state government,* normally accessed with http://www.name of state.gov.
- *Try federal agencies.* Keep in mind that all governmental agencies use .gov in their URLs. Most federal agencies use their abbreviated names in the URL. For example, the Centers for Disease Control and Prevention can be accessed at http://www.cdc.gov and the National Institutes of Health can be accessed at http://www.nih.gov. A search engine such as Yahoo can also help you find agency sites.
- *Try professional health organizations.* You can often use strategies similar to those you used for federal agencies. For example, the American Public Health Association can be accessed at http: //www.apha.org. Nonprofit organizations use .org in their URLs. A search engine can help.
- *Try voluntary health organizations.* Voluntary health organizations are accessed much like professional organizations. They also use .org in their URLs.

Give it a try!

FOR YOUR PORTFOLIO

Create an Action Plan

1. Label one of the dividers in your portfolio "Implementation."
2. Select a format for an action or lesson plan. It should include a description of the topic and target population, objectives, projected schedule, content to be covered, and needed resources. You may also want to include the instructor's name, actual handouts or slides, and other information.
3. Once you have selected the format, complete the plan and have your instructor review it.
4. Make revisions and include the plan in the Implementation section of your portfolio.

9

Program
Evaluation

YOU TRIED ANOTHER PROGRAM FOR TEEN MOTHERS IN your community. This time you assessed their attitudes, beliefs, and perceived needs and based your program development on the assessment. Lots of teens attended the program. Everyone seemed to be having fun. Does that mean the program was effective? Can you assume that the program accomplished what it was supposed to?

Chapter Objectives

1. List purposes of evaluation.
2. Define selected types of evaluation.
3. Describe strategies for conducting process evaluation.
4. Describe strategies for conducting impact evaluation.
5. Describe strategies for conducting outcome evaluation.
6. Create an evaluation plan.

DEFINITION AND PURPOSES

Health professionals frequently assume that the health of their patients, clients, or participants improves as a result of the programs designed for such purposes. However, you should be aware that some health education programs don't work, or health changes as a result of something else. Only effective evaluation can determine for sure. Today, the process of evaluation is multifaceted and begins as soon as program assessment and planning begin. Evaluation is part of the program plan. The strategies from which you may choose are numerous and varied. We give you a brief overview of evaluation practices in this chapter.

Definition

Green and Kreuter (1999) define evaluation as "the comparison of an object of interest against a standard of acceptability" (p. 220). This definition sounds difficult to understand, but both the *object of interest* and *standards of acceptability* are identified by your program objectives. The object of interest is the behavior and the standard of acceptability is the "how much" and "when" parts of the objectives. Let's look at an example from your program for teen mothers. One of your objectives might have been "By the end of the year-long program offered by the public health educator, participants will list at least five benefits of remaining abstinent." In your evaluation the object of interest is "listing benefits of remaining abstinent" and the standard of acceptability is "at least five."

Many individuals believe that the definition for evaluation will change according to the purpose of conducting it. For example, if cost analysis is the major purpose of the evaluation, you might be defining evaluation in terms of **cost-effectiveness** (an assessment of the program costs and how they relate to changes in impact or outcome). On the other hand, if you want to know whether program participants are satisfied with the program, you will probably define evaluation in terms of process (the way in which the program runs).

Purposes

According to Windsor and colleagues (1994), common purposes of evaluation may be

1. To determine the degree of attainment of program objectives
2. To document strengths and weaknesses of the program or components for making decisions and planning
3. To monitor standards of performance and establish quality assurance and control mechanisms
4. To meet the demand for public or fiscal accountability
5. To improve the professional staff's skill in the performance of program planning and implementation

6. To fulfill grant or contract requirements
7. To promote positive public relations and community awareness
8. To determine the generalizability of an overall program or program elements to other populations
9. To contribute to the base of scientific knowledge about health education program design
10. To identify hypotheses about human behavior for future evaluations (pp. 20–21).

TYPES OF EVALUATION

Regardless of the purpose, all forms of evaluation fit into two major categories: formative and summative. **Formative evaluation** has to do with program development and implementation. Its purpose is program improvement (McDermott & Sarvela, 1999). Process evaluation might be conducted during the formative stage of the program. **Summative evaluations** are generally associated with program impacts and outcomes. The specific types of evaluation match the major types of objectives: process, impact, and outcome.

Process Evaluation

In Chapter 7 we defined process as "a series of actions or behaviors resulting in an end." Evaluation of process measures how well the program fulfills the process objectives. A sample process objective evaluation might read, "Did program participants feel that the content of the program met their personal needs?"

Can you see how important it is to write careful *program* objectives? Your evaluation will be directly related to those objectives.

Impact Evaluation

As we said earlier, *impact* refers to aspects of health that change more quickly than health outcomes. Some examples include knowledge levels, weight, and number of cigarettes smoked in a day. Sometimes health determinants or behaviors are both impacts (short-term) or outcomes (long-term) of health programs. If you choose to conduct an impact evaluation, the short-term program effects will be measured and analyzed.

Outcome Evaluation

A health outcome generally deals with determinants of health, such as blood pressure, or health behaviors, such as smoking, rather than health in a broader sense. Health determinants and behaviors can be measured. If you choose an outcome evaluation, the long-term program effects will be measured and analyzed.

THE EVALUATION PLAN

Like the program itself, the evaluation process must have a plan. It should include the procedures you will follow in order to conduct an effective evaluation of the program. The steps in an evaluation plan include, but are not limited to, the following:

1. Writing objectives
2. Developing a study design
3. Creating a timeline
4. Establishing a budget
5. Selecting instruments
6. Identifying data-analysis strategies
7. Identifying implementation plans
8. Determining report style

Writing Objectives

The evaluation plan will have its own objectives. When you think of objectives as road maps, it is easier to understand why you might want to develop objectives that are specific to the evaluation. Your evaluation objectives will be directly related to the program objectives. Imagine that your program objective stated "During the year, the knowledge level of teen mothers regarding safety issues will increase by 25% as a result of four programs presented by the staff health educator at the public health department." Can you identify the objective type? If you said impact, you are absolutely correct. Your evaluation objective will be linked to the program objective, so it might state "Measure the percentage of change in knowledge that occurs between pre- and posttests among women who attend the four safety programs at the community center."

You will have evaluation objectives that link to each of your program objectives and perhaps a few more. You may want to include participant perceptions of the program even if there is no related program objective. After all, regardless of whether the first program was effective (Chapter 7), if participants didn't like it, the word will probably spread and attendance at future programs might be influenced.

Establishing a Budget and Creating a Timeline

The evaluation part of your program should have a separate budget. The steps for developing this budget are the same as those used in the program budgeting: selecting the categories, determining the evaluation phases, estimating costs, documenting in-kind contributions, allowing for contingencies, and calculating the total funding needed. The categories for your evaluation budget will be very similar to those in the program budget. See Table 9.1 for a budget specific to an evaluation project.

TABLE 9.1   Sample Evaluation Budget

Budget Item	Description	Total Cost
Personnel		
Health educator	960 hours $23/hr	$22,080
Secretary	800 hours $14/hr	$11,200
Subtotal		$33,280
Personnel benefits	20% of wages	$ 6,656
Total personnel		$39,936
Supplies		
Printing	100,000 × .04	$ 4,000
Postage	20,000 × .33	$ 6,600
Office supplies		$ 500
Total supplies		$11,100
Services		
Telephone	$150/month	$ 1,800
Total services		$ 1,800
Consultants		
Data processing	25 hours $12/hr	$ 300
Graphic artist	16 hours $25/hr	$ 400
Total consultants		$ 700
Contingencies		$ 500
Total contingencies		$ 500
Indirect costs	15% of total	$ 8,105
Total costs		**$62,141**

A separate timeline for the evaluation will be helpful as well. See Figure 9.1 for a Gantt chart specific to evaluation.

Developing a Study Design

Your plan should include each of the several activities that must take place in the design step of the evaluation. The individuals (program participants) who will be involved in the evaluation must be identified or selected. This group of individuals is called a *sample* from the population (all people in the target audience). The types of evaluation must be identified (process, impact, or outcome), and the methods for conducting the evaluation must be determined. For example, should the program be evaluated through interviews, focus groups, or even clinical tests? As you have learned from other chapters, there are many ways in which information can be collected. Let's discuss some of them in relation to program evaluation.

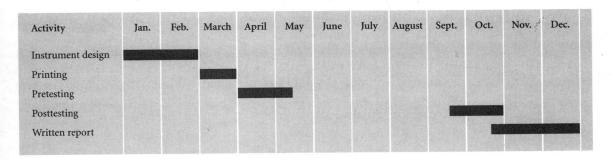

Activity	Jan.	Feb.	March	April	May	June	July	August	Sept.	Oct.	Nov.	Dec.
Instrument design	▬	▬										
Printing			▬									
Pretesting				▬	▬							
Posttesting									▬	▬		
Written report											▬	▬

FIGURE 9.1   Gantt chart for evaluation portion of your program.
Projecting your timeline for the evaluation of your program is just as important as
scheduling program assessment, planning, and implementation. This Gantt chart is
a sample timeline for an evaluation project.

Using Quantitative Data in Evaluation   The ultimate goal of program evaluation, in most cases, is to prove that a specific program causes the effect that we
wish it to. For example, you would probably want to prove that your objectives
were fulfilled as a result of the program you planned for teen mothers. Only one
type of evaluation can prove that a program causes a change. We discussed this
design in Chapter 3 as an experimental study design. If you will remember, it was
the only design in which cause and effect, in relation to disease and agent, could
be demonstrated. The design works in a similar fashion when used in evaluation.
It demonstrates cause and effect in relation to program and behavior change.

*Why is an experi-
mental design neces-
sary to prove cause?*

If you select an experimental design for your evaluation you will need to identify the individuals who will be part of the evaluation with great care. In fact, you
will *randomly select* the individuals who will participate and then *randomly assign*
them to one of two groups, control or intervention. If you will remember, random selection means giving every person in the population the same chance to be
selected for the study; computer programs can be used to ensure randomness.
Random assignment means that once in the study all participants will have equal
chances to be put in the study or the control group. An **intervention** is the program itself or one aspect of it that you would like to study. If you use an experimental design, the two groups of people will be receiving different programs, or
at least one part of the program will be different. In some cases the control group
will not receive any type of intervention.

The specific behavior that you hope your participants will change is called a
dependent variable in an experimental design. The dependent variable will be
measured in both groups of people (those who received the intervention and
those who did not) at two times (before and after the intervention). The degree
to which each group changed their behavior will be compared. You hope that the
group who received your program will have the best results in changing their behavior. A sample evaluation objective for which you might use an experimental
design would be "Participants in the 1-year teen mothers program, presented

by and at the public health department, will score 20% higher on the knowledge scale than control participants."

If the experiment has been carefully conducted, you will be able to say that your program made a difference. If a program truly causes the effect desired, it is said to have **internal validity** (McDermott & Sarvela, 1999). In a carefully designed experiment (one that uses random selection and assignment), you can also claim **external validity** (results can be generalized to other people in the population).

You will have to determine if the experimental design is feasible for your evaluation project. Will you really be able to have two different programs (intervention and control)? Will you be able to make certain that the participants in each group don't talk with one another and contaminate the results? Will there be factors in the community that influence one group of participants but not the other? Experimental designs are not easy; but, even so, we encourage you to strive for the best whenever possible.

Some evaluation designs that are weaker but have potential include one-shot case studies, one-group pretest/posttest designs, and static group comparisons. In the **one-shot case study,** a group that has been involved in a program intervention is posttested only. If you selected this type of intervention, you would want the behavior of interest to be positive after the program. Can you see the flaws in this design? There are many reasons, other than the program, for the behavior to be positive. The program participants might have had positive behaviors before the program even began. Something else, like a TV show or movie, might have precipitated a change in behavior. You would never really know if your program was responsible for the positive behavior.

A pretest is added in the **one-group pretest–posttest design** (McDermott & Sarvela, 1999). In this design, you would be able to measure changes in the behavior after the program was conducted, but you would still not be able to say with certainty that the program itself was responsible for the change. Can you see why? Again, something in the community might have influenced the change.

If two groups will be compared, what problems occur if they aren't pretested?

In the **static group comparison,** you would be able to measure differences in the behavior after the program because two groups are posttested. Only one group has received the program, and neither has been pretested. Once again, you can't be certain that changes are due to the program. The two groups might have been different before they even started. Look at Figure 9.2 for pictorial representations of the quantitative study designs presented.

Using Qualitative Data in Evaluation   Not all data can be quantified; so qualitative studies are used to evaluate some programs. Qualitative designs include focus groups, the Delphi method, interviews, and observation.

FOCUS GROUPS   As you know from Chapter 6, in a *focus-group* design, a small group of people is asked to participate in a discussion. Questions are developed

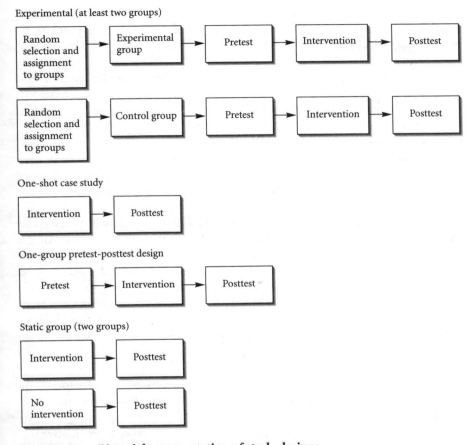

FIGURE 9.2   Pictorial representation of study designs.
Many types of study designs exist and often two or more types of designs will be used in one evaluation project. This figure describes four types of designs.

prior to the discussion and participant comments are audiotaped or recorded in some fashion. A trained facilitator (sometimes called monitor) is present to keep the discussion moving, but this individual does not give opinions or participate in the discussion, other than to clarify what others have said. A second person serves as the recorder so that the facilitator can focus on the process of the discussion. Any number of focus groups can be conducted as long as different people participate in each group.

A difficult issue in a focus-group design is determining who will participate. Will you try to get everyone who has participated in the program to be in a focus group? If there were a large number of people in the program, will you randomly select a few to participate or will you simply invite volunteers? Your decisions will be based on your evaluation objectives, your timeline, and your budget. Keep in mind that if you want a representative sample, you should include all participants or randomly select some of them.

DELPHI TECHNIQUE   You also read a brief description of the *Delphi technique* in Chapter 6. It is another group design, but participants do not meet face-to-face. It is generally used for decision making or consensus building (Raskin, 1974), which can be important evaluation processes if you are trying to determine the value of a health education program.

If you decide to use the Delphi technique, you will need to identify criteria for being included in the study. Your respondents are usually experts in the type of program you are delivering. They will need to commit some time to the study because they will take part in several rounds of surveys.

Round 1 is used for collecting baseline data. Participants will be asked to respond to one or more open-ended questions about their perceptions of the program benefits and weaknesses. When the surveys are returned, you take the responses and put them in a Likert format (items that require a rating). In round 2 participants are asked to respond to the Likert scale. When those surveys are returned, you place the items that have the highest levels of agreement in a list. During round 3 participants rank the items. You then identify the items that are most frequently ranked the highest. Your objective is to see consensus building in the group. A fourth round may be necessary to complete the process.

INTERVIEWS   As you are probably aware by now, *interviews* may be formal or informal, simple or complex. If you select this evaluation design, you might use the same set of questions for all interviewees or you might simply ask people to tell you what they thought of the program. As with other types of qualitative designs, you will have to make decisions about who will be interviewed. Use your evaluation plan as your guide.

OBSERVATION   Like an interview, an *observation* might be formal or informal, simple or complex. An observer might have specific things to look for or might note anything and everything seen. If you select this evaluation method, you will have to decide whether the individuals whom you are observing will be told. People who know they are being observed might change their behavior without even thinking about it. This is called **observer effect.** You will also need to be aware of your own biases. Unless you are careful, your beliefs and attitudes will be reflected in your observation (**observer bias**).

Surveys   *Surveys* can be used in both quantitative and qualitative designs. The type of item or question will determine the kind of data collected. Open-ended items elicit qualitative data, while multiple-choice questions and Likert scales, for example, elicit responses that can be quantified. Surveys are very versatile: They can be used with large or small samples, and they can be conducted over the telephone, through the postal system, in a face-to-face setting, or via e-mail.

As with other evaluation designs, you will have to make decisions about identifying participants. One of the most difficult issues with surveys, however, is determining their appropriateness for your project. For example, surveys that collect information about behaviors, beliefs, and attitudes often use self-report responses. In other words, you are measuring the participants' perceptions, which might not match up with reality. If self-report isn't appropriate for your project, you will want to use another technique, such as an actual observation of behaviors.

Instruments

The instruments used in data collection must be selected, adjusted, and sometimes written. Instrument selection or development should be viewed as an integral part of the evaluation process. If the instrument is medical equipment, for example, it must have protocols (specific procedures) for clinical measurements. The instrument might also be paper-and-pencil questionnaires or surveys.

Developing an instrument is a time-consuming and difficult process. As a result, you might tend to develop evaluation objectives based on available instruments rather than on the program objectives. We agree that every attempt should be made to find an existing instrument that is appropriate; but, if it is not possible, we encourage you to use appropriate development techniques. Let's discuss instrument development as we discuss estimating validity and reliability. Figure 9.3 illustrates a six-step process for instrument development.

Establishing the Framework   Establishing a framework for an instrument is like building a foundation for a house. You need to decide on the best material and style for the foundation. In the case of instrument development, you might choose a theoretical base. If so, a health behavior or learning theory will guide the development process. For example, if social cognitive theory is your foundation, your program and the evaluation will evolve from the theory. One construct in the theory is self-efficacy. One of your program activities, and therefore your evaluation, might focus on this construct. You might also choose criteria for your foundation. Perhaps program participants must achieve a standard set of behaviors (criteria). If so, the evaluation instrument would be guided by these criteria. The good news for you as an evaluator is that you will keep the same framework used during program development. If theory guided the program development, then it will also guide the evaluation.

Developing a Skeleton   You begin by developing a first draft of your instrument. You might start by using an open-ended type of questionnaire that elicits participants' beliefs (Ajzen & Fishbein, 1977); you can talk with individuals who

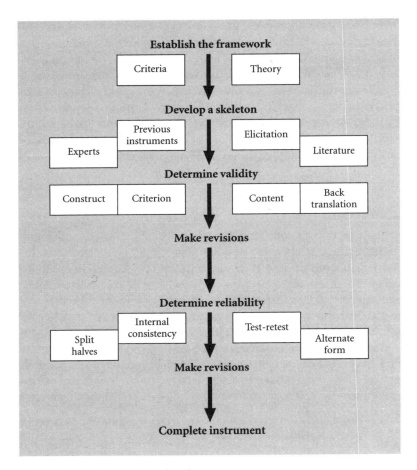

FIGURE 9.3   Instrument development.
Instrument development is a complete task that requires many steps. This illustration provides a model for instrument development.

are expert in the measurement of your behavior of interest; and you can review existing literature for suggested forms and formats.

Special attention must be given to both the format and wording of each item during initial drafting. The difficulty lies in creating items that accurately represent the psychosocial variables of interest (such as attitudes, perceptions, and beliefs) and are appropriate for the target population's culture and local dialect. You will want to search the literature for scale items previously used and adapt those items, if necessary, to the proposed study. Be sure to consider the cultural appropriateness of both the items and the instrument as a whole.

Imagine that you are asked to evaluate a teen pregnancy program that was based on the health belief model. The purpose of one part of the program might have been to increase the likelihood that the teen mothers would select safe ways to discipline their children. You might measure their perceptions of how likely they are to choose inappropriate discipline and their perceptions of the availability of professional services. It will take a certain amount of effort on your part to select the best vocabulary for measuring components of the health belief model, specifically perceptions of susceptibility. You will have to search the literature for an existing instrument. If there is no existing instrument, you will need to find one that was used in a similar situation and adjust it. Once you have developed the skeleton format, estimating validity is the next step.

Instrument Validity   Determining instrument validity begins with attention to the brevity and clarity of the instrument. Establishing instrument brevity and clarity is particularly complicated when cultural sensitivity of the instrument is a priority. Brislin's (1986) guidelines for writing and modifying instrument items suggest using short, simple sentences of less than 16 words. This is no easy task when you should also repeat nouns instead of using pronouns, avoid metaphors and colloquialisms that could shorten the wording, and add sentences and phrases where needed to provide cultural context for key ideas. Only through target community involvement in instrument development can you be sure that the instrument is sufficiently brief and effectively clear.

Once brevity and clarity have been examined, you will want to consider four major types of validity: criterion-related validity, content validity, construct validity, and back translation.

CRITERION-RELATED VALIDITY   When the scoring of an instrument yields results similar to actual observation of the behavior, the instrument is said to have **criterion-related validity.** For example, imagine that a parental discipline survey was developed as an easy way to measure the quality of a teen mother's discipline behaviors. It would have criterion-related validity if it gave the same estimate of discipline quality as did an actual observation of a teen mother disciplining her children. The observed behavior is the criterion. The process requires a statistical procedure called a *correlation* to determine if a relationship exists between a score received on the instrument and a score on the actual performance of the behavior. The resulting number is called a *validity coefficient.* The validity coefficient can range from −1 to +1. For most instruments, you should look for a moderate to high correlation (ranging between .65 and 1) before you use it.

CONTENT VALIDITY   If the instrument accurately reflects an area or domain of knowledge, it has **content validity.** For example, the quality-of-discipline survey would have content validity if it used the word *discipline* and other concepts appropriately. In most cases, no specific, well-defined criteria exist from which to measure content validity. Most evaluators rely on experts in the field to assess it. You would ask a panel of individuals, experts in parental discipline choices, to review the instrument and suggest changes that would make the content stronger.

This practice has merit as long as the people you choose truly have expertise in the content.

CONSTRUCT VALIDITY   The extent to which an instrument reflects its theoretical base is a measure of **construct validity** (Nunnaly, 1978). Construct validation is not a matter of rapid assessment. Much research in using the instrument and follow-up analysis are required. *Factor analysis* (a statistical procedure) may provide you or your statistician with useful information about your theoretically based instrument. This statistical procedure should be used only in combination with expert knowledge of the constructs to be measured to prevent misconceptualization. Individuals with expertise in the theoretical construct being measured are normally asked to assist in establishing the construct validity of an instrument. You will want to establish a second panel of individuals (experts in the health belief model) to review your instrument and suggest changes that would help it reflect the theory in a stronger way. It is important to note that professionals evaluating the construct validity of an instrument may not be familiar with the cultural norms and local dialect of the targeted population. Thus, an instrument thought to be construct-valid could be virtually ineffective if a word distorted meaning within the targeted cultural context.

Plan to involve members of the target culture in your instrument development. The ideal is to enlist the help of health professionals who are familiar with the construct to be measured and who understand the culture and local dialect. When this isn't possible, a combined group effort should include both construct and cultural experts.

BACK TRANSLATION   An instrument designed for one cultural setting and used in a slightly different culture may cause the evaluator to miss aspects of the second culture that are important to the overall picture. The resulting conclusions might then be based on concepts that are nonexistent within the targeted culture or at least partially incorrect. Thus, existing instruments should be used only after modifications are made to fit the specific culture and research situation (Brislin, 1986).

A popular method for validating a translated instrument is called **back translation** (Brislin, 1986). If you choose to have your instrument translated into another language, one bilingual individual translates from the source language to the target language. Another bilingual person then translates the resulting target-language version back to the source language. This process may be repeated several times and the first and last source-language versions compared. If the major concept survives the activity, it is regarded as *etic* (that is, readily available words and phrases exist in the two languages that facilitate concept translation). If the concept does not survive, it is *emic,* or expressible in only the source language.

In addition to its use when two languages are involved, the back-translation process can be used to modify an instrument to the popular jargon of a community. In this instance you would ask "bilingual" translators who understand both the local jargon and the terminology used in the original instrument to be involved in the process.

Selection of bilingual translators is a critical first step in the back-translation process. The ideal is to choose translators who are members of the targeted culture and are keenly familiar with the cultural norms and local dialect of the targeted group. They must also clearly understand the original instrument language and the constructs it is intended to measure. These translators must have an ability to focus on the clear communication of concepts rather than the literal translation of words and phrases. The degree to which they understand both the original instrument and the targeted culture will affect their ability to find target-language equivalents without having to use unfamiliar terms (Brislin, 1986; Feldman & Hollander, 1993; Segall, 1993).

Finding translators who meet the necessary criteria is seldom easy and the ideal is rarely achieved. Translators with differing levels and types of expertise can work as a team. Potential sources are trained professional translators identified by community gatekeepers, health professionals, or university researchers experienced in working with the population as well as members of the cultural group who are studying in a university health program. Because few bilingual individuals are trained translators, a team approach may be more effective.

The results of the back-translation process may seem inconsistent with the original instrument. The critical question to ask in this situation is whether (1) the original instrument concepts survived the process while words and phrases changed or (2) the original concepts were lost in the process. Bringing the translators together with the evaluator to discuss this issue is critical. If the group concedes that the concepts remained intact, the translated instrument is now ready to be subjected to further validation procedures for readability and understandability within the targeted culture. However, if the targeted concept was lost in the process, the evaluator should return to the original instrument. It may be helpful to reword the original following Brislin's guidelines and present the altered version to a new set of translators. Another alternative would be to work with the original translators to create items in the targeted language that do reflect the targeted construct. The resulting instrument can then be further validated.

The rigorous process of back translation cannot fully guarantee that resulting scales will be culturally appropriate. Further work is necessary to validate its utility within the targeted culture. This work includes testing the instrument for readability and understandability with a subsample of the targeted population.

Reliability   Although there are many statistical procedures from which to choose, you might choose one of four basic statistical methods for estimating instrument **reliability** (the instrument's consistency from one testing time to another), including test-retest, split halves, alternate form, and internal consistency.

The test-retest method uses a correlation to document a relationship between scores on the same test after a period of approximately 2 weeks. A weakness of this method, specific to it, involves a memory effect. Individuals retesting may remember their previous answers, and this may result in an overestimation of the reliability of the instrument.

The alternate- or equivalent-form method uses two testing situations (different forms of the same test) given after a period of approximately 2 weeks. A correlation of scores provides a number called the *reliability coefficient.* A weakness for any method using two testing sessions is that true changes in the concept or behavior being measured may decrease the estimated reliability of the instrument.

A split-halves determination can be completed in one testing situation. A correlation between the two halves of an instrument (such as odd-numbered items and even-numbered items) provides the reliability coefficient for each half of the instrument independently.

Internal consistency, normally computed with a statistical procedure called a *Cronbach's alpha,* can also be completed in one testing situation. Internal consistency involves using an item-to-total correlation. Weak items will have a low correlation. A weakness with this method is a possible underestimation of the reliability of the instrument.

A final instrument passes through many stages and revisions. Be sure to include both experts and members of the target audience in the instrument-development process. Once you have developed your instruments, you will be ready to take action.

Implementation

The evaluation plan must include the implementation phase in which the evaluation is conducted. If surveys were selected as the method for collecting data, they would be completed and the data would be coded and analyzed (usually by computer). Coding is a way of preparing data for analysis. A simple example of coding would be assigning a 1 if the participant is a male and a 2 if the participant is a female. The data-analysis software interprets the meaning of the codes.

Data Analysis

When you hear the word statistics *what comes to mind?*

Quantitative Analysis   Sometimes the word *statistics* is used to mean a numerical description of an event such as the frequency of accident-related deaths or incidents of violence in schools. At other times, the word indicates mathematical procedures that are used to test hypotheses (statements of belief or assumptions) or determine reliability and validity.

These two uses of the word *statistics* actually describe two broad categories of statistics: descriptive and inferential. **Descriptive statistics** count and organize data (Kuzma, 1998). You will probably use descriptive statistics in many different ways in your career. Figure 9.4 will help you review ways in which to display descriptive data.

Inferential statistics are used to make comparisons, identify relationships, and draw conclusions about data. It is impossible for us to discuss these tests in enough detail in this chapter; but, if you have not done so already, we encourage you to take a full course in basic statistics so that you can select the best ways to organize and analyze your quantitative data.

Qualitative Analysis   This type of data cannot be represented well with numbers. Conversations, interviews, focus-group discussions, and open-ended survey responses or descriptions of observations are analyzed for patterns or commonalities in meaning. A system of coding is used in qualitative analysis as well as in quantitative but it may involve symbols rather than numbers.

Let us look at an example of qualitative data that might have been collected during our program for teen mothers. Imagine that we asked participants to complete a survey with questions related to their satisfaction with the program. On the survey, one item asked them to describe what they liked about the program. One person wrote, "This program was fun because people I knew were in it with me." Another person wrote, "I really liked this program because I got to go with my friends." Do you see the pattern in the two responses? Both comment about the social aspect (friends or people I know) as a reason for liking the program. You would examine all of the responses for similar patterns in a qualitative analysis. You will not generalize to a larger population of teens as a result of qualitative analysis. In other words, you would not be able to say that all teens will like the program because they are encouraged to come with friends or people they know, but you would be able to say that a common theme among teens that attend the program is the social aspect.

The Evaluation Report

The reporting phase of evaluation may give the appearance of being the easiest, but it can be difficult and time-consuming. Be sure to give it plenty of time. In this phase, the meaning behind the evaluation must be defined and clearly written. In other words, the "so what" must be articulated.

When you write your evaluation report, you must summarize the evaluation activities and express the conclusions that can be drawn from the results. The evaluation report, which is generally prepared at the end of the project, is substantial and formal. According to the National Science Foundation (1997), the evaluation report must consider the following questions:

1. How should the communication best be tailored to meet the needs and interests of a given audience?

Poliomyelitis immunization status of children age 1–4 in central cities
(pop. ≥ 250,000) by financial status, United States, 1969

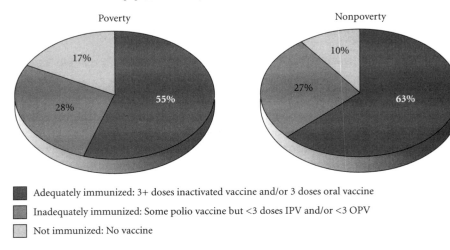

FIGURE 9.4   Displaying descriptive statistics.
Descriptive statistics can be illustrated for your participants or in your reports in a
number of ways. These illustrations provide some examples. Careful thought should
be given to the types of charts or graphs you select so that your results can be clearly
understood. From Descriptive Statistics: Table, Graphs, and Charts, USDHHS, 1980, Atlanta, GA:
Centers for Disease Control.

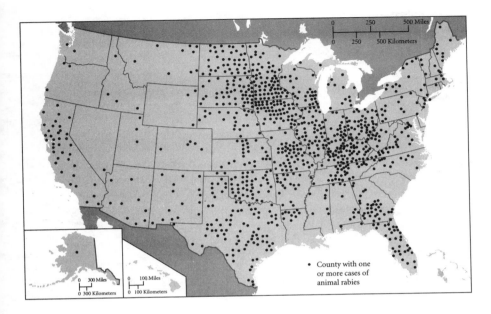

Counties reporting one or more cases
of animal rabies, United States, 1968

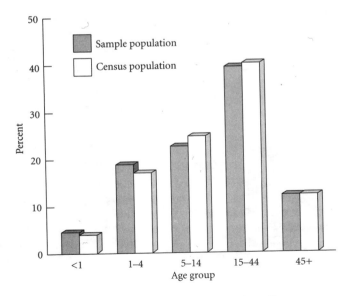

Percent of age distribution of sample population compared to percent of age
distribution of census population immunization survey, sample city, 1970

FIGURE 9.4   **Displaying descriptive statistics.** *(continued)*

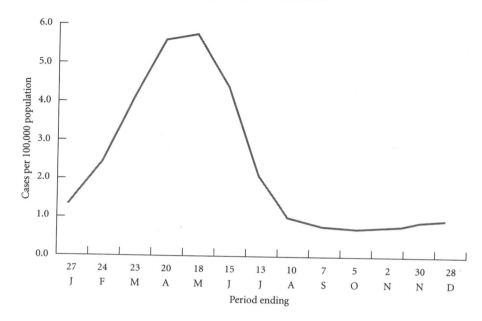

Reported rubella case rates by 13
four-week periods, United States, 1968

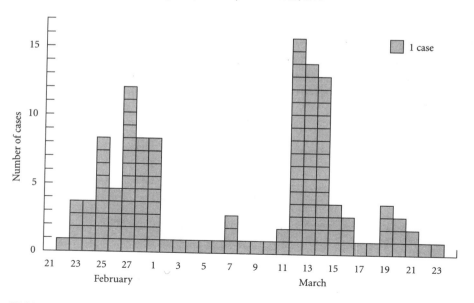

Cases of rash illness, elementary school
sample city, February 22–March 23, 1970

FIGURE 9.4   Displaying descriptive statistics. *(continued)*

2. How should the comprehensive final report be organized? How should the findings of qualitative and quantitative methods be integrated?
3. Does the report distinguish between conclusions based on quantitative data and those that are more speculative?
4. Where findings are reported, especially those likely to be considered sensitive, have appropriate steps been taken to make sure that promises of confidentiality are met?

Determining Audience Needs   In response to the first question, you might decide that the individuals reading the report will need detailed enough information to repeat the program in exactly the same way. If this is the case, each phase of the evaluation must be clearly detailed and thoughtful conclusions prepared. On the other hand, perhaps the audience for the report will be the press. They may be interested primarily in a summary of results and conclusions. This type of report might be shorter but no less thought-out. You might be called on to do both types of report.

Organizing the Report   In general, most reports include some background information, the evaluation objectives, the data-collection methods, a description of data analysis, a listing of the results, and a discussion of conclusions. The report should be well written and interesting to read. If you have used mixed evaluation methods, you will want to include comments and observations as well as statistics. Be sure to proofread, revise, and proofread again. Small errors can detract from the important message you want to give.

Formulating Conclusions   We hope you will consider this section of the report carefully. If your audience is in a hurry, the conclusions will be the focus of their reading. The National Science Foundation (1997) makes the following suggestions for writing the conclusions section of your report:

1. Distinguish carefully between conclusions that are based on quantitative data and those that are more speculative. The best strategy is to start the conclusions section with material that has undergone thorough verification and to place the more subjective speculations toward the end.
2. Provide full documentation for all findings where available. Data-collection instruments, descriptions of the study subjects, specific procedures followed for data collection, survey response rates, refusal rates for personal interviews and focus-group participation, access problems, and the like should all be discussed in an appendix. If problems were encountered that may have affected the findings, possible biases and attempts to correct them should be discussed.
3. Use the recommendations section to express observations and suggestions based on the total project experience. Of course, references to data should be included whenever possible. For example, a recommendation

in the report for the hypothetical project might include the following phrase: "Future programs should provide career-related incentives for faculty participation, as was suggested by several participants." But the evaluator should also feel free to offer creative suggestions that do not necessarily rely on the systematic data collection. (p. 6)

Maintaining Confidentiality   A basic step in maintaining confidentiality is to ask participants to consent to being part of the evaluation. Of course, you will want participants to feel free to say no. They will not feel that confidence has been broken if they understand the evaluation process and how the information you collect will be reported.

It will be important for you to minimize the risks your participants will face. Risks include those that are physical in nature as well as psychological. For example, if you are asking questions that your participants will find embarrassing, they are at psychological risk. If you report something about them that others recognize, you are putting them at psychological risk. If you ask them to do something that could cause injury, that puts them at physical risk. It is up to you to protect them.

When you write your report, present data for a group rather than results specific to individuals. If you are presenting specific comments or observations, do not use identifying information if you can avoid doing so. If a participant can be identified, get permission first. Just remember to be honest, respect your participants, and act with integrity.

IN CONCLUSION

The best health education programs are developed with evaluation in mind. We hope you will take your programs through rigorous process, impact, and outcome evaluations. The instruments you select will need to be valid and reliable.

When you create your evaluation plan, pay special attention to writing your objectives. They should be directly linked to the program objectives. You will also need to create a timeline and budget specific to the evaluation.

You will decide if an experimental design is feasible and determine which qualitative procedures, if any, will be used. We encourage you to use a mixed design (both quantitative and qualitative) in order to collect sound, rich, meaningful, and varied data. Plan your evaluation report as carefully as you have the rest of your process. The report will document your work.

REVIEW QUESTIONS

1. Give examples of process, impact, and outcome evaluations.
2. Describe the steps involved in developing an evaluation plan.
3. List and discuss the categories that might be used in an evaluation budget.

4. Select one type of qualitative design and discuss its strengths and weaknesses.
5. Describe the benefits of using an experimental design.
6. What are the steps in instrument development?
7. Define validity and reliability.
8. Describe the components that should be included in your evaluation report.

FOR YOUR APPLICATION

Creating an Evaluation Plan

In Chapter 7 we asked you to develop a goal and objectives for a program for teen mothers. Now it is time to use them in developing an evaluation plan. Follow the steps provided in this chapter.

FOR YOUR PORTFOLIO

Program Evaluation

1. Have your teacher review your evaluation plan and provide feedback.
2. Revise your plan according to the feedback provided.
3. Ask another health educator for feedback.
4. Revise your plan again.
5. Place a copy of the plan in your portfolio in a new section titled "Evaluation."

10

Coordinating Provision of Health Education Services

"BUT I THOUGHT YOU WERE GOING TO MAKE THOSE phone calls!" You try to keep the exasperation out of your voice, but this is just one of many similar conversations you've had lately. It seems as though no one involved in this new health education program knows what anyone else is doing. What was once a good program idea, both wanted and needed by the community, is becoming an organizational nightmare. You hang up the phone and say out loud "Where did I go wrong?" In desperation, you pull an old textbook off the shelf that you never thought you'd use and look up the term program coordination.

Chapter Objectives

1. Describe the process of cooperation and how to promote it.
2. Identify techniques for conflict resolution.
3. Compare and contrast community development and community organization.
4. List ways in which coalitions and partnerships can be developed.
5. Define *policy* and name its three components.
6. Describe the difference between procedural policy and public health policy.
7. Name four federal agencies that monitor public health policy.
8. Name at least one nongovernmental organization that focuses on public health policy.
9. Summarize the purpose and components of the Patients' Bill of Rights.
10. Describe the process of policy development.
11. Describe tips for making sound decisions about policy development.
12. Practice writing policies.

COOPERATION

Cooperation is a word most of us have heard since our early childhood, along with other phrases such as *play nicely, share, give in,* and *get along.* Most of us can probably remember a time when we were asked to cooperate, but felt that what we were really being asked to do was to give up some level of control and let some other person have her or his way. Because of those kinds of experiences, the idea of cooperation doesn't always excite people. Giving up control over something about which we feel strongly can be a real challenge. However, most of us can also recall a time when we received help from someone else because that person was willing to cooperate. It's a good feeling when you experience one of those rare partnership efforts that truly benefits everyone involved. It usually happens in an atmosphere of cooperation.

Promotion of Cooperation

So what is cooperation? Is it really giving control to another person and following his or her lead? According to *Merriam-Webster's Collegiate Dictionary* (10th ed., 1999), to cooperate is "to act or work with another or others: act together" or "to associate with another or others for mutual benefit." To explore the meaning of cooperation more fully, consider for a moment two important phrases in these definitions. Those are "to act or work together/to associate" and "for mutual benefit."

If a group of people came together to build a small house, no thinking person would expect all members of the group to have the same types of house-building skills and experience. After all, an electrician who could ably wire the house would not necessarily be well-versed in plumbing. Skilled plumbers aren't always good carpenters, and carpenters may know little about applying stucco, aluminum siding, or brick to the outside walls. But each set of knowledge and skills is needed for successful house building.

These differing skills would also likely be needed at different points in the building process. One wouldn't expect the plumbers and electricians to show up, for instance, until the foundation had been laid and the walls framed. If the roofers insisted on doing their job on the day the foundation was poured, we'd likely begin to worry about their competence. And, though each job would be important to the overall goal, each would likely differ from others in the length of time and amount of effort needed.

With so much diversity of effort and focus going on, how would the group be able to achieve any common goal—much less build an entire house? In most house-building efforts, a project foreperson or contractor coordinates the project. This person usually has a blueprint of the house that illustrates how all parts are to be constructed. The contractor uses the blueprints to coordinate individual efforts, constantly checking progress in light of the master house plan. And, because the contractor is the person most aware of the contribution of each group, a full understanding and appreciation of the abilities and efforts of each is paramount to project success.

What can we learn from this illustration about how cooperation works? The concepts are very basic. First, we know that cooperation happens when everyone contributes to the project. However, it is likely that different people must do different jobs at different times, paces, and levels of effort to achieve the common goal. Misperceptions among group members about what others are contributing can lead to jealousy and resentment. A mutual understanding of group-member expectations, from the beginning, is very important.

Second, we know that it helps to have a blueprint and a designated person (or group of people) responsible for coordinating the effort. This person may not necessarily complete individual tasks in the project. Nor does this person need extensive skills in all project task areas. However, the project coordinator should be someone who

- can maintain sight of the big picture and how each individual task fits
- is willing and able to maintain close contact with the project from start to finish
- has strong organizational, communication, and negotiation skills
- can respectfully interact with each project contributor in a positive way

Conflict Resolution

Why Conflict Occurs   Most of us tend to interpret the words and actions of others through the lenses of our personal values (Seelye & Seelye-James, 1996). When values and interpretations differ among individuals, misunderstandings can develop. Consider two highly qualified professionals who are collaborating on a project but have different perceptions about time and commitment. Ann tends to be task-oriented and believes that a committed professional always arrives on time. Ben highly values a cooperative approach and is less concerned about time constraints. Ann interprets Ben's late arrivals to meetings as a sign of low commitment. She decides to take a strong lead to ensure project success. Ben interprets Ann's independent decision making as controlling and aggressive. He stops attending meetings. Mistaken assumptions lead to conflict and the project flounders.

A difference in time orientation is one of the **silent value factors** that are seldom discussed but often contribute to conflict in collaborative efforts (Seelye & Seelye-James, 1996). Though such differences are often expected in cross-cultural situations, they can also influence interaction when no cultural differences are apparent. For example, using formal titles rather than first names may seem cold and distant to some people, whereas using first names can be insulting to others. Avoiding direct eye contact with a member of the other sex may seem respectful to some and devaluing to others. A lecture-based meeting presentation may appear to be the most efficient and logical approach but could cause some of your part-

FOR YOUR INFORMATION 10.1

Assess Your Time Orientation

Differences in time orientation (monochronic versus polychronic) are a common conflict factor. Understanding those differences can be a first step toward conflict resolution.

How monochronic are you?
- ☐ I like to do one thing at a time.
- ☐ I concentrate on the job at hand.
- ☐ I take time commitments (deadlines, schedules) seriously.
- ☐ I am committed to the job.
- ☐ I adhere closely to plans.
- ☐ I am concerned about not disturbing others (follow rules of privacy).
- ☐ I show great respect for private property (seldom borrow or lend).
- ☐ I emphasize promptness in meetings.
- ☐ I am comfortable with short-term relationships.

How polychronic are you?
- ☐ I like to do many things at once.
- ☐ I am highly distractible and frequently interrupt what I am doing.
- ☐ I consider time commitments more of an objective to be achieved, if possible, than a quasi-legal contract.
- ☐ I am committed to people and human relationships.
- ☐ I change plans often and easily.
- ☐ I put obligations to family and friends before work concerns.
- ☐ I consider intimacy with family and friends more important than respecting their privacy.
- ☐ I borrow and lend things often and easily.
- ☐ I base the level of promptness on the particular relationship.
- ☐ I have a strong tendency to build lifetime relationships.

From *Culture Clash: Managing in a Multicultural World* (pp. 25–26), by H. N. Seelye and A. Seelye-James, 1996, Lincolnwood, IL: NTC.

ners to suspect that you feel superior to the group and wish to control it. Understanding these potential differences is the first step to preventing conflict. Because time-orientation differences are a common conflict factor (Seelye & Seelye-James, 1996), we invite you to complete the checklists in FYI 10.1 as a beginning point.

Resolving Differences   How can you avoid conflict that is based on value differences and misinterpretations? Communicate. Communicate clearly by using a variety of written and oral formats. Communicate often by establishing ongoing channels through which information and perceptions are exchanged. Communicate unselfishly by listening as often, or perhaps more often, than you speak.

Communicate to understand. Communicate to problem-solve. Communicate to collaborate.

Communicate. But also keep in mind that, regardless of how hard you work as project coordinator to minimize the potential for conflict, it can still occur. Members of your coalition, task force, or advisory board may agree with the overall goals of the collaborative effort, but strongly differ when it comes to decisions about how to approach a task, the time frame in which it will happen, the location of task events, or who will be involved. What do you do when the cause of the conflict isn't miscommunication but rather disagreement about the process or expected outcomes? The first step is to gain an understanding of the cause of the conflict, what motivates each person involved to disagree.

People often become involved in conflict because they are stakeholders in relation to the argument issue. A **stakeholder** is a person or organization who will likely gain or lose something as a result of the targeted health problem and the efforts made to reduce it. In decision-making situations, most stakeholders are motivated at least in part by what they and the people they represent stand to gain or lose through the decision. That isn't necessarily a bad thing. A diverse representation of community stakeholders can serve as a healthy set of checks and balances in the decision-making process. The protected welfare of various community groups often depends on advocates who look out for their interests. It is likely, however, that some members of such a diverse decision-making group will disagree from time to time. When that happens, your goal as project coordinator will be to facilitate appropriate discussions and negotiations so that the project progresses and, to the extent possible, all groups benefit.

How strong are your negotiation skills? Have you ever attempted to resolve differences between people you care about? If so, you may have concluded at some point that at least one person seemed more interested in personal well-being than the good of all involved. Getting someone like that person to cooperate can be an intellectually and emotionally taxing task and you may have been tempted to use some choice adjectives such as *stubborn, selfish,* and *impossible* in the process.

If you've had a similar experience, you can probably relate to the dilemma some project coordinators face. The ideal is to resolve the conflict in a way that allows all parties involved to reach a mutually satisfying solution. FYI 10.2 contains suggestions for conflict resolution steps (Greenberg, 1999). The first one refers to a technique known as **active listening,** or **reflective listening.** In this technique, each person involved in the discussion is required to orally paraphrase or repeat back what was just said by the other person. The purpose of this exercise is for each person to focus on the thoughts and feelings of others rather than on his or her own personal reactions or interpretations. The person whose statement has been paraphrased is then given the opportunity to correct mistaken interpretations and expand further for deeper understanding.

In our example, Ann and Ben could use active listening to discuss their frustrations and seek conflict resolution. For instance, Ann might say "Ben, I don't

FOR YOUR INFORMATION 10.2

Steps Toward Conflict Resolution

Moving from conflict to resolution often requires a change in attitude and behavior.

From conflict . . .	. . . to resolution
Don't listen.	*Practice active listening.*
Be insensitive.	*Begin with agreement.*
Focus on winning.	*Brainstorm alternative solutions.*
Resist flexibility.	

From *Comprehensive Stress Management* (6th ed., pp. 96–102), by J. S. Greenberg, 1999, Boston: McGraw-Hill.

think you are really committed to this project and it frustrates me." Ben's reflective response could be "You don't think I care about the project? What makes you think that?" Ann might then launch into a description of how Ben is always late for meetings and doesn't seem to care about deadlines. At this point, Ben could respond in at least two different ways. He could abandon the active listening technique, become defensive, and react. On the other hand, he could take a deep breath and attempt to focus on Ann's reasoning and feelings rather than his own. In doing so, his response could be more reflective. "Ann, until now, I didn't realize that my 'late arrivals' irritated you. It isn't because I don't care. It's just that traffic holds me up. Besides, I've been thinking that you don't really want my input on this."

It would then be Ann's turn to paraphrase rather than react. A reflective response could be "Why do you think I don't want your input?" This would allow Ben to explain how hurt he felt when Ann moved ahead on decisions without him, and two mature professionals would have the opportunity to view the situation through the eyes of the other.

Their new appreciation for each other's perspective could then be applied in the next resolution step, finding mutual ground for agreement. In our example, both individuals agreed on the importance of the project, which implies that they share mutual goals. A return to common goals reminds individuals that they are partners rather than adversaries. Competition can then give way to flexible compromise in the third resolution step, brainstorming an alternative solution.

Because Ben and Ann share a common goal, they can compromise in their approach to reaching it. They might, for example, alter meeting schedules and locations to reduce Ben's traffic barriers. Ben could commit to leaving his home earlier and Ann could agree to be more flexible and work on other projects should Ben be late. The two could agree to identify and work toward important deadlines, but adopt a more flexible approach to less time-dependent tasks.

The individual strengths of each person could also be applied more effectively to different aspects of the project. Ben's polychronic strengths could be more effective in interacting with other people who were important to project success, while Ann might prefer to take on a greater responsibility for needed organizational aspects. The two could learn to trust each other more in these responsibilities, respect and appreciate the assets inherent in their differences, and communicate more freely to prevent future misunderstandings. The approach would not guarantee consistently smooth interaction, but effective collaboration could hardly occur without it. The same concepts of individual collaboration and conflict resolution can be applied to group and community settings. Although the processes become more complex in broader interactive settings, some of the same principles apply.

MODES OF COLLABORATION

Community Development

Think back for a moment to other chapters in this textbook in which we've discussed the definitions and roles of communities in health education. By now, you have had the opportunity to explore concepts of how individuals within a community form bonds driven by values, interests, needs, and capacities. We hope you have read those passages about how important it is to involve the community in the earliest stages of needs assessment and maintain participation throughout the phases of program planning, implementation, and evaluation. If so, you may have reached the same conclusion that many others in our profession hold: Community ownership of a health concern and community empowerment to create its own potential solutions are critical to success in community health education efforts.

If community ownership and empowerment are so important, can they be fostered? The answer is "yes and no." In answering this question, we will refer to the processes of community organization and community building. **Community organization** is "the process by which community groups are helped to identify common problems or goals, mobilize resources and, in other ways, develop and implement strategies for reaching the goals they collectively have set" (Minkler & Wallerstein, 1997, p. 241). **Community building** is "the ways in which people who identify themselves as members of a shared community engage together in the process of community change" (p. 241).

Did you note who is expected to instigate action in each of those definitions? The definition of community organization implies that someone other than the community members takes action to *help* the community do what is needed. Traditionally, that "helping someone" has included representatives of health agencies and outside organizations who identified health problems based on epidemiological data and then developed an organizational framework for the community project and guided community members through it (Minkler & Wallerstein, 1997).

In the definition of community building, however, the action is taken by the community members themselves. In its purest interpretation, community building isn't something you can do *to* or *for* a community. It is something that happens when community members engage on their own, using their own ideas and identifying their own strengths. Within this framework, it is the community members who decide on the health issue to be addressed and the steps to be taken (Minkler & Wallerstein, 1997).

Why do we point out these distinctions? What difference will it make in your community health education efforts? In many communities, integrating these distinctions into your attitude and health education approach can make all the difference in the world. If you are not a member of the community and are employed by an outside agency, you will likely be considered a community outsider. Because of mistreatment and exploitation in the past, members of some communities may not readily trust representatives of outside agencies and organizations. To some, the thought of your "empowering them" insultingly implies that, without your agency's help, the community has no power or abilities to solve its own problems. Picture a time when you resented another person trying to tell you how to live your life, and you will likely begin to understand how some community members must feel in these situations. The community-building concept must be integrated into your community organization efforts so that community members will be more likely to think "We're glad you're here" than "Who do you think you are?"

Some practical community building and organization suggestions are listed in FYI 10.3. Ideally, the best place to begin effective community building is with issues the community wants to address. This recalls our discussion of the PRECEDE/PROCEED model in which the health educator is encouraged to begin with a quality-of-life assessment. The types of concerns expressed by communities often involve quality-of-life issues. If you begin there, community members are more likely to involve themselves in your programs over the long term.

All your efforts should be based on one foundation: the notion that the community has at its disposal a variety of resources and abilities needed to address the problem. The goal is to help the community become aware of its existing competencies so that it can capitalize on existing strengths and rectify any existing competency gaps. **Capacity building** and **assets mapping** are terms used to describe how potential community resources, skills, and support networks can be identified and strengthened.

But, wait a minute! Didn't we tell you in an earlier chapter that the health problems you are hired to address will likely already be dictated by agency decisions and available grant money? How can you reconcile the need to target predesignated goals with what we've said here about beginning with community

FOR YOUR INFORMATION 10.3

Community Building and Organization Suggestions

Following these community building and organization suggestions can help a community identify its own health problems and potential solutions.

Support community issues.	Start where the community is and let community members make the decisions. Be a catalyst or facilitator of those decisions, not a decision maker.
Foster issue awareness.	Talk with various groups of community members to raise awareness levels. Offer ideas for how community members might convert concerns into action.
Expedite information collection.	Provide information about where to access resources. If needed, be willing to research information and pass it on to community members.
Develop community competence.	Identify natural leaders and helpers within the community. Help them identify and tap into their own networks of support. Encourage and support collective problem solving and resource development. Emphasize capacity building and assets mapping.
Advocate for the community.	In staff meetings or other settings in which community members are not present, speak on their behalf in a supportive, respectful manner.
Mediate when negotiation is needed.	When needed, help resolve differences between community stakeholders by emphasizing the mutual benefits of cooperation and negotiating mutually acceptable compromise to reach common goals.

Derived from *Community Health Education: Settings, Roles, and Skills for the 21st Century,* by D. J. Breckon, J. R. Harvey, and R. B. Lancaster, 1998, Gaithersburg, MD: Aspen; and "Improving Health Through Community Organization and Community Building," by M. Winkler and N. Wallerstein, 1997, in K. Glanz, F. M. Lewis, and B. K. Rimer, *Health Behavior and Health Education: Theory, Research, and Practice* (pp. 241–269), San Francisco: Jossey-Bass.

concerns? It is possible that the agency decision makers who set those targets are as aware as you of the need for community ownership and, before you were hired, set the wheels in motion for effective community partnerships. You should be able to learn a lot by talking to your superiors and co-workers, along with community members, to gain understanding about how decisions were made.

If you find that the community was not involved in the decision-making process, the concepts and methods of community organization and building should still be applied. You can begin by talking about the targeted health problem with various community groups and gatekeepers, along with representatives of other agencies and community health organizations. Ask for their perceptions about the extent of the problem and potential community-based solutions. If awareness of the problem is lacking, awareness-building messages can be disseminated through the media, town hall meetings, pamphlets, health fairs, presentations to organizations, and focus groups. The time and effort you invest to gain community support will be well worth it in the long run. Without it, your health education programs may be viewed in the community as just another come-and-go event that is best ignored.

Coalitions

Once community support is in place, there are other steps you can take to further develop community organization and foster community building. The asset-mapping and capacity-building efforts should help identify community agencies and organizations other than the one in which you work that could contribute to and benefit from collaborating on community health projects. Shared ideas and resources can streamline costs, reduce duplication, and improve the quality of resulting programs (Payne, 1999). For these reasons, we encourage you to consider forming a coalition.

A **health coalition** is an organized group of individuals who act on behalf of the agencies, organizations, and community subgroups they represent to collaboratively target a specific community health issue. Coalitions are often formally structured with written goals and designated responsibilities (Parker et al., 1998). They can be useful throughout all aspects of a community health effort, offering guidelines and resources for everything from needs assessment to program evaluation (Payne, 1999). It is important, however, that specific coalition tasks remain consistent with designated goals.

One way of using a coalition in an effective manner is to ask its members to brainstorm a list of immediate and long-range objectives and tasks that, if accomplished, can help the coalition meet its goals. For example, consider a fictitious coalition whose primary goal is to reduce the incidence of HIV infection among adolescents in the community. There are several different tasks or projects a coalition could initiate to help accomplish this goal. Among them could be a needs assessment to identify HIV/AIDS-related attitudes, knowledge, and risk behaviors among local adolescents; an HIV/AIDS awareness campaign through

List some of the tasks a coalition could initiate or support to reduce the incidence of HIV infection among adolescents in your community.

1. Carefully research the partner organization's stated/actual goals, activities, history, and reputation within the community.

2. Establish clear goals, expectations, and responsibilities. Verify them at all organizational levels.

8. Frequently celebrate accomplishments and express appreciation for partner contributions.

3. Establish clear channels for decision making, communication, task completion, and reporting.

Partnership development guidelines

7. Evaluate periodically to document progress, analyze/adjust methods, and monitor perceptions.

4. Distribute written meeting summaries and ask for feedback.

6. Meet regularly to communicate, trouble-shoot, and encourage.

5. Clearly delineate individual and group tasks, responsibilities, and deadlines.

FIGURE 10.1   Guidelines for establishing effective partnerships.
These guidelines can facilitate mutually beneficial outcomes.

local newspapers and radio and television stations; a telephone AIDS hotline to which adolescents could call to ask questions; and an HIV testing and referral program that adolescents could readily access. Each of these activities would match the coalition goal of reducing the incidence of HIV infection. Each could be carried out over time and, in some cases, simultaneously if varying clusters of coalition members served as leaders and members of subgroup task forces.

A coalition of this breadth would require careful coordination and consistent communication among coalition members. Each task force would need clearly communicated directives, specific objectives, and designated deadlines by which a particular task objective should be met. Consistent periodic coalition meetings, with task-force reports requested at each meeting, offer the accountability check needed to encourage progress. The person asked to coordinate this effort could be you.

Keep in mind that coalitions aren't always a good choice. Coalitions can help you accomplish more than you could within the capacity of your single agency and community contacts. However, coordinating a coalition usurps a large amount of time, energy, and resources. And barriers to progress can arise with coalitions if individual members push personal agendas or continue to react negatively to earlier problems with other coalition members. So, before you form one, carefully consider its usefulness and cost in light of your community's intended objectives. Invest the time needed to know all you can about potential coalition members and how they are viewed by the community before inviting them to the table.

Partnerships

In some instances, a coalition may be deemed less desirable than a simpler partnership established between your agency and a single community group or organization. The political lines and historical perspectives are often less complicated in these types of partnerships. Thus, progress on designated tasks can, in some ways, advance more quickly. However, the simpler partnership approach can also reduce the scope of what you are able to accomplish because you will have fewer resources and contacts.

A partnership with a community organization is a good place to start when the task you've been hired for can be adequately accomplished through the partnership capacities. You and your partner organization can establish clearly stated goals and objectives and initiate important tasks. Then, as the work progresses and the need for broader involvement arises, other groups can be invited to join in your well-established efforts. The guidelines in Figure 10.1 can help you establish a strong partnership from the beginning.

THE ROLE OF POLICY IN SERVICE COORDINATION

When was the last time you heard someone mention the word *policy* in a conversation? You might have been in a department store attempting to return some merchandise. Or you could have been in your supervisor's office asking why changes couldn't be made. If you've ever been told you couldn't do something because it would violate a policy, you may be tempted to think the purpose of any policy is to make life difficult. Yet, despite occasional frustrations, most of us recognize that, when needed, a carefully developed and applied policy has its merits.

Policy Defined

Green and Kreuter (1999) defined **policy** as "the set of objectives and rules guiding the activities of an organization or administration" (p. 190). This definition is relatively easy to use because it touches on two important characteristics of a policy: rules and objectives.

Procedural Policy An organization's **procedural policy** is the set of rules and regulations by which an institution or organization operates. Procedural policy serves as a guideline for *how* things are accomplished. For example, suppose you worked in a hospital patient education program and had a great idea for a health education program you'd like to develop for the hospital's employees. How would you go about gaining permission to develop it? And, if permission were granted, what do you think would be the rules about using hospital time versus your own time to work on it? Where would you go to gain access to supplies and other resources? Who would need to see memos about its development and who would sign off on important papers and contracts? The answers to such questions would depend on organizational regulations, the procedural policies that guide such things as how decisions are made, resources are requisitioned, tasks are accomplished, and reports are disseminated.

Procedural policies often only focus on how tasks are to be accomplished. They don't always explain why the task should be initiated in the first place. Examining the reason for the task or health program takes us back to the policy definition provided by Green and Kreuter (1999), which includes organizational objectives as part of a policy's driving force. Adding an objective component to the definition creates a more complete perspective on policies and policy development. Objectives that are clearly stated in an organization's written policies help justify the health services and promotion programs provided by that organization. They help organizational decision makers stay on track as they make choices about what they will do and for whom it will be done.

Public Health Policy   Developing policy to help decision makers stay on track also works at the national level. Many national initiatives to enhance the well-being of U.S. citizens begin as national policies. National policies do not have to be health-specific to have an impact on our nation's health. Policies that affect housing, education, and crime control, for example, influence the health and well-being of U.S citizens.

FEDERAL POLICYMAKERS   However, specific components of the federal government are charged to direct and monitor health-specific policy development. As we have stated in previous chapters, the Department of Health and Human Services holds primary responsibility for national health services and initiatives in the United States. National health policies are largely generated and maintained within this organization through four important agencies. One of those, the Health Resources and Services Administration, directs health policy initiatives and service programs to underserved and special-needs populations, particularly through the Office of Minority Health and the Office of Rural Health Policy. The Centers for Disease Control and Prevention promote health policy as it relates to prevention initiatives for specific health issues, such as chronic disease prevention, environmental health, and injury prevention. The Health Care Financing Administration administers federal involvement in the Medicare and Medicaid programs and is responsible for policy development related to those programs.

The fourth agency, the Agency for Health Care Policy and Research, supports research and subsequent policy development that improves the quality of health care, reduces health care costs, and broadens health service access. The *Criteria for Evaluating Internet Health Information* (AHCPR, 1999) summarized in FYI 10.4 is an example of information provided in a policy paper published by that agency. Information about other agencies can be found in Appendix D.

FOR YOUR INFORMATION 10.4

Criteria for Evaluating Internet Health Information

The following criteria for evaluating Internet health information show examples of information provided in a policy paper.

Credibility   includes the source, currency, relevance or utility, and editorial review process for the information

Content   must be accurate and complete, and an appropriate disclaimer must be provided

Disclosure   includes informing the user of the purpose of the site, as well as any profiling or collection of information associated with using the site

Links   evaluated according to selection, architecture, content, and back linkages

Design   encompasses accessibility, logical organization (navigability), and internal search capability

Interactive   include feedback mechanisms and means for exchange of information among users

Caveats   clarification of whether site function is to market products and services or is a primary information content provider.

From *Criteria for Assessing the Quality of Health Information on the Internet—Policy Paper,* by Mitretek Systems Health Information Technology Institute, 1999. Retrieved May 24, 2000 from the World Wide Web: http://hitiweb.mitretek.org/docs/policy.html.

POLICIES AND THE LEGISLATURE   Public policies are often put into effect as a political law, ordinance, or resolution (Breckon, 1997). Ideas for legislated health policy initiatives can originate from a variety of sources, including members of Congress, the executive branch, committees, or special interest groups. Once introduced as a bill, a health-related policy initiative will be submitted to a legislative committee that will likely conduct hearings on the proposed bill and, subsequently, rewrite, amend, approve, or reject the bill. A bill that has been approved by a committee is then placed before the Senate or House of Representatives for consideration. A number of health agencies and organizations are actively involved in efforts to influence health policy legislation. In Chapter 12, we will explore this advocacy process in more detail.

The Patients' Bill of Rights

A current health policy concern that has received national attention is the concept of protecting patients' rights in relation to health care (Reardon, 1999). In 1998, President Clinton directed the Department of Health and Human Services and

FOR YOUR INFORMATION 10.5

Patients' Bill of Rights

The Patients' Bill of Rights focus on accessibility to quality health care among health care consumers.

1. Consumers have the right to receive accurate, easily understood information and some require assistance in making informed health care decisions about their health plans, professionals, and facilities.
2. Consumers have the right to a choice of health care providers that is sufficient to ensure access to appropriate high-quality health care.
3. Consumers have the right to access emergency health services when and where the need arises.
4. Consumers have the right and responsibility to fully participate in all decisions related to their health care.
5. Consumers have the right to considerate, respectful care from all members of the health care system at all times and under all circumstances.
6. Consumer must not be discriminated against in the delivery of health care services consistent with the benefits covered in their policy or as required by law based on race, ethnicity, national origin, religion, sex, age, mental or physical disability, sexual orientation, genetic information, or source of payment.
7. Consumers who are eligible for coverage . . . must not be discriminated against in marketing and enrollment practices based on race, ethnicity, national origin, religion, sex, age, mental or physical disability, sexual orientation, genetic information, or source of payment.
8. Consumers have the right to communicate with health care providers in confidence and to have the confidentiality of their individually identifiable health care information protected.
9. Consumers have the right to a fair and efficient process for resolving differences with their health plans, health care providers, and the institutions that serve them, including a rigorous system of internal review and an independent system of external review.

From *Report to the Vice President of the United States: Status of Implementation of the Consumer Bill of Rights and Responsibilities in the Department of Health and Human Services,* by U.S. Department of Health and Human Services, 1998 (November 2). Retrieved November 15, 1999, from the World Wide Web: http://aspe.os.dhhs./gov/health /vpreport.htm.

other federal agencies to comply with the Consumer or Patients' Bill of Rights (USDHHS, 1998c). As can be noted in FYI 10.5, these rights focus on accessibility to quality health care. There appears to be a growing sentiment that current managed health care initiatives are not working and that drastic measures are in order to return the power of health care decision making to the doctor and patient rather than health maintenance organizations (HMOs) (Online News-Hour, July–December 1999; Reardon, 1999). Current trends seem to favor the patients' rights movement; Congress passed a law in 1999 to allow patients to sue their HMOs in the event of being refused needed health care. In the wake of that legislation, some HMOs have voluntarily relinquished the health care decision-making power back to physicians (Online NewsHour, July–December 1999).

A number of nongovernment organizations and institutes keep watch on legislative health policy initiatives and attempt to keep the public informed of their own views. One of those, the National Center for Policy Analysis (NCPA, 1999) has recently analyzed and discussed the adequacy of the Patients' Bill of Rights, along with other health policy issues. It might be worth your while to visit the NCPA Web site and consider the viewpoint presented there. You can obtain a list of other policy-minded organizations by visiting the Web site of the National Center for Public Policy (see Appendix D).

The Process of Policy Development

National public health policies serve as guidelines for establishing health program priorities in the United States. For instance, laws that prohibit alcohol use among minors and national campaigns to prevent alcohol abuse are direct outcomes of public and health policies. But why do those specific policies exist and how were they developed?

Decision Making   The Healthy People 2000 and 2010 goals described in Chapter 1 are a product of national health policies. But why did the policy developers target the specific health problems described in those documents and not others? Health policies have historically been driven by economic, social, and political concerns (Ibrahim, 1985). Epidemiological statistics such as mortality and morbidity rates are often categorized by demographic characteristics (such as age, gender, ethnicity, and socioeconomic status) to identify groups at risk. The impact of existing health services and programs on the health status of these groups is also considered. And, in some instances, a politically influential figure can be instrumental in swaying policy decisions (Ibrahim, 1985). These three components (existing needs, current program impact, and available support) are important considerations in any effort to develop health policies.

Most new policies are developed because someone perceived a need for change. Perhaps you have recently benefited from a new university policy that expanded library operation hours. Why would university officials put such a policy in effect when they know it will cost more money? It is because they have considered you, their client, and have deemed it worth the expense and effort to meet your needs. But how did they know you needed those changes? We hope they didn't guess. The appropriate approach would have been to survey a representative sample of students to find out about library access needs and interests, consult with library administrators to assess their perceptions of need and feasibility, and test the newly designed service to observe the degree to which the change would make a difference. These actions would be taken before the proposed policy was officially enacted to ensure a *cost-effective* approach.

In the same manner, health policy development should be based on sound needs-assessment efforts and careful interpretation of the results. A scientific investigation into existing health status and needs in a population is the first critical component of policy development. Perceived needs among population members and the professionals who deliver health programs should be identified in this step.

Second, the availability of resources and the feasibility of being able to maintain the proposed policies must also be considered. The overwhelming list of needs within some communities can confuse policy developers. The goal is to develop policies that reflect a balanced perspective, one that considers actual and perceived needs in light of service feasibility.

This balanced perspective can then help you move to the third component of policy development, that of soliciting support from those who have the resources and political influence to assist with policy adoption. We will discuss this issue more fully in Chapter 12 when we address advocacy concepts. For now, it is sufficient to know that political power is a critical component of policy development and adoption.

Writing Policy   Green and Kreuter (1999) state that a well-written policy has three components: "(1) the clear statement of a problem (or potential problem) that needs attention, (2) a goal to mitigate or prevent that problem, and (3) a set of strategic actions to accomplish that goal" (p. 386). With those three requirements in mind, where would you begin in the process of policy development? Assume, for a moment, that you work for a large manufacturing company in which many of the employees smoke cigarettes. The company decision makers have already identified the problem, which is that employees are smoking on the job. You've been asked to write a policy that will help them address that problem.

Follow Green and Kreuter's three-component guidelines to write a smoke-free-environment policy for a company.

Your statement of the problem could be written in a number of ways, as long as it identified the problem of smoking employees. The second part of the policy, a goal to mitigate or reduce the problem, would likely include a statement about reducing the frequency of smoking on the job or creating a smoke-free environment. The third part, the set of strategic actions needed to accomplish that goal, would likely be difficult to put into effect, especially if you realized that any policy you created could upset some of your employees.

The nature of the policy you would develop and strategies used to implement it would greatly depend on your philosophy and goal. If your ultimate goal were to have no smokers on the payroll, your strategic approach could embrace quick, drastic action, such as posting no-smoking signs throughout the building and automatically firing any employee caught violating the rule. If, on the other hand, you desired to keep smokers in your employ but still maintain a smoke-free environment, you might take a more gradual approach that provided advance notice to employees, designated smoking areas, and smoking cessation classes for employees who smoke. Your goal would dictate your policy and how you applied it.

IN CONCLUSION

The concept of synergism is a prime example of how we view the connection between collaboration and policy development. **Synergism,** in this context, would mean that the partnership efforts of collaborating parties would produce a greater effect than the sum of efforts independently exerted by each party. Effective coordination of health programs and services is dependent on a collaborative effort toward policy development and goal attainment. Your efforts toward these goals may not always produce the desired effect and, even when they do, the results sometimes emerge very slowly. However, even in small, gradual increments, synergism can be powerfully effective.

When the time comes for you to serve as the coordinator of a collaborative project, we suggest that you display the word *synergism* in a place where you and your partners will frequently notice it. The reminder may help you work through some long days. It may also cause you to smile when you come to the point where synergism has finally been achieved.

REVIEW QUESTIONS

1. Describe the process of cooperation and how to promote it.
2. Identify techniques for conflict resolution.
3. Compare and contrast community development and community organization.
4. List ways in which coalitions and partnerships can be developed.
5. Define policy and name its three components.
6. Describe the difference between procedural and public health policy.
7. Name four federal agencies that monitor public health policy.
8. Name at least one nongovernmental organization that focuses on public health policy.
9. Summarize the purpose and components of the Patients' Bill of Rights.
10. Describe the process of policy development.
11. Describe tips for making sound decisions about policy development.
12. Practice writing policies.

FOR YOUR APPLICATION

Creating a Community Coalition

Select a local age- or ethnicity-specific community subgroup and a health problem it faces. Create a proposal for a coalition whose primary goal would be to address the health problem in the community group you selected. Your proposal should include

- a coalition mission statement and goals (Each goal should represent a specific project or task needed to accomplish the stated mission.)

- a list of strategies/programs and skills/resources needed to accomplish each goal
- a list of national and state organizations, agencies, and the like that could potentially provide some needed support (Specifically describe what each could provide, such as information, materials, guidance.)
- a list of local organizations, agencies, institutions, and other community groups who may have a vested interest in the well-being of the targeted group (List the potential contribution each could make to attain the coalition mission and goals and the benefits it might derive from its contribution.)
- a description of regular channels of communication, decision making, and reporting recommended for the coalition to follow
- a timeline for the coalition to follow in completing designated tasks

FOR YOUR PORTFOLIO

Coordinating a Health Event

Contact a local community organization leader or public school teacher who is interested in health promotion. Volunteer to help coordinate a health fair, seminar, or other health-related event that will involve organizational members as learning educators. For example, members of a senior citizens center may enjoy helping elementary students implement a school health fair. Submit to the director or teacher a written project plan containing project goals and objectives, specific strategies and methods you will use, a timeline, and a list of resources and potential event participants. Provide references the leader may contact to inquire about your abilities and dependability. Create a "Coordinating (Responsibility V)" division for your professional portfolio and place in it pictures, letters of appreciation, and other documentation of your coordinating efforts.

11

Acting as a Resource Person

YOU KNOW THAT, AS A HEALTH EDUCATOR, YOU WILL fill the role of resource person. But what does that mean? Do you need to know everything there is to know about health? Do you need to know every important person in health care and be well versed in every computer program as well as the Internet? The good news is, absolutely not! If you are capable of all this you are special indeed and unlike every other person in the world. No one can know and do everything. What you can do is know how to access information and where to go for help.

Chapter Objectives

1. Describe the jobs of other health care professionals.
2. Identify the importance of volunteers.
3. Discuss consultative relationships.
4. Define networking.
5. Describe and compare computer sources of information, including the World Wide Web, online databases, and online journals.
6. Discuss health care agencies that might be resources for the community.
7. Describe government-provided insurance, including Medicaid, Medicare, and supplements.
8. Describe private insurance options, including HMOs, PPOs, and fee-for-service plans.
9. Describe government agencies that serve as health resources.

WHAT IS A RESOURCE PERSON?

One of your responsibilities will be to know how to get information, where to find available services, and who will be able to help in a given situation. A good resource person doesn't have to know everything but, rather, knows where to find information and services. In this chapter we discuss a few of the types of resources, including people, computers, and organizations.

PEOPLE AS RESOURCES

People are the world's most valuable resources. The wisdom, knowledge, and skills that a diverse group of individuals can bring to a project are immense. We encourage you to appreciate the wealth of human resources you have available to you.

Health and Allied Health Professionals

Think of as many different health professions as possible. How could these professionals help a resource person?

Health professionals can offer much knowledge and many types of skills that might benefit your health education programs. Some job descriptions follow, but many other professionals might also serve as resources.

- *Dental hygienists and dentists.* Hygienists help people keep their teeth clean, and they conduct an initial assessment of the integrity of the teeth and gums. Most importantly, the hygienist teaches people how to care for their teeth and prevent problems. The dentist diagnoses and treats problems that occur with teeth and gums. Among the specialty areas in dentistry are endodontics (treatment of roots of teeth) and oral surgery.
- *Nurses.* Most of us know about nurses. We have seen them in a variety of settings ranging from schools to hospitals. They observe, assess, and record signs and symptoms; administer medications and treatments; and provide patient instruction. You are probably most familiar with registered nurses, who have either a two-year diploma or a bachelor's degree in nursing. Licensed practical or vocational nurses train in one year. They have fewer responsibilities regarding treatment and must be supervised by a registered nurse.
- *Nutritionists.* These professionals, also called dieticians, are trained to blend the science of nutrition with the planning and preparation of meals. They work in many settings, such as hospitals and schools, and may counsel groups of people or work one-on-one with individuals. As you can see, education is a large part of their job.

- *Occupational therapists.* The goal for the occupational therapist is to help individuals develop and maintain daily living skills. The people with whom they work may be mentally, physically, developmentally, or emotionally challenged, Occupational therapists may work in a client's home or in a health care facility.
- *Physical therapists.* Physical therapists, like occupational therapists, also help individuals restore function. A primary difference is that physical therapists generally work with individuals who have experienced normal functioning in the past and have had an injury occur to remove their ability to function. They will work less with daily living skills and more on the functioning of a joint or limb.
- *Physicians.* We assume that all of you have seen a physician at some time in your life. They are involved primarily in the treatment of disease but are beginning more frequently to address prevention. They use a wide variety of equipment and practice primarily in their private offices and health care facilities. The term *physicians* refers to medical doctors (M.D.) and doctors of osteopathy (D.O.). D.O.s use traditional forms of treatment, including medicines and surgery, but they place special emphasis on the musculoskeletal system. Many M.D. and D.O. specialty areas exist; perhaps you can name a few.
- *Respiratory therapists.* These therapists are literally concerned with the breath of life. They might be involved in diagnosis, treatment, or maintenance of the highest quality of respiratory function possible. They use a variety of equipment at a person's home or in a health care facility. They teach patients about their respiratory status and how to improve it.
- *Other therapists.* Other types of therapy include art therapy, dance therapy, recreational therapy, music therapy, pet therapy, and horticulture therapy. The primary goal of each is to help people attain and maintain independence. The wide variety of therapy types allows therapists to combine their interest in health with other interests; and they allow patients to use the medium of choice to improve their functional capacity.
- *Ultrasound, X-ray, and imaging technicians.* Technological advancements have opened a number of jobs for imaging technicians. An increasing number of imaging techniques do not use X-rays, including ultrasound and magnetic resonance scans. Each type of imaging requires specific knowledge and skills.

We learned just how much other health professionals can serve as resources recently when we were seeking some specific information on the dollar value of lives saved through early detection of breast cancer. We searched the online databases and the Web but could not find the specific information we needed. We mentioned the problem to one of our students, an X-ray technician. She had the information we needed within five minutes. What an incredible resource we had without realizing it. We hope you won't make the same mistake.

Volunteers

Almost any health-related agency for which you will work will depend on volunteers. "If the trend toward fewer government services for disadvantaged and ill individuals continues, the need for unpaid volunteers will increase" (Penner & Finkelstein, 1998, p. 525).

In fact, "lack of money to purchase health care coupled with societal forces and sociodemographic factors limit the ability of poor families to achieve and maintain adequate health status" (Beardain & Grantham, 1993, p. 2). Volunteers, both health professionals and lay individuals, help increase the amount of health-related services provided by community programs (Penner & Finkelstein, 1998). In fact, they may be the only hope for some agencies to make a difference in the health status of people in their community.

Sometimes the magnitude of dismal news shared in the media gives us the impression that few people choose to be helpful and giving. However, volunteerism is alive and well in this country. Half of the people in the United States volunteer their time with service organizations. They volunteer an average of four hours per week and provide billions of dollars worth of services annually (Penner & Finkelstein, 1998).

You will need to know something about who volunteers and why they do so in order to recruit and retain the people you need. People who volunteer often have more education and higher incomes than those who do not. Married people, especially married women, volunteer more frequently (Zweigenhaft, Armstrong, Quintis, & Riddick, 1996). However, the number of men who volunteer is increasing, as is the percentage of elders (Chambre, 1993).

People volunteer for various reasons (Snyder, 1993), often a combination of factors. Some of the reasons people give for choosing to volunteer include personal satisfaction, professional responsibility, perceived community need, desire to help others (Ward, 1998); commitment to service, business networking, career development (Ellis, 1993); recreation, a desire to make friends (Glascoff, Baker, & Glascoff, 1997); and recognition.

If in the future you need volunteers in your work, we encourage you to tailor recruitment and retention efforts for specific types of individuals. Creating an environment where volunteers can make a difference in health status requires more than just providing an opportunity to volunteer. A comprehensive understanding of why people volunteer, what barriers prevent them from volunteering, and what keeps them motivated to continue to volunteer may improve the volunteer experience and have a powerful impact on the effectiveness of volunteer services. Volunteers will also need training and development opportunities. We hope you will accept the challenge of maximizing your volunteer resources through a respectful understanding of them as individuals.

Consultants

Consultants, people you hire to assist with a specific project or program, can offer a combination of five abilities: expertise, perspective, authenticity, friendship, and accomplishment (Bellman, 1990). Let's discuss these abilities in a little more detail.

Expertise   This ability pertains to a special knowledge or skill. You might, for example, want to hire a consultant to help you evaluate a specific program. According to Bellman (1990, p. 129), you may want to use a consultant's expertise for one or more of several reasons:

1. You may not have the knowledge and skills yourself.
2. You may have the knowledge and skills but not the time.
3. You may not be in the right position to do the work.
4. You may not want to do the work yourself.

Be honest with consultants about why you are hiring them. If you happen to be serving as a consultant yourself, be sure to find out why you are being hired.

Perspective   This ability involves assistance in "seeing the world in a new way." For example, sometimes an organization or program isn't running smoothly because an individual or individuals are not performing in the way that they should. For example, we were assisting public health personnel to access information and found that they rarely used the Internet as a tool. We made the assumption that they lacked the skills to use the Internet. However, according to Bellman (1990, p. 131), the lack of performance isn't usually lack of skills, as normally perceived by supervisors, but instead faulty perceptions about the use of skills. For example, the people concerned

- see the situation in a way that precludes using the skills that would be appropriate to the situation.
- don't understand that the skills might be necessary.
- are scared to use the skills they have because of perceived consequences.
- don't want to use their skills because they think it would be inappropriate.
- don't know when to use their skills because no one has indicated that the skills are needed.
- suffer in some way when they use their skills.

In our case, the individuals with whom we were working mistakingly believed that they were not allowed to use the Internet. In either case, lack of training or the need for a new perspective, a consultant can assist.

Authenticity   A consultant can help people in an agency recognize the true nature of the organization. Earlier we talked about seeing the world in a new way, but authenticity is "seeing" reality. The consultant must be personally authentic (know and understand self) in order to add this dimension to the consulting process.

Friendship   Bellman (1990) notes that characteristics that we expect from our friends are the same characteristics that we should expect in a consulting relationship:

- We want friends to be honest.
- We expect our friends to allow us to take responsible risks.
- We want to be able to talk about what is important to us with our friends and to be taken seriously.
- We want to accomplish things, reach goals shoulder to shoulder, and enjoy our accomplishments with our friends.
- We want be able to talk with friends about concerns, knowing that they will be supportive.

Although friendship might seem out of place in a business relationship, the elements of friendship we have listed are necessary to honest appraisal and true teamwork.

Accomplishment   The normal expectation from a consulting relationship is that results will be achieved. Obviously, results are the bottom line for hiring a consultant. We caution you, however, to be careful in the way you define *results*. Sometimes we have personal agendas for accomplishments that are not based in reality. For example, if you hire someone to help you evaluate a program, you cannot demand that the results show the program in a completely positive light. Accomplishment in this case is gaining information that will help you improve your program. You might also want to think in terms of small successes. Give yourself and your programs credit for the process of improvement, not just the final outcome.

The negative side of consulting is the financial cost. In cases where you are "stuck," due to overwork, lack of skills, inability to gain perspective, or whatever reason, the benefits of hiring a consultant may outweigh the costs in a dramatic way. A consultant can save a program or project.

Networking

Have you heard people talking about networking but just couldn't really get a handle on what it means? Networking is an important tool for serving as a resource person. Look at Figure 11. 1 and you will see the kinds of connections that meeting and getting to know people actually bring. For example, if you meet and share information with person A, you have the potential of gaining resources from persons A, B, and C. Person A knows and talks with B and C; and if you ask,

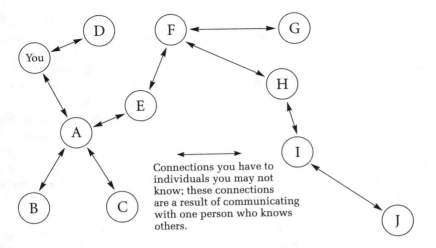

FIGURE 11.1   Networking.
Networking is a key factor when you are serving as a resource person and when you are seeking resources. Communicating with a couple of key individuals could be of great benefit to you and your agency.

he or she will most likely be willing to pass along your name, needs, or skills. Networking can take you even further because each individual knows other individuals. The key to networking is that you place yourself in situations where you can meet and talk with other professionals. You must be willing to discuss your needs as well as those skills you are willing to share with others. Professional conferences, workshops, and other professional development activities are good places to start networking.

COMPUTERS AS RESOURCES

The World Wide Web

As you know, the World Wide Web (WWW), part of the Internet, is a network of servers that connect together with links. The **links** help an individual at one computer access files at another site. A link generally goes to a **home page** (the introductory page to a Web site). The home page often acts as a table of contents or guide to the site's other pages and links to more sites (McLean, 1996). For example, if you go to the Texas Woman's University home page at **http://www4@twu.edu**, you will find a list of phrases like Virtual Visit, Departments, and Student Services. If you put the cursor on one of the phrases, you will note that it turns into a small hand, indicating a link to another page. You simply click on the link, and your Web browser will retrieve the page from where it is stored and display it on your computer.

Links between sites are made with the help of hypertext. **Hypertext** also helps the user find information through key words and phrases. You know you are using hypertext to access information when you type in "http:" as part of the address. HTTP stands for hypertext transport protocol (Daniel & Balog, 1997).

A Web **browser** is software that helps you view the World Wide Web on your computer. According to Daniel and Balog (1997), "there are three basic types of Web browsers: full screen browsers (e.g., Lynx), graphical browsers (e.g., Netscape or Mosaic), and line mode browsers" (p. 261). Full screen browsers differ from the other browsers in putting just text on the screen. The others show text and graphics and provide other services. If you want to know more about browsers, you might visit **http://www. browsers.com.** As a World Wide Web user, you travel from one **Uniform Resource Locator** (URL) to another. The URL is a Web address.

The Web's contribution to health education can be phenomenal: Health facts can be at your fingertips in seconds, but you need to make sure that the information you choose is indeed factual (see the discussion later in the chapter). You may also need to protect yourself from frustration over the plethora of addresses, types of sites, and contradictory information. You probably have a favorite search tool, but if not, try one of those mentioned in the following paragraphs.

Search Tools

Search Engines   A **search engine** is a database created by software that searches the Web for titles and phrases. In other words, when you initiate a search using a search engine, you are not searching the Web itself but, rather, the search engine database. The numerous search engines all have similarities, but they differ in size and in the types of Web pages they list. Some of the most well-known search engines are AltaVista (**http://www.av.com**), Excite (**http://www.excite. com**), HotBot (**http://www.hotbot.com**), InfoSeek (**http://www.infoseek.com**), Lycos (**http://www.lycos.com**), and WebCrawler (**http://www.webcrawler .com**). AltaVista is probably the largest and fastest database, but HotBot may be easier to use (Kennedy, 1999). Although they are all similar in ways, you must be the judge of which is "best for you." We encourage you to try them all and compare your results.

Search Agents   Use of a **search agent** involves searching the Web live. In general, the search agent software will query search engines or directories for the specific information you are requesting. According to Kennedy (1999), some of the best-known search agents are Copernic (**http://www.copernic.com**), Dogpile (**http://www.dogpile.com**), and MetaCrawler (**http://www.metacrawler.com**). Unfortunately, search agents usually provide only a limited number of hits per site they search.

Directories   A **directory** is a database with a number of Web sites listed for each topic. Directories may even be compiled by people rather than computer software

(Kennedy, 1999). Web sites are categorized by subject, date, and even format. Some well-known directories are Yahoo (**http://www.yahoo.com**), About.com (**http://www.about.com**), and LookSmart (**http://www.looksmart.com**). Yahoo is probably the largest database, but About.com includes expert guides with each topic.

Other Online Databases

Don't forget about professional journals when you are seeking information. Sometimes the ease of gathering information electronically makes seeking and reading professional journals less attractive. However, as you will learn in a later section of this chapter, the information you collect must be verified through research. Because professional journals are generally the means by which research is disseminated, it is vitally important that you stay abreast of what they report.

Locating professional articles has become as simple as searching the Web. Large databases that archive articles and abstracts exist for most professions. For example, Medline is a database compiled by the U.S. National Library of Medicine that archives articles and abstracts from approximately 3,500 medical journals. Other databases that health educators might find useful include Psychlit (psychology-related journals) and ERIC (educational journals). Most databases for professional journals can be accessed via the Web, but we suggest that you visit your library and use the CD-ROM versions at least once so that you get to know your library resources. There are so many more than you can imagine. You will truly appreciate the library only if you visit and use it.

A health education journal published online is *The International Electronic Journal of Health Education*. As with hard-copy journals, you must pay for a subscription, and there is a schedule of publication. Although you have the option of printing a hard copy of a journal article if necessary, you will not have to store or dispose of a pile of journals. This plays a small but important role in preserving the environment in which we live.

Analyzing Computer Resources

Think about a time when you used information from the Web for a paper or other class assignment. How did you know that the information you used was accurate and appropriate? Did you think about accuracy? There are actually three categories to consider when analyzing a source of information: accuracy, appropriateness, and adequacy. Figure 11.2 illustrates these categories.

When you find information on the Web, is it always meaningful and correct?

Accuracy   The term **accuracy** refers to the correctness of the information. We can all agree that you need to present the most accurate information possible. If you are a member of the Health Education Directory, an electronic mailing list for health educators, you have read discussions about **urban myths.** These are anecdotes and supposed facts that are widely disseminated but have no accuracy. An example of such a myth is the claim that antiperspirants cause cancer. The assertion

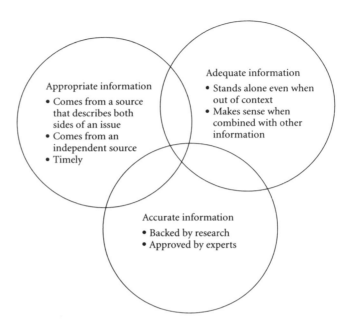

FIGURE 11.2   Guidelines for analyzing electronic sources of information.
As you know, the Internet can provide massive amounts of information. Unfortunately, some of the easiest Internet sources to access don't provide reliable unbiased information. This model can provide you with guidelines for analyzing your computer sources of information.

sounds plausible. You might hear that an antiperspirant blocks sweat glands and, further, that a blocked sweat gland might result in cellular changes that, in turn, can result in cancer. Despite the apparent plausibility of the claim, current research does not document a relationship between antiperspirants and cancer.

Unfortunately, many pieces of information are related as fact, even though they have no empirical basis. Empirical research would involve an experimental study design. Recall from Chapter 3 that an experimental design is a type of research study that uses at least two groups of subjects, one for the intervention and another for comparison. When you present information, be sure to identify the experimental studies that document what you are saying.

Sometimes research isn't enough to document the accuracy of information because of the presence of bias or flaws in some research designs. In cases like these, it may be wise to check the opinions of experts in the field to verify information you are presenting. To find expert opinion, check the databases for peer-reviewed journals; experts will have published articles on their area of concentration.

Appropriateness   The **appropriateness** of information can be determined by assessing its source. If the source presents two or more different perspectives accompanied by citations, it may be more appropriate than sources offering just one perspective. You can be more confident that the information is not based on one biased viewpoint. But look for evidence of bias if the source is a for-profit organization or is funded by an organization that wishes to propound a specific viewpoint.

Timeliness of information is also important. You usually need the most current information or enough background material for a historical perspective. Determine your specific needs, but make a deliberate decision about the time issue rather than accept information no matter when it was written.

Adequacy   The **adequacy** of information has to do with its depth. For example, the short sentence "Smoking causes health problems" has meaning by itself. It can be backed by research that is current and independent. It is not likely to be misconstrued even if it stands alone. Some statements need to be supported by additional information that is also accurate and appropriate in order to have meaning. For example, the statement "Herbal preparations can enhance health" does not stand alone. Many herbal preparations haven't even been studied. If you are discussing herbs, you will want to give actual information. It is up to you to make certain that the information is adequate either by itself or in combination with additional information.

ORGANIZATIONS AS RESOURCES

Voluntary Health Organizations

We introduced voluntary health organizations in Chapter 2. These organizations can have a powerful impact on the health of a community. It will be important for you to get to know which are available in your community and network with the professionals staffing them. Some brief descriptions of a few of the many voluntary health organizations follow. Appendix D lists URLs for these and other organizations.

- *The American Cancer Society.* This organization is dedicated to helping people who face cancer through research, patient services, early detection, treatment, and education. The national office is located in Washington, D.C., but the organization has state and local affiliates.
- *The American Lung Association.* Fighting lung disease for more than 90 years, the American Lung Association is a leader in tobacco education and regulation. It has a strong focus on the prevention of lung diseases like asthma, tuberculosis, pneumonia, and emphysema.
- *March of Dimes.* Four major problems threaten the health of America's babies: birth defects, infant mortality, low birth weight, and lack of prenatal care. The March of Dimes has adopted goals to bring us closer to the

day when all babies will be born healthy. The goals include a commitment to "reduce birth defects by 10%, reduce infant mortality to 7 per 1,000 live births, reduce low birth weight to no more than 5% of all live births, and increase the number of women who get prenatal care in the first trimester of their pregnancy to 90%" (March of Dimes, 1999a, p. 1).

- *Muscular Dystrophy Association.* This voluntary health agency is working to defeat 40 neuromuscular diseases through worldwide research, comprehensive services, and public health education.
- *National Kidney Foundation.* The National Kidney Foundation seeks to prevent kidney and urinary tract diseases. It also seeks to improve the health and well-being of individuals and families affected by these diseases and increase the availability of all organs for transplantation.
- *Cystic Fibrosis Foundation.* The mission of the Cystic Fibrosis Foundation is to assure development of ways to improve the quality of life for individuals with this disease.
- *American Red Cross.* This organization has multiple functions and services. The primary mission, however, is to help prevent, prepare for, and cope with emergencies. Approximately 30 million people are assisted each year.
- *The National Academies of Practices.* This organization is dedicated to quality health for all. The members, nominated by individuals in their prospective fields, serve as the nation's distinguished, interdisciplinary policy forum, addressing public policy, education, research, and inquiry.

Organizations That Deliver Health Care

Most of us are aware of the typical organizations that deliver health care: hospitals with emergency rooms, community outreach clinics or health centers, and doctors' offices. Much education is provided by these organizations. Unfortunately, health information is not always presented appropriately or in a culturally sensitive manner. The timing of information presentation is also not always beneficial to the patient. For example, providing education during a crisis in the emergency room is not generally effective. Nevertheless, these organizations can offer outstanding resources.

Even schools can serve as health-related resources. Public Law 94-142 requires that all children in the United States be provided free and appropriate public education. Because some children need health care in order for education to be meaningful, schools have implemented many health services. Among them are physical therapy, occupational therapy, counseling, speech therapy, and nursing services (Rodman et al., 1999).

Insurance Companies   Insurance companies affect health care delivery tremendously because they create and sell the plans that cover our health care expenses.

There are two broad categories of insurance with which you should be familiar: private (fee for service and managed care) and government.

PRIVATE—FEE FOR SERVICE   Insurance is about money. In 1992, $840 million, or approximately 14% of the nation's income, went to health care (Rasell, Bernstein, & Tang, 1993). Insurance helps people cover the cost of health care. Two basic categories of private insurance exist: payment after and payment before services are delivered. Before the 1990s, payment after the delivery of services, or **fee for service,** was the most common form of health insurance (Baker & Baker, 1999). Today, almost all insurance provides predetermined-per-person delivery of services. Each insurance company will negotiate with the health care delivery institution and physician the fee that will be paid for each service. Therefore, hospitals and physicians may receive different amounts for the same services from various insurance companies.

PRIVATE—MANAGED CARE   The concept of **managed care** refers to a "means of providing health care services within a network of health care providers" (Baker & Baker, 1999, p. 26). In the managed care model, all health care services for an individual are coordinated and provided by the network. The network consists of health care providers and agencies that agree to be members. **Health maintenance organizations (HMOs)** are the most common type of managed care plan. Several varieties of HMOs currently exist, but they all have similarities. The insurance company pays a preset monthly fee to the health care providers who belong to the HMO. An insured individual must use the providers who are designated in the plan or pay higher fees. Health care providers employed by the insurance company review cases and play a role in the selection of health care. The insurance company may charge physicians in some way if they order services that are not suggested by the company.

Most plans cover hospital services (surgical and emergency room), long-term care services, home care, primary care physician (PCP) visits, selected lab work, radiology, and pharmaceutical needs, Unfortunately, many managed care organizations include only limited mental health services. And yet millions of people each year need services for mental health. Dental and eye care are often covered under separate plans.

Preferred provider organizations (PPOs) are another type of private insurance plan. Similar to HMOs, they consist of a panel of providers that range from hospitals to specialty physicians. The panel members provide utilization review or a review of the services ordered by a physician. They make recommendations about the necessity of services, and the physician is expected to follow those recommendations. Doctors may be charged in some way for services that are deemed unnecessary. People who select PPOs must use the providers who are members of the plan or pay higher fees, The types of services offered are very similar to those offered in the HMO plans. See FYI 11.1 for a list of managed care terms that you might need to know in the future.

FOR YOUR INFORMATION 11.1

List of Managed Care Terms

Managed care is difficult to understand at times. It is made so by the use of terms that aren't commonly used. The following are definitions for some of the common managed care terms.

Term	Definition
Managed care	"The means of providing health care services within a network of health care providers" (Baker & Baker, 1999)
Fee for service	Payment after the delivery of health care services
Capitation rates	Predetermined upper limit for treatment cost
Case managers	Individuals in the employ of the insurance company who oversee and manage treatment for an individual receiving health care
Copayment fees	Predetermined fee for which the insured is responsible
Deductibles	Predetermined amount of money that the insured will pay before insurance coverage begins
Formularies	Descriptions of approved treatment regimes
Gatekeeper physicians	The physician who determines the need for and authorizes specialty health care
Utilization review	Review and management of treatment selected by physicians who are members of the HMO or PPO
Preventive medicine	Health care delivery before the occurrence of disease or disease progression

HMOs and PPOs create problems for many ethnic Americans and other underserved U.S. populations. The motivation behind HMOs is to decrease expenses, not improve health status. The basis of the HMO or PPO model is that physicians and patients overutilize the health care system. In order to solve the problem, the physician becomes the gatekeeper to prevent unnecessary services. We know, however, that many ethnic Americans and poor people, in fact, do not access health care as often as do European Americans and people from middle- or upper-income families. They also have poorer health.

When ethnic Americans and other underserved individuals arrive at their HMO, they may have a backlog of illnesses. Their course of illness is likely to be longer and more severe due to lack of adequate housing, food, and clothing. Compounding these problems is the fact that utilization review is based on statistical norms for European Americans. It will be important for you to understand insurance and find ways to help those who are hurt by our current insurance programs.

GOVERNMENT INSURANCE   In 1965, legislation established "Health Insurance for the Aged and Disabled" as part of the Social Security Act (Baker & Baker, 1999). Known as **Medicare,** this insurance program has two parts called simply Part A and Part B. Part A covers hospital stays, and Part B covers other health care. An individual chooses to purchase Part B. Anyone working in the United States pays a tax to cover Part A Medicare. Part B is charged to the individuals, generally through deductions from Social Security benefit payments.

Medicaid was also established in 1965 as part of the Social Security Act. This program was created to assist needy individuals with health care expenses. Although the federal government provides broad eligibility criteria, each state sets its own specific criteria and payment rates for services. This is the largest program for helping people with low incomes to pay for health care.

Other government programs include the Department of Veteran Affairs health programs, migrant health care services, mental health services, drug and alcohol services, and Indian health care services.

Government Agencies   We discussed the National Institutes of Health (NIH) and the Centers for Disease Control and Prevention (CDC) in Chapter 2. These two agencies have a powerful influence on the health of the nation. You will find more detailed information about each in the paragraphs that follow. Keep in mind, however, that even government agencies that don't seem to be health-related can have great influences on health (AARP, 1999).

NATIONAL INSTITUTES OF HEALTH   The NIH mission is "to uncover new knowledge that will lead to better health for everyone" (NIH, 1999, p. 1). The NIH, housed in Bethesda, Maryland, has 25 institutes and centers (FYI 11.2). It is one of the eight agencies of the Public Health Service, which is part of the Department of Health and Human Services. The institutes work toward their mission by conducting research in their own laboratories; supporting research at universities, medical centers, and other institutions; and assisting in the training of research investigators.

The NIH has supported about 50,000 **principal investigators** (scientists who take the lead in a research project) in conducting health-related research. The agency employs more than 15,000 people—from research scientist to support personnel.

According to the NIH (1999, pp. 4–5), research it supported played a role in the following accomplishments:

- Mortality from heart disease, the number one killer in the United States, dropped by 36% between 1977 and 1999.

FOR YOUR INFORMATION 11.2

NIH Institutes and Centers

The NIH consists of both institutes and centers. You may wish to call or visit the Web site for a specific institute.

Center for Information Technology (formerly Division of Computer Research and Technology, OIRM, TCB)
301-496-6203

Center for Scientific Review (formerly Division of Research Grants)
301-435-0714

John E. Fogarty International Center (FIC)
301-496-2075

National Cancer Institute (NCI)
301-435-3848

National Center for Complementary and Alternative Medicine (NCCAM)
301-496-1712

National Center for Research Resources (NCRR)
301-435-0888

National Eye Institute (NEI)
301-496-5248

National Heart, Lung, and Blood Institute (NHLBI)
301-496-4236

National Human Genome Research Institute (NHGRI)
301-402-0911

National Institute on Aging (NIA)
301-496-1752

National Institute on Alcohol Abuse and Alcoholism (NIAAA)
301-443-3860

National Institute of Allergy and Infectious Diseases (NIAID)
301-496-5717

National Institute of Arthritis and Musculoskeletal and Skin Diseases (NIAMS)
301-496-8188

- Death rates from stroke decreased by 50% during the same period.
- Improved treatment and detection methods increased the relative 5-year survival rate for people with cancer to 60%.
- Paralysis from spinal cord injury can be significantly reduced by rapid treatment with high doses of a steroid.
- Long-term treatment with anticlotting medicines cuts stroke risk from a common heart condition known as atrial fibrillation by 80%.
- In schizophrenia, where suicide is always a potential danger, new medications reduce troublesome symptoms such as delusions and hallucinations in 80% of patients.
- Chances for survival increased for infants with respiratory distress syndrome, an immaturity of the lungs, due to development of a substance to

National Institute of Child Health and Human Development (NICHD)
301-496-5133

National Institute on Deafness and Other Communication Disorders (NIDCD)
301-496-7243

National Institute of Dental and Craniofacial Research (NIDCR)
301-496-4261

National Institute of Diabetes and Digestive and Kidney Diseases (NIDDK)
301-496-3583

National Institute on Drug Abuse (NIDA)
301-443-1124

National Institute of Environmental Health Sciences (NIEHS)
919-541-3345
301-402-3378

National Institute of General Medical Sciences (NIGMS)
301-496-7301

National Institute of Mental Health (NIMH)
301-443-4513

National Institute of Neurological Disorders and Stroke (NINDS)
301-496-5751

National Institute of Nursing Research (NINR)
301-496-0207

National Library of Medicine (NLM)
301-496-6308

Office of the Director (OD)
301-496-1766

Warren Grant Magnuson Clinical Center (CC)
301-496-2563

From *NIH Overview,* prepared by the Office of Communications and Public Liaison, August 1999. Retrieved December 28, 1999, from the World Wide Web: http://www.nihigov/welcome/nihnew.html.

prevent the lungs from collapsing. In general, life expectancy for a baby born today is almost three decades longer than it was for one born at the beginning of the century.

- Those suffering from depression now look forward to returning to work and leisure activities, thanks to treatments that give them an 80% chance to resume a full life in a matter of weeks.
- Vaccines protect against infectious diseases that once killed and disabled millions of children and adults.
- Dental sealants have proved 100% effective in protecting the chewing surfaces of children's molars and premolars, where most cavities occur.
- In 1990, NIH researchers performed the first trial of gene therapy in humans.

CDC   As you know from Chapter 2, the CDC mission is to "promote health and quality of life by preventing and controlling disease, injury, and disability" (1999a, p. 1). The CDC, whose main office is in Atlanta, Georgia, includes 11 centers, institutes, and offices. Refer to the CDC organizational chart in Chapter 2. The CDC works toward its mission by pledging the following to the American people (1999a, p. 1):

- To be a diligent steward of the funds entrusted to it
- To provide an environment for intellectual and personal growth and integrity
- To base all public health decisions on the highest-quality scientific data, openly and objectively derived
- To place the benefits to society above the benefits to the institution
- To treat all persons with dignity, honesty, and respect

The CDC employs almost 8,000 people who have 170 occupations. The employees work in 10 locations across the United States with CDC facilities.

IN CONCLUSION

Although you don't need to know everything and every person in the field of health, you do need to be able to access and use resources. You should begin by understanding your most valuable resource: people. Health care professionals can offer you knowledge and skills that you alone cannot hope to attain in one lifetime. They and others might serve as volunteers or form a vital network for you. In all cases, respect is the first word to remember. People are invaluable and must be treated so.

In today's world, technology is not only a resource but also a necessity. Your ability to find information and present it depends on your mastery of computer technology. And of course, health care changes every day with the improvement of diagnostic and treatment modalities based in technology.

Don't forget organizations. Although you may access them through the Web, it is your understanding of their importance that will guide you in the search. The world has resources too numerous to count. It is up to you to find, understand, respect, and use them effectively.

 ## REVIEW QUESTIONS

1. Identify three health professionals other than health educators and describe how each might serve as a resource for a health educator.
2. List five reasons people might volunteer. What can you do to help maintain volunteers?
3. Describe the five abilities that a consultant might bring to a client.

4. Define networking and discuss its importance.
5. Identify the differences between search engines, search agents, and directories.
6. Select one health-related organization and go to the Web to collect more information about it. Write several paragraphs describing your findings.

FOR YOUR APPLICATION

Recruiting and Keeping Volunteers

Pretend that you work for a voluntary health association.

Select a specific agency and create a hypothetical activity in which that agency might be involved.

Develop a list of methods you will use to recruit volunteers for the activity you have chosen.

Make a second list of methods you will use to keep those volunteers.

FOR YOUR PORTFOLIO

Recruiting Volunteers

1. Make a divider for your portfolio labeled "Resource Person."
2. Review the "For Your Application" activity.
3. Develop a flyer that you could use to recruit the volunteers for your hypothetical activity.
4. Include all of the information a volunteer will need to make a decision about volunteering.
5. Have your instructor check your work.
6. Revise the flyer.
7. Put it in the Resource Person section of your portfolio.

12

Advocating for

Health

THERE ARE SO MANY HEALTH ISSUES IMPACTING YOUR community—so many problems and so little money. Sometimes it seems as if all of the money in the world wouldn't help anyway. You may be feeling frustrated because much more than new programs is needed to address these problems. You may need to advocate for policy changes and legislative actions. This chapter will discuss how you might go about advocating for health.

Chapter Objectives

1. Define advocacy.
2. Identify methods of advocating for health issues.
3. List tips for writing advocacy letters, using media, and visiting policy makers.
4. Describe the impact of environment on community health.
5. Discuss the importance of selected chronic diseases and disorders in community health.
6. Describe issues related to addictions.
7. Identify social issues that require advocacy.

ADVOCACY

Advocacy is actively working to change the social, political, legal, economical, and medical environments; it is working to make a change in society. It is standing up for individuals who cannot speak for themselves. When used correctly and effectively, advocacy can have a tremendous impact on the health of the public. Leaders in the discipline of health education increasingly recognize that the discipline's mission is to address not just individual health but also the social, political, and economic structures that serve as barriers to community health and well-being. Health educators serve as leaders in addressing conditions that diminish health. However, many health educators go through professional preparation programs that do not provide any information or training in advocacy (Ward & Koontz, 1999).

You've heard the word advocacy *but what does it really mean?*

The process of advocacy is many things to many people. It might be lobbying on Capitol Hill in Washington, D.C., with the purpose of educating and influencing policy makers, encouraging insurance companies to cover prevention services, or standing up at a school board meeting to campaign for a comprehensive health education curriculum. Advocacy can be local or national, can be directed toward policy makers of all kinds, and can be used to change many environments. See FYI 12.1 for some terms you may come across while advocating (Ward & Koontz, 1999).

Among the basic tools of advocacy are knowledge, coalitions and partnerships, lobbying, grassroots activities, media, personal communication or legislative advocacy, and technology.

Knowledge

Information, of course, is the basis of knowledge. We have talked about information gathering in several chapters. We have discussed assessing individual and community needs through various methods, and we have discussed the library, the Internet, and many other sources of information. In the case of advocacy, information and knowledge provide you with the power to affect others. We are not suggesting that to be an advocate you have to be an expert. But you do need enough knowledge to be able to provide adequate decision-making information for those to whom you are advocating.

Coalitions and Partnerships

Coalitions involve organizing individuals or organizations into a team that can work toward a common goal. Remember our discussions about asset-based assessment? As noted in Chapter 6, coalition development is a form of asset building. See FYI 12.2 for a list of guidelines for creating a coalition. The child protection teams that many cities have are good examples of coalitions. In the case of a child protection team, the coalition comprises people from all of the agencies in the city that might be able to help abused children.

FOR YOUR INFORMATION 12.1

Advocacy Terms

Following are some of the common terms used in advocacy, which may help you when you become involved in the advocacy process.

Advocacy.   Actively working to change the social, political, legal, economical, and medical environments; it is making a change in society.

Lobbying.   To conduct activities aimed at influencing public officials and especially members of a legislative body on legislation.

Appropriations.   Money that has been set aside by formal action for a specific purpose.

Entitlements.   A government program providing benefits to members of a specified group or the funds supporting or distributed by such a program.

Discretion.   The power of free decision or latitude of choice within certain legal bounds.

Constituent.   One who authorizes another to act as agent.

Note. Definitions for *lobbying, appropriations, entitlements, discretion,* and *constituents* are from *Merriam-Webster's Collegiate Dictionary,* 10th ed., 1999, Springfield, MA: Merriam-Webster.

From "Putting Advocacy into Action" by S. E. Ward and N. Koontz, 1999. *Eta Sigma Gamma Monograph, 17*(2), 36–40.

Lobbying

Lobbying is a form of advocacy. The difference between the two is sometimes subtle. A lobby generally focuses on a specific target, and the lobbyist is paid. Advocacy can be focused but is generally broader, covering more issues. You need to be aware that if a state or federal agency employs you, you cannot represent that organization through lobbying. You may advocate for health issues as an individual, but you cannot serve as a paid lobbyist. The American School Health Association and other professional organizations hire lobbyists to talk with policy makers about health issues.

Grassroots Activities

These are activities whose impetus comes from the people rather than city officials or even area health educators. You can help individuals or groups within your community mobilize to effect change in health-related policies. The Vision Project in Denton, Texas, is an outstanding example of grassroots activity. A few

FOR YOUR INFORMATION 12.2

Building a Coalition

Coalitions are groups of individuals (generally representing agencies that can provide resources) working toward a common goal. Building a coalition should be done with thoughtful planning. The following provides some tips for doing so.

Define objectives.
Identify resources.
Select initial members.
Obtain endorsements.
Hold a meeting.
Prepare purposes.
Maintain membership through follow-up.

From APHA *Advocates' Handbook: A Guidebook for Effective Public Health Advocacy,* by American Public Health Association, 1999, Washington, DC: APHA.

individuals wanted to improve and strengthen the city. They knew they could not do it by themselves, and they knew that city officials could not accomplish what they had in mind. They realized they needed input and help from a wide variety of people. They wanted to hear what others thought would make the city of Denton better. The organizers held focus groups where anyone could participate and offer suggestions. Hundreds of people participated, and many ideas were shared, many of which were health-related. Eventually, planning and then action teams took the ideas, developed objectives, and carried them forward. As a result, the City of Denton now has a family resource center that helps families access health services.

Media

If you choose to advocate through the media, you might employ news releases, letters to the editors, editorial board meetings, radio interviews or talk shows, and news conferences Each can be used effectively in advocating for health. See FYI 12.3 for some general media advocacy tips and FYI 12.4 for suggestions regarding specific media.

Legislative Advocacy

This type of advocacy is actually a form of personal communication with legislators (local, state, or federal). You can communicate with your legislators by

FOR YOUR INFORMATION 12.3

Media Advocacy

You will want to make a careful selection of the types of media you will use for successful advocacy of your issue. This list provides some tips for advocacy use in general.

Establish a relationship with journalists.
Don't give up.
Think diffusion curve (local is best for the majority of people).
Use current issues.
Create a "hook" or way to create immediate interest.
Be a trustworthy and accessible source.
Have confidence.

From *APHA Advocates' Handbook: A Guidebook for Effective Public Health Advocacy*, by American Public Health Association, 1999, Washington, DC: APHA.

writing letters, calling, visiting, or e-mailing (American Public Health Association [APHA], 1999). In general, you want to know about the person with whom you will be communicating—his or her philosophies and voting records on health issues. After all, if your legislator is a smoker and is heavily supported financially by tobacco companies, you probably won't gain much by discussing tobacco control with him or her. It is important to establish a positive working relationship with your legislator by contacting the office before you visit and providing some preliminary information. You will probably talk with a staff member during this preliminary call and perhaps even during the visit. Don't be put off by this. Staff members will take your information to the legislator, especially if you provide accurate information succinctly and in a straightforward fashion.

The timing of your visit or letter determines the potential impact. A letter or visit that provides information after a vote has been made is meaningless, even if the information would have changed the vote. On the other hand, a letter or visit immediately before an impending vote might play an important role in changing the vote. In order to time your communication well, you need to learn about the legislative process and keep abreast of the issues that are being addressed. The Internet can help you stay up-to-date.

Writing Your Legislator   Letters can be effective means of influencing legislation. Your letters can be sent via postal mail, fax, or e-mail. The same guidelines apply to each format. See FYI 12.5 for tips for writing your policy maker.

FOR YOUR INFORMATION 12.4

Media Formats

Consider any or several of the types of media for your advocacy campaign. This will help you compare them.

Media Format	Tips
News releases	Provide name of organization.
	Provide contact name.
	Include a headline.
	Convey release time and end time.
	Keep it short (1–2 pages).
	Use pyramid structure with strong lead.
	Use plain language, short sentences, quotes.
	End with "tag" (description of group).
Letters to editors	Be brief and concise (one concept in 250 words).
	Refer to other stories.
	Include contact information.
Editorial board meetings	Call the editorial page editor.
	Prepare for the meeting.
	Present your issue.
	Follow up.
Radio or television interviews	Arrange the appearance.
	Familiarize yourself with the program.
	Prepare for the interview.
	Conduct the interview.
	Dress professionally.
	Look at the host if on TV (avoid notes).
	Sit up straight but don't be stiff.
	Don't guess at the answers.
News conferences	Determine the location.
	Notify the news media.
	Call the journalists.
	Have resources available (such as fact sheets).
	Select a moderator.
	Make a presentation (3–5 people make statements and then allow for questions).
	Follow up (conduct interviews and make calls after event).

From *APHA Advocates' Handbook: A Guidebook for Effective Public Health Advocacy,* by American Public Health Association, 1999, Washington, DC: APHA.

FOR YOUR INFORMATION 12.5

Tips for Writing to Your Policy Maker

Your policy maker will pay attention when he or she receives a number of letters about one issue. People are often fearful of writing to a policy maker and will need your encouragement. These tips might provide some assistance. Keep the following tips in mind as you correspond with your policy makers.

- Be accurate and pay attention to detail. Use the proper form of address and correct spelling of the policy maker's name.
- Whenever possible and appropriate, use your organization's letterhead.
- Remember to identify yourself as a constituent.
- Identify yourself as a public health professional in the text of your letter. Whenever possible, list your official title and any professional degrees after your signature.
- Short letters are best—try to keep them to one page. Don't use jargon or confusing technical terms.
- Concentrate on a single issue. Letters should cover only one topic or bill and be timed to arrive while the issue is alive.
- Praise, praise, praise. If your legislator pleases you by supporting a public health issue, write and say so.

In addition, there are important points to remember regarding the substance of your letter.

- State your purpose for writing at the outset.
- Correctly identify the legislation. If you are writing about a specific bill, remember to describe it by its official title and number, as well as by its popular name.

Adpted from *APHA Advocates' Handbook: A Guide for Effective Public Health Advocacy,* by American Public Health Association, 1999, Washington, DC: APHA.

Visiting Your Legislator   Making a personal visit to your legislator can have a powerful impact on policy decisions. Legislators want to know how their constituents feel about the issues being addressed. Your visit will be more impressive if a large group of you contact a number of legislators about the same issue. FYI 12.6 presents tips for making a personal visit to your policy maker.

Whether you are writing a letter or making a personal visit, you need to be fully informed regarding those health issues for which you will advocate. A few of the important issues at the beginning of the 21st century include addictions, chronic diseases, mental health, environment, and social issues. The sections that follow give brief overviews of some of these issues.

FOR YOUR INFORMATION 12.6

Tips for Making a Personal Visit to Your Policy Maker

Making a personal visit to policy makers can be a powerful influence on them. The following are tips for arranging a meeting with your policy maker:

- Send a letter or a fax, or call to request an appointment. If you want to meet with your legislator in the district, send the request to the district office. If you will be visiting the capital, send the letter to that office.
- Be sure to identify yourself as a constituent and address the letter to the legislator and to the attention of the appointment scheduler. Include information about who you are, the nature of your visit (identify what you want to discuss), when you would like to meet, and the names of any friends or colleagues who may accompany you.
- After a few days, follow up by calling the office to which you sent the letter and ask to speak with the appointment scheduler or the administrative assistant who handles appointments. Explain who you are and why you are calling. Refer to the letter you sent to the office. If the legislator is un-available at that time or will not be in the area on the date you would like to meet, the appointment scheduler may offer you another date or time or may provide you the opportunity to meet with the legislative staff member who handles the issue you want to discuss.
- Send a letter or make a phone call confirming the appointment.

Keep the following tips in mind when conducting a meeting with your policy maker:

- Arrive on time. If meeting with a staff member, be sure you have the correct contact name. Do not underestimate the power of the staff person in helping to shape the policy maker's opinions and positions on issues or a particular piece of legislation.
- Bring two or three colleagues with you. Prior to the meeting, you should agree on what points will be made and which points each of you will discuss.
- Try to deliver your message in three minutes. Be sure to introduce yourself and your colleagues and explain why you are concerned with the issue and your expertise regarding the issue. Be concise, polite, and professional.
- Be prepared to answer questions. Clearly explain your interests and issues.

Adpted from *APHA Advocates' Handbook: A Guide for Effective Public Health Advocacy,* by American Public Health Association, 1999, Washington, DC: APHA.

ADDICTIONS

Forms of addiction include the commonly recognized alcohol and drug addictions as well as the less well recognized excessive gambling addiction (Pavalko, 1999). Addiction or its negative consequences warrant grave concern in most communities. However, even when addiction isn't present, high-risk behaviors create problems within communities.

Addiction is not easy to define. What is probably the most widely used definition involves a combination of psychological, social, and biological factors (Shaffer, 1999). Addiction may or may not involve physical dependence. No instrument or test measures addiction perfectly, even though many screening tools exist (Shaffer, 1999). Shaffer's three C's offer a way of identifying the existence of addiction (1999, p. 2). They include

- Craving to compulsion—behavior that is motivated by emotions found along the craving to compulsion spectrum. Craving can range from a mild desire to an overwhelming impulse to act. A compulsive behavior is a powerful repetitive pattern of action.
- Continuity—continued involvement with the drug or activity in spite of adverse social, psychological, or biological consequences.
- Control problems—loss of control, a subjective sense that one no longer can control one's behavior.

Each of us voluntarily chooses behaviors hundreds of times a day. What makes us behave the way we do? We have posed this question before, but we would like you to think about it again. Let's look at our behaviors from a perspective slightly different from those presented in earlier chapters. Among other things, our behaviors are influenced by their consequences. According to Young (1999), we learn both simple and complex behaviors through **operant conditioning.** The concept of operant conditioning is fairly simple. If something positive results from a behavior, that behavior is more likely to be repeated. It can be difficult, however, to recognize the "something positive." It may be a small feeling or emotion, or it might be something concrete like a grade. Behaviors that result in the avoidance of negative experiences are also more likely to be repeated. For example, if we feel less fatigue after sleeping a full eight hours, we are more likely to continue the practice of getting adequate sleep.

Sometimes behaviors become addictive through operant conditioning. An individual repeatedly performing a behavior that results in a positive consequence learns that the positive consequence can be consistent with continued behavior. Before long, even if the positive consequence doesn't occur every time, the behavior continues. Neuroscientists are also finding that pathways exist in the brain for organizing our responses to consequences (Young, 1999). In other words, the pathways assist in operant conditioning.

Addictive drugs enter the brain and influence the body's **neurotransmitters,** which assist the brain's nerve cells to communicate with one another (Young, 1999). There are many neurotransmitters and many drugs. Different drugs influence different transmitters or the same transmitters in different ways. Other addictive behaviors may also influence neurotransmitters. Some neuroscientists believe that addictive drugs also may influence brain levels of dopamine—a substance critical for learning.

If nothing else, this discussion should clue you in to the fact that addiction is very complex and not easily overcome. It is not an issue of will power. Treatment generally requires a combination of strategies, some of which might include prescribed medicines.

Alcohol

Gordis (1999) reports that around 60% of adults in the United States use alcohol. Of those users, approximately 14 million people, or one in 13, abuse alcohol. Many millions more behave in risky ways as a result of alcohol use. An estimated $167 billion is spent and approximately 100,000 deaths occur each year because of alcohol use. Apart from the economic burden of alcohol misuse and abuse, the magnitude of the social and psychological impact is far too great to even imagine.

Some research indicates that moderate use of red wines might enhance cardiovascular health. However, excessive alcohol use can cause liver damage and contribute to heart disease (Gordis, 1999). Pregnant women who drink even moderately can put their babies at risk of fetal alcohol syndrome and other problems. Because of the tremendous burden that alcohol misuse and abuse places on our communities, we must advocate for more education and research on alcohol. Two legislative actions have been shown to be effective with adolescents: The drinking age has been increased to 21 years in all states, and some states have set the maximum blood alcohol limit in young drivers to .02%.

Drugs

Tucker (1999) reports that the "1997 federal drug-control budget was $16 billion, and two-thirds of it was allocated to law enforcement agencies" (p. 19). The United States uses a total control, "zero tolerance," philosophy toward drug addiction. This means that we choose to eliminate the source—and theoretically that elimination should decrease the problem. Is the philosophy working? According to Tucker (1999, p. 21), there are five serious flaws with the philosophy:

1. It is virtually impossible to halt illegal drug trafficking.
2. History documents that people find ways to get psychoactive drugs.
3. Negative consequences, such as increased criminal activity, increase.

4. Other countries are negatively affected. For example, herbicide programs to destroy drug crops in Peru created ecological damage.
5. Public health and health education interventions are ignored.

It may be time to consider *harm-reduction* policies as a step on the way to total abstinence. "Harm reduction is a public health approach aimed at reducing the harmful consequences of substance use for both the user and the community" (Tucker, 1999, p. 21). An example of a harm-reduction program is making bleach or sterile needles available to IV drug users to help control the spread of HIV. Acceptance of the harm-reduction philosophy will require changes in laws, health policies, and even current treatment approaches. We challenge you to think critically about harm reduction versus zero tolerance.

Education seems to be most effective when combined with other community activities (Gordis, 1999). Providing facts and figures alone does not change alcohol consumption. As you can see, communities that will be successful in decreasing the devastating problems that result from alcohol and drug misuse must be willing to bring science, education, community resources, and policy together. Only a combined, well-conceived effort will make a difference with these complex issues.

Gambling

As with alcoholism, there is a continuum of risky gambling behavior, ranging from problem gambling to compulsive gambling and addiction to it (Pavalko, 1999). The American Psychiatric Association lists diagnostic criteria for pathological gambling in the *Diagnostic and Statistical Manual of Mental Disorders,* 4th edition. As you can see from the list in FYI 12.7, addicted gamblers are preoccupied with gambling. They seem to need more and more; the wagers and potential financial losses become great. Addicted gamblers experience withdrawal symptoms when they are not gambling (Pavalko, 1999), and they often try to keep their gambling a secret. The size of their wagers and subsequent financial losses may well be beyond the gambler's means—encouraging illegal activities to obtain money.

Addicted gamblers report that the feeling of "action," or living on the edge, is what they desire (Pavalko, 1999). They will lose track of other things, like time, need for food and sleep, and relationships. People who are addicted to gambling may well have other addictions. However, gambling addiction is a great deal more silent than other addictions. There are no physical signs, and most people in a community are not aware of the addiction. The hidden nature of the problem makes it difficult to address. An awareness campaign may be the only logical place to start. After awareness, what philosophy for addressing the problem would you support? Are you in favor of harm reduction, or zero tolerance, or increased regulation?

FOR YOUR INFORMATION 12.7

Diagnostic Criteria for Pathological Gambling

Pathological gambling has become a serious problem for many people in the United States today. Awareness that pathological gambling exists is the first step in helping communities protect their members from its devastating consequences.

The American Psychiatric Association's Diagnostic Criteria for Pathological Gambling

1. Preoccupied with gambling (preoccupied with reliving past gambling experiences, handicapping, or planning the next venture, or thinking of ways to get money with which to gamble).
2. Needs to gamble with increasing amounts of money in order to achieve the desired excitement.
3. Restlessness or irritability when attempting to cut down or stop gambling.
4. Gambles as a way of escaping from problems or relieving dysphoric mood (feelings of helplessness, guilt, anxiety, or depression).
5. After losing money gambling, often returns another day in order to get even ("chasing" one's losses).
6. Lies to family members or others to conceal the extent of involvement with gambling.
7. Illegal acts (forgery, fraud, theft, embezzlement) are committed in order to finance gambling.
8. Has jeopardized or lost significant relationship, job, or educational or career opportunity because of gambling.
9. Reliance on others to provide money to relieve a desperate financial situation caused by gambling (a bailout).
10. Repeated unsuccessful efforts to control, cut back, or stop gambling.

Source: *Diagnostic and Statistical Manual of Mental Disorders*, 4th ed., by American Psychiatric Association, 1994, Washington, DC: Author.

CHRONIC DISEASES

Cardiovascular Diseases

Diseases of the heart and its blood vessels (**cardiovascular diseases**) are the nation's leading cause of death (American Heart Association [AHA], 1999). They kill more people than the next seven leading causes of death put together. The economic burden of cardiovascular disease in 1998 was $274.2 billion. This figure includes costs of health care providers' services, hospital stays, medications, and lost productivity for the approximately 1,100,000 Americans who had heart attacks that year. The psychosocial burden of the disease is hard to determine. Imagine the number of family and friends, worksites, and communities affected when more than 2,600 Americans die of cardiovascular diseases each day (AHA, 1999).

One form of cardiovascular disease, **coronary artery disease (CAD)**, occurs when the arteries that supply the heart itself are damaged or blocked by **atherosclerosis.** When these arteries don't work sufficiently, oxygen can't reach the heart muscle. Without oxygen the muscle fiber will die, just as will any other tissue in the body. Atherosclerosis is the buildup of fat, connective tissue, and other substances that may result in partial or complete blockage of the artery (Donatelle, Snow, & Wilcox, 1999). Death of heart muscle is called **myocardial infarction.**

As with many other chronic diseases, there is no single cause of cardiovascular disease. Remember the web of causation presented in Figure 3.9? It illustrates the true complexity of coronary artery disease. Some behaviors or factors, however, are known to directly influence the development of CAD. These **risk factors** include smoking, **hypertension** (high blood pressure), high blood cholesterol, and lack of physical activity. Other factors that also contribute, although less directly, include age, sex, the presence of diabetes, obesity, and levels of stress.

The magnitude of influence that a disease like CAD has on a community and nation make it an important health education issue to address. Because lifestyle so heavily influences the onset of the disease, its incidence can continue to be decreased by healthy lifestyle changes among Americans. Advocating for prevention dollars would make a lot of sense. But how far should we go? We have made effective policy changes and laws regarding alcohol and tobacco use. Should we do so for the behaviors that cause CAD? We encourage you to spend time considering difficult issues like this.

Cancer

Characterized by disorderly growth of cells, **cancers** cause much of the morbidity and mortality in the United States and the world. Almost any part of the body can develop cancer; however, most new cases are of five types (Green & Ottoson, 1999). For men, these are prostate, lung, colorectal, bladder, and non-Hodgkin's lymphoma. For women these are lung, breast, colorectal, ovarian, and uterine. As you know, if not successfully treated, the cancer cells may travel or **metastasize** from the primary site to another site.

In any given community, you will note that the incidence of cancer increases with age. There are racial or ethnic differences in most communities as well. For example, according to Green and Ottoson (1999), Hispanic, Chinese, Filipino, and Japanese women have a lower mortality rate (15 per 100,000) from breast cancer than do Black, White, or native Hawaiian women (25 per 100,000). The largest cancer killer, lung cancer, kills more men than women, although this trend is changing with time. Over the last century, both men and women have seen increases in lung cancer deaths; however, recently, deaths among women continue to increase, while the death rates are declining among men (Green & Ottoson, 1999).

Genetics   Genetics can influence cancer rates. Women who have mothers, aunts, or sisters who have had breast cancer are more likely to develop it than are women without a family history of the disease. Be cautious with this information. Sometimes women hear it and believe that, because they do not have a family history of breast cancer, they won't get it. This belief could prevent them from conducting breast self-exams or seeking mammograms. Although these are forms of secondary prevention, they can save many lives by detecting cancer at a stage in which it can be treated.

Lifestyles   Most cases of cancer are associated with behaviors chosen by the patient. As you know, sun exposure, exposure to **carcinogens** (cancer-causing substances) in the air or at work, exposure to tobacco, and diet influence cancer rates. High-fat diets seem to be of greatest concern, but it is also important to follow all of the dietary guidelines suggested and approved by the U.S. Food and Drug Administration. See Figure 12.1 for the food pyramid.

Tobacco   Tobacco use is responsible for about one-third of all cancer deaths (Green & Ottoson, 1999). In fact, it is the leading preventable cause of death, in general, in the United States (USDHHS, 1990). Unfortunately, 80% of people who smoke start before they are 18 years of age (CDC, 1998a). The number of people under 18 who are smoking increased in the 1990s; thousands of teens start smoking each day. According to survey results, an increasing number of adolescents used smokeless tobacco or spitting tobacco, as it is termed by the American Cancer Society, in the 1980s and early 1990s. White adolescent males have the highest prevalence rate—above 10% (USDHHS, 1994). Nonsmokers are also greatly affected by tobacco because they are exposed to **secondhand,** or **sidestream, smoke.** When people are in a room with a lit cigarette, the cigarette smoke that floats into the air (and that they inhale) contains more tar, nicotine, carbon monoxide, and ammonia than that drawn into the lungs of a smoker.

Although cancer is a primary consequence of tobacco use, many other health problems are also a result. For example, cigarette smoking is related to heart disease and stroke. It impairs the respiratory system so seriously that respiratory diseases like **chronic obstructive lung disease (COLD), emphysema,** and **chronic bronchitis** are prevalent among smokers. COLD is generally a combination of respiratory diseases that cause obstruction of breathing (Hales, 1994). Emphysema results from overdistension of the air sacs (alveoli) in the lungs, and chronic bronchitis is a consistent irritation of the bronchi of the lung. Other

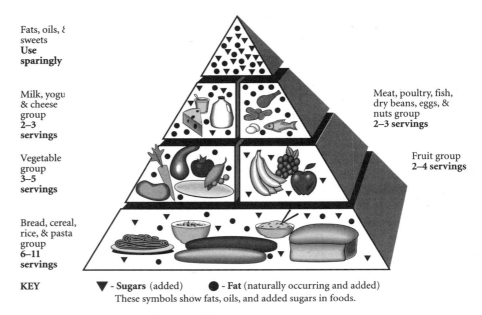

Fats, oils, & sweets
Use sparingly

Milk, yogu & cheese group
2–3 servings

Vegetable group
3–5 servings

Bread, cereal, rice, & pasta group
6–11 servings

Meat, poultry, fish, dry beans, eggs, & nuts group
2–3 servings

Fruit group
2–4 servings

KEY   ▼ - **Sugars** (added)   ● - **Fat** (naturally occurring and added)
These symbols show fats, oils, and added sugars in foods.

FIGURE 12.1   Food guide pyramid.
The Food Guide Pyramid is a quick, easy way to help individuals or groups understand what constitutes a healthy diet. You may want to use it in an advocacy campaign for school curricula that teaches about healthy diets. From *Food Guide Pyramid*, by U.S. Department of Agriculture, Human Nutrition Information Service, 1992, Home and Garden Bulletin No. 249.

tobacco-related health problems include gum disease, ulcers, low-birth-weight babies, and fertility problems.

The sheer numbers of people involved with tobacco either directly or indirectly make advocacy for control and prevention of tobacco use imperative. Appropriations to CDC prevention programs are also a valid advocacy target.

ENVIRONMENT

The environment is a major determinant of health. Environmental health encompasses many aspects of life, such as air, water, and food quality; waste disposal; insect, rodent, and animal control; and noise control (Morgan et al., 1997). Let us consider food, water, and air quality in more depth.

Food Quality

We presented some information about infectious disease in Chapter 3. As you remember, food, air, and water can be major modes of transmission for microorganisms that, in turn, can cause a variety of diseases that threaten the health of a community. In order to assist people in your community to protect themselves against these communicable diseases, it is important for you to know how to control microorganisms. Oxygen, temperature, food and moisture, pH, and osmotic pressure all influence the growth of microorganisms. They also affect control.

Some microorganisms need oxygen in the environment in order to survive (**aerobic organisms**), while others must live in an oxygen-free environment (**anaerobic organisms**). Still others survive with or without oxygen (**facultative organisms**). Because so many microorganisms that spoil food are aerobic, many foods are vacuum-packed (without oxygen). Of course, vacuum-packed food is not protected from anaerobic or facultative microorganisms.

Temperature requirements also vary among microorganisms. Some need very hot temperatures to grow, while others need warm, cool, or cold temperatures. Organisms that thrive at moderate temperatures will most likely survive in the human body and make people sick. It is important to prevent the survival of these microorganisms in foods. How would you go about doing so? We hope that you said you would keep food cold or hot. In other words, temperatures warmer than 113°F and colder than 60°F can control many microorganisms.

Microorganisms require food and water much as humans do. Effective methods for cleaning eating and cooking utensils and food preparation areas can prevent microbial infection. Unseen particles can provide excellent food for organisms. Dried foods last longer than fresh foods full of moisture. People who live in very humid climates learn quickly to put food items in airtight containers.

Pathogens live best in a pH of approximately 7.0. The level of acidity determines pH; therefore, adding an acid or alkaline like citric acid or vinegar can protect foods. Of course, many foods won't taste good with citric acid or vinegar, so other means of protection (such as refrigeration) are necessary.

Salt influences growth of microorganisms by influencing the osmotic pressure. **Osmosis** is the movement of two fluids capable of being mixed together through a membrane until they are in equal concentration on either side of the membrane. Salt-curing food protects food by putting it in an environment that will remove moisture from food through osmosis. Health educators play an important role in teaching people to prevent the growth of microorganisms in their food. Safe food issues may be important targets for advocacy.

Water Quality

Water, one of the world's most important resources (Morgan et al., 1997), influences most aspects of human life. It is a major component of the human body as well as the earth. As you can see in Figure 12.2, the hydrologic cycle, water is continually recycled. The quality of air influences water content while it is in the atmosphere. Microorganisms, chemicals, and minerals in the ground also influence the content of water. The Environmental Protection Agency (EPA)

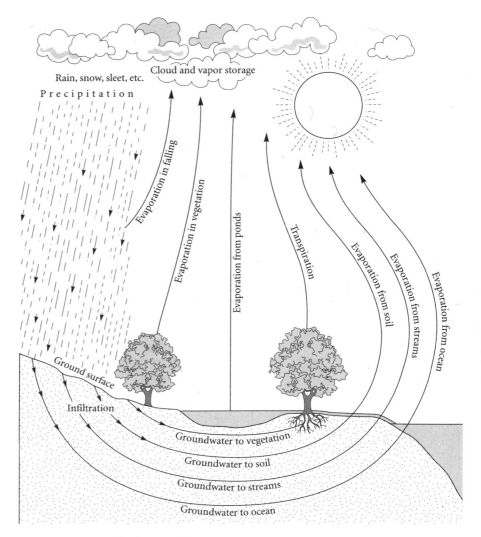

FIGURE 12.2   Hydrologic cycle.
The amount of water on our planet never changes; it is continually recycled. Pollutants in the air and ground enter our water supply. Environmental protection must occur at all stages of the hydrologic cycle. From *Environmental Health,* by M. T. Morgan et al., 1997, Englewood, CO: Morton.

has identified standards for drinking water. However, we must consider water-protection strategies throughout the cycle. We must continue to develop strategies for improving air quality and preventing toxic chemicals from entering ground and surface waters. At the same time, we must encourage environmentally sound industry growth and crop protection for the nation's farmers.

Air Quality

Many living organisms on earth must breathe a combination of 78% nitrogen, 21% oxygen, and 1% of a mixture of argon, carbon monoxide, and other gases. Unfortunately, many other gases and substances enter the air and cause pollution. Sources of air pollution can be human-made or natural. Some natural sources include forest fires, dust storms, volcanic eruptions, decay of organic materials, pollen, and molds. Although human behavior influences even natural sources of pollution, humans directly influence the air with fumes from cars, industrial pollutants, and other substances.

Pollution can be either prevented or addressed once it is a problem. Morgan et al. (1997, p. 222) suggest the following strategies:

Prevention

1. Control population growth.
2. Reduce the need for energy.
3. Enhance fuel-dependent units such as gas engines.
4. Recycle resources and prevent loss of metals and chemicals into the environment.
5. Emphasize quality in products (such as cars) so they will last longer.
6. Encourage repair of products rather than supporting remove-and-replace practices.
7. Reduce our dependency upon conveniences and our desire for affluence.
8. Reduce our dependency upon fossil fuels.
9. Find new nonpolluting sources of energy (such as wind, tidal, and solar energy).

Treatment

1. Remove pollutants after combustion by using scrubbers and electrostatic precipitators at industrial facilities.
2. Add lime and other materials to raise the pH of lakes, streams, and the soil damaged by acid rain.
3. Support improved methods of emission control.
4. Research new methods of removing pollutants in emissions.
5. Find ways to convert pollutants to resources.
6. Improve catalytic conversion in automobiles.

MENTAL HEALTH

Eating Disorders

When most of us think about eating disorders, we think about behaviors involving food, such as eating too much or too little. Although indeed part of an eating disorder, these behaviors are only a small part of a very complex picture.

You have probably heard of the three major types of eating disorders: anorexia nervosa, bulimia nervosa, and binge eating. **Anorexia nervosa** involves long-term fasting to some degree of starvation. Symptoms vary for each individual; however, excessive weight loss, sensitivity to cold, skin problems, cavities, and gastrointestinal problems may indicate the presence of anorexia (Center for Eating Disorders, 1999).

Like anorexia nervosa, **bulimia nervosa** involves a preoccupation with food and appearance. People with bulimia may eat a very large amount of food and then induce vomiting. Misuse of laxatives, diuretics, exercise, and diet pills may also be common among these individuals. **Binge-eating disorder** is characterized by excessive overeating for a period of days, weeks, or months.

Millions of people in the United States are affected by eating disorders, including people of all ages. Most of those afflicted are adolescent or young adult women (Center for Eating Disorders, 1999). Approximately 10% of those with anorexia and bulimia are thought to be males, but 25% of individuals with binge-eating disorders are thought to be males. Males with eating disorders are more likely to have been teased about weight or to have experienced success at sports after weight loss (Center for Eating Disorders, 1999). Sports that require weight control, like gymnastics, dance, and wrestling, put young athletes at risk. Coaches often encourage—or, in some cases, demand—stringent weight control, putting athletes in no-choice situations.

As with most chronic diseases and disorders, no single cause for eating disorders can be identified. Stress, poor self-image, the need for control, the need for achievement, and difficulty controlling emotions may influence the onset of an eating disorder. The media have contributed to the development of harmful perceptions we have about the size of our bodies. In media presentations, thinness and success seem to be linked.

Body image is how we "see" our body and the feelings we have about it. Some individuals over- or underestimate the actual size of their bodies. This misperception may lead to extreme body image dissatisfaction and unhappiness. For some, it may also trigger an obsessive need to be thinner and a cycle that spirals downward. The individual finds that losing a little weight doesn't increase the feeling of happiness, so more weight is lost. Eventually, excessive weight loss begins to bring about other health problems.

Treatment of eating disorders may be *inpatient* (involves admission into a treatment facility) or *outpatient* (no admission). In either case, the approach to treatment will involve cognitive and behavioral therapies in which people are helped to realize they do have an eating disorder and to examine the possible issues causing it. Pharmaceutical approaches—that is, the use of medications—are also used. The individuals and their families work together during treatment. Without treatment, approximately 20% of people with eating disorders do not survive. Although treatment effectiveness needs further research, at this time around 60% of individuals who receive treatment do improve (Center for Eat-

FOR YOUR INFORMATION 12.8

Learning More About Eating Disorders

Eating disorders make up a group of disorders that aren't always easy to diagnose or treat. It is important that health educators and community members know where to get help for these serious problems. For information about eating disorders, you can call your local mental health association or you can call:

- Eating Disorders Awareness and Prevention
  800-931-2237
- National Association of Anorexia Nervosa (ANAD)
  847-831-3438
- Anorexia Nervosa and Related Eating Disorders (ANRED)
  503-344-1144
- National Eating Disorders Organization (NEDO)
  918-481-4044
- Center for the Study of Anorexia and Bulimia
  212-233-3444

From *Frequently Asked Questions*, by Center for Eating Disorders. Retrieved January 3, 2000, from the World Wide Web: http//www.eatingdisorders.com /faq/htm.

ing Disorders, 1999). See FYI 12.8 for a list of places to learn more about eating disorders.

Prevention of eating disorders may be as difficult as identifying the cause. However, much can be accomplished through education. Health education at both home and school regarding well-balanced diets, the benefits and pleasure of moderate exercise, and the deception of advertising may play a large role in prevention. Can you see why comprehensive health education in schools would be an appropriate advocacy target?

Depression

Depression is influenced by electrolyte imbalances and hormone and vitamin deficiencies. It is caused by a chemical imbalance in the brain and may have a genetic component. Some of the symptoms of depression include anxiety, sadness, feelings of helplessness, loss of interest, feelings of guilt, change in sleep or eating habits, fatigue, and restlessness (Center for Eating Disorders, 1999). Depression can be effectively treated with pharmaceuticals and therapy. The difficulty lies in finding a health care provider who is knowledgeable about its treatment and willing to work with a person until the most effective treatment combination is discovered. This process can be frustrating, but the message of "don't give up" is applicable in the treatment of depression. The frequent lack of insurance coverage for mental health issues is also a problem.

Stress

Stress has been seen over time from three perspectives. The first conceptualizes stress as a stimulus from the environment that causes discomfort. According to this perspective, events or situations that cause the discomfort are called **stressors,** and research is conducted on the impact of stressors on the human being. The second perspective views stress as a response. Research focuses on the types of responses (physiological and psychological) humans have to stressors. The third perspective sees stress as a continual transaction between a person and the environment. Sarafino (1990) uses all three perspectives to define stress as "the condition that results when person/environment transactions lead the individual to perceive a discrepancy—whether real or not—between the demands of a situation and the resources of the person's biological, psychological, or social systems" (p. 77).

When we *appraise* (consider through the process of thought) an event or situation, we are likely to determine that it is irrelevant, good, or stressful. If an event is appraised as stressful, the body will react. Hans Selye described a series of biological reactions that people experience when stress is prolonged. Figure 12.3 charts the general adaptation syndrome. The syndrome has three phases: alarm reaction, resistance, and exhaustion. The alarm stage involves a fight-or-flight reaction in which your body will release the hormones epinephrine, norepinephrine, and cortisol—these increase heart rate and blood pressure. The alarm stage serves a useful purpose in a real short-term emergency. But the human body can't continue to survive in this alarm stage. If stress continues, but not at the level to cause death, the second phase will involve resistance. In resistance, the body remains physiologically aroused but not to the extent of the alarm phase. In this phase, the body is not as able to protect itself from new stressors. It becomes vulnerable to health problems such as high blood pressure and an impaired immune system. The third stage, exhaustion, occurs with severe long-term stress. Disease and physiological damage are much more likely. As in the first stage, death can occur.

As a health educator, you will need to understand stress and ways of addressing it. Stress-coping strategies range from taking a walk to taking medications. We encourage you to get to know more about these through either self-study or a class. It is equally important to address stress by removing stressors where possible. It becomes all to easy to expect the victim of stress to control it rather than to remove the problem itself. In some cases, the community environment may be responsible for the presence of stressors. Safety, access to services, access to educational opportunities, housing, employment, violence, and socioeconomic

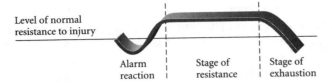

FIGURE 12.3   General adaptation syndrome.
Hans Selye described a three-phase series of biological reactions that people experience with prolonged stress. During the first and third phases, an individual is more prone to injury. From *Fit and Well: Core Concepts and Labs in Physical Fitness and Wellness*, 1st ed., by T. D. Fahey, P. M. Insel, & W. T. Roth, 1994, Mountain View, CA: Mayfield.

status are all social issues that contribute to community stress. As with the individual, prolonged community stress will result in a sickened community. Will you be able to help?

SOCIAL ISSUES

Violence

You probably have noted that many of the issues we have discussed in this and other chapters are complex and difficult to understand. The same is true for violence. There is a strong connection between poverty and the risk of victimization. There is also a connection between poverty and level of crime (Kilmer & Price, 1995a). Some psychologists believe that turning to violence may be an attempt to change a feeling of powerlessness.

Areas with high crime have more gang activity, substance abuse, access to guns, and unsafe schools. Unsafe schools result in poorer educational opportunities, which in turn lead to fewer alternative activities and more crime (Kilmer & Price, 1995d). Increased substance abuse leads to more violence among youth, and access to guns leads to more unintentional shootings as well as criminal violence. Around 3,000 children under 20 die each year of accidental shootings. This situation is truly a vicious cycle.

Increases in community violence are associated with juvenile victimization. One in four crime victims is juvenile (Kilmer & Price, 1995b), and homicide is the second leading cause of death among those 15 to 24 years old in the United States. African American and Hispanic males bear the burden of victimization and homicide.

The media don't help the situation. In fact, some believe that the media glorify violence and, in some ways, victimization. Others believe that television and movies portray violence so frequently that viewers lose their sense of horror toward it. The relationship between violence and media has not been adequately studied. It is a complicated issue.

Domestic violence occurs when an individual abuses his or her intimate partner (Kilmer & Price, 1995c). This type of violence is expressed in many forms, including hitting, punching, kicking, verbal abuse, sexual assault, threat of injury with a deadly weapon, social isolation, and murder. Children who witness domestic violence are traumatized and terrorized. Long-term effects of witnessing violence toward a loved one might lead to problems in physical and mental health as well as cognitive development.

Child abuse can also take many forms, including physical abuse, neglect, sexual abuse, and emotional abuse. Home is the most dangerous place for some children because parents are the most frequent perpetrators of child abuse. An estimated 2.5% of the nation's children may have experienced abuse, but true numbers are hard to determine because many cases of abuse remain unreported. Abuse leads to more abuse; children who are abused often abuse their own children.

Solving the problems of violence and abuse will never be easy. People who are involved frequently have poor coping skills, high stress, and a history of family violence and substance abuse. They often live in poverty and are socially isolated. The target of advocacy must go much deeper than just elimination of violence. The root causes must be addressed before any major changes will be seen in levels of violence and abuse.

IN CONCLUSION

Health educators must unite and advocate for important health issues. The power of many voices can make a difference in health outcomes. Advocacy is not a single activity. Knowledge, coalitions and partnerships, lobbying, grassroots activities, media, and legislative advocacy are excellent advocacy tools. Be sure to use the tips and guidelines for advocacy that other advocates have found to be useful.

 REVIEW QUESTIONS

1. List and define the advocacy terms presented in this chapter.
2. Compare and contrast four advocacy tools.
3. Describe topics you feel are important to cover in a training session for people who wish to visit a policy maker.
4. Select two health issues that you believe warrant advocacy. Write a few paragraphs giving important facts about your issues.
5. Using the health issues you selected in question 4, analyze the differences between the philosophies of harm reduction and control.
6. Identify a health issue that is not presented in the chapter but that you consider an important advocacy topic. Justify your choice.

FOR YOUR APPLICATION

Preparing for Advocacy

1. Select a health issue that you think warrants further advocacy in your state.
2. Collect some information about the issue.
3. Create a one-page fact sheet that you could give to other health educators who would be willing to join you in advocating for the issue.
4. Ask some of your classmates to comment on or make additions to your fact sheet.

FOR YOUR PORTFOLIO

Putting Advocacy to Practice

1. Select a health issue that warrants further advocacy or use the one that you selected in "For Your Application."
2. Write a letter to one of your state legislators (preferably the individual from your home district) about your selected issue.
3. Use the tips provided in this chapter.
4. Ask your instructor to read your letter and provide feedback.
5. Revise your letter and send it to your legislator.
6. Put a copy in the Resource Section of your portfolio.

PART III

Communicating Health Education Needs

Communicating Health and Health Education Needs

THE TEENAGER SHIFTS HER BABY TO THE OTHER HIP AND opens the pamphlet you just handed to her. "Oh, how she needs this information," you think to yourself. But will the pamphlet convince her to get her baby immunized? Did the explanation you gave make sense to her? She's so young and has much to learn about parenting. And there are other needs in her life. The few minutes you have to convince her to come back next week are fading. You feel that every word counts. But are they the right words?

Chapter Objectives

1. Specify the skills necessary for effective communication.
2. Practice effective communication skills.
3. Name and describe each component of the health communication model.
4. Explain what is meant by iatrogenic health education disease.
5. Explain the difference between persuasive communication and coercion.
6. Name and give an example of each of the six stages of health communication.
7. Describe effective writing tips.
8. Identify effective speaking techniques.

EFFECTIVE COMMUNICATION

Communicate, communicate, communicate. We attempted to make a strong point in Chapter 10 about how important communication can be in collaboration and conflict-resolution efforts. In other chapters we also discussed the usefulness of careful communication in a variety of health education efforts (see FYI 13.1). We didn't, however, address the issue of what communication is and how you can apply it in a variety of ways to be an effective health educator. Effective communication is the backbone of our profession. It permeates all seven areas of responsibility and can become your most valuable tool as you interact with community members to conduct needs assessments and plan, implement, and evaluate programs. It is particularly useful in the process of community capacity building, which we described in Chapter 6, because you may need it to help community members raise broader community awareness about an existing health problem, influence public opinion about the need to address the problem, and mobilize support from institutional, political, and community leaders and stakeholders (Heaven, 1999).

The absence of clear communication can quickly lead you astray when you are attempting to serve as a resource person or program coordinator (Seelye & Seelye-James, 1996). Miscommunication can foster frustration and resentment and destroy important working relationships. It can result in wasted time and resources when you have to backtrack and reconstruct project components. It can also affect your credibility in the community and reduce community members' motivation to become involved.

Communication is also important within the context of the basic philosophies of health education that we discussed in earlier chapters. If the primary goal of community health education were to force people to do what we believe is best for them, the communication process would be simple. We would merely need to clearly state what we expect from people and graphically describe the consequences for those who do not comply. We would no longer need a textbook chapter focused on communication because most people are already familiar with how direct orders are communicated.

We do need this chapter, however, because community health education is not primarily about enforcing directives. It is, instead, about helping people to help themselves. From this perspective, the focus isn't on you, the health educator, and what you expect. The decision-making power lies in the hands of the people you serve. Their beliefs, expectations, values, desires, and concerns will ultimately dictate their health-related behavior. Your role is to facilitate their decisions by providing information, resource access, and guidance as needed. And, in some instances, you may also discover a need to persuade, motivate, and encourage healthy choices.

That's where the need for effective communication enters the picture. Designing something intended to communicate—like the immunization pamphlet given to the young mother in our opening scenario—can be a challenge.

FOR YOUR INFORMATION 13.1

Health Communication–Related Topics in Earlier Chapters

Review the following chapter sections to broaden perspectives about health communication.

Chapter	Health Communication–Related Topic
5	Communication styles (of traditional cultures)
6	Community participation and capacity building
7	Multiple intelligences
8	Social marketing and the theory of the diffusion of innovation
9	The evaluation report
10	Collaboration and conflict resolution
11	Obtaining accurate information from resources
12	Methods of advocating for health

How does one persuade a young woman whose life views are different from yours that the temporary discomfort of an injection is a good thing if it protects her baby from disease? You already know the answer. It begins with effective communication.

Communication Defined

"I communicated to him that I was going to finish the job. He just didn't listen!" Can you imagine hearing this statement made in a tone of frustration? We can! Few things are more irritating than to believe you have communicated with another person and, later, discover that the person didn't understand at all. Do you think whoever our speaker is referring to simply didn't listen? It's possible. Picture two people, Vanessa and Tyson, who are busily putting away groceries. Vanessa talks as she works. Tyson interjects a few "um-hums" here and there as he places cans on a shelf. What Vanessa doesn't know is that, for some reason, Tyson didn't hear what she thinks he heard. Days later, Vanessa discovers through a friend that Tyson did not believe she had told him about her plans and reacted negatively when she carried them out. Miscommunication led to misunderstanding, and problems resulted.

There could be a number of reasons for this miscommunication, including the actions and thoughts of both people involved. True communication depends on both the giver and the receiver of a message. However, accurate communication depends not only on the people involved but also on the nature and quality of the message itself and the channel through which the message is delivered.

FOR YOUR INFORMATION 13.2

Health Communication Model

This model shows a linear flow of health communication that reminds us to consider factors that influence each component and shape the degree to which clear, effective communication occurs.

SENDER ———→ MESSAGE ———→ MEDIUM ———→ RECEIVER

From *Health Education: Learner-Centered Instructional Strategies,* 4th ed., by J. S. Greenberg, 1997, New York, NY: McGraw-Hill.

Communication is defined as "an act or instance of transmitting, . . . a technique for expressing ideas effectively." But the process is a bit more complex than it seems. To understand it more clearly, we introduce you to a useful model.

List possible contributors to the kitchen scenario miscommunication.

Health Communication Model   Jerrold Greenberg (1995) is a well-known health educator who has contributed much to what is known in our profession about the process of health communication. His **health communication model** illustrates how communication works (FYI 13.2). On the surface, the communication process seems simple. The *sender* (Vanessa in our illustration) attempts to convey a *message* (that she plans to do something) through a communication *medium,* or channel of message delivery (orally, as she puts away groceries), to the *receiver* (Tyson). That sounds simple enough, doesn't it? However, if the process is so simple, why does miscommunication occur? Let's explore the possibilities as they relate to each of the four model components.

SENDER   Have you ever been totally certain that you said something in a particular way only to discover later that what you said and what you thought you said were two different things? Perhaps you made a statement in conversation and immediately realized that your wording conveyed something other than what you intended. Such situations can be embarrassing, but they are a useful example of how the sender plays an important role in the communication process.

How the sender processes information, decides upon the message to be conveyed, and formulates the message to be expressed are critical to message development. Possible contributing factors to the miscommunication in our illustration may have included inconsistencies between what Vanessa intended to say or believed she said and what she actually stated. A clearly communicated message begins with careful decision making and message construction on the part of the sender.

Before we move on to the second component of the model, let's discuss who the sender is in most health education situations. Greenberg (1995) points out that most health educators think of themselves as the message senders. After all, we are the ones hired to communicate health education messages. But isn't the sender also considered the originator of the message? The sender in our illustration certainly originated her message about her plans. But are health educators truly the originators of health education messages about, for example, the effect of exercise and diet on one's health? Or are we simply the messenger, the deliverer, the medium through which the message is sent? Greenberg (1995) maintains that society is the true health education message sender and that we, as health educators, are the message conduit. Understanding that difference serves as a reminder that we must carefully consider the accuracy and quality of the message we are sending before we send it.

MESSAGE   In our example involving the two grocery-bearing friends, we know little about the message itself. We know only that it was about some decision Vanessa had made about something she planned to do. Whether that decision was a good idea and how it would affect others seems irrelevant to our discussion about how it was miscommunicated. However, as a health educator, the nature of the messages you will be asked to convey is a critical issue. It's important to consider message accuracy and message appropriateness.

Many confusing health-related messages are transmitted to our society through the news media, infomercials, books, magazines, and the Internet. Many of them are products of sensationalized half-truths, money-making schemes, or misguided individuals who mean well but mistakenly believe and spread inaccurate health information. As a health educator, you are professionally responsible for the accuracy of the health messages you deliver. That is why it is important for you to understand research methodology and the difference between evidence-based fact and opinion. We invite you to revisit Chapter 11, where we discuss the importance of knowing where to go for accurate information as a resource person. And, for each message you send, be sure to first consider who originated that message and on what research evidence it was based.

Message appropriateness is another important aspect to be considered. For example, the message that regular exercise can positively contribute to one's health may be accurate. But the term "regular exercise" can mean different things to different people. What would be considered an appropriate exercise type, frequency, and intensity for one person might place another at risk of injury. We need only compare the exercise needs of an Olympic athlete to those of a formerly sedentary 80-year-old adult to understand the importance of adapted messages. Messages about exercise or any other health issue should be presented in a way that is appropriately tailored to match the needs and abilities of the message receivers.

As we stated in Chapter 8 when we discussed social marketing and the diffusion of innovation theory, presenting the message in a way that appropriately appeals to individual values and readiness for change increases the chance that the message will be accepted. Some individuals in our society suffer from what is referred to as iatrogenic health education disease (IHED) (Greenberg, 1995). Though IHED isn't truly a diagnosable disease, the phrase is used to describe a state of mind in which a person feels overwhelmed by the onslaught of health-risk messages. As a result, the person believes that trying to live a healthy lifestyle is futile and gives up on trying to maintain healthy behaviors. If you have ever heard someone say, "We all have to die of *something!*" or "Oh, *everything* causes cancer!" you may have been listening to a person suffering from IHED. To guard against this, your messages should be appropriately tailored to the receiver's sense of what is reasonable and worthwhile.

MEDIUM   As we stated earlier, Greenberg (1995) would likely contend that you, the health educator, are the message medium, the channel through which the health message is delivered. From a different perspective, pamphlets, Web pages, oral presentations, newspaper articles, and public service announcements (PSAs) could also be considered examples of a message medium. Whether you consider yourself or these message delivery channels as the medium, it is important that you pay close attention to how health messages are delivered.

You may have noted in our miscommunication illustration that both parties were busily putting away groceries as the message was delivered. Can you imagine Vanessa bending down to put something on a bottom shelf just as she began her message about her plans? While her back was turned Tyson could have momentarily stepped into a closet pantry and never even heard her statement. Or, through the noise and shuffle of activity, he may have heard only part of what she said. In either event, one could conclude that the chosen message channel left a lot to be desired.

This is why the selected message medium or channel is so important. Your message can be accurate and appropriately adapted to your intended audience. It may be worded in a way that effectively appeals to audience needs, values, and levels of readiness for acceptance. Yet, with all those important components in place, the communication process still may break down due to a faulty message medium. That medium must be a consistently reliable channel to the audience, one that can be depended upon to deliver the message to the right place at the right time. Return to Chapter 8 for more detail about placing your message appropriately.

RECEIVER   Finally, we arrive at the place in which blame was placed in the beginning. Vanessa's comment that "He just didn't listen!" placed all the blame at Tyson's feet. We've already considered the possibility that it wasn't Tyson's fault, that the problem could lie with the sender, message, or medium. But let's reconsider. After all, Tyson was providing some indication that he was listening with each "um-hum" he offered. It is possible that Vanessa clearly stated her plans in an audible format, and Tyson was there all along to receive every word, but didn't. He may not have been really listening at all. Or he may have been listening but didn't really place importance on what she said and, thus, quickly forgot it. Or he may have listened carefully but, because he and Vanessa process information differently, may have placed an entirely different interpretation on what she said.

The receiver obviously plays an important role in the message communication process. In health education settings, the receiver could be the person whose health needs you are attempting to assess and address with health programs. It could also be the community gatekeeper or stakeholder whose support you need in your assessment and programming efforts. The receiver could be someone whose resources you hope to attain for use in your efforts through grants, donations, or volunteered services. In each of these situations, knowing your communication goal is important.

The Communication Effect

Before developing a specific message and choosing an audience-appropriate medium or message channel, the message sender should carefully consider the desired communication effect, or outcome. For instance, is the purpose of a message to simply provide information, or is it intended to persuade the message receiver to adopt a particular health attitude or behavior? The difference in these two desired effects could drastically alter your communication approach.

There was a time when public educators believed that we needed only to impart health-related knowledge to bring about positive changes in health behavior. If we simply told people, for example, that smoking causes cancer and regular exercise can help prevent heart disease, then people would automatically stop smoking and start exercising—or so it was believed. Thus, we needed only to bridge knowledge gaps with informative health messages, and all people everywhere would live healthier lives. Right? Wrong!

You may recall our discussions in previous chapters about the multitude of factors that influence health attitudes and behaviors. You may also remember that knowledge about health is only one factor, which, in the face of all those other influences (such as values, habits, peer pressure), carries very little weight on its own in health-related decisions. That is why developing effective health communication messages is such a challenge. In addition to providing needed health information in a format that is easily understood, the messages you send must also appeal to the message receiver's value system. They must motivate your receivers to overcome any perceived barriers that might prevent them from adopting healthy attitudes and behaviors.

Persuasive Communication   If health communication focused only on developing clearly stated health information, you, as a health educator might not be needed. After all, many professional disciplines train their members to clearly present information. However, there is a real art to knowing how to assess and adapt health-related messages to the needs and values of a variety of audiences and to package those messages in ways that can persuade the receiver to change health-related attitudes and behaviors.

This art is known as **persuasive communication.** A return to our discussion in Chapter 8 about the theory of diffusion of innovation could be helpful in understanding this art within the context of mass communication. We encourage you to develop persuasive communication skills and seek opportunities to practice applying them through a variety of media (see "For Your Portfolio"). Never forget, however, that persuasive communication is not the same thing as **coercion,** which leans toward manipulating or even forcing people to do what you want. The decision to adopt or reject a health-related attitude or behavior is not yours as the health educator. Your job is to provide needed information, training, and resources for positive health behavior change and to attempt to respectfully persuade and encourage the adoption of attitudes and behaviors that are clearly in the best interests of your audience. However, the decision belongs to the message receiver, not you. Adopt a respectful approach in your health communication efforts, and you will likely avoid crossing the line between the professionally appropriate tone of persuasive communication and inappropriate coercion.

Regardless of the targeted receiver and the purpose of your message, the receiver is the pivotal component in the communication process. The receiver is the component over which you, the health educator, have the least amount of control. For that reason, it is critical that you learn all you can about the receiver's thought processes, needs, values, and preferred communication channels.

Learning Styles and Information Processing   People think in different ways, and that's why communication can sometimes be a challenge. The ideas formulated by the message sender do not always match the thought processes of the receiver. What may seem to you to be a perfectly clear pamphlet about the need for immunizations may not make any sense at all to another person. Or perhaps your pamphlet helps clarify the issue for one mother, but she would achieve full understanding more readily by listening to oral testimony from another teenage mother who provides the same information but in story form.

Differences in learning and information-processing (cognitive) styles have been researched for years (Anderson & Adams, 1992; Bean, 1996), and much of this information is reflected in the multiple intelligences model we described in Chapter 7. Here we wish to add only that understanding the differences in individual information processing represented in the model will greatly enhance your communication efforts.

Some controversy exists in the literature about whether learning and communication-style differences can be detected across cultures. Numerous studies have been cited as growing evidence that distinct cultural differences exist in relation to these styles (Anderson & Adams, 1992; Cushner, 1994). Others argue that such studies do not provide conclusive evidence (Kitano, 1997). As with other cultural differences, these distinctions appear to emerge among groups of individuals who closely adhere to their cultural roots. In fact, some scholars suggest that culture shapes not only what one thinks, but also how one thinks and learns (Cushner, 1994).

We call this to your attention to make two points. First, as the cultural diversity of our society grows, so will the need to offer your communication message in multiple formats and channels. Second, we caution you to carefully consider both sides of the cultural distinction argument so that you don't make the mistake of either ignoring culture-specific differences or of stereotyping those who wear certain cultural labels. Whenever time and resources allow, a balanced, multiple-strategy approach is a good idea.

COMMUNICATION STRATEGIES AND PRINCIPLES

Now that you have a firm understanding of the communication process and your role and purposes in health communication, we can begin to explore strategies that have been proven to enhance the likelihood of successful communication. We first present some general strategies for the development and implementation of health communication. We follow that with some broad communication principles and strategies that can be adapted to most media. In subsequent sections, we also provide basic guidelines for selected media.

Stages of Health Communication

The circle in Figure 13.1 illustrates six stages of health communication (NIH, 1995) that, when followed, can help you develop effective messages. Note that the first three, shaded in gray, are steps you should take before the communication is implemented. After reading the earlier chapters in this book, you should be able to anticipate that a thorough needs assessment and detailed plan are recommended before any health education effort begins. This includes efforts toward effective health communication.

Let's pretend for a moment that you work in the community education division of a health maintenance organization and have been asked to enhance awareness in the local lesbian community about the need for annual well-woman checkups. You begin with stage 1, planning and strategy selection, which entails a preliminary needs assessment. As you would in a needs assessment for any health education program, you first study existing data and then collect new data to fill in any information gaps. The goal is to identify specific subgroups within the lesbian community who may be least likely to obtain annual checkups and gain an understanding of the factors that influence that choice. (Return to Chapter 6 for a reminder of needs-assessment components and strategies.) Stage 1 would end with clearly defined communication goals and objectives that are designed to address influencing factors.

You would then be ready to move on to stage 2, to select communication channels and materials that best match your targeted audience's needs and preferred information sources (such as specific radio stations, newspapers, and organizational newsletters). We encourage you to solicit as much input as possible

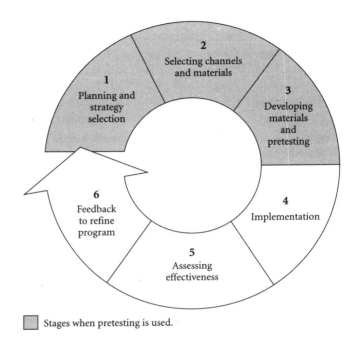

Stages when pretesting is used.

FIGURE 13.1   Stages of health communication.
Following these six stages of health communication can help to develop effective communication messages. From *Making Health Communication Programs Work: A Planner's Guide,* by National Institutes of Health, 1995, Atlanta: USDHHS (NIH Pub. 92-1493). Retrieved November 28, 1999, from the World Wide Web: http://rex.nci.nih.gov/NCI_Pub_Interface/HCPW/OVER.HTM.

from community members; in doing so, expect to receive a variety of suggestions about channels and formats. Individuals who wear the same label do not necessarily access the same communication channels. Find out about communication channels that have been used in the past to reach members of the community, and analyze existing communication materials to determine strengths and weaknesses of past and current efforts.

Communication channels for the lesbian community can be very complex due to within-group diversity and the fact that members seldom cluster into geographically distinct locations. In other words, the definition of the lesbian community follows the same distinctions and limitations we discussed in earlier chapters when attempting to identify other recognized community groups. You may, for instance, be able to access some members of the lesbian community through organizations whose specific purpose is to provide service to and support the community. However, some lesbians who wish to avoid discrimination and mistreatment do not access information through these organizations. They may, however, receive your message about the need for annual checkups via their lesbian friends who do participate in those organizations. Or you may more readily reach these women through local newspapers and television stations that are considered more mainstream.

It is a good idea to draft and test (stage 3) several different message channels (such as brochures, videos, or public service announcements on radio). Ask community gatekeepers and health experts with knowledge about local lesbian culture to critique each and provide suggestions. Then pilot-test the revised message formats and channels and obtain feedback from representatives of the intended audience. Ask those representatives to give you their honest impressions of the message and its format, the degree to which the message could be understood, recalled, and accepted as important and culturally appropriate. Make revisions based on their feedback.

In our example, let us assume that the outcome of the first three stages was the development of a pamphlet designed to persuade lesbians to value annual well-woman checkups and overcome barriers that often prevent them from obtaining the checkups. Your pamphlet also contains a list of women's health clinics in which the well-woman checkup process is designed to address the needs and concerns of lesbians. You also train volunteers from the community to present this information at local organizational meetings and worship centers that specifically serve the lesbian community. In their presentations, the volunteers distribute the pamphlets and appeal to the audience to attend one of the clinics and encourage others in the community to do the same.

In addition, you decide to develop a public service announcement (PSA) for radio in which the message deliverer identifies herself as a lesbian and provides a testimonial about how she used to avoid well-woman checkups but, through a chance screening experience, was diagnosed and treated for ovarian cancer, a condition for which she'd never considered herself to be at risk. The PSA ends with a heartfelt appeal to the listener to break through the barriers and go in for a checkup. Listeners are then given a phone number they can call to get the list of local women's health clinics that is also provided in the pamphlet.

You now have implemented three different communication channels (stage 3). The radio PSA serves as one. The volunteer presenters who also distribute the pamphlet serve as a second channel. And, if the presenters' audiences respond to the appeal, the pamphlet alone may serve as a third as it finds its way into the hands of other lesbians who never hear the presentation. How will you know whether all three channels are working and whether you should continue to invest time and money into all three? That's where stages 5 and 6 come in. You won't know unless you track the messages.

You can choose from several tracking strategies. You could ask your volunteer presenters to keep records of the frequency and location and date of each presentation, the number of people who attend them, and the number of pamphlets distributed at the end of each meeting. You could also record the number of times the PSA was aired with dates and time of day noted. But those counts would only tell you how often you presented the message. They would tell you nothing about whether the intended communication effect or outcome was a result and which channel was responsible. That is, did the communication increase the frequency of annual well-woman checkups among targeted members of the lesbian community?

Measuring the communication effect would require a different kind of tracking, one that would allow you to survey those who received the message to learn about how they perceived the message and whether it motivated them to complete an annual checkup. After your campaign begins, you could also survey those who attended the clinics listed in the pamphlet to determine whether any were motivated to make an appointment by one of the communication channels and, if so, which one. A review of Chapter 9 can help you consider other evaluation possibilities. For our purposes here, note that evaluation and revision are important components of health communication.

General Communication Principles

The National Institutes of Health (1995) have provided an overview of how the public commonly perceives health messages (FYI 13.3). Understanding these perceptions can help you shape your health messages so that they are more likely to be accepted. First, the NIH points out that few people understand the concept of health risk. That is why the public is more likely to strongly react to such low-risk possibilities as homicides and accidental deaths that are often sensationalized by the news media. Yet they may ignore information about chronic diseases (such as heart disease, stroke, diabetes) that represent a greater health risk (are a more likely possibility) for most Americans.

To counter this imbalance, it might seem logical to focus our communication efforts on risk-awareness messages. However, messages that frighten the audience can backfire by producing feelings of helplessness and denial. If you have ever heard a person say "Everything causes cancer," you likely understand the dangers of using *fear tactics* in your communications. A well-balanced message can include an explanation of related health risks, but should not target fear as the intended outcome.

In the same sense that few people understand health risk, the general public has little confidence in or understanding of scientific research (NIH, 1995). People tend to embrace easy solutions and absolute answers and expect to find them in scientific research results; they have little patience with discussions about the need to replicate studies over time to test for consistency. Few understand how variability in study participant numbers and characteristics, methods used, and research settings can bias results. Even fewer know the difference between an association that only proves two factors coexist and a well-designed cause-and-effect study. For this reason, oversimplified news media coverage of a man who drank throughout his life and lived to be 100 years old, for instance, can quickly become accepted as conclusive evidence that alcohol intake increases longevity.

FOR YOUR INFORMATION 13.3

Public Perceptions About Health Messages and Suggested Communication Strategies

These suggested communication strategies (right column) are based on what is known about common public perceptions (left column) and how they affect people's acceptance of health messages.

Common Public Perceptions	Suggested Communication Strategies
• Few people understand the concept of health risk.	• People personalize new information.
• Fear tactics sometimes backfire.	• Focus on positive outcomes of positive behaviors. (Avoid fear tactics.)
• The public may not believe or understand science.	• Minimize use of scientific jargon.
• People respond to easy solutions and absolute answers.	• Keep messages simple.
• People tend to live for today, not tomorrow.	• Accentuate immediate health and nonhealth benefits.
• Health may not be a priority.	• Personalize messages.
• Individuals do not feel personally susceptible.	• Suggest "do-able" first-step solutions.
• The public holds contradictory beliefs.	

From "How the Public Perceives Health Messages," in *Health Communication Processes That Work,* by National Cancer Institute, 1999. Retrieved November 28, 1999, from the World Wide Web: http://rex.nci.nih.gov/NCI_Pub_Interface/HCPW/HOME.HTM.

The irony in this is that few people dwell on the future, and long-range health risks and related information are seldom a priority (NIH, 1995). These tendencies apply especially to the younger members of our society and to those at lower socioeconomic levels. But no matter who your audience is, your health messages should emphasize immediate health and nonhealth benefits to adopting healthy lifestyles. An example would be to explain how regular exercise results in immediate stress reduction and weight management benefits, to show that people who exercise report more positive perceptions about life and are more productive. These short-range, non-health benefits may create a greater message appeal and have greater impact than would a discussion about how exercise can reduce risk of long-range heart disease.

Our perceptions about personal susceptibility to a particular health problem are usually lower than our actual risk rates (NIH, 1995). Yet individuals can also hold contradictory beliefs about how people, in the abstract, are susceptible to a multitude of health dangers. To return to an earlier example, picture a smoker who doesn't believe he or she is at personal risk of developing lung cancer but insists that all things cause cancer. The smoker may believe that we will all eventually die of cancer anyway and that quitting smoking will do little to change that. To counter low levels of *perceived susceptibility* and *contradictory beliefs,* design your messages in a way that personalizes the issue and provides clear, simple suggestions that won't overwhelm your message receiver.

Strategies for Selected Communication Media

You have access via the Internet to a very useful Web page called the Community Toolbox (**http://ctb.lsi.ukans.edu**). This Web page is sponsored by a variety of professional working groups, organizations, and foundations whose members are interested in promoting community health and community development (University of Kansas, 1999). From it, you can download skill-building information on over 150 community health topics. Among those topics are a variety of practical "how to" articles that relate to the development and use of professional presentations, fact sheets, pamphlets, PSAs, and grant proposals. The Web site provides a much broader array of resources than what we have mentioned here. We invite you to visit this and other Web sites listed in Appendix D for more detailed information about health communication theory, principles, and skills.

Writing for Success   An important first step in good writing is knowing *why* you are writing and for *whom* the message is intended. Then create an outline or cognitive map of your intended message so that you have a clear vision of the major points you wish to communicate. A number of different types of writing styles and formats could be appropriate, depending on your writing purpose and audience. These can range in complexity and length from single-statement public service announcements to brief informational brochures and flyers to full articles intended for a general audience or a professional community. Across these formats, however, there are some general rules of thumb you can follow for effective writing (FYI 13.4).

In many cases, the most powerful, thought-provoking statements are those that are clear and concise (Henson, 1995). Marketers have known for years that people tend to respond to short slogans they can easily remember. We need only to watch an evening of television and pay attention to the myriad of commercial jingles to find examples of that concept. Good writers follow the same guideline by deleting unnecessary words or phrases and simplifying sentence structure. An example of this practice would be to convert the statement "People who really care about each other should never let each other drive while under the

FOR YOUR INFORMATION 13.4

Rules of Thumb for Good Writing

Practicing these rules will enhance the efficacy of your health education messages.

To prepare for writing:

- Identify why you are writing.
- Identify your audience.
- Create a message outline or cognitive map.

To write concisely:

- Use active voice.
- Delete unnecessary words.
- Avoid strings of prepositional phrases.

To adapt materials to the intended audience:

- Use SMOG or your word processing program to determine reading levels.
- Use back translation to determine cultural appropriateness.

To correct mistakes and evaluate finished products:

- Edit more than once.
- Pilot test materials.

influence of alcohol" to a more concise version like "Friends don't let friends drive drunk."

Three additional tips for concise writing are to avoid excessive use of prepositional phrases, delete unnecessary words, and use verbs in an active voice. Consider the statement "The attitudes of the community are so powerfully strong that the program offered by our agency will need to focus on them." The phrases "the attitudes of the community" and "the program offered by our agency" could be shortened to "community attitudes" and "agency program." The words "so powerfully" in the phrase "so powerfully strong" could be deleted without losing meaning. Sentences should always be in the *active voice;* make the organization or person who will do the action (the agency) the subject of the sentence and use a verb in the active voice. Thus, a shorter statement could be "The agency program should focus on the strong community attitudes." "For Your Application" at the end of the chapter contains an editing exercise that will allow you to practice this simplification process.

The SMOG formula presented in FYI 13.5 can be used to adapt your written materials to specific audience reading levels. More specific guidelines for its application can be accessed through the Community Toolbox Web page. Your word processing program probably has a feature that can help you assess readability. The back translation process described in Chapter 9 can help you adapt your message to a culturally appropriate format. Because you will likely have spent a great deal of time working with the material at this point, you will need to submit the final draft to people who can read it with a fresh eye and suggest further changes. Don't skip this step! A final edit by other health experts and community leaders, followed by a pilot test among community members, can save you the cost and embarrassment of distributing materials that contain misspelled words, incomplete sentences, or confusing text. The Community Toolbox Web page also contains specific guidelines for materials development and pretesting. This final step will be worth the investment.

INFORMATIONAL PIECES FOR LAY NEWSLETTERS   We encourage you to consider regular newsletter mailings to keep community members apprised of agency or program activities and related national and local news. A number of word processing programs contain newsletter templates that are simple to use. Access to the Internet for late-breaking health news and graphics makes newsletter production simpler than ever. Before you develop your own, study newsletter content and layouts from a variety of sources and apply the tips for good writing provided in FYI 13.4. As with brochures and pamphlets, advice from a graphic artist or journalist can improve the quality of your product.

BROCHURES AND PAMPHLETS   An effective brochure or pamphlet should have a single theme. You cannot cover all aspects of a particular health topic in one brochure. As stated earlier, use an outline and keep the message simple. For example, if the purpose of your brochure or pamphlet is to convince a teenage mother to obtain immunizations for her baby, limit your message to reasons why she should get them and where she can get them. Don't get bogged down into related but unnecessary details about, for example, the human immune system or symptoms of childhood diseases. Apply the rules of thumb listed in FYI 13.4 and use bulleted lists where appropriate. Enlist the help of an experienced graphic artist or photographer for advice about layout, graphics/visuals, typefaces, and paper. We live in a fast-paced, visually stimulated society. So visual appeal is extremely important.

LETTERS AND MEMOS   Frequent letters and memos sent through the postal service or via electronic mail can be an effective tool for keeping a variety of team members apprised of your progress and plans. As with other written materials, brevity is important. Try to limit letters to one page and memos to one or two

FOR YOUR INFORMATION 13.5

The SMOG Readability Formula

The SMOG readability formula is commonly used to determine the reading level of written materials. To calculate the SMOG reading grade level, begin with the entire written work that is being assessed and follow these four steps:

1. Pick 30 sentences,* 10 each from near the beginning, in the middle, and near the end of the text.
2. From this sample of 30 sentences, circle all of the words containing three or more syllables (polysyllabic words), including repetitions of the same words, and total the number of words circled.
3. Estimate the square root of the total number of polysyllabic words counted. This is done by finding the nearest perfect square and taking its square root.
4. Finally, add a constant of 3 to the square root. This number gives the SMOG grade, or the reading grade level that a person must have reached if he or she is to fully understand the text being assessed.

*Visit the Community Toolbox Web site for details about pamphlets and fact sheets: http://rex.nci.nih.gov/NCI_Pub_Interface/HCPW/APPEN.HTM.

SMOG Conversion Table

Total Polysyllabic Word Counts	Approximate Grade Level
0–2	4
3–6	5
7–12	6
13–20	7
21–30	8
31–42	9
43–56	10
57–72	11
73–90	12
91–110	13
111–132	14
133–156	15
157–182	16
183–210	17
211–240	18

From *Making Health Communication Programs Work: A Planner's Guide,* by National Institutes of Health, 1995, Atlanta: USDHHS (NIH Pub. 92-1493). Retrieved November 28, 1999, from the World Wide Web: http://rex.nci.nih.gov/NCI_Pub_Interface/HCPW/APPEN.HTM.

paragraphs. When appropriate, use a business-style heading that lists "Date," "To," "From," and "Re" so that readers can quickly identify the purpose and content of the letter or memo.

PROFESSIONAL ARTICLES   Most professional journal articles follow a thesis-based structure, meaning that they begin by introducing the reader to a specific question, problem, or issue (Bean, 1996). The introduction explains why the question or issue is significant by reviewing and citing professional literature on the subject. If the paper is a *scientific article*, meaning that it describes and reports the results of an experiment or applied program, a description of the methods or program implemented should follow the introduction section. Then come the description of the results or outcomes, a discussion of the strengths and weaknesses of the study or program, and the author's interpretations and conclusions (Garrard, 1999). The article must also include a bibliographical format that allows you to cite each source used. Each journal has its own *author guidelines*, usually printed in every issue, that describe how to format a manuscript you plan to submit. Pay careful attention to these guidelines and study several past volumes of your target journal to note commonly published topics and writing styles.

Manuscripts submitted for publication in professional journals are usually subjected to a rigorous review process before they are placed in print. The journal editor who receives your manuscript will first read it to determine whether your manuscript topic matches journal goals and readership interest. If the editor believes so, he or she will then send out copies of your manuscript to journal reviewers who have knowledge about your manuscript topic. Each reviewer will submit a recommendation about whether the manuscript should be rejected, accepted for publication as written, or accepted if certain revisions are made. In the case of the last recommendation, the reviewer will also provide directions for suggested manuscript changes. The editor will then synthesize responses from all reviewers and make a decision about rejection or acceptance of your manuscript for publication in the journal. If "accepted with revisions," you may ask the editor to clarify suggestions before submitting a revised manuscript. It sometimes takes as long as a year or two for a manuscript to progress from your seed of an idea through manuscript development and submission to a printed journal article. Writing for publication takes lots of practice, patience, and persistence. We recommend that you begin by looking for opportunities to be a co-author with professors who have publication experience.

Speaking for Success   Think back to the last time you heard a good speaker deliver a message. What made you think the speaker was so good? It probably had something to do with your degree of interest in the speech topic. However, an interesting topic isn't the only characteristic of a good speech. A good speaker can make almost any topic sound interesting. But good speakers don't grow on trees. They usually have developed their speaking skills over time. FYI 13.6 lists the qualities of a good speaker, many of which you can develop with practice.

FOR YOUR INFORMATION 13.6

Qualities of a Good Speaker

The qualities of a good speaker go beyond good preparation and include skills related to verbal and nonverbal communication.

A good speaker

Begins the speech with an attention-catching statement or story.
Tells the audience what to expect in the speech.
Limits the speech to 3 or 4 main points.
Includes the whole audience through frequent eye contact.
Uses stories and illustrations where appropriate.
Uses pleasant and appropriately animated facial expressions.
Uses an outline to enhance flow.
Never reads notes to the audience.
Projects the voice to the back of the room.
Uses differing voice inflections and appropriate nonverbal body language.
Speaks slowly, clearly, and concisely.
Uses visuals to illustrate major points.
Involves the audience as much as possible.
Summarizes the speech by reiterating its major points.
Limits the speech to the designated time frame.

TELEPHONE VOICE   The tone of voice you use in a telephone survey or business conversation can make a difference in how well your words are accepted. In most cases, using a slightly lower and deeper tone than you usually use in common conversation can convey warmth and confidence. Practice speaking in a calm, carefully concise manner and enunciate your words distinctly. Adopt a cheerful telephone demeanor, even when talking to a difficult person, and you will be surprised about the results.

PRESENTING FOR LAY AUDIENCES   Three key elements to a successful community presentation are the right background conditions, the right preparation, and the right delivery (Wadud, 1999). You can gain understanding and some control over the background conditions by studying your prospective audience. Ask questions about their demographics (for example, age, socioeconomic status, ethnicity), knowledge about and attitudes toward the presentation topic, and their expectations of you and your presentation. Consider recruiting key stakeholders and community gatekeepers to attend the presentation to motivate them to see the need for community action. Whenever possible, study the presentation

FOR YOUR INFORMATION 13.7

Presentation Preparation Steps

Following these simple presentation preparation steps can strengthen message delivery and acceptance.

Write a clear, brief presentation objective.
Develop a presentation outline.
Select supporting materials.
Create visual aids.
Practice.

From "Making Community Presentations," by E. Wadud, 1999, in *Community Tool Box,* chapter 1, section 6, edited by B. Berkowitz and J. Schultz. Retrieved November 28, 1999, from the World Wide Web: http://ctb.lsi.ukans.edu/tools/cl/cls6f.shmtl.

setting ahead of time to check room size, temperature, acoustics, seating arrangements, and audiovisual equipment. Find out in advance who will be present to help you adjust things at the last minute if needed.

Good preparation begins with a clear presentation objective. Let's return to our earlier example in which you were asked to address the need for well-woman checkups among members of the lesbian community. Pretend that you are preparing to make one of the community presentations we described, and let's work through some basic preparation steps (FYI 13.7).

Your written objective might state that you wish to convince members of the audience to get an annual well-woman checkup and encourage others in the community to do the same. Your main presentation points should contain information designed to persuade your audience (that is, reach your presentation objective). For example, your points could include a brief description of the risks involved in bypassing annual well-woman checkups, an acknowledgment of past barriers to checkups for members of the lesbian community, a summary of how some women's health clinics have begun to address the problem and are accessible, a list of the benefits of participating, and directions for calling to set up an appointment. You could then create bulleted lists under each of your selected main points that would contain key subpoints for each. From there, you could expand your outline into a full presentation.

Write a one-sentence presentation objective and three main presentation points.

We recommend that you use a software program for slide presentations to develop your outline. Most programs will allow you to add detailed notes beneath each slide created, and you can then convert the results to a variety of visual formats, including computerized slides projected onto a screen with a data projector, 35mm slides for a more traditional slide projector, overhead transparencies, or even paper printouts for poster displays. FYI 13.8 contains some valuable design

FOR YOUR INFORMATION 13.8

Tips for Creating Effective Visual Aids

These tips for creating effective visual aids approve the appearance and acceptance of the health message.

- Limit each visual to one main idea.
- Use no more than 6–8 lines of text per graphic or slide.
- Use bulleted lists and key phrases rather than sentences.
- Use plain language; avoid jargon.
- Double-space between text lines.
- Use large, bold, crisp fonts.
- Check for visibility from the back of the room.
- Only show information you plan to discuss.
- Plan to quote and clarify each graphic or slide.
- Turn off the projector lights when you have no slides to project.
- Cover the next graphic or slide until you are ready to address it.
- Use chart formats effectively:
     Horizontal bars: to compare categories
     Vertical bars: to show change over time
     Line graphs: to show trends across time periods
     Pie charts: to show amounts as a percentage of the total

From "Making Community Presentations," by E. Wadud, in *Community Tool Box*, chapter 1, section 6, edited by B. Berkowitz and J. Schultz. Retrieved November 28, 1999, from the World Wide Web: http://ctb.lsi.ukans.edu/tools/cl/cls6f.shmtl.

tips for any visual format used (and you can use multiple formats in the same presentation).

Don't forget to practice your presentation (Wadud, 1999). What looks good on paper doesn't always sound good in an oral format, and the length of time needed for the presentation will likely be important. Begin with an opening sentence that will grab your audience's attention. At the end, summarize the main points you just delivered and appeal to your audience's values and concerns as they relate to your presentation topic. Memorize the key points of the presentation so you can concentrate on a professional delivery, but plan to use your presentation notes to help you stay focused.

As you practice your presentation, visualize speaking to your audience or stand in front of a mirror. Concentrate on projecting your voice to the back of the room, but in a relaxed, expressive tone that exudes appropriate levels of enthusiasm and confidence. Work on including all members of the audience through frequent eye contact and avoid turning your back to the audience when referring to visual aids. Instead, stand to the side of the visual and face the audience as you describe the visual.

PRESENTING FOR PROFESSIONAL AUDIENCES   Much of what we recommended for community presentations also holds true when presenting to professional audiences. However, where professional and technical terminology is considered jargon and should be avoided in community presentations, it is more likely to be understood and expected among professional audiences. We suggest that you use professional terminology among your professional peers to enhance your credibility as well as audience understanding. This does not mean your language will be obscure or your meaning hard to discern. Your first object should still be communication. Professional audiences are also more likely to expect and appreciate your knowledge of the professional literature and how your work relates to other studies and theories. We encourage you to develop a strong research and theory-based understanding of your work so that you can convey to your professional peers how your work contributes to universal understandings. When presenting at professional conferences, it often helps to provide a handout to your audience that contains an abstract of your presentation and a list of references or recommended readings. Expect some audience members to want to contact you later to learn more about your work and explore future collaborative efforts. Maintaining contact with your professional peers through professional conferences and seminars can be your professional lifeline. We highly encourage you to participate in professional meetings and present your work so that others may learn from and add to your understanding.

IN CONCLUSION

We have already emphasized the value of strong communication skills within each of the seven areas of responsibility. We strongly encourage you to begin developing these skills immediately and practice them as often as possible. "For Your Portfolio" provides a suggestion that will help you incorporate several communication formats into one experience and document them in your professional portfolio.

Whether you are attempting to communicate with people face-to-face in personal conversations or group presentations, through written media, or public service announcements, the basic concepts remain the same. State your message clearly and concisely. Remember that simple statements and messages are often powerful motivators. Use visuals and illustrations whenever appropriate. And communicate your message in a variety of formats as frequently as possible. Communicate to inform. Communicate to empower. Communicate to progress.

REVIEW QUESTIONS

1. Describe some skills that are necessary for effective communication.
2. Name and describe each component of the health communication model.

3. Explain what is meant by iatrogenic health education disease.
4. Explain the difference between persuasive communication and coercion.
5. Name and give an example of each of the six stages of health communication.
6. List at least five effective writing tips.
7. Name at least six characteristics of a good speaker.

FOR YOUR APPLICATION

Learning to Write Concisely

Convert each of the following sentences into a more concise statement by rewriting to avoid excessive prepositional phrases, deleting unnecessary words, and using active voice. Ask a friend to do the same and compare your results.

1. The incredibly high incidence of hypertension among males of African American descent has been reduced by education programs.
2. The common opinion that AIDS is something that happens only to members of the gay community is held by students who attend the local high school.
3. Educational programs that prevent needless accidental injuries have been designed by a large number of the employees of the agency.
4. Preventive health services that are available and affordable were already mandated by the members of the community.

FOR YOUR PORTFOLIO

Gaining Communication Experience

Volunteer to deliver a health education presentation to a local community group. Thoroughly research the professional literature and use Internet resources listed in Appendix D of this text to obtain the information you need and ideas about how to communicate it. Create a slide presentation, poster, and/or informational pamphlet or flyer to be distributed to your audience at the end of the presentation. Ask the audience and, if possible, an experienced presenter to evaluate your presentation and materials. Create a "Communication" (Responsibility VII) division for your professional portfolio and place in it your presentation documentation and the materials you develop. Adapt your style and delivery for future presentations in accordance with evaluation suggestions.

14

Quality of Life and Future Trends

THE ELDERLY WOMAN LEANS BACK IN HER CHAIR AND absentmindedly pushes her glasses back up her nose. She gives you a knowing, tolerant look and says, "Honey, I ain't never had a need for that before. Don't see why I should start now." She's talking about the low-fat diet you just described to her. You knew before you started that it would be a tough sell—in some ways tougher than explaining the complexities of her diabetic condition. Now you're compelled to discuss changes in eating habits, habits that developed over a lifetime for a person who has overcome more of life's challenges than you may ever face. How do you convince her that such a drastic lifestyle change could make a difference in her quality of life? What does quality of life mean to her?

Chapter Objectives

1. Analyze the quality-of-life issues in communities today.
2. Discuss the health needs that may arise in the future as a result of what is happening in the world and in U.S. communities today.
3. Describe predicted changes in health care systems and their potential influence on health education opportunities in the community.
4. Describe predicted job-market growth patterns as they relate to community health education.
5. Name the seven areas of responsibility of an entry-level health educator and the three responsibility areas currently being considered for advanced-level health educators.
6. Name at least two emerging technologies and provide at least two examples of how a health educator may use each.
7. Describe insights and approaches that may be useful to health educators of the future.

QUALITY OF LIFE

It is fitting that we end this textbook with an in-depth focus on the importance of **quality of life** in our society and how it may be influenced by future societal and professional trends. Your grasp of this topic could shape your personal and professional future. It truly is that important. Yet we realize that a single chapter in a solitary textbook cannot possibly cover all you need to understand about the topic. Consider this chapter a starting point, and expect to learn more about quality of life over the course of your lifetime.

What Is High Quality of Life?

You may remember that quality of life holds a place of distinction in the PRE-CEDE/PROCEED model (see Chapter 6) as one of the primary community factors in needs assessment and program planning. Yet one of the most exasperating characteristics of studying quality of life is that it is so difficult to define and measure. Green and Kreuter (1999), the creators of the PRECEDE/PROCEED model, define quality of life as "the perception of individuals or groups that their needs are being satisfied and that they are not being denied opportunities to pursue happiness and fulfillment (p. 54)." *Satisfied needs, happiness,* and *fulfillment* are key terms in this definition because they help us shape what we're looking for when assessing a community's quality of life.

Quality of life is a broad topic that obviously entails more than just the absence or presence of disease or disability in one's life. Many non-health-related factors can influence one's sense of a life fulfilled. Employment, family relationships, financial stability, and educational experience are only a few life factors that can affect one's level of satisfaction. Yet the irony is that these and other factors do not necessarily dictate satisfaction levels for every person. You probably know of someone, for instance, who has experienced financial hardships or had little educational experience but is still satisfied with life in general. You may also know of at least one person who has more money than most and an impressive number of academic degrees but still appears to be less than satisfied or happy in life.

Green and Kreuter (1999) cite a number of variables that have been measured as **quality-of-life indicators.** Those can fall under a variety of categories, including psychological and spiritual (specific examples are comfort, self-esteem), social and economic (alienation, unemployment), family (happiness, crowding), and health outcomes (performance, absenteeism). For a more complete list, refer back to Figure 6.5, in which 17 potential quality-of-life indicators are listed as part of the PRECEDE/PROCEED model.

As you have likely already gathered, quality of life can be measured, but only with the input of your target community or individual client. The phrase "the perception of individuals and groups" in Green and Kreuter's (1999) definition of quality of life reminds us that, ultimately, only the individuals and groups with whom we work can decide how quality of life is defined. So how will you know if

List some nonhealth-related factors that can influence one's sense of life fulfillment.

a community is experiencing high or low levels of quality of life? Ask. You may find it useful to return to our description of Maslow's hierarchy of needs (Chapter 2) to review different types of needs and how they relate to perceptions about quality of life.

Quality of Life and the Health Education Process

By now, you should be familiar enough with the quality-of-life issue to understand that it is intricately connected to health. As we saw in earlier chapters, few people engage in health-related behaviors for health reasons only. It isn't necessarily the desire for a longer life or the absence of disease that primarily motivates people to adopt healthy behaviors. The ultimate motivating factor is how that behavior is expected to help one feel, function, or look (Green & Kreuter, 1999). Good health, an outcome of healthy behavior, is often viewed only as the connecting bridge to quality of life.

Another important point is that the connection between health and quality of life isn't always linear or unidirectional. As we discussed in Chapter 1, quality-of-life indicators (social indicators) can be affected by and affect a community's health. Figure 14.1 illustrates how health problems, lifestyle and environmental problems, and a single quality-of-life concern (poverty; see Chapter 5) can affect one another in a reciprocal relationship. The result can be a depressing downward spiral in a community's well-being.

The good news is that the same illustration could be converted to show a positive relationship, leading to an upswing, if well-planned, long-range, multifaceted efforts were invested to address all three areas. This broader approach would require more than health education and promotion. It would call for you to use the concepts and methods we've discussed throughout this textbook to form community-based coalitions, advocacy groups, and broad collaborative teams. We hope that not all the members of these teams would be health educators. You would also need the help of social workers, anthropologists, statisticians, politicians, businesspersons, clergy, nurses, physicians, dentists, and a host of others. You would also need to develop the skills and savvy needed to make these broader approaches more of a common reality in our health profession practice. The key to accomplishing these goals is your ability to adapt to future changes in our society.

FUTURE TRENDS

Don't you wish you could have been given a personal guidebook at birth that contained all the specific instructions for life you would ever need? Perhaps an individualized crystal ball would have been better. It would have had some interesting visual potential and would have been a change from reading. Knowing the future could save you many anxious moments spent worrying about specific job and career-path decisions. Of course, knowing everything about the future could

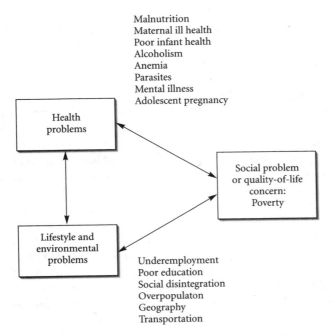

Malnutrition
Maternal ill health
Poor infant health
Alcoholism
Anemia
Parasites
Mental illness
Adolescent pregnancy

Health problems

Social problem
or quality-of-life
concern:
Poverty

Lifestyle and
environmental
problems

Underemployment
Poor education
Social disintegration
Overpopulaton
Geography
Transportation

FIGURE 14.1   Reciprocal relationships between health, lifestyle and environ-ment, and quality of life: poverty.

From *Health Promotion Planning: An Educational and Ecological Approach,* 3rd ed., by L. W. Green and M. W. Kreuter, 1999, Mountain View, CA: Mayfield, p. 88.

be a bit overwhelming and might rob us of our sense of adventure. But there are times when a glimpse of what is coming could be of help. One way of knowing how to streamline your professional-development efforts is to look at current trends in health needs and approaches to community health.

Predictions for Future Health-Related Needs

The future of the health education profession will depend on the **supply and de-mand** of health education products (such as healthy lifestyles, quality of life) and services (such as ways to develop healthy lifestyles and enhance quality of life). Demand depends upon the degree to which customers want or need the product or service and are willing and able to purchase it. We provide here an overview of evolving health needs at the global and national level, along with a look at how the changing health care system will affect you.

Global Health Trends   The World Health Organization (WHO, 1999b) states that, due to socioeconomic development and technological advances, the world as a whole is moving toward a healthier, longer life span. In response, the organ-ization is shifting from a global focus on survival endeavors to one of improving the well-being of humanity. WHO has identified four major trends that will have increasing influence on the global health status. These include "rapid urbanization, new and re-emerging infectious diseases, chronic diseases, the Global Teenager and population aging" (WHO, 1999b).

RAPID URBANIZATION   The earth's population is growing at an astronomical rate. An estimated 5.7 billion people lived on the planet in 1995. That number is projected to reach 9.4 billion by 2050, 10.4 billion by 2100, and 10.8 billion by 2150 (United Nations Secretariat, 1998). This growth rate gives rise to growing concerns about our ability to maintain a **sustainable environment** for all those people. In a sustainable environment, such factors as housing, education, health and nutrition, and the use of natural resources keep adequate pace with population growth and distribution patterns (WHO, 1996). In other words, a sustainable environment is one in which the people who live in it have access to what they need to live.

Related to the issue of increasing population is the world's rapid urbanization (WHO, 1999b). Forty-five percent of the world's population lived in urban areas in 1995. By 2025, that proportion is expected to increase to 60%. People are flocking to cities all over the world to be closer to jobs and other resources. As more children are born in those areas, city boundaries will expand by necessity.

The downside of rapid urban growth is crowding and stress. Those who can afford to move out of crowded inner-city areas and into more attractive suburbs leave behind those who face poverty and marginalization. The result is often inadequate housing, poor waste disposal and sanitation systems, and stress-induced violence and accidents. It is possible that, as the urbanization phenomenon grows, so will the number of people living in this poverty gap.

We've painted a dim picture of the world's future. But the World Health Organization doesn't see it that way. WHO maintains that urbanization also offers us the opportunity to develop healthy cities, to pool our concentrated resources to create positive environments. The organization refers to it as the preferred future:

> We create an environment in which everyone's health is promoted and protected —whether this is in schools, workplaces or the home. An environment in which the air is clear, the water safe, and where health, transport and waste management services are well managed and effective. An environment in which everyone enjoys access to social amenities such as safe play areas for children. An environment in which the different "players"—civilians young and old, industries and companies, municipal authorities, nongovernmental organizations and public utilities—work together to optimize use of the resources, skills and capacities that are often abundant in urban areas. In short, a healthy city that meets needs for work, learning, rest and play (WHO, 1999b).

NEW AND REEMERGING INFECTIOUS DISEASES   When smallpox was eradicated from the globe in the 1970s, some believed we would soon eradicate virtually all infectious diseases (WHO, 1999b). We have made great strides in vaccine development and immunization programs. However, a number of bacteria strains have become resistant to medicines and new and reemerging microbes are still a problem. In fact, WHO states that at least 30 new disease-causing organisms were identified between 1980 and 2000. Expected to trouble us most are multi-drug-resistant strains of tuberculosis, AIDS, and a resurgence of malaria.

The Center for Population and Development Studies at the Harvard School of Public Health (HSPH) houses a Burden of Disease Unit (**http://www.hsph.harvard.edu/organizations/bdu/**). Experts from this unit have worked with WHO, the World Bank, states, and other countries to measure death and disability on global and national scales. In a report titled *The Global Burden of Disease* (HSPH, 1999), these experts predict that deaths due to infectious diseases will drop despite increases in HIV and tuberculosis. They point to current efforts in antibiotic development and control technologies that, if rigorously attended to in the future, should be able to keep up with expected infectious disease emergencies. To counter increasing risks from infectious diseases, WHO (1999b) calls for an integration of existing and new developments in

- vaccines, molecular biology, and genetic engineering.
- communications technologies to detect and contain infectious diseases across national boundaries.
- modification of negative developments in world travel and trade as well as land use and ecology to prevent the emergence and spread of microbes.

EXPANDING CHRONIC DISEASES   The good news is that life expectancy across the globe is increasing and many are enjoying socioeconomic improvements (WHO, 1999b). The bad news is that, as people live longer and adopt unhealthy Western lifestyle habits (such as smoking, sedentary living, and high-fat diets), a global epidemic of chronic diseases such as heart disease, cancer, diabetes, and depression is expected (WHO, 1999b). Yet we have at our disposal the know-how and resources to combat the spread. The exciting news is that you, as a future health educator, are part of the potential solution!

CHANGING DEMOGRAPHICS   You probably remember from your Chapter 4 readings that the U.S. population is aging. That is also true from a global perspective (WHO, 1999b). In 1999, 580 million people over the age of 60 were living in the world. By 2020, that number is expected to exceed 1 billion. As more people live longer, the primary challenge will be to help individuals develop and sustain their well-being into old age. The focus will continue to rest on healthy lifestyle behaviors such as exercise, diet, and abstinence from tobacco. Newly expanding needs will center on efforts to help the elderly remain active in their communities, maintain and develop new social contacts, and engage in intergenerational activities (WHO, 1999b).

Though the highest proportion of population expansion will be among the elderly, the world's adolescent population will continue to grow as well. WHO (1999b) has coined the phrase **global teenager** to emphasize the emerging changes in how this age group, worldwide, will view and function in emerging societies. As is already common in the United States and other developing countries, more and more adolescents will face the kinds of lifestyle choices common to those living in Western affluence. WHO (1999b) encourages us to consider and address in the future the health-influencing values and lifestyles conveyed by mass media, mass tourism, and mass marketing.

Health Trends in the United States   Chapters 4 and 5 of this textbook describe current and projected health issues among age- and ethnicity-specific subgroups in the United States. As you read the global predictions made already in this chapter, you were likely able to envision the role U.S. health would play within that global picture. The United States is a developed country that enjoys relative affluence and comfort in comparison to less-developed (developing) countries of the world. Our Westernized sedentary lifestyle and access to high-fat, low-fiber foods will continue to influence the increase in chronic disease rates.

We stated in Chapter 4 that the incidence of heart disease in the United States has decreased in recent years. While that is true, it still remains at the top of the list for leading causes of deaths overall. And it is still true that heart disease and cancer combined account for 60% of all deaths in the United States (PAHO, 1998). Thus, the existing emphasis by health educators on the lifestyle behaviors associated with these two is expected to continue.

Despite recent victories in infectious-disease control, the United States is not immune to rising threats from drug-resistant bacterial and microbial infections faced by the rest of the world. As travel and business connections around the globe increase, so will exposure to worldwide health risks for all people on the planet. The United States will be no exception.

Experts from the Harvard School of Public Health Burden of Disease Unit (HSPH, 1999) bring to our attention another health issue predicted to greatly affect the United States and the world. The greatest cause of disability worldwide is depression, and the number of individuals affected by it is rapidly rising (Demko, 1997). Depression rates and resulting disability will also likely rise in the United States in the forms of unipolar and bipolar depression, alcohol abuse, schizophrenia, and obsessive-compulsive disorder.

Trends in Health Care   As world demographics, economy, and health needs change, so will the way in which we deliver health care. Changes in health insurance coverage and health service delivery are already evident. We present here some common trends in both areas.

CHANGES IN HEALTH INSURANCE COVERAGE   In Chapter 2 we discussed the culture of poverty and how individuals with no health insurance are more likely to use hospital emergency departments for their usual source of health care than they are to seek preventive medical services in a doctor's office. Trends in health care show that private health insurance coverage continues to decline (Krause,

1999). Reasons for this trend include increased health insurance costs and changing employment patterns. For example, a 111% increase in premium costs for employer-sponsored health insurance occurred between 1988 and 1996. As a result, many small firms dropped coverage altogether and others moved to hire part-time employees for whom coverage is not required (Krause, 1999). That trend is expected to continue into the next decade.

An increasing number of uninsured people rely on Medicaid and other publicly funded health programs (Krause, 1999). Federal and state health programs are currently designed to address the health insurance needs of poor children and the elderly, with some benefits available to low-income pregnant women and disabled adults. Fewer companies are offering insurance coverage packages to their retirees, a population that may not yet meet Medicare's requirement that they be 65 or over or Medicaid's low-income or disability requirements. The burden of providing health care for these growing numbers of uninsured adults will remain with many state and local public hospitals and clinics.

To counter these predicted trends, the National Governors' Association (Krause, 1999) reports that some states are

- implementing surveys to estimate numbers of the uninsured by city and region.
- reforming employer-sponsored and individual insurance markets by using purchasing pools, enacting small-group reforms, and creating high-risk pools to increase health insurance coverage.
- increasing coverage to eligible children and their families through a program called the State Children's Health Insurance Program.

CHANGES IN THE HEALTH CARE SYSTEM   As changes in demographics, health needs, and health insurance coverage occur, we can also expect to see changes in health care delivery. Some of these changes are already apparent in the ways hospitals and clinics are adjusting their focus and adapting operations and facilities. The managed health care system introduced in the 1990s radically altered the way health care is delivered (McKahan, 1999). Gone are the days of extended hospital stays and high profits. The new focus is on patient outcome and cost reduction—without sacrificing the quality of care. Thus, the current trend is for hospitals to consolidate and streamline the patient care process (Family Education Network, 1999). Such consolidation often entails grouping similar patient populations and moving services closer to them, streamlining paperwork through computerized records systems, and broadening staff skills and responsibilities.

While some hospitals are shutting down due to decreased inpatient numbers, many others are renovating and converting available space to accommodate changing health care needs (McKahan, 1999). For example, the number of hospital-based outpatient services is expected to increase by 30% by 2005. Many hospitals are rebuilding to accommodate these needed services and are converting existing space for a variety of other uses.

Predictions for the Future of the Community Health Education Profession

As we return to our supply-and-demand illustration, you probably understand that business profits depend not only on the nature of the product or service demanded but also on a businessperson's ability to supply a quality product or service in an efficient, cost-effective manner. The future of the health education profession rests, to some degree, on the ability of its members to effectively position themselves to meet the demand, to make a difference in people's lives.

It is a potentially exciting time in the history of the community health profession. Across the globe, health organizations and professionals are moving toward community-oriented health promotion concepts that match the philosophy and methods of our profession. The World Health Organization (WHO, 1998) hosts periodic international conferences to discuss and plan global health promotion strategies. The first of these was held in Ottawa, Canada, in 1986. From it emerged the **Ottawa Charter for Health Promotion,** which outlined five strategies to build healthy public policy, create supportive environments, strengthen community action, develop personal skills, and reorient health services (WHO, 1997). The charter has served as a cornerstone for worldwide health promotion efforts through the years, including those emerging from subsequent international conferences (WHO, 1998).

In 1998, WHO set forth a resolution on health promotion based on five strategic priorities developed during the fourth international conference held in Jakarta, Indonesia. These five priorities, known as the **Jakarta Declaration** (WHO, 1997), include the resolve to

- promote social responsibility for health
- increase investments for health development
- consolidate and expand partnerships for health
- increase community capacity and "empower" the individual in matters of health
- secure an infrastructure for health promotion

Based on these and other resources, Brick Lancaster (1999), CDC Associate Director for Health Education Practice and Policy, outlined some potential trends for the future of the community health profession. In addition to demographic, urbanization, and disease shifts (already discussed in this chapter), he emphasized the need to address community health issues within the broader context of social, economic, and environmental systems. Health education and promotion will be viewed as a *social investment* because the results of improved health status can strengthen a community's capacity and enhance its quality of life. Health educators will need to become more involved in public policy development as the shift continues from individual to community-based efforts.

How will these changes affect you? What we have discussed here is *your future* if you choose to develop a career in the health profession. The specific area of the profession in which you work will dictate the degree to which you will experience these trends. But if our society continues to move as predicted, these community-oriented trends will shape the job market you face and the skills you need.

Trends in the Job Market   Every two years, the **National Bureau of Labor Statistics** (NBLS, **http://www.bls.gov**) compiles an employment outlook report for the coming decade (Bowman, 1997). In the most current report (NBLS, 1998), total employment is projected to increase by 14% from 1996 to 2006. Ethnic diversity, proportion of women, and age of the labor force are also expected to increase (Bowman, 1997). Jobs requiring an associate degree or higher are expected to grow most rapidly (NBLS, 1998). And because computer technology occupations are rapidly expanding (Bowman, 1997), training in that area is likely to be important in most health-related positions.

According to the National School-to-Work Learning and Information Center (1999), 60% of today's high school students will work in jobs that do not yet exist. Health assessment and treatment occupations (health service occupations) are the fastest-growing employment areas (Silvestri, 1997). In fact, half of the 30 fastest growing occupations in the United States are related to health care (Bowman, 1997). Opportunities for self-employment in that arena are also expected to abound, but education and training will be important.

The job market in the health profession is definitely changing (NBLS, 1998); and with determination and strong skills development, you could position yourself for an exciting future. The U.S. Department of Health and Human Services maintains a Web page titled "Employment Opportunities/Job Resources on the Internet" (**http://www.hhs.gov/progorg/ohr/jobs/morejobs.html**). Another potentially useful job search Web site is called the Health Promotion Career Net (**http://www.hpcareer.net**). We encourage you to visit the site for information about health-related employment opportunities and links to other useful sites.

Coordinators of the University of North Texas Public Health Program (UNTPHP, 1999) compiled from the Department of Health Services and other sources a summary of health-related job market trends and lists of projected employment opportunities (**http://www.hsc.unt.edu/education/public_health/trends_research.htm**). Current personnel shortages in community and public health have been identified in the areas of epidemiology, biostatistics, environmental and occupational health, public health nutrition, public health nursing, and public health and preventive medicine. Emerging technology and the broadening perspectives on socioeconomic issues will also expand the need for more health planners and policy makers across the globe.

A call for more health educators is also expected in the future (UNTPHP, 1999). Rising health insurance costs are already driving corporate leaders to look to employee wellness programs for potential cost-containment solutions. The

---

FOR YOUR INFORMATION 14.1

Potential Health Education Employment Settings

These potential health education employment settings can be useful when deciding about courses to take, skills to develop, and jobs to explore.

Public and private schools
Institutions of higher education
State and regional health agencies
Federal health agencies
Corporate wellness programs
Alternative health practices
Voluntary health agencies
Advocacy organizations
Pharmaceutical companies
Health maintenance organizations
International health organizations

---

worldwide AIDS epidemic should continue to increase the demand for health educators. And, in many developing countries, health educators will find opportunities to work in the areas of disease prevention, nutrition, maternal and child health, population control, sanitation, and industrial hygiene. FYI 14.1 contains a list of potential employment settings and key issues.

Trends in Needed Skills   "What do you want to be when you grow up?" You were probably asked that question when you were a child. If you are working on a college degree, you may still be in the process of answering the question for yourself. Just as we have throughout this textbook, we continue to assume that your future plans involve the health profession. Perhaps you plan to become a community health education specialist or, at least, to infuse some aspect of community health concepts and skills into your future work endeavors. If so, we applaud you, for you are obviously aware of how much of the health profession and health care industry are moving toward a stronger community-oriented base (Lancaster, 1999). Health professionals in a variety of settings are increasingly challenged by the need to understand and use community-based concepts and methods. Some of them have not had the opportunity you have, through this textbook and other sources, to be trained in those important skills.

AREAS OF RESPONSIBILITY   To what skills are we referring and how will you be able to use them in the future? Appendix A contains a complete list of the seven areas of responsibility that currently define the entry-level competencies needed to practice effective community health education. The National Commission for Health Education Credentialing (NCHEC), American Association for Health Education (AAHE), and the Society for Public Health Education (SOPHE) have worked to expand the competencies and subcompetencies of those seven and add three additional responsibility areas for advanced or graduate-level practitioners. FYI 14.2 contains a list of these three advanced-level responsibilities and competencies as described in *A Competency-Based Framework for Graduate-Level Health Educators* (NCHEC, AAHE, and SOPHE, 1999). A more complete and updated description of these and their subcompetencies can be obtained through the NCHEC Web site (see Appendix D). A Competencies Update Project Advisory Committee (CUPAC) is expected to continue working on these responsibilities through the spring of 2001 (NCHEC, 1999). At some point in your career, you may need to develop skills in these areas to position yourself for professional advancement and promotion.

EMERGING TECHNOLOGIES   Technology-based occupations are projected to be the fastest-growing job industry (NBLS, 1998). Demands for technological skills will continue to spill over into health employment areas as computer applications, teleconferencing, electronic mail (e-mail), and Internet use become more commonplace. Many health-related employment settings are participating in this high-tech development. Depending upon your future work environment, you may be constantly challenged to master and use new technologies as they develop.

In contrast, access to these technology resources remains limited in some health employment and community settings. Where this is true, you may need to adapt to limited access, develop creative alternatives, search for ways to enhance technology access and use in the work environment, and personally invest in the equipment and services needed to maintain personal access to a rapidly changing world. To be prepared for high- and low-tech working environments, we recommend that you seek training and experience in using health education methods conducive to both scenarios.

In keeping with the introductory nature of this textbook, FYI 14.3 provides a brief overview of existing and developing technologies; Web site resources are listed in Appendix D, and we invite you to explore them for more in-depth study. As these technologies evolve, the categories we have set up in FYI 14.3 are becoming less distinct. We have grouped the technologies in the way we believe most people think of them.

We strongly encourage you to invest in your personal training so that you can become well-versed in such areas as word processing and data management, information retrieval and analysis, electronic mail systems, and Web page design. Most universities offer full courses in which you can learn the intricacies of technology use. Some health education departments offer technology-based health education courses through which you can learn to access, use, and develop online health information. We also encourage you to join at least one professional health

FOR YOUR INFORMATION 14.2

Three New Areas of Graduate Responsibility in Health Education

These three areas of graduate responsibility in health education are important skills for those working on masters and doctoral degrees in health education.

Area of Responsibility VIII
Applying Appropriate Research Principles and Techniques in Health Education

Competency A: Conduct a thorough review of the literature.
Competency B: Use appropriate qualitative and quantitative research methods.
Competency C: Apply research principles to health education practice.

Area of Responsibility IX
Administering Health Education Programs

Competency A: Develop and manage fiscal resources.
Competency B: Develop and manage human resources.
Competency C: Exercise organization leadership.
Competency D: Obtain acceptance and support for programs.

Area of Responsibility X
Advancing the Profession of Health Education

Competency A: Provide a critical analysis of current and future needs in health education.
Competency B: Assume responsibility for advancing the profession.
Competency C: Apply ethical principles as they relate to the practice of health education.

From *A Competency-Based Framework for Graduate-Level Health Educators,* by National Commission for Health Education Credentialing, American Association for Health Education, and the Society for Public Health Education, 1999, Allentown, PA: NCHEC.

education mailing list through which you can stay informed and actively participate in online discussions about current health issues.

INSIGHTS AND APPROACHES   In addition to technology skills, you will need to develop insights and approaches to community health education that match the evolving philosophy and successful methods of our profession. Throughout this

Overview of Technology Resources for Health Educators

This overview of technology resources for health educators provides basic information about computer, Internet, and telecommunication applications.

	Specific Application	General Use
Computer Applications	Word processing	Helps develop, store, print documents, letters, pamphlets, newsletters, flyers, questionnaires, memos, etc.
	Spreadsheets/ statistical programs	Compute numerical/statistical calculations/ create tables and graphs for budgets/expense accounts, quantitative research/assessment data, etc.
	Computer-assisted instruction (CAI)	Interactive tutorials that help one learn about a specific health topic and/or practice skill development through games, simulations, and other activities.
	Filing/database programs	Files, manipulates, and prints mailing lists, client records, inventories, etc.
	Special-purpose software	Examples: desktop publishing (newsletters, pamphlets, etc.), professional presentations (outlines and visuals for transparencies, slide projectors, computerized projectors), health-risk appraisals (compute individual health status and risks based on individual input), health education planning programs.
Internet Applications	Electronic mail (e-mail)	Exchange messages within minutes with a person or a group of people. Attach documents/files or links to Internet Web sites. Join mass mailing lists (listservs) on which you can post to and read messages from all members of a list.
	Online info & database searches	Use online search engines to find topic-specific Web resources. Visit health agency/organization and online journal Web sites to tap into databases, resources, and current health information. (See Appendix D.)
	Web page development	Develop your own personal or agency health education Web page. Enroll in a university course and learn how!
	Online education	A number of universities offer online courses and workshops. Check university Web sites for more information.

(continued)

FOR YOUR INFORMATION 14.3, *continued*

Telecommunications	Specific Application	General Use
	Teleconferencing	Telephone/television/satellite technology connects sites for meetings/conferences. People in connected settings can see/converse with each other and share visuals through television monitors and microphones.
	Interactive classrooms	Educators can now simultaneously teach more than one classroom of individuals via the teleconferencing technology described above.
	Voice mail	Customize your phone's number/type of rings and voice-mail greeting. Date, save, and forward messages. Simultaneously send a single message to a group of people on a special mailing list you create.

From *Community Health Education: Settings, Roles, and Skills for the 21st Century,* 4th ed., by D. J. Breckon, J. R. Harvey, and R. B. Lancaster, 1998, Gaithersburg, MD: Aspen; *Health Promotion Planning: An Educational and Ecological Approach,* 3rd ed., by L. W. Green and M. W. Kreuter, 1999, Mountain View, CA: Mayfield; and "Using Computer Technology for Health Education," by A. Taub, 1997, *International Journal of Health Promotion 4,* 5.

textbook we have introduced these insights and approaches into discussions pertinent to specific skills and concepts. We have summarized them in FYI 14.4. If you adopt them, these suggestions should help you keep abreast of health and job-market trends as they develop and effectively meet the health education needs of tomorrow's communities. Though the list was created with a bit of "tongue in cheek" attitude, the concepts match the path our profession and the health care industry seem to be taking.

Despite appearances, the pairs listed in FYI 14.4 do not necessarily contradict each other. We encourage you to think on both global and local levels. As we described in Chapter 2, the RISE approach to community identification can help you approach issues and problems from these two perspectives. It is extremely important to understand your target community on a local basis, to adapt your health programs and services to local perspectives, needs, and capacities. But you should also remember that no individual or community functions in total independence of others. Advances in technology and world trade make the world seem smaller. Viewing your community within the context of global health can help you more accurately understand local influences, predict trends in health issues and resource availability, and tap into outside resources as needed to enhance your community's quality of life.

FOR YOUR INFORMATION 14.4

Insights and Approaches for Future Success: Apparent Contradictions

These insights and approaches for future success are not as contradictory as they may seem at first glance.

Think globally.
Think locally.

Remain current.
Know your history.

Know a lot.
Assume you don't.

Be patient.
Dig in.

Be flexible.
Be consistent.

Use creativity.
Honor tradition.

Be a team player.
Be a leader.

Work hard.
Have fun.

We also recommend that you strive to be a trendsetter and a historian. You'll need to remain current on health issues and trends, as well as the technologies used to access information and deliver services. Active participation in professional organizations is a relatively easy way to keep abreast of new discoveries and current trends. This type of information will be commonly available to you through professional conferences where you can network with others who address similar community issues and needed solutions. We encourage you to be willing to present the methods and results of your own work through conference presentations so that others can glean from your experiences.

The journals published by these professional organizations can also be a valuable information resource that will help you remain current; they can also be an outlet through which you can share your local community's ideas and successes.

Do not hesitate to contact your current or former university professors for help in conference presentations and journal publications. Many of them have experience in professional research, presentation, and publications and would likely view such a partnership with you as mutually beneficial and rewarding.

Few factors are more dangerous to the success of a community health program than a health professional who thinks she or he knows it all but relies only on past training and knowledge. Most communities, health issues, and potential solutions are in constant flux. To remain effective, assume that there is always more to learn, and take the frequent initiative to do so. So that you'll "know a lot," establish a regular period (at least one day a month) in which you read the professional literature and visit reliable Internet sources. To broaden your community perspective, visit and revisit community organizations and information sources, attend community events, remain actively involved in the community, and listen to its members. Approach each community event, reading, and Internet visit with the attitude that there is always more to learn. It goes without saying that few members of your target community will appreciate a "know-it-all." Be confident in your training and experience, but always assume there is more to learn.

One of the more difficult skills of our profession is the ability to discern when to wait and when to get busy. We suggest that you adopt a patient attitude when looking at community health issues from a broad perspective. Wide-sweeping community change takes time, and the results will likely emerge slowly. However, immediate action in small program increments can be an effective way to get things started. When necessary, initiate small tasks with reachable goals at the beginning of a community effort. Advertise ongoing progress and celebrate small accomplishments. Gradually build on those while remaining patient with broader, long-range goals. Constantly remind all involved of both the short- and long-range perspectives. Work to become a patient visionary.

Flexibility and consistency are two important assets that can be developed. If you follow the community-based precepts and methods recommended in this textbook, you will discover that you are not the ultimate decision maker. You will need to be flexible with your own perceptions of how things should be accomplished. Some community members may choose approaches that seem to be less efficient or effective than the approach you would personally take. But community empowerment calls for flexibility in that area. Under some circumstances, you may need strong skills to keep your partners and yourself on track, keeping your eyes on specific goals and the tasks needed to get you there. The key is to remain consistent with specific goals and objectives but flexible in how they are obtained.

At times, new and creative ideas are critical to community health success. Be willing to try something new if you think it will appeal to targeted members of your community. Community members can be a wonderful resource for creative ideas. However, be careful to study and appreciate community traditions and honor them, if appropriate, in the midst of your efforts. Close interaction with a variety of community members and gatekeepers, as well as periodic needs assessments and pilot tests, will help you maintain a needed balance.

How can one be a team player and a leader at the same time? Good leaders do not dictate to others. They lead by example. They ask for frequent input from all involved and are quick to follow the lead of others who have good ideas, abilities, and experience. It is more important to a good leader that the task be successfully accomplished than it is to be recognized as the person who accomplished it. In the spirit of team effort, a good leader is as willing to empty the trash and clean the bathroom, for example, as he or she is to make tough organizational decisions.

Shared governance, the process by which decision making and power are shared by all group members, is a sign of good leadership and part of being a team player. The leader who effectively practices and benefits from shared governance is one who understands the human need for self-governance, individual choice, and personal accomplishment. Model it and expect it from others. Be a good leader by being a good team player.

Hard work can be fun. You'll have more fun when you know the work you are doing has a purpose and you can see evidence that it makes a difference. We encourage you to adapt your daily activities to specific goals and objectives. Make a list of daily tasks that can be readily accomplished within the confines of your resources. Practice positive time- and stress-management techniques so that you remain focused on true priorities and eliminate needless, time-consuming trivia. List daily accomplishments and mentally celebrate them. Practice **cognitive self-rehearsal** in which you frequently remind yourself about the positive aspects of your work, what you enjoy about it, and what you've accomplished so far. Learn to enjoy it. Work hard. Have fun.

IN CONCLUSION

We live in a rapidly evolving society in which change is the only true constant. Picture a teacher you once knew who seemed to fall behind the times and thereby lost the opportunity for personal growth and professional contribution. Staying abreast of needed information and skills will require an ongoing commitment on your part, particularly after you graduate. Some health educators who are working in the field find it difficult to carve out of their busy schedules the time needed for professional development. In light of the rapid pace at which our profession is changing, we urge you to view continual renewal as a necessity rather than a luxury. To be adequately equipped for the future of health education, we encourage you to

* develop a deep-rooted understanding of community health education within the context of broader social structures and quality of life.

- pay close attention to predicted trends, and embrace new ideas and technologies as they develop.
- reach beyond the confines of course expectations and grade incentives, and view learning as your lifeline to your professional future.
- adopt and implement a plan for professional development beyond graduation.

We challenge you to adopt the mind-set of a lifelong learner. May all your professional endeavors be worth the climb.

REVIEW QUESTIONS

1. Analyze the quality-of-life issues in communities today.
2. Discuss the health needs that may arise in the future as a result of what is happening in the world and in U.S. communities today.
3. Describe predicted changes in health care systems and their potential influence on community health education opportunities.
4. Describe predicted job-market growth patterns as they relate to community health education.
5. Name the seven areas of responsibility of an entry-level health educator and the three responsibility areas currently being considered for advanced-level health educators.
6. Name at least two emerging technologies and provide at least two examples of how a health educator may use each.
7. Describe insights and approaches that may be useful to health educators of the future.

FOR YOUR APPLICATION

Addressing Quality-of-Life Issues

Interview three people whose ages, cultures, and lifestyles differ from one another's. Ask each to describe his or her personal definition of quality of life and the specific health issues that affect it. Use the results to

- compare responses across interviews and identify similarities and differences
- identify at least two professional disciplines outside of your own that could help enhance the quality of life of your interviewees
- brainstorm potential efforts that could involve representatives of these disciplines in a collaborative effort

FOR YOUR PORTFOLIO

Polishing Your Portfolio

Review the narrative of your philosophy of health education (Chapter 1, "For Your Portfolio"). Critique it in light of what you have learned from this textbook, particularly from this chapter, about quality of life and future trends. Revise the narrative to more accurately reflect your current perspectives about health, health education, and your role as a future health educator. Ask two health professionals who are working in your targeted employment area to review your entire portfolio (see Appendix C) and suggest format and content changes. Continue to add portfolio content as you progress through your degree program. Don't wait until graduation to seek out profession-related work and volunteer experiences. Carve time from your busy schedule to prepare yourself for the job market of the future.

Appendix A

Seven Areas of Responsibility for Entry-Level Health Educators

RESPONSIBILITY I—ASSESSING INDIVIDUAL AND COMMUNITY NEEDS FOR HEALTH EDUCATION

Competency A: Obtain health-related data about social and cultural environments, growth and development factors, needs, and interests.

Subcompetency

1. Select valid sources of information about health needs and interests.
2. Utilize computerized sources of health-related information.
3. Employ or develop appropriate data-gathering instruments.
4. Apply survey techniques to acquire health data.

Competency B: Distinguish between behaviors that foster and those that hinder well-being.

Subcompetency

1. Investigate physical, social, emotional, and intellectual factors influencing health behaviors.
2. Identify behaviors that tend to promote or compromise health.
3. Recognize the role of learning and affective experiences in shaping patterns of health behavior.

Competency C: Infer needs for health education on the basis of obtained data.

Subcompetency

1. Analyze needs-assessment data.
2. Determine priority areas of need for health education.

RESPONSIBILITY II—PLANNING EFFECTIVE HEALTH EDUCATION PROGRAMS

Competency A: Recruit community organizations, resource people, and potential participants for support and assistance in program planning.

Subcompetency

1. Communicate need for the program to those who will be involved.
2. Obtain commitments from personnel and decision makers who will be involved in the program.
3. Seek ideas and opinions of those who will affect or be affected by the program.
4. Incorporate feasible ideas and recommendations into the planning process.

Competency B: Develop a logical scope and sequence plan for a health education program.

Subcompetency

1. Determine the range of health information requisite to a given program of instruction.
2. Organize the subject areas, comprising the scope of a program in logical sequence.

Competency C: Formulate appropriate and measurable program objectives.

Subcompetency

1. Infer educational objectives facilitative of achievement of specified competencies.
2. Develop a framework of broadly stated, operational objectives relevant to a proposed health education program.

Competency D: Design educational programs consistent with specified program objectives.

Subcompetency

1. Match proposed learning activities with those implicit in the stated objectives.
2. Formulate a wide variety of alternative educational methods.
3. Select strategies best suited to implementation of educational objectives in a given setting.
4. Plan a sequence of learning opportunities building upon and reinforcing mastery of preceding objectives.

RESPONSIBILITY III—IMPLEMENTING HEALTH EDUCATION PROGRAMS

Competency A: Exhibit competency in carrying out planned educational programs.

Subcompetency

1. Employ a wide range of educational methods and techniques.
2. Apply individual or group process methods as appropriate to given learning situations.
3. Utilize instructional equipment and other instructional media effectively.
4. Select methods that best facilitate practice of program objectives.

Competency B: Infer enabling objectives as needed to implement instructional program in specified settings.

Subcompetency

1. Pretest learners to ascertain present abilities and knowledge relative to proposed program objectives.
2. Develop subordinate measurable objectives as needed for instruction.

Competency C: Select methods and media best suited to implement program plans for specific learners.

Subcompetency

1. Analyze learner characteristics, legal aspects, feasibility, and other considerations influencing choices among methods.
2. Evaluate the efficacy of alternative methods and techniques capable of facilitating program objectives.

3. Determine the availability of information, personnel, time, and equipment needed to implement the program for a given audience.

Competency D: Monitor educational programs, adjusting objectives and activities as necessary.

Subcompetency

1. Compare actual program activities with the stated objectives.
2. Assess the relevance of existing program objectives to current needs.
3. Revise program activities and objectives as necessitated by changes in learner needs.
4. Appraise applicability of resources and materials relative to given educational objectives.

RESPONSIBILITY IV—EVALUATING EFFECTIVENESS OF HEALTH EDUCATION PROGRAMS

Competency A: Develop plans to assess achievement of program objectives.

Subcompetency

1. Determine standards of performance to be applied as criteria of effectiveness.
2. Establish a realistic scope of evaluation efforts.
3. Develop an inventory of existing valid and reliable tests and survey instruments.
4. Select appropriate methods for evaluating program effectiveness.

Competency B: Carry out evaluation plans.

Subcompetency

1. Facilitate administration of the tests and activities specified in the plan.
2. Utilize data-collecting methods appropriate to the objectives.
3. Analyze resulting evaluation data.

Competency C: Interpret results of program evaluation.

Subcompetency

1. Apply criteria of effectiveness to obtained results of a program.
2. Translate evaluation results into terms easily understood by others.

3. Report effectiveness of educational programs in achieving proposed objectives.

Competency D: Infer implications from findings for future program planning.

Subcompetency

1. Explore possible explanations for important evaluation findings.
2. Recommend strategies for implementing results of evaluation.

RESPONSIBILITY V — COORDINATING PROVISION OF HEALTH EDUCATION SERVICES

Competency A: Develop a plan for coordinating health education services.

Subcompetency

1. Determine the extent of available health education services.
2. Match health education services to proposed program activities.
3. Identify gaps and overlaps in the provision of collaborative health services.

Competency B: Facilitate cooperation between and among levels of program personnel.

Subcompetency

1. Promote cooperation and feedback among personnel related to the program.
2. Apply various methods of conflict reduction as needed.
3. Analyze the role of health educator as liaison between program staff and outside groups and organizations.

Competency C: Formulate practical modes of collaboration among health agencies and organizations.

Subcompetency

1. Stimulate development of cooperation among personnel responsible for community health education program.
2. Suggest approaches for integrating health education within existing health programs.

3. Develop plans for promoting collaborative efforts among health agencies and organizations with mutual interests.

Subcompetency

1. Plan an operational, competency-oriented training program.
2. Utilize instructional resources that meet a variety of inservice training needs.
3. Demonstrate a wide range of strategies for conducting inservice training programs.

RESPONSIBILITY VI—ACTING AS A RESOURCE PERSON IN HEALTH EDUCATION

Competency A: Utilize computerized health information retrieval systems effectively.

Subcompetency

1. Match an information need with the appropriate retrieval system.
2. Access principal online and other database health information resources.

Competency B: Establish effective consultative relationships with those requesting assistance in solving health-related problems.

Subcompetency

1. Analyze parameters of effective consultative relationships.
2. Describe special skills and abilities needed by health educators for consultation activities.
3. Formulate a plan for providing consultation to other health professionals.
4. Explain the process of marketing health education consultative services.

Competency C: Interpret and respond to requests for health information.

Subcompetency

1. Analyze general processes for identifying the information needed to satisfy a request.
2. Employ a wide range of approaches in referring requesters to valid sources of health information.

Competency D: Select effective educational resource materials for dissemination.

Subcompetency

1. Assemble educational material of value to the health of individuals and community groups.
2. Evaluate the worth and applicability of resource materials for given audiences.
3. Apply various processes in the acquisition of resource materials.
4. Compare different methods for distributing educational materials.

RESPONSIBILITY VII—COMMUNICATING HEALTH AND HEALTH EDUCATION NEEDS, CONCERNS, AND RESOURCES

Competency A: Interpret concepts, purposes, and theories of health education.

Subcompetency

1. Evaluate the state of the art of health education.
2. Analyze the foundations of the discipline of health education.
3. Describe major responsibilities of the health educator in the practice of health education.

Competency B: Predict the impact of societal value systems on health education programs.

Subcompetency

1. Investigate social forces causing opposing viewpoints regarding health education needs and concerns.
2. Employ a wide range of strategies for dealing with controversial health issues.

Competency C: Select a variety of communication methods and techniques in providing health information.

Subcompetency

1. Utilize a wide range of techniques for communicating health and health education information.
2. Demonstrate proficiency in communicating health information and health information needs.

Competency D: Foster communication between health care providers and consumers.

Subcompetency

1. Interpret the significance and implications of health care providers' messages to consumers.
2. Act as a liaison between consumer groups and individuals and health care provider organizations.

From *A Framework for the Development of Competency-Based Curricula for Entry Level Health Educators,* by National Task Force on the Preparation and Practice of Health Educators, 1985, Allentown, PA: National Commission for Health Education Credentialing.

Appendix B

Code of Ethics for the Health Education Profession

PREAMBLE

The Health Education profession is dedicated to excellence in the practice of promoting individual, family, organizational, and community health. Guided by common ideals, Health Educators are responsible for upholding the integrity and ethics of the profession as they face the daily challenges of making decisions. By acknowledging the value of diversity in society and embracing a cross-cultural approach, Health Educators support the worth, dignity, potential, and uniqueness of all people.

The Code of Ethics provides a framework of shared values within which Health Education is practiced. The Code of Ethics is grounded in fundamental ethical principles that underlie all health care services: respect for autonomy, promotion of social justice, active promotion of good, and avoidance of harm. The responsibility of each Health Educator is to aspire to the highest possible standards of conduct and to encourage the ethical behavior of all those with whom they work.

Regardless of job title, professional affiliation, work setting, or population served, Health Educators abide by these guidelines when making professional decisions.

ARTICLE I: RESPONSIBILITY TO THE PUBLIC

A Health Educator's ultimate responsibility is to educate people for the purpose of promoting, maintaining, and improving individual, family, and community health. When a conflict of issues arises among individuals, groups, organizations, agencies, or institutions, Health Educators must consider all issues and give priority to those that promote wellness and quality of living through principles of self-determination and freedom of choice for the individual.

Section 1

Health Educators support the right of individuals to make informed decisions regarding health, as long as such decisions pose no threat to the health of others.

Section 2

Health Educators encourage actions and social policies that support and facilitate the best balance of benefits over harm for all affected parties.

Section 3

Health Educators accurately communicate the potential benefits and consequences of the services and programs with which they are associated.

Section 4

Health Educators accept the responsibility to act on issues that can adversely affect the health of individuals, families, and communities.

Section 5

Health Educators are truthful about their qualifications and the limitations of their expertise and provide services consistent with their competencies.

Section 6

Health Educators protect the privacy and dignity of individuals.

Section 7

Health Educators actively involve individuals, groups, and communities in the entire educational process so that all aspects of the process are clearly understood by those who may be affected.

Section 8

Health Educators respect and acknowledge the rights of others to hold diverse values, attitudes, and opinions.

Section 9

Health Educators provide services equitably to all people.

ARTICLE II: RESPONSIBILITY TO THE PROFESSION

Health Educators are responsible for their professional behavior, for the reputation of their profession, and for promoting ethical conduct among their colleagues.

Section 1

Health Educators maintain, improve, and expand their professional competence through continued study and education; membership, participation, and leadership in professional organizations; and involvement in issues related to the health of the public.

Section 2

Health Educators model and encourage nondiscriminatory standards of behavior in their interactions with others.

Section 3

Health Educators encourage and accept responsible critical discourse to protect and enhance the profession.

Section 4

Health Educators contribute to the development of the profession by sharing the processes and outcomes of their work.

Section 5

Health Educators are aware of possible professional conflicts of interest, exercise integrity in conflict situations, and do not manipulate or violate the rights of others.

Section 6

Health Educators give appropriate recognition to others for their professional contributions and achievements.

ARTICLE III: RESPONSIBILITY TO EMPLOYERS

Health Educators recognize the boundaries of their professional competence and are accountable for their professional activities and actions.

Section 1

Health Educators accurately represent their qualifications and the qualifications of others whom they recommend.

Section 2

Health Educators use appropriate standards, theories, and guidelines as criteria when carrying out their professional responsibilities.

Section 3

Health Educators accurately represent potential service and program outcomes to employers.

Section 4

Health Educators anticipate and disclose competing commitments, conflicts of interest, and endorsement of products.

Section 5

Health Educators openly communicate to employers expectations of job-related assignments that conflict with their professional ethics.

Section 6

Health Educators maintain competence in their areas of professional practice.

ARTICLE IV: RESPONSIBILITY IN THE DELIVERY OF HEALTH EDUCATION

Health Educators promote integrity in the delivery of health education. They respect the rights, dignity, confidentiality, and worth of all people by adapting strategies and methods to the needs of diverse populations and communities.

Section 1

Health Educators are sensitive to social and cultural diversity and are in accord with the law, when planning and implementing programs.

Section 2

Health Educators are informed of the latest advances in theory, research, and practice, and use strategies and methods that are grounded in and contribute to development of professional standards, theories, guidelines, statistics, and experience.

Section 3

Health Educators are committed to rigorous evaluation of both program effectiveness and the methods used to achieve results.

Section 4

Health Educators empower individuals to adopt healthy lifestyles through informed choice rather than by coercion or intimidation.

Section 5

Health Educators communicate the potential outcomes of proposed services, strategies, and pending decisions to all individuals who will be affected.

ARTICLE V: RESPONSIBILITY IN RESEARCH AND EVALUATION

Health Educators contribute to the health of the population and to the profession through research and evaluation activities. When planning and conducting research or evaluation, Health Educators do so in accordance with federal and state laws and regulations, organizational and institutional policies, and professional standards.

Section 1

Health Educators support principles and practices of research and evaluation that do ño harm to individuals, groups, society, or the environment.

Section 2

Health Educators ensure that participation in research is voluntary and is based upon the informed consent of the participants.

Section 3

Health Educators respect the privacy, rights, and dignity of research participants and honor commitments made to those participants.

Section 4

Health Educators treat all information obtained from participants as confidential, unless otherwise required by law.

Section 5

Health Educators take credit, including authorship, only for work they have actually performed and give credit to the contributions of others.

Section 6

Health Educators who serve as research or evaluation consultants discuss their results only with those to whom they are providing service, unless maintaining such confidentiality would jeopardize the health or safety of others.

Section 7

Health Educators report the results of their research and evaluation objectively, accurately, and in a timely fashion.

ARTICLE VI: RESPONSIBILITY IN PROFESSIONAL PREPARATION

Those involved in the preparation and training of Health Educators have an obligation to accord learners the same respect and treatment given other groups by providing quality education that benefits the profession and the public.

Section 1

Health Educators select students for professional preparation programs based upon equal opportunity for all and the individual's academic performance, abilities, and potential contribution to the profession and the public's health.

Section 2

Health Educators strive to make the educational environment and culture conducive to the health of all involved and free from sexual harassment and all forms of discrimination.

Section 3

Health Educators involved in professional preparation and professional development engage in careful preparation; present material that is accurate, up-to-date, and timely; provide reasonable and timely feedback; state clear and reasonable expectations; and conduct fair assessments and evaluations of learners.

Section 4

Health Educators provide objective and accurate counseling to learners about career opportunities, development, and advancement and assist learners with obtaining secure professional employment.

Section 5

Health Educators provide adequate supervision and meaningful opportunities for the professional development of learners.

Approved: Coalition of National Health Education Organizations, November 8, 1999, Chicago, IL

Appendix C

A Professional Portfolio for Health Educators

Created by Eva Doyle and Susan Ward, Texas Woman's University

PORTFOLIO PURPOSE

A common dilemma for college graduates in any field is that potential employers often prefer to hire people with "job-related experience." Students who concentrate on earning a degree may not be able to simultaneously gain that preferred work experience. A professional portfolio that contains evidence of your work, even if the work was generated through course assignments, can help potential employees more clearly understand and appreciate the full extent of your training and skills. Your portfolio can be used as

- A professional development guide that helps you
  - Identify strengths in your current skill and experience levels
  - Target areas for improvement
- A conversation starter in informal interviews with health professionals in the field. Ask them to
  - Describe skills/experiences you would need for employment in their work setting
  - Provide suggestions for portfolio format and content
- A point of reference for internship/practicum and employment interviews
  - Place the words "Portfolio upon request" at the bottom of your résumé and take the portfolio with you for interviews
  - If asked to leave the portfolio with an interviewer, ask for a future appointment date so you can ask for feedback (and pick up the portfolio)
  - Keep duplicate copies of portfolio content on file in case of accidental loss

A SUGGESTED PORTFOLIO FORMAT

Place your portfolio in a three-ring binder notebook with the six components listed below included. Type all materials neatly, including the tabs for the dividers! For the portfolio and title pages, use larger fonts and center titles on the page.

1. *Title Page.* Create a title page that says "Professional Portfolio" (typed, centered in large, neat letters). Below it, provide your name, address, and phone number.
2. *Contents Page.* Include a contents page that lists "Philosophy of Health Education," "Résumé" and then each of the nine titles (see "Portfolio Sections").
3. *Philosophy of Health Education.* Write a brief summary of your personal philosophy as it relates to the health education profession (one-half to a full page). Include in it how you see your role as a health educator in helping people develop healthy lifestyles.
4. *Résumé.* Follow the philosophy page with your one-page résumé (see "Your Résumé").
5. *Dividers and title pages.* Behind the résumé, place a tabbed divider, immediately followed by a title page, for each section.

YOUR RÉSUMÉ

The exact format you use on your résumé is up to you and dependent on your experience and employment goals. It should be concise, simply worded, neatly formatted, free of errors, and printed on quality paper. Many universities have support services that help students prepare résumés. Enlist the help of experienced professionals! Some sections you may want to consider and ask experts for advice about are listed below.

Personal Contact Information

Center at the top of the résumé your name, postal address, phone number, and e-mail address. Make it easy for a potential employer to contact you!

Your Professional Goal

You may choose not to include a professional goal in your résumé. In many cases, a carefully worded cover letter can accomplish what is needed more readily. However, if you choose to include one, do so *only* when applying for a specific job and adapt your goal to that job description.

Computer and Language Skills

List the types of computers (such as Mac, PC) and software programs (such as specific word processing, data spreadsheet, presentation, and Web design programs) with which you are familiar (include e-mail and the Internet). Also list languages other than English in which you have been trained or are proficient.

Educational Experience

List all completed degrees (including an associate degree) and the degree on which you are now working (include an expected graduation date). Include your G.P.A. if it is at least 3.00.

Work Experience

Expert advice varies about how much and which types of work experience to include in a résumé. Some suggest that you list only experiences from the past ten years and include only employment experiences in which you worked for three months (such as substantial summer jobs) or more (at least six months for "non-summer" jobs). Some suggest that you include extensive internship experiences in this, even if they weren't paid positions. Others suggest that internship descriptions belong under the heading of "volunteer experiences." The general rule of thumb is that each résumé heading should include a minimum of two different experience listings under it.

Volunteer Experience

List one-time events (help with a fundraiser or health fair) and long-term volunteer experience (serving as a mentor or on an ongoing committee). Provide brief descriptions of your responsibilities and accomplishments within each.

Student Activities and Honors

Include here your memberships in student organizations and officer or committee memberships you held. If you have made the dean's list or received an award, scholarship, or other type of honor, list it here.

References

Unless specifically requested in a job announcement, do not place a list of references on your one-page résumé. Have a list on file that you can submit later and state at the bottom of your résumé that "Professional references are available upon request" (or "Professional references and portfolio available upon request"). Contact people *before* naming them as a reference to ensure that they will feel comfortable providing positive feedback about your abilities. When asked to submit references, always contact your references to tell them to expect a phone call.

PORTFOLIO SECTIONS

The following nine sections are based on the assumption that you wish to document your ability to perform skills relevant to the Seven Areas of Responsibility of an entry-level health education specialist, an internship or practicum you have completed as part of the requirements within your degree program, and your community volunteer experience. We suggest that you adapt these to your specific needs and experience. Listed beneath each section heading are samples of the kinds of materials you may wish to include. These are not exhaustive lists. Be creative in how you display your experiences. Separate each section with a tabbed divider and section title page.

Section I: Assessing Individual and Community Needs for Health Education

- Copies of needs-assessment questionnaires/surveys you've created
- Descriptions of any needs-assessment projects in which you've participated (include photographs, description of target population, materials used, results, etc.)
- "Mock" needs assessments you've completed for a course project
- A paper you've written that describes or documents the health needs of a population

Section II: Planning Effective Health Education Programs

- Program plans you developed as part of a course project
- "Real" health education programs you helped develop (through internship, courses, volunteer work, etc.)

Section III: Implementing Health Education Programs

- Documentation of implemented programs (pictures of health fairs, thank-you letters from program directors, flyers used to advertise events you helped implement, etc.)
- Evidence of actual program implementation (flyers, pictures, etc.). (Place program plans in Section II.)

Section IV: Evaluating Effectiveness of Health Education Programs

- Instruments or plans you designed to evaluate a health education program or organization

- Evaluation summaries of a program or activity that *you* wrote or helped implement

Section V: Coordinating Provision of Health Education Services

- Health education programs or activities you coordinated (perhaps you arranged for the guest speaker, made room reservations, coordinated food offered, etc.)
- A health fair or other special community event that you coordinated

Section VI: Acting as a Resource Person in Health Education

- Descriptions/examples of any resource kits or directories you developed
- Presentations in which you provided information about where to go to get help, information, or resources (include its outline, objectives, and any handouts)
- Documentation of any volunteer work on a resource hotline or other resource or information-related endeavor

Section VII: Communicating Health and Health Education Needs, Concerns, and Resources

- Health education flyers, brochures, or other materials you developed to disseminate health-related information
- Presentations (outline, objectives, and related handouts) that provided information about a particular health-related topic. (This should not duplicate Section VI.)

Section VIII: Internship/Practicum Experiences

All materials related to your internship or practicum experiences should go here, including project objectives, written summaries, letters of appreciation, pictures of activities, etc. There may be some overlap between this and other sections. For example, you may have developed a health fair for your internship. If so, list the activity in this section and state that related materials can be found, for example, in Sections II and III.

Section IX: Community Service

Documentation of organizational membership and activities should go here, including acknowledgment of membership in organizations, certificates, or letters of appreciation for any volunteer work or activity, etc.

Appendix D

Health Agency, Organization, and Resource List

PROFESSIONAL DEVELOPMENT AND THE JOB MARKET (SELECTED SITES)

Bureau of Health Professions (under HRSA) http://www.hrsa.gov/bhpr

National Center for Health Workforce Information & Analysis (Bureau of Health Professions, HRSA) http://www.hrsa.gov/bhpr/ORP/wiaa.htm

National Commission for Health Education Credentialing http://www.nchec.org

PROFESSIONAL ASSOCIATIONS (SELECTED SITES)

American Association for Health Education http://www.aahperd.org/aahe/aahe-main.html

American Medical Association http://www.ama-assn.org

American Psychological Association http://www.apa.org

American Public Health Association http://www.apha.org

American School Health Association http://www.ashaweb.org

Association for Worksite Health Promotion http://www.awhp.org

National Wellness Institute http://www.nationalwellness.org

Society for Public Health Education http://www.sophe.org

COMMUNITY HEALTH EDUCATION
TECHNIQUES (SELECTED SITES)

Community Toolbox http://ctb.lsi.ukans.edu

Diversity Rx http://www.diversityrx.org

Guide to Community Preventive Services (under OPHS)
http://web.health.gov/communityguide

NATIONAL HEALTH AGENCIES, OFFICES, AND CENTERS

U.S. Department of Health and Human Services (USDHHS) http://www.hhs.gov

Administration for Children and Families (ACF) http://www.acf.dhhs.gov

Administration on Aging (AOA) http://www.aoa.dhhs.gov

Agency for Healthcare Research and Quality (AHRQ)
http://www.ahcpr.gov

Agency for Toxic Substances and Disease Registry (ATSDR)
http://www.atsdr.cdc.gov

Centers for Disease Control and Prevention (CDC) http://www.cdc.gov

Food and Drug Administration (FDA) http://www.fda.gov

Health Care Financing Administration (HCFA) http://www.hcfa.gov

Health Resources and Services Administration (HRSA)
http://www.hrsa.dhhs.gov

Indian Health Service (IHS) http://www.ihs.gov

National Institutes of Health (NIH) http://www.nih.gov

Program Support Center (PSC) http://www.psc.gov

Substance Abuse and Mental Health Services Administration (SAMHSA)
http://www.samhsa.gov

Centers for Disease Control and Prevention (CDC, under USDHHS) http://www.cdc.gov

Associate Director for Minority Health http://www.cdc.gov/od/admh

Epidemiology Program Office http://www.cdc.gov/epo

National Center for Chronic Disease Prevention and Health Promotion
http://www.cdc.gov/nccdphp

National Center for Environmental Health http://www.cdc.gov/nceh

National Center for Health Statistics http://www.cdc.gov/nchs

National Center for HIV, STD, and TB Prevention http://www.cdc.gov/nchstp/od

National Center for Infectious Diseases http://www.cdc.gov/ncidod

National Center for Injury Prevention and Control http://www.cdc.gov/ncipc

National Immunization Program http://www.cdc.gov/nip

National Institute for Occupational Safety and Health http://www.cdc.gov/niosh

National Vaccine Program Office http://www.cdc.gov/od/nvpo

Office of Communication, Division of Media Relations http://www.cdc.gov/od/oc/media

Office of Genetics and Disease Prevention http://www.cdc.gov/genetics

Office of Global Health http://www.cdc.gov/ogh

Office of Health and Safety (OhASIS) http://www.cdc.gov/od/ohs

Office of Women's Health http://www.cdc.gov/od/owh

Health Resources and Services Administration (HRSA) http://www.hrsa.dhhs.gov (selected sites)

Bureau of Health Professions http://www.hrsa.dhhs.gov/bhpr

Bureau of Primary Health Care http://www.bphc.hrsa.gov

Center for Public Health Practice http://www.hrsa.dhhs.gov/CPHP

HIV/AIDS Bureau http://www.hrsa.dhhs.gov/hab

Maternal and Child Health Bureau http://www.mchb.hrsa.gov

Office for the Advancement of Telehealth http://telehealth.hrsa.gov

Office of Minority Health http://www.hrsa.dhhs.gov/OMH

Office of Rural Health Policy http://www.nal.usda.gov/orhp

National Institutes of Health (NIH, under USDHHS) http://www.nih.gov

National Cancer Institute http://www.nci.nih.gov

National Eye Institute http://www.nei.nih.gov

National Heart, Lung, and Blood Institute http://www.nhlbi.nih.gov

National Human Genome Research Institute http://www.nhgri.nih.gov

National Institute of Allergy and Infectious Diseases http://www.niaid.nih.gov

National Institute of Arthritis and Musculoskeletal and Skin Diseases
http://www.nih.gov/niams

National Institute of Child Health and Human Development
http://www.nichd.nih.gov

National Institute of Deafness and Other Communication Disorders
http://www.nih.gov/nidcd

National Institute of Dental and Craniofacial Research
http://www.nidr.nih.gov

National Institute of Diabetes and Digestive and Kidney Diseases
http://www.niddk.nih.gov

National Institute of Environmental Health Sciences
http://www.niehs.nih.gov

National Institute of General Medical Sciences http://www.nih.gov/nigms

National Institute of Mental Health http://www.nimh.nih.gov

National Institute of Neurological Disorders and Stroke
http://www.ninds.nih.gov

National Institute of Nursing Research http://www.nih.gov/ninr

National Institute on Aging http://www.nih.gov/nia

National Institute on Alcohol Abuse and Alcoholism
http://www.niaaa.nih.gov

National Institute on Drug Abuse http://www.nida.nih.gov

Office of Public Health and Science (OPHS, under USDHHS)
http://www.surgeongeneral.gov/ophs

Office of Disease Prevention and Health Promotion
http://odphp.osophs.dhhs.gov

Office of Emergency Preparedness http://ndms.dhhs.gov

Office of HIV/AIDS Policy
http://www.surgeongeneral.gov/ophs/hivaids.htm

Office of International and Refugee Health
http://www.surgeongeneral.gov/ophs/oirh.htm

Office of Military Liaison and Veterans Affairs
http://www.surgeongeneral.gov/ophs/ovaml.htm

Office of Minority Health Resource Center http://www.omhrc.gov

Office of Population Affairs http://www.hhs.gov/progorg/opa

Office of Research Integrity http://ori.dhhs.gov

Office of the Surgeon General http://www.surgeongeneral.gov

Office on Women's Health http://www.4woman.gov/owh

President's Council on Physical Fitness and Sports http://www.surgeongeneral.gov/ophs/pcpfs.htm

Other Government Agencies

Environmental Protection Agency (EPA) http://www.epa.gov

Occupational Safety and Health Administration (OSHA, under Department of Labor) http://www.osha.gov

International Organizations and Resources

Office of Global Health (under CDC) http://www.cdc.gov/ogh

Pan American Health Organization http://www.paho.org

World Health Organization http://www.who.org

GENERAL HEALTH-RELATED INFORMATION AND DATA SOURCES

CDC Wonder (Centers for Disease Control) http://wonder.cdc.gov

Fastats (Centers for Disease Control) http://www.cdc.gov/nchs/fastats

Health Finder (U.S. Department of Health and Human Services) http://www.healthfinder.gov

Health Statistics (Centers for Disease Control) http://www.cdc.gov/od/oc/media/healthstats.htm

Health Topics A to Z (Centers for Disease Control) http://www.cdc.gov/health/diseases.htm

National Bureau of Labor Statistics http://stats.bls.gov

National Center for Health Statistics http://www.cdc.gov/nchs

National Center for Policy Analysis http://www.ncpa.org

National Center for Public Policy http://www.public-policy.org

National Health Information Center http://nhic-nt.health.org

U.S. Census Bureau http://www.census.gov

VOLUNTARY HEALTH ORGANIZATIONS AND FOUNDATIONS (SELECTED SITES)

Alzheimer's Association http://www.alz.org

American Cancer Society http://www.cancer.org

American Diabetes Association http://www.diabetes.org

American Heart Association http://www.americanheart.org

American Lung Association http://www.lungusa.org

American Red Cross http://www.redcross.org

Arthritis Foundation http://www.arthritis.org

Council on Foundations http://www.cof.org

Cystic Fibrosis Foundation http://www.cff.org

Epileptic Foundation of America http://www.efa.org

Foundation Center of New York http://www.foundationcenter.org

Leukemia Society of America http://www.leukemia.org

Lupus Foundation of America http://www.lupus.org

March of Dimes for Birth Defects www.modimes.org

Muscular Dystrophy Association http://www.mdausa.org

National Kidney Foundation http://www.kidney.org

National Osteoporosis Foundation http://www.nof.org

National Safety Council http://www.ncs.org

Planned Parenthood Federation of America
http://www.plannedparenthood.org

Robert Wood Johnson Foundation http://www.rwjf.org

ETHNIC AND MINORITY INFORMATION RESOURCES

General Information Sources

Diversity Rx http://www.diversityrx.org

Ethnomed http://healthlinks.washington.edu/clinical/ethnomed

Family and Community Violence (under OMH) http://www.fcvp.org

Healthy People 2010 http://www.health.gov/healthypeople

Initiative to Eliminate Racial and Ethnic Disparities in Health
http://raceandhealth.hhs.gov

Institute for Minority Health Research
http://www.sph.emory.edu/bshe/imhr

Minority and Ethnic Groups (CDC)
http://www.cdc.gov/nccdphp/minority.htm

Minority Health Network http://www.pitt.edu/~ejb4/min

The Minority Health Professional Foundation
http://www.minorityhealth.org

Office of Minority Health http://www.omhrc.gov

U.S. Census Bureau Reports (ethnicity- and poverty-specific)
http://census.gov/population/www/pop-profile

American Indian/Native American Health Resources

Association of American Indian Physicians http://www.ionet.net/~aaip

Center for American Indian Research and Education
http://www.caire.org

Code Talk (Office of Native American Programs, HUD)
http://www.codetalk.fed.us

Indian Health Service (IHS) http://www.ihs.gov

Hispanic American Health Resources

Chicano/Latino Net Health http://clnet.ucr.edu/research/health.html

Latino Cardiovascular Health Resources (National Heart, Lung, and Blood Institute) http://www.nhlbi.nih.gov/health/prof/heart/latino

Midwest Latino Health, Research, Training, and Policy Center (University of Illinois at Chicago) http://www.uic.edu/jaddams/mlhrc/mlhrc.html

The National Alliance for Hispanic Health http://www.hispanichealth.org

National Hispanic Medical Association http://home.earthlink.net/~nhma

African American Health Issues

African American Program (American Diabetes Association)
http://www.diabetes.org/africanamerican

Black Health Net http://blackhealthnet.com

Asian and Pacific Islander Health Information Resources

Asian and Pacific Islander American Health Forum
http://www.apiahf.org/contact5.html

Association of Asian Pacific Community Health Organizations
http://www.aapcho.org

AGE- AND GENDER-SPECIFIC INFORMATION RESOURCES

Specific Populations (under CDC)
http://www.cdc.gov/nccdphp/populati.htm

Maternal and Infant Health

March of Dimes for Birth Defects Foundation http://www.modimes.org

Maternal and Child Health Bureau http://www.mchb.hrsa.gov

Mothers and Infants (Centers for Disease Control)
http://www.cdc.gov/nccdphp/mothers.htm

National Healthy Mothers, Healthy Babies Coalition
http://www.hmhb.org

Office of Adolescent Pregnancy Programs (Office of Population Affairs,
USDHHS) http://www.hhs.gov/progorg/opa/titlexx/oapp.html

Children

Administration for Children and Families (ACF) http://www.acf.dhhs.gov

American Academy of Child and Adolescent Psychiatry
http://www.aacap.org

Children and Adolescents (under CDC)
http://www.cdc.gov/nccdphp/children.htm

National Institute of Child Health and Human Development
http://www.nichd.nih.gov

National Resource Center for Health and Safety in Child Care (under
Maternal and Child Health Bureau, HRSA) http://nrc.uchsc.edu

Adolescents and Young Adults

Adolescent Health "On-Line" (American Medical Association)
http://www.ama-assn.org/adolhlth

Children and Adolescents (under CDC)
http://www.cdc.gov/nccdphp/children.htm

Texas Youth Commission Office of Prevention http://www.tyc.tx.us

Youth Risk Behavior Surveillance System (under CDC)
http://www.cdc.gov/nccdphp/dash/yrbs

Middle-Aged Adults

Health Conditions of the Americas (under PAHO)
http//:www.paho.org/english/country.htm

[See disease/health issue-specific organizations, CDC, NIH, and OPHS]

Older Adults

Administration on Aging (under USDHHS) http://www.aoa.dhhs.gov

American Association of Retired Persons (AARP) http://www.aarp.org

National Institute on Aging (under NIH) http://www.nih.gov/nia

Older Adults (under CDC) http://www.cdc.gov/nccdphp/older.htm

Women's Health

Mothers and Infants (under CDC)
http://www.cdc.gov/nccdphp/mothers.htm

Office of Women's Health (under CDC)
http://www.cdc.gov/od/owh/whhome.htm

Office on Women's Health (under OPHS)
http://www.4woman.gov/owh/aboutowh.htm

Women's Health (under CDC) http://www.cdc.gov/nccdphp/women.htm

Men's Health

Men's Health (under CDC) http://www.cdc.gov/nccdphp/men.htm

ONLINE SEARCH HELPS AND JOURNALS

Directories

About.com http://www.about.com

LookSmart http://www.looksmart.com

Yahoo http://www.yahoo.com

Search Agents

Copernic http://www.copernic.com

Dogpile http://www.dogpile.com

MetaCrawler http://www.metacrawler.com

Search Engines

Alta Vista http://www.altavista.com

Excite http://www.excite.com

HotBot http://www.hotbot.com

Lycos http://www.lycos.com

Webcrawler http://www.webcrawler.com

Journals (selected sites)

American Journal of Epidemiology
http://www.jhsph.edu/Publications/JEPI

American Journal of Health Behavior http://www.ajhb.siu.edu

International Electronic Journal of Health Education
http://www.kittle.siu.edu/iejhe

Journal of Health Communication http://www.aed.org/JHealthCom

For additional listings and descriptions of health-related Web sites, refer to M. J. Kittleson (1997). *Web sites for health professionals.* Sudbury, MA: Jones and Bartlett (www.jbpub.com).

References

AARP. (1999 March/April). Social Security: A woman's prerogative. *Modern Maturity*, p. 76.

Advocacy Summit. (1999). *Tobacco prevention and control appropriations.* (Fact Sheet). Washington DC: Society of Public Health Education.

Agency for Health Care Policy and Research [AHCPR]. (1999). *Criteria for assessing the quality of health information on the Internet—Policy paper.* Retrieved November 14, 1999, from the World Wide Web: http://hitiweb.mitretek.org/docs/policy.html.

Airhihenbuwa, C. O. (1990). A conceptual model for cultural appropriate health education programs in developing countries. *International Quarterly of Community Health Education, 11,* 53–62.

Ajzen, I. (1991). The theory of planned behavior. *Organizational Behavior and Human Decision Processes, 50,* 179–211.

Ajzen, I., & Fishbein, M. (1977). Attitude-behavior relations: A theoretical analysis and review of empirical research. *Psychological Bulletin, 84,* 888–918.

Alward, R. R., & Camunas, C. (1991). *The nurse's guide to marketing.* Boston, MA: Delmar.

American Cancer Society [ACS]. (1999). *American Cancer Society.* Retrieved December 13, 1999, from the World Wide Web: http://www.links2go.com/more/www/cancer/frames.html.

American Heart Association. (1997). *Heart and stroke statistical update.* Dallas: Author.

American Heart Association. (1999). *Heart and stroke facts.* Dallas. Author.

American Lung Association [ALA]. (1999). *American Lung Association.* Retrieved December 13, 1999, from the World Wide Web: http://lungusa.org.

American Public Health Association [APHA]. (1975). The role of official local health agencies. *American Journal of Public Health, 65*(2), 189–193.

American Public Health Association. (1999). *APHA Advocate's Handbook.* Washington DC: Author.

American Speech-Language-Hearing Association. (1999). *Language skill disorders.* Retrieved September 22, 1999, from the World Wide Web: http://www.healthtouch.com/levl/leaflets/aslhaO58.htm.

Anderson, J. A., & Adams, M. N. (1992). Acknowledging the learning styles of diverse student populations: Implications for instructional design. In L. L. B. Border and N. Van Note Chism (Eds.), *Teaching for diversity* (pp. 19–33). San Francisco: Jossey-Bass.

Armstrong, T. (1994). *Multiple intelligences*. Alexandria, VA: Association for Supervision and Curriculum Development.

Baker, J. J., & Baker, R. W. (1999). *Health care finance: Basic tools for nonfinancial managers*. Gaithersburg, MD: Aspen.

Bandura, A. (1977). *Social learning theory*. Englewood Cliffs, NJ: Prentice-Hall.

Bean, J. C. (1996). *Engaging ideas: The professor's guide to integrating writing, critical thinking, and active learning in the classroom*. San Francisco: Jossey-Bass.

Beardain, R. P., & Grantham, J. B. (1993). The use of volunteerism in indigent health care. *Journal of Health and Social Policy, 5*(1), 1–7.

Becker, M. H. (Ed.). (1974). The health belief model and personal health behavior. *Health Education Monographs, 2* (entire issue).

Bellman, G. M. (1990). *The consultant's calling: Bringing who you are to what you do*. San Francisco: Jossey-Bass.

Benbow, N., Wang, Y., & Whitman, S. (1998). The big cities health inventory, 1997. *Journal of Community Health, 23*(6), 471–489.

Bennett, C. E., and Martin, B. (1998). *The Asian and Pacific Islander population*. (U.S. Census Bureau Report.) Retrieved April 27, 2000, from the World Wide Web: http://census.gov/population/www/pop-profile/aipop.htm.

Bornstein, D. (1996). *The blind men and the elephant: A Hindu fable by John Godfrey Saxe*. Retrieved July 31, 1999, from the World Wide Web: http://www.milk.com/random-humor/elephant_fable.html.

Bowman, C. (1997). Employment outlook, 1996–2006: BLS projections to 2006—Summary. *Monthly Labor Review*, November, 3–5. Retrieved December 29, 1999, from the World Wide Web: http://www.bls.gov/pdf/emp11s97.pdf.

Breckon, D. J. (1997). *Managing health promotion programs: Leadership skills for the 21st century*. Gaithersburg, MD: Aspen.

Breckon, D. J., Harvey, J. R., & Lancaster, R. B. (1998). *Community health education: Settings, roles, and skills for the 21st century*. Gaithersburg, MD: Aspen.

Brislin, R. W. (1986). The wording and translation of research instruments. In W. J. Lonner & J. W. Berry (Eds.), *Field methods in cross-cultural research* (pp. 137–164). Beverly Hills, CA: Sage.

Burke, M., Wieser, P., & Keegan, L. (1995). Cultural beliefs and health behaviors of pregnant Mexican-American women: Implications for primary care. *Advances in Nursing Science 17*(4), 37–52.

Campinha-Bacote, J. (1998). Africans-Americans. In L. D. Purnell and B. J. Paulanka (Eds.), *Transcultural health care: A culturally competent approach* (pp. 53–73). Philadelphia: F. A. Davis.

Carlson, W. D., & Grady, R. (1993). *Preparing a grant proposal for the federal government*. Unpublished paper presented at Texas Woman's University Fall Faculty Development Seminar, October.

Carnevale, A. P., Gainer, L. L., & Meltzer, A. S. (1990). *Workplace basics*. San Francisco: Jossey-Bass.

Center for Eating Disorders. (1999). *Frequently asked questions*. Retrieved December 13, 1999, from the World Wide Web: http://www.eating-disorder.com/faq.htm.

Centers for Disease Control and Prevention. (1997a). Deaths and death rates for the 10 leading causes of death in specific age groups, by race and sex: United States, 1995. *Monthly Vital Statistics Report, 45*(11). Retrieved June 23, 1999, from the World Wide Web: http://www.cdc.gov/nchswww/SSBR/1c7bb_a.htm.

Centers for Disease Control and Prevention. (1997b). Summary of notifiable diseases, United States, 1996. *Morbidity and Mortality Weekly, 45*(53), 7–84.

Centers for Disease Control and Prevention. (1998a). *Chronic diseases and their risk factors: The nation's leading causes of death.* Atlanta: USDHHS.

Centers for Disease Control and Prevention. (1998b). *Youth risk behavior surveillance system—United States 1997.* Retrieved June 16, 1999, from the World Wide Web: http://www.cdc.gov/nccdphp/dash/yrbs/ov.htm.

Centers for Disease Control and Prevention. (1999a). *Centers for Disease Control and Prevention.* Retrieved December 13, 1999, from the World Wide Web: http://cdc.gov/about cdc.htm.

Centers for Disease Control and Prevention. (1999b). *A coordinated school health program: The CDC eight component model of school health programs.* Retrieved August 11, 1999, from the World Wide Web: http://www.cdc.gov/nccdphp/dash/cshpdef.htm.

Centers for Disease Control and Prevention. (1999c). Trends in HIV-related sexual risk behaviors among high school students—Selected U.S. cities, 1991–1997. *Journal of School Health, 69*(7), 255–257.

Chambre, S. M. (1993). Volunteerism by elders: Past trends and future prospects. *The Gerontologist, 33*(2), 221–228.

Chicago Public Library. (1997). *Chicago timeline: 1958—Our Lady of the Angels school fire.* Retrieved April 16, 2000, from the World Wide Web: http://38.221.132.101/004chicago/timeline/ourlady fire.html.

Children's Defense Fund. (1998). *The state of America's children—Yearbook 1998.* Washington, DC: Author.

Cohen, M. N. (1989). *Health and the rise of civilization.* New Haven: Yale University Press.

Cushner, K. (1994). Preparing teachers for an intercultural context. In R. W. Brislin & T. Yoshida (Eds.), *Improving intercultural interactions: Modules for cross-cultural training programs* (pp. 109–128). Thousand Oaks, CA: Sage.

Cystic Fibrosis Foundation. (1999). *Cystic Fibrosis Foundation.* Retrieved December 13, 1999, from the World Wide Web: http://centraltx@cff.org.

Daniel, E. L., & Balog, J. E. (1997). Utilization of the World Wide Web in education. *The Journal of School Health 28*(5), 260–267.

Deeds, S. G. (1992). *The health education specialist: Self-study for professional competence.* Los Alamitos, CA: Loose Canon.

del Pinal, J. (1998). *The Hispanic population.* Washington, DC: U.S. Census Bureau. Retrieved May 27, 1999, from the World Wide Web: http://www.census.gov/population/www/pop-profile/hisppop.html.

Demko, D. (1997, July 29). *WHO gauges global depression.* ThirdAge Media. Retrieved December 28, 1999, from the World Wide Web: http://coltraine.thirdage.come/cgi-bin/NewsPrin.cgi.

Dever, G. E. (1990). *Community health analysis: Global awareness at the local level* (2nd ed.). Gaithersburg, MD: Aspen.

Dinger, M. K., & Parsons, N. (1999). Sexual activity among college students living in residence halls and fraternity or sorority housing. *Journal of Health Education, 30*(4), 242–246, 260.

Doll, R. C. (1992). *Curriculum improvement: Decision making and process* (8th ed.). Boston, MA: Allyn and Bacon.

Donatelle, R., Snow, C., & Wilcox, A. (1999). *Wellness choices for health and fitness.* Belmont, CA: Wadsworth.

Ellis, S. J. (1993). Volunteerism as an enhancement to career development. *Journal of Employment Counseling, 30*(3), 127–132.

Epp, J. (1986). Achieving health for all: A framework for health promotion. *Canadian Journal of Public Health, 77*(6), 393–407.

Evans, A. S. (1978). Causation and disease: A chronological journey. *American Journal of Epidemiology 108,* 254–255.

Fahey, T. D., Insel, P. M., & Roth, W. T. (2001). *Fit and Well: Core Concepts and Labs in Physical Fitness and Wellness.* Mountain View, CA: Mayfield.

Family Education Network. (1999). Global health trends from *The world health report, 1999.* In *Information please almanac.* Boston, MA: Author. Retrieved December 9, 1999, from the World Wide Web: http://couponsurfer.infoplease.com/ipa/A0779166.html.

Feldman, R. H., & Hollander, R. B. (1993, November/December). Issues in cross-cultural and international health education research. *Health Education,* 11–15.

Fors, S. W., Crepaz, N., & Hayes, D. M. (1999). Key factors that protect against health risks in youth: Further evidence. *American Journal of Health Behavior, 23*(5), 368–380.

Foundation Center of New York. (1999). *Mission and role of our libraries.* Retrieved August 11, 1999, from the World Wide Web: http://www.foundationcenter.org/newyork/ny_mission.html.

Friedman, G. D. (1994). *Primer of epidemiology* (4th ed.). New York: McGraw-Hill.

Friis, R. H., & Sellers, T. A. (1999). *Epidemiology for public health practice* (2nd ed.). Gaithersburg, MD: Aspen.

Garrard, J. (1999). *Health sciences literature review made easy: The matrix method.* Gaithersburg, MD: Aspen.

Gilmore, G. D., & Campbell, M. D. (1996). *Needs assessment strategies: For health education and health promotion* (2nd ed.). Madison, WI: Brown and Benchmark.

Glanz, K., Lewis, F. M., Rimer, B. K. (Eds.). (1997). *Health behavior and health education: Theory, research, and practice.* San Francisco: Jossey-Bass.

Glascoff, M. A., Baker, J. B., & Glascoff, D. W. (1997). Successfully promoting volunteerism by offering extrinsic rewards in a personal health course: A pilot study. *Journal of School Health Education, 28*(4), 219–223.

Gold, R. S., Green, L. W., & Kreuter, M. W. (1998). *Enabling methods of planning and organizing within everyone's reach (EMPOWER).* Sudbury, MA: Jones and Bartlett.

Gordis, E. (1999). Research on alcohol problems. *National Forum: The Phi Kappa Phi Journal, 79*(4), 24–27.

Green, L. W., & Kreuter, M. W. (1999). *Health promotion planning: An educational and ecological approach* (3rd ed.). Mountain View, CA: Mayfield.

Green, L. W., & Ottoson, J. M. (1999). *Community and population health* (8th ed.). Boston: WBC/McGraw-Hill.

Greenberg, J. S. (1995). *Health education: Learner-centered instructional strategies* (3rd ed.). Madison, WI: Brown and Benchmark.

Greenberg, J. S. (1999). *Comprehensive stress management* (6th ed.). Boston: McGraw-Hill.

Hales, D. (1994). *An invitation to health* (6th ed.). Redwood City, CA: Benjamin/ Cummings.

Harvard School of Public Health [HSPH]. (1999). *The global burden of disease and injury: Executive summary.* Retrieved December 28, 1999, from the World Wide Web: http:// www.hsph.edu /organizations/bdu/gbdsum6.pdf.

Health Sponsorship Council. (1999). *Street Skills.* Retrieved September 22, 1999, from the World Wide Web: http://www.healthsponsorship.co.nz/streetskills.html.

Heaven, C. (1999). Communicating information about health and community development issues. In B. Berkowitz & J. Schultz (Eds.), *Community tool box.* Retrieved November 27, 1999, from the World Wide Web: http://ctb.lsi.ukans.edu /tools/cl /cls3f. html.

Henry, J., & Ward, S. E. (1999). The art and science of health education. Unpublished paper.

Henson, K. T. (1995). *The art of writing for publication.* Needham Heights, MA: Allyn and Bacon.

Hill, S. C., & Drolet, J. C. (1999). School-related violence among high school students in the United States, 1993–1995. *Journal of School Health, 69*(7), 264–272.

Hochbaum, G. M. (1958). *Public participation in medical screening programs: A sociopsychological study.* PHS Publication No. 572. Washington, DC: U.S. Government Printing Office.

Howard, B. V., Lee, E. T., Cowan, L. D., Devereaus, R. B., Galloway, J. M., Go, O. T., Howard, W. J., Rhoades, E. R., Robbins, D. C., Sievers, M. L., & Welty, T. K. (1999). *Rising tide of cardiovascular disease in American Indians: The Strong Heart study. Circulation, 99,* 2389–2395. Retrieved April 27, 2000, from the World Wide Web: http:// www.circulationaha.org.

Ibrahim, M. A. (1985). *Epidemiology and health policy.* Rockville, MD: Aspen.

Indian Health Service [IHS]. (1999). *About the Indian Health Service.* Washington, DC: Author. Retrieved July 16, 1999, from the World Wide Web: http://www.ihs.gov.

Ireland, J. D. (1999, June). *Udana VI.4, Tittha Sutta, various sectarians (1).* Buddhist Publication Society. Retrieved July 31, 1999, from the World Wide Web: http://world. std.com /~metta/canon/khuddaka/udana/ud6-4.html.

Jack, L., Harrison, I. E., & Airhihenbuwa, C. O. (1994). In A. C. Matiella (Ed.), *The multicultural challenge in health education* (pp. 51–72). Santa Cruz, CA: ETR Associates.

Joint Committee on Health Education Terminology. (1991). Report of the 1990 Joint Committee on Health Education Terminology. *The Journal of Health Education, 22*(2), 105–106.

Kennedy, A. J. (1999). *The Internet: The Rough Guide 2000.* New York: Rough Guide.

Kilmer, D., & Price, T. (1995a). *Characteristics of families experiencing violence.* Retrieved December 13, 1999, from the World Wide Web: http://www.oseda.missouri.edu / kidcnt /reports/violence/nspcomm.html.

Kilmer, D., & Price, T. (1995b). *Community violence and children.* Retrieved December 13, 1999, from the World Wide Web: http://www.oseda.missouri.edu /kidcnt /reports/ violence/nspcomm.html.

Kilmer, D., & Price, T. (1995c). *Family violence and children.* Retrieved December 13, 1999 from the World Wide Web: http://www.oseda.missouri.edu /kidcnt /reports/violence/ nspcomm.html.

Kilmer, D., & Price, T. (1995d). *Where youth violence and environment intersect.* Retrieved December 13, 1999, from the World Wide Web: http://www.oseda.missouri.edu / kidcnt /reports/violence/nspcomm.html.

Kitano, M. K. (1997). A rationale and framework for course change. In A. I. Morey & M. K. Kitano (Eds.), *Multicultural course transformation in higher education: A broader truth* (pp. 1–17). Boston: Allyn and Bacon.

Kolb, D. G. (1992). The practicality of theory. *The Journal of Experiential Education, 15*(2), 24–29.

Komro, K. A., Perry, C. L., Veblen-Mortenson, S., Williams, C. L., & Roel, J. P. (1999). Peer leadership in school and community alcohol use prevention activities. *Journal of Health Education, 30*(4), 202–208.

Kotler, P., & Zaltmane, G. (1971). Social marketing: An approach to social change. *Journal of Marketing, 35*(3). 3–12.

Kraft, R. J. (1988). A call to action and reflection. In R. J. Kraft & M. Sakofs (Eds.), *The theory of experiential education* (pp. 1–3). Boulder, CO: Association for Experiential Education.

Krause, N. (1999, June 4). *Trends in private health insurance coverage.* Health Policy Studies Division, National Governor's Association, Center for Best Practices, Washington, DC. Retrieved December 9, 1999, from the World Wide Web: http://www.nga.org/Pubs/IssueBriefs/1999/990604HealthIns.asp#Summary.

Kuzma, J. W. (1998). *Basic statistics for the health sciences.* Mountain View, CA: Mayfield.

Lancaster, B. (1999, December). *Trends, issues, and partnerships in health education and health promotion.* Workshop conducted at the Annual Convention of the Texas Association for Health, Physical Education, Recreation, and Dance, Austin, Texas.

Landrum-Brown, J. (2000). *Black English.* Retrieved May 8, 2000, from the World Wide Web: http://www.staff.uiuc.edu/~jlandrum/BlkEng.html.

Lankard, B. A. (1995). *New ways of learning in the work-place.* Columbus, OH: ERIC Clearinghouse on Adult, Career, and Vocational Education. (ERIC Document Reproduction Service No. 377 311).

Lasker, R. D. (1997). *Medicine and public health: The power of collaboration.* New York: The New York Academy of Medicine.

MacKenzie, E. C., & Brown, W. H. (1986). *How to prepare a competitive proposal.* Louisiana State University: Louisiana Agricultural Experiment Station.

March of Dimes. (1999a). *March of Dimes.* Retrieved December 13, 1999, from the World Wide Web: http://www.marchofdimes.org.

March of Dimes. (1999b). *On an average day in the United States.* Retrieved July 12, 1999, from the World Wide Web: http://www.modimes.org/HealthLibrary2/factsfigures/avgday.htm.

Marlowe, B. A., and Page, M. L. (1998). *Creating and sustaining the constructivist classroom.* Thousand Oaks, CA: Corwin Press.

Maslow, A. (1954). *Motivation and personality.* New York: Harper & Row.

Matocha, L. K. (1998). Chinese-Americans. In L. D. Purnell and B. J. Paulanka (Eds.), *Transcultural health care: A culturally competent approach* (pp. 163–188). Philadelphia: F. A. Davis.

McDermott, R. J., & Sarvela, P. D. (1999). *Health education evaluation and measurement: A practitioner's perspective* (2nd ed.). Boston: McGraw-Hill.

McKahan, D. (1999). Health care facilities: Current trends and future forecasts. *The Academy Journal.* Retrieved December 9, 1999, from the World Wide Web: http://www.e-architect.com/pia/acadjour/articles/07/article07a.asp.

McKenzie, J. F., & Jurs, J. L. (1993). *Planning, implementing, and evaluating health promotion programs.* New York: Macmillan.

McKenzie, J. F., Pinger, R. R., & Kotecki, J. E. (1999). *An introduction to community health* (3rd ed.). Sudbury, MA: Jones and Bartlett.

McKenzie, J. F., & Smeltzer, J. L. (1997). *Planning, implementing, and evaluating health promotion programs: A primer* (2nd ed.). Boston: Allyn & Bacon.

McLaughlin, G. (1969). SMOG grading—a new readability formula. *Journal of Reading, 12*(May), 639–646.

McLean, D. D. (1996). *Use of computer-based technology in health, physical education, recreation, and dance.* Washington DC: ERIC Clearinghouse on Teaching and Technical Education (ERIC Document Reproductions Service N. ED 390 874).

Miller, D. F., & Price, J. H. (1997). *Dimensions of community health.* Boston: McGraw-Hill.

Minkler, M., & Wallerstein, N. (1997). Improving health through community organization and community building. In K. Glanz, F. M Lewis, and B. K. Rimer (Eds.), *Health behavior and health education: Theory, research and practice* (2nd ed.) (pp. 241–269). San Francisco: Jossey-Bass.

Miranda, B. F., McBride, M. R., & Spangler, Z. (1998). Filipino-Americans. In L. D. Purnell and B. J. Paulanka (Eds.), *Transcultural health care: A culturally competent approach* (pp. 245–272). Philadelphia: F. A. Davis.

Mish, F. C. (Ed.) (1999). *Merriam-Webster's Collegiate Dictionary* (10th ed.). Springfield, MA: Merriam-Webster, Incorporated.

Montano, D. E., Kasprzyk, D., & Taplin, S. H. (1997). The theory of reasoned action and the theory of planned behavior. In K. Glanz, F. M. Lewis, and B. K. Rimer (Eds.), *Health behavior and health education: Theory, research, and practice* (2nd ed.) (pp. 85–112). San Francisco: Jossey-Bass.

Morgan, M. T., et al. (1997). *Environmental health* (2nd ed.). Englewood, CA: Morton.

Morris, J. N. (1975). *Uses of epidemiology* (3rd ed.). Edinburgh: Churchill Livingstone.

Muscular Dystrophy Association. (1999). *MDA.* Retrieved December 13, 1999, from the World Wide Web: http://www.mdusa.org.

Nadler, L., & Nadler, Z. (1987). *The comprehensive guide to successful conferences and meetings.* San Francisco: Jossey-Bass.

National Association of County Health Officials [NACHO]. (1991). *APEX/PH, Assessment protocol for excellence in public health.* Washington, DC: Author.

National Bureau of Labor Statistics [NBLS]. (1998, February 5). *1998–99 edition of the occupational outlook handbook published.* Retrieved December 29, 1999, from the World Wide Web: http://www.bls.gov/news.release/ooh.nws.htm.

National Center for Health Statistics [NCHS]. (1996). *Health, United States, 1995.* Hyattsville, MD: Public Health Service.

National Center for Health Statistics. (1997). Report of final mortality statistics, 1995. *Monthly Vital Statistics Report, 45*(11), pp. 23–33.

National Center for Health Statistics. (1999a). *Health, United States, 1999.* Hyattsville, MD: Author. Retrieved January 11, 2000, from the World Wide Web: http://www.cdc.gov/nchswww/products/pubs/pubd/hus/99mortal.htm.

National Center for Health Statistics. (1999b). *National Vital Statistics Report 47*(18). Retrieved June 21, 1999, from the World Wide Web: http://www.cdc.gov/nchswww/fastats/births.htm.

National Center for Policy Analysis [NCPA]. (1999). *Health issues: The cost of patient's rights legislation.* Retrieved November 15, 1999, from the World Wide Web: http://www.ncpa.org/pi/health/pd071499a.html.

National Commission for Health Education Credentialing [NCHEC]. (1999, June). *Competencies Update Project: Status Report*. Retrieved December 30, 1999, from the World Wide Web: http://www.nchec.org/cupproj.htm.

National Commission for Health Education Credentialing [NCHEC], American Association for Health Education [AAHE], and the Society for Public Health Education [SOPHE]. (1999). *A competency-based framework for graduate-level health educators*. Allentown, PA: NCHEC.

National Healthy Mothers, Healthy Babies Coalition [HMHB]. (1999). *Healthy Mothers, Healthy Babies News 13*(2).

National Institute on Alcohol Abuse and Alcoholism [NIAAA]. (1988, January 14). *Age of drinking onset predicts future alcohol abuse and dependence* (Press release). Rockville, MD: National Institutes of Health.

National Institutes of Health [NIH]. (1995). *Making health communication programs work: A planner's guide*. NIH Publication No. 92-1493. Atlanta: USDHHS. Retrieved November 28, 1999, from the World Wide Web: http://rex.nci.nih.gov/NCI_Pub_Interface/HCPW/HOME.HTM.

National Institutes of Health. (1999). *NIH overview*. Retrieved December 13, 1999, from the World Wide Web: http://www.nih.gov/welcome/nihnew.html.

National Kidney Foundation. (1999). *National Kidney Foundation*. Retrieved December 13, 1999, from the World Wide Web: http://www.kidney.org/general.

National School-to-Work Learning and Information Center. (1999). *Future trends*. Retrieved December 9, 1999, from the World Wide Web: http://www.scps.k12.fl.us/Stw/trends.htm.

National Science Foundation. (1997). *User-friendly handbook for mixed method evaluation*. Retrieved February 7, 1999, from the World Wide Web: http://www.her.nsf.fov/HER/REC/pubs/NSF97-1531/start/htm.

Norbeck, J. (1995). Who is our consumer? Shaping nursing programs to meet emerging needs. *Journal of Professional Nursing, 11*(6), 325–331.

Novartis Foundation for Sustainable Development. (1999). *A short course in social marketing*. Retrieved September 22, 1999, from the World Wide Web: http://www.foundation.novartis.com/social_marketing.htm.

Nunnaly, J. C. (1978). *Psychometric theory*. New York: McGraw-Hill.

Office of Disease Prevention and Health Promotion [ODPHP]. (1988). *Disease prevention/health promotion: The facts*. Palo Alto, CA: Bull.

Office of Prevention, Texas Youth Commission. (1999). *A summary of "Youth violence, guns, and illicit drug markets."* Retrieved December 13, 1999, from the World Wide Web: http://www.tyc.state.tx.us/prevention/youthvio.htm.

Online NewsHour. (1999, July–December). *Patients' Bill of Rights: A health spotlight report*. Retrieved April 21, 2000, from the World Wide Web: http://www.pbs.org/newshour/bb/health/july-dec99/patients_index.html.

Online NewsHour. (1999, October 29). *Online focus: President Clinton*. Retrieved November 14, 1999, from the World Wide Web: http://www.pbs.org/newshour/bb/health/july-dec99/clinton_privacy.html.

Paisano, E. L. (1998). *The American Indian, Eskimo, and Aleut population*. U.S. Census Bureau. Retrieved April 27, 2000, from the World Wide Web: http://www.census.gov/population/www/pop-profile/amerind.html.

Pan American Health Organization [PAHO]. (1998). United States of America. *Health conditions in the Americas.* Retrieved June 21, 1999, from the World Wide Web: http://www.paho.org/english/country.htm.

Parker, E. A., Eng, E., Laraia, B., Ammerman, A., Dodds, J., Margolis, L., & Cross, A. (1998). Coalition building for prevention. In R. C. Brownson, E. A. Baker, L. F. Novick, (Eds.), *Community-based prevention: Programs that work.* Gaithersburg, MD: Aspen.

Parker, R. C. (1999). *Ten steps to better Web sites, part 1.* Retrieved November 6, 1999, from the World Wide Web: http://designrefresher.i-us.com/septore.html.

Pavalko, R. M. (1999). Problem gambling. *National Forum: The Phi Kappa Phi Journal 79*(4), 28–32.

Payne, C. A. (1999). The challenges of employing performance monitoring in public health community-based efforts. *Journal of Community Health, 24*(2), 159–170.

Payne, R. K. (1998). *A framework for understanding poverty* (2nd ed.). Baytown, TX: RFT.

Penner, L. A., & Finkelstein, M. A. (1998). Dispositional and structural determinants of volunteerism. *Journal of Personality and Social Psychology, 74*(2), 525–537.

Perry, C. L., Williams, C. L., Veblen-Mortenson, S., Toomey, T. L., Komro, K. A., Anstine, P. S., McGovern, P. G., Finnegan, J. R., Forster, J. L., Wagenaar, A. C., & Wolfson, M. (1996). Project Northland: Outcomes of a community wide alcohol use prevention program during early adolescence. *American Journal of Public Health, 86,* 956–964.

Powell, K. B. (1999). Correlates of violent and nonviolent behavior among vulnerable inner-city youths. In J. G. Sebastian & A. Bushy (Eds.), *Special populations in the community* (pp. 39–48). Gaithersburg, MD: Aspen.

Prochaska, J. O., Redding, C. A., & Evers, K. E. (1997). The transtheoretical model and stages of change. In K. Glanz, F. M. Lewis, and B. K. Rimer (Eds.), *Health behavior and health education: Theory, research, and practice* (2nd ed.) (pp. 60–84). San Francisco: Jossey-Bass.

Project Wild Handbook. (1995). Durham, NC: Duke University. Retrieved February 29, 1999, from the World Wide Web: http://www.duke.edu/web/PWILD/handbook/processing.html.

Purnell, L. D. (1998). Mexican-Americans. In L. D. Purnell and B. J. Paulanka (Eds.), *Transcultural health care: A culturally competent approach* (pp. 163–188). Philadelphia: F. A. Davis.

Radley, A. (1995). *Making sense of illness: The social psychology of health and disease.* London: Sage.

Rasell, E., Bernstein, J., & Tang, K. (1993). Utilization review and financial risk-shifting: Compensating patients for cost containment injuries. In V. R. Randall, *Impact of managed care organizations on ethnic Americans and underserved populations.* Retrieved December 4, 1999, from the World Wide Web: http://www.udayton.edu/~health/manage02.htm.

Raskin, M. S. (1994). The Delphi Study in field instruction revisited: Expert consensus on issues and research priorities. *Journal of Social Work Education 3*(1), 75–89.

Reardon, T. R. (1999, September 23). *Pass Norwood-Dingell patient protection bill.* American Medical Association (Released statement). Retrieved November 15, 1999, from the World Wide Web: http://www.ama-assn.org/advocacy/statemnt/990923.htm.

Reed, E. S. (1996). *The necessity of experience.* New Haven: Yale University Press.

Rodman, J., Weill, K., Driscoll, M., Fenton, T., Hill, A., Salem-Schatz, S., & Palfrey, J. (1999). A nationwide survey of financing health-related services for special education students. *Journal of School Health 69*(4), 133–139.

Salpolsky, R. (1998). How the other half heals. *Discover, 19*(4), 49–52.

Sarafino, E. P. (1990). *Health psychology: Biopsychosocial interactions.* New York: John Wiley.

Satcher, D. (2000, January 25). *Healthy people 2010: A path to the future* (Press Release). U.S. Department of Health and Human Services.

Schon, D. A. (1987). *Educating the reflective practitioner.* San Francisco: Jossey-Bass.

Schust, C. A. (1997). *Community health education and promotion: A guide to program design and evaluation.* Gaithersburg, MD: Aspen.

Sebastian, J. G. (1999). Definitions and theory underlying vulnerability. In J. G. Sebastian & A. Bushy (Eds.), *Special populations in the community* (pp. 3–9). Gaithersburg, MD: Aspen.

Seelye, H. N., & Seelye-James, A. (1996). *Culture clash: Managing in a multicultural world.* Lincolnwood, IL: NTC.

Segall, M. H. (1993). *Cross-cultural psychology: Human behavior in global perspective.* Monterey, CA: Brooks/Cole.

Shaffer, H. J. (1999). On the nature and meaning of addiction. *National Forum: The Phi Kappa Phi Journal 79*(4), 9–14.

Silvestri, G. T. (1997). Employment outlook, 1996–2006: Occupational employment projections to 2006. *Monthly Labor Review,* November, 58–83. Retrieved December 29, 1999, from the World Wide Web: http://www.bls.gov/pdf/emp11o97.pdf.

Simpson, C. E. (1998, August/September). What must we do to meet Healthy People goals? *Closing the Gap,* August/September, p. 4.

Snow, H. (1992). *The power of team building: Using ropes techniques.* San Diego: Pfeiffer.

Snyder, M. (1993). Basic research and practical problems: The promise of a "functional" personality and social psychology. *Personality and Social Psychology Bulletin 19*(3), 251–264.

Spector, R. E. (1996). *Cultural diversity in health and illness* (4th ed.). Norwalk, CT: Appleton and Lange.

Steinaker, N. W., & Bell, M. R. (1979). *The experiential taxonomy: An approach to teaching and learning.* New York: Academic Press.

Still, O., & Hodgins, D. (1998). Navajo Indians. In L. D. Purnell and B. J. Paulanka (Eds.), *Transcultural health care: A culturally competent approach* (pp. 423–447). Philadelphia: F. A. Davis.

Stretcher, V. J., & Rosenstock, I. M. (1997). The health belief model. In K. Glanz, F. M. Lewis, and B. K. Rimer (Eds.), *Health behavior and health education: Theory, research, and practice* (2nd ed.) (pp. 41–59). San Francisco: Jossey-Bass.

Swartz, M. (1990). Infant mortality: Agenda for the 1990's. *Journal of Pediatric Health Care 4,* 169–174.

Timmreck, T. C. (1998). *Epidemiology.* Boston: Jones and Bartlett Publishers.

Travis, J. W. (1990). *Wellness for helping professionals.* Mill Valley, CA: Wellness Associates.

Tucker, J. A. (1999). From zero tolerance to harm reduction. *National Forum: The Phi Kappa Phi Journal 79*(4), 19–23.

United Nations Secretariat (1998, February). *World population projections to 2150.* Population Division of the Department of Economic and Social Affairs, United Nations Secretariat, New York. Retrieved January 4, 2000, from the World Wide Web: http://www.undp.org/popin/wdtrends/execsum.htm.

United States Census Bureau [USCB]. (1997a). *Poverty: 1997 highlights.* Washington, DC: Author. Retrieved June 23, 1999, from the World Wide Web: http://www.census.gov/hhes/poverty/poverty97/pov97hi.html.

United States Census Bureau. (1997b). *Poverty 1997: People and families in poverty by selected characteristics: 1989, 1996, and 1997.* Washington, DC: Author. Retrieved June 23, 1999, from the World Wide Web: http://www.census.gov/hhes/poverty/poverty97/pv97est1.html.

United States Census Bureau. (1998). *Selected economic characteristics of people and families, by sex and race: March 1998.* Washington, DC: Author. Retrieved June 23, 1999, from the World Wide Web: http://www.census.gov/population/socdemo/race/black/tabs98/tab02.txt.

United States Census Bureau. (1999a). *Resident population estimates of the United States by age and sex: April 1, 1990 to April 1, 1999.* Retrieved June 21, 1999, from the World Wide Web: http://www.census.gov/population/estimates/nation/intfile2-1.txt.

United States Census Bureau. (1999b). *Resident population estimates of the United States by sex, race, and Hispanic origin: April 1, 1990 to April 1, 1999.* Population Estimates Program, Population Division, U.S. Census Bureau. Retrieved June 23, 1999, from the World Wide Web: http://www.census.gov/population/estimates/nation/intfile3-1.txt.

United States Census Bureau. (1999c). *Selected social characteristics of the population, by sex, region, and race: March 1998.* Retrieved June 23, 1999, from the World Wide Web: http://www.census.gov/population/socdemo/race/black/tabs98/tab01.txt.

United States Census Bureau. (1999d). *Selected social and economic characteristics for the 25 largest American Indian tribes: 1990.* Retrieved July 17, 1999, from the World Wide Web: http://www.census.gov/population/socdemo/race/indian/ailang2.txt.

United States Department of Agriculture [USDA]. (1993). Code of federal regulations 7 (parts 210–299). Washington, DC: U.S. Government Printing Office.

United States Department of Health and Human Services [USDHHS]. (1990). *Healthy People 2000: National health promotion and prevention objectives.* DHHS Publication No. 91-51212. Washington DC: U.S. Government Printing Office.

United States Department of Health and Human Services. (1991a). *Healthy Communities 2000: Model standards.* Washington, DC: U.S. Government Printing Office.

United States Department of Health and Human Services. (1991b). *Healthy People 2000: National health promotion and disease prevention objectives.* DHHS Publication No. PHS90-50212. Washington, D.C.: U.S. Government Printing Office.

United States Department of Health and Human Services. (1994). *Preventing tobacco use among young people: A report of the Surgeon General.*

United States Department of Health and Human Services. (1995). *Healthy People 2000 progress review for American Indians and Alaskan Natives* (Announcement, February 15). Hyattsville, MD: Public Health Service. Retrieved June 21, 1999, from the World Wide Web: http://odphp.osophs.dhhs.gov/pubs/hp2000/progrvw/INDIAN.HTM.

United States Department of Health and Human Services. (1997a). *Healthy People 2000 review, 1997.* Hyattsville, MD: Public Health Service.

United States Department of Health and Human Services. (1997b). *Healthy People 2000 progress review: Hispanic Americans* (Announcement, April 29). Hyattsville, MD: Public Health Service. Retrieved June 21, 1999, from the World Wide Web: http://odphp.osophs.dhhs.gov/pubs/hp2000/progrvw/Hispanics/HispanicAm.htm.

United States Department of Health and Human Services. (1997c). *Healthy People 2000 progress review: Asian Americans and Pacific Islanders* (Announcement, September 13). Hyattsville, MD: Public Health Service. Retrieved June 21, 1999, from the World Wide Web: http://odphp.osophs.dhhs.gov/pubs/hp2000/progrvw/Asians/AsianAm.htm.

United States Department of Health and Human Services. (1998a). *President Clinton announces new racial and ethnic health disparities initiative* (Announcement, February 21). White House Fact Sheet, HHS Press Office, Hyattsville, MD: Author. Retrieved May 20, 1999, from the World Wide Web: http://raceandhealth.hhs.gov/pres.htm.

United States Department of Health and Human Services. (1998b). *Healthy People 2000 progress review: Black Americans* (Announcement, October 26). Hyattsville, MD: Public Health Service. Retrieved June 21, 1999, from the World Wide Web: http://odphp.osophs.dhhs.gov/pubs/hp2000/progrvw/blacks.htm.

United States Department of Health and Human Services. (1998c). *Report to the vice president of the United States: Status of implementation of the Consumer Bill of Rights and responsibilities in the Department of Health and Human Services.* Released November 2, 1998. Retrieved November 15, 1999, from the World Wide Web: http://aspe.os.dhhs.gov/health/vpreport.htm.

Universal Design. (1999). *Shortcuts to disabilities.* Retrieved September 22, 1999, from the World Wide Web: http://thinkquest.phillynews.com/tq1977/11719/data/accessibility.html.

University of Kansas. (1999). *Community health toolbox: Bringing solutions to light.* Retrieved November 28, 1999, from the World Wide Web: http://ctb.lsi.ukans.edu.

University of North Texas Public Health Program [UNTPHP]. (1999). *Job market trends.* Retrieved December 9, 1999, from the World Wide Web: http://www.hsc.unt.edu/education/public_health/trends_research.htm.

Wadud, E. (1999). Making community presentations. In B. Berkowitz and J. Schultz (Eds.), *Community tool box (chapter 1, section 6).* Retrieved November 28, 1999, from the World Wide Web: http://ctb.lsi.ukans.edu/tools/cl/cls6f.shtml.

Wallerstein, N. (1992). Powerlessness, empowerment, and health: Implications for health promotion programs. *American Journal of Health Promotion 6,* 197–205.

Walter, S. L. (1997). *Preparing a budget for a literacy program.* Retrieved on August 4, 1999, from the World Wide Web: http://gamma.sil.org/liguallinks/library/literacy/krz2000/715.htm.

Ward, M. (1998, March). Embracing volunteerism. *School Foodservices and Nutrition,* 24–31.

Ward, S. E., & Koontz, N. (1999). Putting advocacy into action. *Eta Sigma Gamma Monograph 17*(2), 36–40.

Weiler, R. M., Dorman, S. M., and Pealer, L. N. (1999). The Florida school violence policies and programs study. *Journal of School Health 69*(7), 273–279.

Weinreich Communications. (1999). *What is social marketing?* Retrieved September 22, 1999, from the World Wide Web: http://www.socialmarketing.com/whatis.html.

Windsor, R., Baranowski, T., Clark, N., and Cutter, G. (1994). *Evaluation of health promotion, health education, and disease prevention programs* (2nd ed.). Mountain View, CA: Mayfield.

World Health Organization [WHO]. (1996). Sustainable human settlements development in an urbanizing world, *Habitat Agenda* (Section IV C). Retrieved January 4, 2000, from the World Wide Web: http://www.unhabitat.org/agenda/ch-4c-4.html.

World Health Organization. (1997). *The Jakarta declaration on health promotion for the 21st century.* Retrieved December 30, 1999, from the World Wide Web: http://www.ldb.org/vl/top/jakdec.htm.

World Health Organization. (1998, January 28). *Resolution of the executive board of the*

WHO. Retrieved December 30, 1999, from the World Wide Web: http://www.who.int/hrp/hpres98.htm.

World Health Organization. (1999a). *A healthy future for all.* Retrieved December 9, 1999, from the World Wide Web: http://www.who.int/hpr/expo/futures01.html.

World Health Organization. (1999b). *Health for all.* Retrieved August 11, 1999, from the World Wide Web: http://www.who.org/aboutwho/en/healthforall.htm.

Young, A. M. (1999). Addictive drugs and the brain. *National Forum: The Phi Kappa Phi Journal 79*(4), 15–18.

Zuckoff, M. (1995). More and more claiming American Indian heritage. *Boston Globe,* April 18, 1995.

Zweigenhaft, R., Armstrong, J., Quintis, F., & Reddick, A. (1996). The motivations and effectiveness of hospital volunteers. The *Journal of Social Psychology 136*(1), 25–34.

Credits

Chapter 1 Fig. 1.1 Adapted from *Uses of Epidemiology,* Third Edition, by J. N. Morris. Copyright © 1975 Churchill Livingstone, Inc. With permission of the publisher.

Chapter 2 FYI 2.1 http://www.amhrt.org. With permission from the American Heart Association. FYI 2.2 http://www.rwif.org/main.html. With permission from The Robert Wood Johnson Foundation.

Chapter 3 Fig. 3.1 Adapted with permission from *Epidemiology for Public Health,* Second Edition, by R. H. Friis and T. A. Sellers. Copyright © 1999 Aspen Publishers, Inc. Fig. 3.5 From *Environmental Health,* Second Edition, by M. T. Morgan et al. Copyright © 1997 Wadsworth Publishing Company. Reprinted with permission of Wadsworth, a division of Thomson Learning. Figs. 3.6, 3.7, 3.8 From *An Introduction to Epidemiology,* Second Edition, by T. C. Timmreck. Copyright © 1998 Jones and Bartlett Publishers, Sudbury, MA. www. jbpub.com. Reprinted with permission of the publisher. Fig. 3.9 From *Primer of Epidemiology,* Fourth Edition, by G. D. Friedman, 1994, McGraw-Hill. Reproduced with permission from The McGraw-Hill Companies.

Chapter 5 Fig. 5.1 From "A Conceptual Model for Culturally Appropriate Health Education Programs in Developing Countries" by C. O. Airhihenbuwa, *International Quarterly of Community Health Education, II,* 1990, pp. 53–62. Used with permission from the author. FYI 5.2 From *Health Promotion in Diverse Communities* by V. M. Gonzalez, J. T. Gonzalez, V. Freeman, and B. Howard-Pitney, 1994, Stanford Center for Research in Disease Prevention. With permission from Stanford University Health Promotion Resource Center.

Chapter 6 Figs. 6.7, 6.8 From V. J. Strecher and I. M. Rosenstock, "The Health Belief Model" in *Health Behavior and Health Education: Theory, Research, and Practice,* edited by K. Glanz, F. M. Lewis and B. K. Rimer, 1997, Jossey-Bass. Reprinted by permission of John Wiley & Sons, Inc. Fig. 6.9 From J. O. Prochaska, C. A. Redding, L. L. Harlow, J. S. Rossi, and W. F. Velicer, 1994, "The Transtheoretical Model of Change and HIV Prevention: A Review," *Health Education Quarterly* 21(4), pp. 471–486. Reprinted by permission of Sage Publications, Inc.

Chapter 8 Fig. 8.2 From "Implementing Comprehensive School Health Education: Educational Innovations and Social Change" by L. J. Kolbe and D. C. Iverson, 1981, *Health Education Quarterly* 8, 57–80. Copyright © 1981 Sage Publications, Inc. Reprinted by permission of the publisher. Fig. 8.3 From L. Nadler and Z. Nadler, *The Comprehensive Guide to Successful Conferences and Meetings,* 1987, Jossey-Bass. Reprinted by permission of Jossey-Bass, Inc., a subsidiary of John Wiley & Sons, Inc. Fig. 8.4 From Ronald C. Doll, *Curriculum Improvement: Decision Making and Process,* Ninth Edition, 1996, Allyn & Bacon. Copyright © 1996 by Allyn & Bacon. Reprinted by permission from the publisher. FYI 8.6 From "Designing Access to the WWW Pages," http://www.atacess.org/design.html. Retrieved on May 9, 2000, Alliance for Technology Access, 1999. Reprinted with permission from Alliance for Technology Access.

Chapter 10 P. 221 Definition of "cooperation" by permission from *Merriam-Webster's Collegiate® Dictionary,* Tenth Edition. Copyright © 1999 by Merriam-Webster, Incorporated. FYI 10.1 From H. N. Seelye and A. Seelye-James, *Culture Clash: Managing in a Multicultural World,*

1996, NTC Publishing Group. Copyright © 1996 NTC Publishing Group. Used with permission of the publisher. FYI 10.4 From Mitretek Systems Health Information Technology Institute, *Criteria for Assessing the Quality of Health Information on the Internet — Policy Paper.* Retrieved November 14, 1999, from the World Wide Web: http://hitiweb.mitretek.org/docs/policy.html.

Chapter 12   FYI 12.1 By permission. From *Merriam-Webster's Collegiate® Dictionary,* Tenth Edition. Copyright © 1999 by Merriam-Webster, Incorporated; and from "Putting Advocacy into Action" by S. E. Ward and N. Koontz, 1999. *Eta Sigma Gamma Monograph (The Health Education Monograph Series)* 17(2), p. 37. Used with permission from the publisher. FYI 12.2, 12.3, 12.4, 12.5, 12.6 From APHA, *Advocates' Handbook: A Guidebook for Effective Public Health Advocacy,* 1999. With permission from the American Public Health Association. FYI 12.7 From American Psychiatric Association: *Diagnostic and Statistical Manual of Mental Disorders,* Fourth Edition. Copyright © 1994 American Psychiatric Association. Reprinted with permission from the publisher. Fig. 12.2 From *Environmental Health,* Second Edition, by M. T. Morgan et al. Copyright 1997 Wadsworth Publishing Company. Reprinted with permission from Wadsworth, a division of Thomson Learning.

Chapter 13   FYI 13.2 From *Health Education: Learner-Centered Instructional Strategies,* Fourth Edition, 1997. Reproduced with permission of The McGraw-Hill Companies. p. 288 Definition of "communication." By permission. From *Merriam-Webster's Collegiate® Dictionary,* Tenth Edition. Copyright © 1999 by Merriam-Webster, Incorporated. FYI 13.7, 13.8 From "Making Community Presentations" by E. Wadud, in *Community Tool Box,* Chapter 1, Section 6, http://ctb.lsi.ukans.edu, Work Group on Health Promotion and Community Development, The University of Kansas, Lawrence, Kansas. Reproduced with permission.

Chapter 14   FYI 14.2 Reprinted with permission from *A Competency-Based Framework for Graduate-Level Health Educators* by National Commission for Health Education Credentialing, American Association for Health Education, and the Society for Public Health Education, 1999.

Appendix A   From *A Framework for the Development of Competency-Based Curricula for Entry-Level Health Educators* by National Task Force on the Preparation and Practice of Health Educators, 1985, National Commission for Health Education Credentialing. Reprinted with permission from Health Education Credentialing, Inc., Society for Public Health Education, and American Association for Health Education.

Appendix B   Code of Ethics for the Health Education Profession. Reprinted with permission from Ethics Task Force Coalition of National Health Education Organizations.

Index